LIKE A TREE
BY RUNNING WATER

She did it all! These words summarize the story of Katherine Russell, better known to Californians as Mother Mary Baptist Russell, pioneer founder of the Sisters of Mercy in California. The story of this remarkable woman is one that speaks of courage in the face of opposition and hardship, of dedication to those society has forgotten, of ingenuity and creativity in responding to the crises and needs of post-Gold Rush California.

Born in pre-famine Ireland, Mary Baptist learned about hardship and poverty through the experience of the Irish people. Moved by an urgent longing to be of service to the poor and by a desire to dedicate her life to God, she entered the Sisters of Mercy in Kinsale, Co. Cork, Ireland in 1848. Just six years later she set out with seven of her sisters on a journey which would make her one of the "pioneer makers of Northern California." Her story, even 150 years later, is one that stirs in the reader a sense of wonder and amazement at the breadth of her accomplishments.

Arriving in San Francisco in 1854, Mary Baptist started the first Catholic Hospital in California, negotiated with the State to care for its young women delinquents, its indigent sick and its aged. No challenge was too much for her or for her sisters. They quickly responded to the health care needs of the city during the cholera epidemic of 1855 and again in the small pox epidemic of 1868. She built a House of Mercy to shelter domestic servants and protect them from exploitation, ministered to women caught in the web of prostitution and addiction, set up elementary schools and academies. Mary Baptist was the first woman to be given permission to visit prisoners in San Quentin. Her work did not end there. She established a registry office to find jobs for willing workers, provided food for the unemployed during California's severe depressions, and found time to set up natural history museums and educational displays.

Mary Baptist did not confine her work to San Francisco. She established a convent and school in Sacramento in 1857 where her sisters quickly became an integral part of the city. They were its first visiting nurses and opened St. Joseph Academy where generations of women were educated for leadership and service. During the great flood of 1861, with the city under water for almost six months, the sisters ministered by boat to those in need. In 1863 Mary Baptist extended her works to Grass Valley, concentrating on education and care for orphans.

In the midst of all this activity, Mary Baptist found time to write lengthy letters to friends, family and governmental agencies. These letters have been collected in this work and join with her story in presenting a woman worth remembering, one who was called by her contemporaries the "best known charitable worker on the Pacific Coast."

Like a Tree by Running Water

The Story of Mary Baptist Russell,
California's First Sister of Mercy

Mary Katherine Doyle, RSM

Blue Dolphin Publishing

Published by Blue Dolphin Publishing, Inc.
P.O. Box 8, Nevada City, CA 95959
Orders: 1-800-643-0765
Web: www.bluedolphinpublishing.com

ISBN: 1-57733-149-4 softcover
ISBN: 1-57733-150-8 hardcover

Library of Congress Cataloging-in-Publication Data

Doyle, Mary Katherine, 1944-
  Like a tree by running water : the story of Mary Baptist Russell, California's
first Sister of Mercy / Mary Katherine Doyle.
      p. cm.
  Includes bibliographical references and index.
  ISBN 1-57733-149-4 (softcover : alk. paper) — ISBN 1-57733-150-8
(hardcover : alk. paper)
  1. Russell, Mary Baptist, 1829-1898. 2. Sisters of Mercy—Biography.
3. Superiors, Religious—California—San Francisco—Biography. 4. Russell,
Mary Baptist, 1829-1898—Correspondence. 5. Superiors, Religious—
California—San Francisco—Correspondence. I. Title.

BX4705.R74D69 2004
271'.9202—dc22

                                                        2004008894

Cover photo by Mary Katherine Doyle, RSM

Printed in the United States of America

10   9   8   7   6   5   4   3   2   1

Mary Baptist Russell
Pioneer Foundress, Sisters of Mercy in California

They shall be like a tree planted by water,
sending out its roots by the stream. It
shall not fear when heat comes, and its
leaves shall stay green; in the year of drought it
is not anxious, and it does not cease to bear fruit.

Jeremiah 17:8

Table of Contents

Introduction

I first met Katherine Russell when I was eighteen. It happened one day when wandering around our convent library. There I discovered her life hidden amidst the various volumes. It was the beginning of a forty-year fascination with this remarkable woman better known to us as Mary Baptist Russell, California foundress of the Sisters of Mercy.

As a young Sister of Mercy I was captured by the courage and passion that caused Katherine Russell to travel far beyond her native Ireland to a country wild and untamed. It seemed as though her energy had no limit. She became a model and inspiration for me. As my life moved on, Mary Baptist had a magnetic impact on me. At each turn of my journey she surfaced with renewed wisdom, with renewed challenge. She was no longer simply a larger-than-life hero but became for me a source of vision and encouragement. Challenges dotting my life found precedent in hers.

Then there was mystery, mysteries that I could never solve. How did she acquire the type of education that prepared her for leadership when she was raised in an area which historically denied education to Catholic families? How could she be so involved in such a wide variety of activities and yet be so adept at them all? Why is there so much silence about the contributions of this woman religious[1] and those like her in feminist historical works detailing women's contributions in the Far West?

Finally, after walking with Katherine for most of my life, I realized she had much to teach us, much to say to the realities of life at the beginning of this new millennium. Hers was a life that needed a storyteller to give it voice and color.

It was during the 1980s when I felt a deep need to share Mary Baptist's story with others, to be her storyteller. She had always been important to me, but as world events unfolded, I believed her life provided paradigms to shape our response to many of the issues facing today's Sisters of Mercy. Indeed, her life speaks to all who long to serve persons who are economically poor, uneducated, infirm or in need. Still, there was very little material with which to work. Only two biographies of Mary Baptist have been written, one by her brother Matthew, published in 1902, and the second by Sister Mary Aurelia McArdle in 1954. Beyond these two slim volumes, only a few articles were written over the years. Each deepened the story but none put all the pieces together; none seemed to capture the essence of this women known to her contemporaries as Mother Mary Baptist Russell.

The task of the storyteller is two-fold. It demands honoring the facts of a person's life, not omitting anything in order to make the person fit a preconceived image. It also demands seeing that person through the eyes of her own time and culture. Matthew Russell told Mary Baptist's story with all the love and devotion of a younger brother. He spoke of her inner character, her accomplishments, and gathered together as many of her letters as he could. In his book, Father Matthew notes that the letters of Mary Baptist's early years in California seem to have been lost. To be more sweeping, many of her letters have been lost or remain yet to be found.

It was the search for Mary Baptist's lost letters that sustained my interest. Each new letter seemed to add a new dimension to her character. Each new find suggested that more letters were to be discovered. In the mid-eighties, four letters surfaced unexpectedly at the motherhouse of the Holy Family Sisters in Fremont, California. Soon after, another came to light that gave new insight into the scope of her interests. It was as though Mary Baptist wanted to tell her story in her own words. The woman whom I initially believed to be quite terse in written correspondence turned out to be just the opposite in her letters to family and friends. She wrote detailed descriptions of her experience, everything from death-bed conversions to her first visit to a gold mine. These letters have been gathered together in this volume, and to my amazement they number almost 100.

The second part of the storyteller's charge is to place the subject within the time and culture of her period. Matthew could not include the feel of her environment or the challenges she faced in a culture so different from her native roots. Mary Baptist lived in three worlds: the world of early nineteenth century Ireland, the world of post-Gold Rush California, and the world of California as it developed into a prosperous and dynamic state. Each differed so much that Mary Baptist had to dance the dance of constant adaptation. Reading the signs of the times was part and parcel of her everyday experience. As Mary Baptist moved to respond to the ever-changing landscape of life, she reached out to new areas and new ministries. This she did with absolute fidelity to the vision of Mercy deeply ingrained in her spirit.

Mary Baptist was not a rugged individualist. She was solidly connected to both her own family and her religious Sisters. Her community of Mercy was not limited to the Sisters who co-labored with her in the California mission. It extended to her Kinsale community and to the extended family of Mercy foundations throughout the United States. Her letters show that she sought their advice, gave advice in return, and saw herself as engaged in a common endeavor. She carried on a lively correspondence with her Sisters in Newry and Kinsale, apprising them of events and begging their prayers and assistance.

No story of Mary Baptist would be complete without an introduction to some of the other women of Mercy who exerted great influence upon her life: Mother Mary Francis Bridgeman and Mother Mary deSales Reddan, among others. Mary Baptist would be the first to protest too great an attribution of accomplishment to her. She was part of a community of women, all contributing to the mission. Many of their acts of courage and deeds of outstanding charity are shadowed in historical silence. It seems to have been the norm for the early Sisters in San Francisco to remain hidden from publicity and acclaim.

It is the dynamic of historical silence that has most surprised me as I pursued the story of Katherine Russell. In a wide variety of books published about the early days of San Francisco and its growth as a city, no mention is made of her or her Sisters' influence in the city, yet she is one of the pioneer makers of California. Even works on the religious figures of the time such as John B. McGloin's *California's First Archbishop* or John Dwyer's *Condemned to the Mines* either ignore the contributions of Mary Baptist and her Sisters or else relegate their contributions to just a few sentences. A quick review of women highlighted in collections about women in the West shows no mention of her or any of the other pioneer women religious, yet they were instrumental in building the educational and health-care institutions needed for a lawless city to be transformed to an urban center of commerce, culture, and political power. It has only been since the turn of the new millennium that note of her has been made in such books as *Fascinating Women in California History* by Alton Pryor and *Famous American Women, A Biographical Dictionary from Colonial Times to the Present*, edited by Robert McHenry.

Mary Baptist had a heart for history, keeping for herself the job of annalist for the San Francisco community. We are indebted to her for carefully preserving in the San Francisco annals transcriptions of the important letters she sent to others as well as the anecdotal materials she included in these important documents. The shadow side of this reality is that she rarely spoke of herself, only of others. Only in her letters and in the reminiscences of those who knew her do we find hints about her style, her sense of humor, and her perspectives on the issues of her day.

One of the most intriguing aspects of Mary Baptist is her spiritual vision. Again, it is hard to pinpoint her spiritual discipline or her inner struggles, but we do find some clues in her instructions to her Sisters and in her later letters. There are other clues to be found in examining the books she read, the devotions she promoted and the rule of life that she followed. These sources taken as a whole give us a type of spiritual portrait of the world of the Spirit that grounded everything Mary Baptist did. The title of this book, *Like A Tree by Running Water,* was chosen because it captures her inner source of strength. Taken from the Prophet Jeremiah, it reflects her ability to remain constant in times of struggle as well as in times of success because she was rooted in God.

It is important to say a few words about the letters of Mary Baptist that you will find throughout this story. The letters have been gathered from primary sources discovered in archival collections, and from secondary sources derived from books written at the beginning of the twentieth century. Many have been gathered from the annals of the Regional Communities of the Sisters of Mercy in Burlingame and in Auburn, California. The main secondary sources are *The Life of Mother Mary Baptist Russell* and *Three Sisters of Lord Russell of Killowen and Their Convent Life,* both written by Father Matthew Russell, and Volumes Three and Four of *Leaves from the Annals of the Sisters of Mercy* by Mother Mary Austin Carroll.

In working with these materials, it became clear to me that Mary Baptist rarely used punctuation when she wrote social letters. There are times when small connecting words are omitted. I have taken the liberty of supplying punctuation when possible and have formatted the letters in a way that makes them more "reader friendly." I ask forgiveness in advance for this liberty, but it is my intent to introduce you to her spirit and heart in the most direct way possible. Each letter is annotated and any clarifying information that was available has been added by way of introduction to each text.

No work such as this can be done without a great deal of practical assistance and loving encouragement from others. I want to thank my Auburn Regional Community for allowing me to pursue this passion of mine. I can never express the depth of gratitude I have for their patient listening to my discoveries over the past fifteen years and their gentle prodding to finish the story! I also want to express my appreciation and thankfulness to my Burlingame Sisters who have provided abundant encouragement and enthusiasm for the work. For the past seven years they have never failed to ask: "How is your Baptist book coming?"

In researching Mary Baptist's life I undertook a pilgrim journey retracing the movement of her life. This pilgrimage took me to her birthplace in Newry, Co. Down, Northern Ireland, and then down to Kinsale, Co. Cork, where she spent the first six years of her life as a Sister of Mercy. My journey was blessed with the assistance of three wonderful archivists, Sister Evelyn Kelly of the Sisters of Mercy in Newry, Sister Patricia Quinlin of the Sisters of Mercy in Kinsale, and Father Stephen Redmond, SJ, archivist for the Jesuit Community in Dublin. Each gave freely of their expertise, time and assistance and provided both materials and insight illuminating Mary Baptist's early years.

My journey was made easy by the hospitality of friends who provided a home for me during my trip. To Michael and June Murphy who opened their home to me; to my Sister in Mercy, Sister Assumpta Wallace, who was guide and companion during my trip; and to my sisters at St. Joseph Convent, Kinsale, and Our Lady of Mercy Convent, Newry, who helped me experience the spirit of Mercy as Mary Baptist must have known it.

Special thanks are due to Marilyn Gouailhardou, RSM, Burlingame Regional Community archivist, and Mary Helena

Sanfilippo, RSM, who were instrumental in gathering the resources for this collection. I am especially grateful to Margaret Mitchell, RSM, Michelle Gorman, RSM, and Colleen Gregg who spent hours listening to the story and offering their encouragement and critique of the manuscript. My life and this story are blessed by their wisdom.

To those who were willing to review the text and offer wisdom and suggestions: Mary Loyola MacDonald, RSM, Ellen FitzGerald, RSM, Kerry Wood, Elizabeth Dossa, Barbara Pauley, Michelle Gorman, RSM, Marilyn Gouailhardou, RSM, Jeffrey Burns and Mary Elizabeth Schiele, my grateful thanks. To my publisher Paul Clemens and his staff at Blue Dolphin Publishing—you have made this work come to life and I am most grateful. Finally, I want to thank those who have traveled this way with me. To Thomas More Newbold, C.P., Mary Celeste Rouleau, RSM, Marie Eloise Rosenblatt, RSM, and my MAST companions, and all the members of my Auburn Regional Community: You have encouraged and supported me and believed that telling Mary Baptist's story was important. May it be all that you hoped it would be.

And now, for you who are about to meet Katherine Russell for the first time or to renew her acquaintance, may you find in her a friend and inspiration for your own journey.

Part I

Seafield at Killowen, the childhood home of Mary Baptist

How pleasant is home to the weary!
In heav'n may we feel it one day!

But ah! Though the charms I have chanted
Have dear to my memory grown,
I think of thee more, O Rostrevor!
Because thou art near to Killowen.

Matthew Russell, S.J.
"A Picnic at Rostrevor"
From *Idyls of Killowen*

I

Out of the Green Earth

Understanding the character and vision of Katherine Russell, called in religion Mother Mary Baptist, requires us to journey back in time to another century and another world, the world of the nineteenth century Ireland. The century's political, social, economic, and religious climate, with its curious blend of romanticism and realism, emerging social consciousness and economic harshness, was a significant factor in shaping Katherine's response to the world around her, both before and after her entry into the Sisters of Mercy. The intersection of these Victorian currents and the Russell family story creates a portrait that is captivating and intriguing.

The recollections of the Russell family life left to us by Matthew and Sarah Russell, Katherine's brother and sister, are important elements in reconstructing this portrait.[1] Their rich insights into the style and pattern of Russell family life provide clues to the outstanding success of its family members. The family gave to the world four Sisters of Mercy: Lily, Sister Mary Aquin; Sarah, Mother Mary Emmanuel; and Katherine, Mother Mary Baptist and their aunt Sister Mary of Mercy Russell. Matthew Russell, S.J., the youngest of the family, was founder and editor of *The Irish Monthly,* while his older brother Lord Charles Russell, in 1894, became the first Catholic since the Reformation to hold the office of Lord Chief Justice in England.

The Russells were a blend of Norman and Celtic ancestry. Arthur Russell, Katherine's father, was a descendant of Normans who settled in Lecale in the 12ᵗʰ century when, as a reward for military service, an early ancestor was awarded lands in this County Down barony. Two centuries later, in 1316, the first Russell was created Baron of Killough, a little seaport in the eastern part of the county. The Russell clan expanded through the years and broke off into four distinct branches, each of which is credited with faithfulness to their Catholic heritage, deep patriotism for Ireland, and political savvy.[2] These qualities would take root in the Russell children, descendents of the Ballystrew branch of the family.

The vicissitudes of Catholic landholders were part of the family story, a story of forfeited estates, oppression and ultimate restoration through the support of Protestant friends, and the determination of Russell women. One such story was the tale of Mary Russell, whose husband died in the Cromwellian wars and whose lands were confiscated as a result.[3] Mary was not the type to give up without a struggle. Like the persistent widow of the Gospel, she decided to appeal directly to Charles II, the English monarch. She walked from Holyhead to London and, as the story goes, flung herself before the King asking for justice. Her appeal was successful.[4]

Over and over again the Russell family stories tell of the price paid for seeking freedom and justice. Members fighting against the oppressive rule of their times often met defeat or death. The family was then subject to loss of property or punishment. The bonds of friendship experienced by the Russells must have transcended any sectarian lines; however, for each time friends of the Protestant tradition intervened to assist the family in retaining lands and property for the next generation. This intervention was necessitated due to the penal laws, which limited Catholic land holdings.[5]

Katherine's mother, Margaret Mullin, also had family stories that fueled the fires of patriotism and quickened the thirst for justice. In later years Sarah Russell, herself a Sister of Mercy, would recall a story told by her mother. "I have heard my mother tell stories of '98. Her father was a captain of a merchant ship; he was drowned at sea. Her mother married a second time—Mr. Moore of Belfast. One day, in 1798, she was standing at the door of her house—my mother was then seven years old—with a baby in her arms, when a soldier coming up spoke rudely to her. Mr. Moore was standing by. He expostulated with the soldier, whereupon the latter made a lunge of the bayonet at my grandmother, and drove the point through the baby's eye. The child was killed on the spot, and then the soldier ran away. Mr. Moore followed him to the barracks and told what happened. But all the satisfaction Mr. Moore got was that he was sent to gaol [sic] for six weeks. My mother often told us this story, and other stories of those terrible times."[6]

Suffering and hardship were not limited to the generations preceding Katherine's parents, Arthur and Margaret. Arthur Russell grew up in Killough along with his brother Charles. Their father, a corn merchant, did not live to see the birth of Katherine nor the remarkable influence of his son Charles, who would become President of Maynooth College in 1857. Lacking land, Arthur looked to the sea for his future. He became a member of the merchant marine and eventually the captain of his own ship.

Arthur Russell courted Margaret Mullin in the early 1800s, but his courting came to naught. Margaret married John Hamill, a Belfast merchant. This marriage came to a sudden end with the unexpected death of Mr. Hamill in 1820. Like her mother before her, Margaret was left a young widow with six children to raise. Even though John Hamill provided well for his family, it must have been difficult for Margaret to face an uncertain future with such young children. Adding to her grief, death would visit once more. Mary Hamill, her young daughter, died before her mother would find new happiness and strength in her marriage to Arthur Russell who, having said good-bye to the seafaring life, was ready once more to seek Margaret as his wife. He purchased the Southwark brewery and established residence in Newry, a commercial center rivaling Belfast. This time his quest was successful and the two married in July 1825.[7] Over the next decade six Russell children, Mary, Elizabeth (Lily), Katherine, Sarah, Charles, and Matthew, were added to their Hamill stepbrothers and sisters, James, Thomas, Arthur, Margaret, and Ann. All in all, the family would eventually number thirteen, not counting the Governess, Miss Margaret O'Connor, and extended family members.

The values and priorities of the Russell parents found expression in every detail of family life. Priority was placed on faith, education, patriotism, simplicity, and love for those who were poor. At first the family lived on Queen Street in Newry, then called Ballybot. Arthur Russell purchased a residence there, and in this house Katherine was born in 1829. As the family grew, Arthur built a larger residence on the property as well as two additional houses that were leased out. One tenant was Captain Verner, brother of one of the leading members of the Orange party.[8] Captain Verner's daughter Jane would be swept off her feet by a young Irish patriot, John Mitchel, author of the *Jail Journal*.[9] The Mitchel family lived in close proximity to the Russells, as did many other Irish political figures of the time.[10]

The political nature and leanings of the Russell family were part of their spirit. Margaret Russell was deeply sympathetic to the struggle for Irish independence and reform. Catholic Emancipation was achieved only two weeks before Katherine's birth on April 18, 1829. This event brought her mother special joy as she cried over Katherine, calling her "her first free-born child."[11]

The early years of Katherine's life were spent in an affectionate, bustling home. Sarah recollects:

> Our old house in Ballybot I can recall as a very well furnished one, and each bedroom distinguished by a name taken from its style,

such as the white room, blue, chintz, or green room. The fine long hall, good, cosy breakfast parlor, large dining and drawing rooms, the kitchen and our own two nurseries—a day and a night one. Then the busy brewery yard, full of drags, horses, men and barrels, Newfoundland dogs—Leo and Pompey—and terriers with forgotten names. The garden with apples, the special fruit pictured still distinctly, and the flowers.[12]

It was a peaceful life for the family, rich with friends and thriving commerce. Sarah recalls that friends remembered the Russell household at Ballybot as one that was full of young people. "It must have been a very pleasant house, for there were so many young people, our step-sisters and brothers, and those dear Belfast friends, and our uncles and aunts and cousins of our father's, many of them contemporaries of our elder sisters. Newry seems to have been a half-way house from Killough; and many a happy gathering I have heard of, where music, singing, dancing, riddles, round games joined in by all, young and old, made the evenings go quickly."[13] This seemingly idyllic scene was not without sorrow. Thomas Hamill, one of Margaret's older children, helped his stepfather run the brewery. This well-liked and playful brother died of fever in 1834, leaving the family to mourn the loss of another sibling.

By 1838 Arthur Russell's health began to fail and the brewery was sold for an advantageous price. Like many of the wealthier families of Ireland, the Russell family planned to move to France where educational opportunities would be greater for the older girls, Mary and Lily (Elizabeth). The move would also provide a warmer climate for the ailing Arthur Russell. By this time the Hamill children were pursuing their own careers. James ventured to South America; Arthur, who had replaced his brother as his stepfather's assistant in the brewery, was now free to study law. Ann Hamill became the first sibling to follow a religious vocation when she entered the Poor Clares. Margaret was married to a rising young attorney, Peter Gartlan, under whom Arthur would apprentice.[14] Everything was ready for the family's move to France, or so it seemed.

The family had moved out of its main house to one of the rental houses. Just when clothes and belongings were packed and their departure imminent, Mary, the eldest Russell daughter, came down with the "fever" and died suddenly on June 28, 1838. Sarah describes the scene years after the event: "I remember well that morning. We were all dressed in white and brought down to the back parlor where Mary lay dead, and dear Mamma seated in deep mourning beside her remains. R.I.P. She was a sweet, lovable, clever child, just over 12 years old."[15] The death occurred on the very day of Queen Victoria's coronation. Though lights danced throughout Newry, the Russell home was cloaked in darkness. Arthur Hamill, Mary's stepbrother, and James McHenry would stand sentry all night to explain that the darkness was for mourning, not for a lack of loyalty. With this death, all plans of France vanished.

For seven years the Russell youth had spent their summers in Killowen, where two carriages full of seniors and visitors from Newry came each Sunday to relax, share stories and enjoy the sea. On such occasions the house became so full that the little Russells found their bed transformed into a temporary dinner table when no room remained at the family table. Killowen was just two and a half miles away from Rostrevor, a favorite destination during the summer. It was to Killowen, a seaside place of solitude, rest, and beauty, that the Russells retired after Mary's death.[16]

The natural beauty of Killowen created a bond with nature in Katherine. She would always love the ocean, and little wonder. Seafield, the Russell home, faced the sea on one side and the mountains on the other. Sarah tells us that Seafield was,

> small, about sixteen acres, beautifully situated on the shores of Carlingford Lough, and immediately opposite that old historic town, whose old castle (King John's) was distinctly visible from

our house, along with the ruins of the Dominican Abbey and the pretty village of Carlingford.

The house was old-fashioned and comfortable, but rather small; so a new wing was built soon after. The fields lay sloping to the seashore and to the midday sun. That same sun was visible "from the rising to the going down thereof." Behind us were the Slieve Ban and Croagh Shee Mountains, while before us lay the broadest part of the Carlingford Lough.[17]

The circumstances of health and unexpected loss that drew the Russells to their new home proved to be a blessing, providing the children with experiences different from urban life. Climbing mountains, swimming in the sea, and observing the cycles of nature were part of their everyday life at Killowen.

It is clear from family recollections that the Russells' economic situation does not match the image of poverty-stricken Ireland in the early nineteenth century. The family was not wealthy, nor were they poor. They were best described as upper middle class. Due to wise provisions made by John Hamill, Margaret came to her second marriage financially secure. Arthur Russell was a good steward and able to provide his large family with opportunities for education, the arts, and an engagement with the political tides of his time. The monies they had they used wisely.

Matthew Russell, the youngest in the family, commented on the frugal nature of their upbringing especially after the death of his father. As a Jesuit he was asked to meditate on the question, "Do I love Poverty as a Mother?" Matthew responded:

I think I do in theory, partly because I had a mother who was worthy of that sacred name. She was not weak or selfish; she loved her children with a true and wise love. No children, I think, of our social standing could be brought up with fewer toys or less pocket-money; but we were thoroughly happy and content. If she saw us cowering over the fire on a cold day, she would say *Tut! Tut!* in a cheerful way, as if to upbraid us for being soft and unmanly. But she kept us well supplied with all substantial comforts and in good health; and on limited means she educated us for our work in life and kept out of debt; nay, she gave much money in the incessant driblets of charity and large sums for religious purposes, and she served many people in their need. She never gave expensive dinners to friends, but she managed to give them pleasant evenings at our populous fireside, which satisfied the claims that hospitality had upon her under her peculiar circumstances as a widow with a large young family dependent on the prudent usury of not a very large number of thousands.[18]

At Seafield, the education of the children was placed in the hands of Miss Margaret O'Connor, who acted as a live-in governess for the family. The curriculum, as Sarah remembers it, comprised "English (which we learned thoroughly), History (English, Roman and Grecian), French, Botany, Natural Philosophy, Astronomy, Music, Drawing. On starry nights Miss O'Connor would show us the constellations and planets, so that we learned them and loved to be star-gazing. The flowers, too, were pulled to exemplify what botany taught."[19]

The rhythm of schooling was rarely interrupted. The parlor was designated as the classroom and given over to that purpose until near dinner. The only person who seemed able to change that pace was Arthur Russell, who would sometimes come and ask Miss O'Connor's permission to have the children go out to the meadow to pull the dandelion flowers before they multiplied or, at other times, to assist with weeding the garden. It was a trade of study for work.

Formal study was complemented by the intellectual life of the family itself. Sarah notes: "Our good uncles and aunts kept dear Father always well supplied with newspapers besides some we got ourselves. The standard works of that time we got in the same way or from other kind friends. Scott, Banim, Miss Edgeworth, Dickens, Thackeray etc., etc., were familiar reading in our house. Greer's Lending Library in Newry had no steadier customers."[20] Religious books were also part of the regular reading material of the family. Part of the Sunday ritual involved each child reading aloud a chapter of the Bible after dinner.

By 1844 it was decided that Mrs. Russell would take the Russell children to Belfast to expand their educational opportunities. Both Katherine and Lily were placed in a private school, while Charles was enrolled first in Mr. Harkin's School and later in St. Malachy's College. Matthew was sent to Mr. Harkin's school where one of his early learnings was that everyone did not share the political views of his family. The patriotic Margaret had sent Matthew off with a "Repeal cap,"[21] a type of Scottish cap with green shamrocks on it and the word Repeal. He was promptly "mobbed by young urchins in the street."[22] Returning home hatless, he changed his style of attire. After a few months the younger children, Matthew and Sarah, returned to their father in Seafield.

Education and politics seem to have gone together for the Russells. They were deeply connected to the political currents of the time. Sarah tells us,

> Our evenings were all spent together, so that we heard of the public events of the day from newspapers, which would occasionally be the reading, or we heard our seniors discussing them. In the stirring times of the Monster Meetings our grand Liberator was the figure ever before us. With what enthusiasm every word would be listened to! Ardent patriots and warm loyal Catholics as both Father and Mother were, and from our earliest days hearing these great subjects talked about, it would be unnatural if any of us could turn anything but true warm-hearted Irish Catholics.[23]

Daniel O'Connell, known as the Great Liberator,[24] became an almost mythic character for the younger Russells. Sarah remembers that her whole ambition and prayer was to see him. During one of her trips to Dublin with her mother, Mrs. Russell took her to Conciliation Hall where Sarah's ambition was fulfilled. The sighting of Ireland's "Liberator" was a high point of memory for her.

Moore's "Irish Melodies" provided another hook into patriotic spirit for the younger children. These patriotic songs were sung by Mrs. Russell as part of family life. They were her favorite melodies. The extent of political awareness within the Russell family home is made clearer in Sarah's recollections.

> In our almost isolated home, having no social neighbors whatever and few visitors from a distance, the lives and actions of distinguished men of the day seemed to stand more prominently before us than they would otherwise have done. O'Connell, Moore, Wellington, and others of that day were well known to us. When the State Trials were going on, every line in the papers was listened to with intense interest by old and young. O'Connell's imprisonment was a subject for family mourning; while his liberation, 6 September, 1844, brought universal exultation.[25]

With such grounding, it is little wonder that members of the family would enter political life. Charles Russell would be drawn to the Young Ireland movement that was actively engaged in working for governmental and legislative reforms. Members of the Hamill family also would be involved in the political and legal life of Ireland. Margaret Hamill's husband, Peter Gartlan, was one of three called upon to defend O'Connell and others in the State Trial of 1844, while Arthur Hamill devoted his career to law. Katherine herself would maintain a keen interest in Irish politics throughout her lifetime, even though she was thousands of miles away.

The Russell parents were an interesting blend of style. Arthur was remembered for his great gentleness and kindness as well as his ability to see the best in things. Touching stories or tales of magnanimous action easily moved him. Sarah describes her father as a man of great sensitivity and compassion.

> Kindly-hearted he truly was; no one ever heard his hard word. If any of us did wrong and Mother was showing her displeasure, he would take the culprit's part (if penitent) and the well-remem-

bered words, 'Margaret, let by-gones be by-gones,' or 'Forget and forgive,' would get us pardon from her. One little lesson of his often served me since. I was standing at the parlour window, watching the rain pouring down the panes, and I said, 'Such a horrible day!' and dear Father, who overheard me, said, 'Oh, child, don't say that. You don't know but some poor farmer has been praying for that rain and God has sent it to him.[26]

Mrs. Russell translated her upright character into parenting practices, demanding from her children utmost honesty, integrity, and the desire to do their best. Margaret's model of discipline left lasting impressions on the children. For spending their Sunday collection money on candy and ruining their muffs with yellow sugar, the oldest culprit, Lily, was sent back to own up to Bishop Michael Blake that the girls had taken the Church's money. For telling an untruth, the same young culprit had to don the "white sheet" of a penitent and stand at the gateway where carts and people would definitely notice her. Another well-remembered violation had to do with abusing the possession of the household keys and helping themselves to cheese without permission. This breach of trust earned Katherine and Sarah three days of silent waiting before finding out what their punishment would be. For Sarah the hardest part was the clear message that trust had been broken, a grave failing.[27]

Matthew notes that his sister's recollections of the punishments received by the Russell children "illustrate the firmness with which this wise mother corrected the faults of her children, that unwearying maternal vigilance which lets nothing that is blameworthy escape without blame, while it teaches its stern lessons with an evenness of justice that, along with a wholesome fear, inspires confidence and love. There never was a gloomy day in that well-disciplined house."[28] While this comment might be idealized, it is clear that a strong bond of love and respect existed between Margaret and her children. They would do anything for her and she gave her life in their cause.

In some ways Margaret Russell was almost larger than life. She was Spartan in her simplicity and discipline of life, but she joined that with a tender care for those who were poor. Mrs. Russell has been described as "very much the head of the house. She was a handsome, clever woman, clear-headed and strong-willed, having excellent business qualities and possessing a composure and dignity of character, which her life and letters to a great extent reveal."[29] One thing is certain: she had tremendous influence over the life decisions of her sons, guiding them away from what she considered risky career options to more secure employments. Following her advice, both Arthur Hamill and Charles Russell delayed their study of law. In Katherine's case, her mother's influence guided the future Mother Mary Baptist away from the Sisters of Charity to the newly founded Sisters of Mercy. Katherine's younger sister Sarah longed to join her sister in San Francisco but her longing was not to be satisfied. Mrs. Russell objected to Sarah's plan to join Mary Baptist. She had already given two daughters to Mercy, Lily and Katherine. Reluctant to ask such a sacrifice of her mother, Sarah changed her plans and remained in Newry entering the newly founded Mercy community there.

No discussion of the Russell family life would be complete without reflecting upon their religious practice. The Russells had a "faith in action" model of Catholicism. While living in Ballybot, the children were sent to the cathedral for Mass each Sunday. Their task was to bring home some word said in the sermon. This was an important duty and demanded concentration. Sarah would later lament that before the "word" could be safely committed to memory, it would fade and the sermon end before another memorable one could be captured.[30]

Sunday was kept as a strict day of rest. Unnecessary cooking, cleaning, and even playing the piano (except to accompany hymns) was forbidden, yet the day was celebrated as special. Sunday fare was matched by Sunday dress. Card playing was not allowed but story-telling, games, and the like made the evenings enjoyable. First Communions and Confirmations were major events.

Once more it is the family chronicler, Sarah, who gives insight into the spiritual practice of the group:

> We were rather piously inclined all of us, and we had a little association of our own and conferences on holy subjects. I remember the subject proposed in one of them by Kate was, 'What was the best way to become a Saint?' And the unanimous opinion was 'to do our daily duties as well as ever we could, and to do all in the presence of God to please Him'—a wise one surely, and containing as high a spirituality as I, for my part, have ever learned since."[31]

Study was not the only element of religious practice. Mortifications also played a part. Their penitential practice was characterized by a concentration on little things like not taking the best potato or giving in to thirst. The children followed their own path, sometimes without their parents' notice. Once, the eager penitents decided to limit themselves to one glass of milk per day. Their parents did not discover this practice until the last week of Lent because the senior Russells had observed their own fast until noon, thereby leaving the children to eat by themselves. Once discovered, the limitation on milk was quickly stopped.[32]

Father Charles Russell, Katherine's uncle, played an important part in stirring the religious ardor of the family. Father Russell, usually referred to as Dr. Russell, was a remarkable man in his own right. He entered Maynooth in 1826 just a year after the Russells married. By 1835 he was appointed professor of humanities and later became the chair for ecclesiastical history. Dr. Russell was a close friend of John Cardinal Newman, who said of him, "My dear friend Dr. Russell, President of Maynooth, had perhaps more to do with my conversion than any one else. I do not recollect that he said a word on the subject of religion. He was always gentle, mild, unobtrusive, uncontroversial. He let me alone."[33] In 1842 "Uncle Charles" gave each of the young Russells a Roman Missal. The children were now able to follow the priest as Mass was celebrated and join with him in offering up this prayer of thanksgiving and praise.

In 1845 this life of faith would deepen and expand when the family returned to Ballybot after the death of Arthur Russell. In their sorrow the remaining Russells found comfort and strength in their religious practice. In Sarah's words, "It was not in social pleasure, however, that our happiness lay, but in the riches of religious enjoyment that opened up to us."[34] Morning Mass, reception of the sacraments, sermons, teaching catechism, and attending vespers now became part of the regular rhythm of Russell life.

The same year would mark a transition in the life of the Russells and in the life of Ireland itself. The cold winds of famine and death touched the land; the face of poverty seared itself on human faces. If death had not intervened, perhaps the Russells would have remained in their secluded Seafield; but, as it was, Arthur's frail health simply ebbed away. The gentleness of character that marked his life was even more apparent in his last days. He was uncomplaining, prayerful, and patient. By May 1845, Margaret, Arthur and Sarah had gone to Arthur Hamill's home in Newry so that Mr. Russell could be near doctors. Still his decline continued. With death imminent, Lily, Kate and Charles were summoned home from Belfast, Matthew brought up from Killowen. Arthur died on May 28, 1845, with his children gathered around his bed. His last word was "Margaret."[35]

What followed changed the course of Katherine's life and gave to California its pioneer Mercy foundress.

II

Touched by the North Wind

The death of Arthur Russell marked a profound change in the style of family life within the Russell home. Seafield was now a lonely, sad place for them and Margaret decided to move her orphaned family back to Ballybot. The move came in December 1845. The Jennings family, close friends of the Russells, welcomed the bereaved family, providing them comfort and hospitality in the midst of their grief. It was the beginning of a gentle time for the family. Small social gatherings renewed their spirits, while access to religious devotions and sacramental life sharpened their commitment to live according to Gospel values.

During this three-year period, 1845-1848, Katherine experienced, first hand, service to those who were poor or suffering. Although Katherine was taught the full range of the arts, music, drawing, singing and poetry, Sarah tells us she gave them all up. "… She thought she would never need them in after life; for she had made up her mind to be a Nun in an Order which served the poor only. She entered with all her heart into the religious advantages our new life presented and joined to it earnest, self-sacrificing service of the poor."[1]

Ireland was just beginning to experience the long winter of famine that resulted in widespread poverty, desperation and death. Results of the potato blight were everywhere and touched

St. Joseph's Convent, Kinsale, from which the eight California Pioneers departed for their mission to San Francisco

every family. Mrs. Russell was deeply engaged in providing as much relief as possible to those in need. As President of the Ladies' Societies which provided clothing and relief for the poor starving people of Newry, she set an example for her children of direct service to the poor. Clothes and food were given out daily, and Kate, then seventeen, was a zealous member of her mother's society. "Each lady had a certain number of articles of clothing given to her to make or get made weekly; so between sewing when at home, visiting the sick and poor in their houses, or calling from door to door of the better-off portion of the community for their weekly subscription, I can safely say Kate's whole time was devoted to the benefit of the poor."[2]

The famine brought in its wake disease and devastation. Cholera and the "fever" moved through the populace. In Newry a Workhouse had been opened in 1841. The institution was set up for those who were unable to support themselves: the old, infirm, and those with physical or mental disabilities. Destitute children were also included. By 1842 the Newry workhouse had admitted 222 persons. Six years later the residents would number 1,283. An additional 1,824 persons were receiving what was called "outdoor relief."[3]

Typical workhouse rations were limited to ten ounces of meal per day plus three ounces of potatoes. Milk was supplied only for the noon meal. Rations for outdoor relief consisted primarily of Indian meal.[4] The increasing numbers of paupers strained the workhouse system, resulting in greater reduction of food and services. Crowding hastened the spread of disease. Reports from the medical officers of the period repeatedly speak of the inadequacies of the facilities and the danger of more deaths from disease. Discipline in the workhouse was severe in hopes of making the workhouse unattractive and thereby a "last resort."[5]

The combined natural and political nature of the famine was not lost upon Katherine. While nature was responsible for the fungal disease that blighted crop after crop, it was the economic philosophy of the day that caused an inadequate response to this disaster. Following the *laissez faire* philosophy of free and uncontrolled trade, English governmental leaders failed to intervene in meaningful ways. Limitations on food relief, restrictions on who could receive aid, arbitrary administration by Guardians and the draining of exports from Ireland, all fueled the fires of devastation. Attitudes such as those held by the Duke of Cambridge tended to dismiss the true nature of the famine. Speaking in 1846, the Duke noted that: "they all knew Irishmen could live upon anything, and there was plenty of grass in the fields, even though the potato crop should fail."[6] In spite of the great hunger that existed in the country, between October 1845 and January 1846 some 30,000 oxen, bulls and cows, over 30,000 sheep and lambs and 100,000 pigs were exported to England.[7]

Irish nationalists proved totally ineffective in the face of the suffering. Irish politicians battled over theoretical issues of repeal, cooperation with the English Whig party, and land reform, while the people they represented were locked in a battle to protect their children from starvation. One-eighth of the population of Ireland died during these years, and another one-eighth emigrated in hopes of a better life. The political system was powerless to stem the tide. For Katherine and her family, famine wore a human face. She lived in the midst of the suffering and saw its ravages. Sarah again is our chronicler:

> The famine years are too well known in history to require any description. Indeed I would not attempt it, but surely they were years of such utter destitution, misery, starvation, and despair, that we may pray to God never to witness the like again. Business was nearly at an end in towns; no such things as fairs and weekly market held.... I remember one day seeing a woman, thin and haggard, with a little pale ghost of a child catching her thin skirt while she carried a burden under her arm. And what was it? The coffin with the remains of her little child which she was conveying to the graveyard of the Old Chapel to be buried.[8]

Sarah goes on to lament that in a country where death is honored and the bereaved embraced as family; no family or friend was there to relieve and comfort the grieving mother. Sickness and death had become too commonplace. Katherine, true to her commitment to aid those in need, befriended the woman and would see that "pale ghost of a child" grow up to become a Sister of Mercy.[9]

By 1848 Katherine knew she wanted to be a Sister of Charity. The work of Mother Mary Aikenhead's Sisters was attractive to Katherine because it matched her own desire to work among the poor. Katherine sought her mother's permission and that of the Reverend Michael Blake, bishop of her diocese. Although her inclination was to the Sisters of Charity, Katherine chose to allow the Bishop Blake to have the deciding word.[10]

Bishop Blake, a close friend of Mercy Foundress Catherine McAuley, was anxious to establish a foundation of Sisters of Mercy in his diocese and saw in Katherine Russell the realization of this hope. With this in mind he guided the young applicant to the new order. As a condition of his permission he asked that she return to Newry whenever he was able to found a Convent of Mercy. From this point on, Katherine was at peace with the decision to embrace the Sisters of Mercy as her order of choice.

With the initial decision made, it was now time to select a specific foundation of Mercy to enter. Katherine was a woman of northern Ireland. She was shaped and molded by its beauty and its political climate. Her preference was to stay in the north, but the only foundation of Mercy established in the north of Ireland at that time was the Derry convent. The works of this foundation included a pension school.[11] Because she wanted to work only with the poor, Katherine chose to look elsewhere. She sought the advice of Dr. Charles Russell, her uncle, in this important decision. He, along with her stepbrother Arthur, was Katherine's guardian. Among Dr. Russell's friends was Dr. Denis Murphy, Bishop of Cork where the Sisters of Mercy had recently opened a Convent in Kinsale. Uncle Charles recommended that this foundation be considered for the aspiring Sister of Mercy.

Mrs. Russell set about checking on the fervor and character of this community. She and Katherine visited the foundation and found it much to Mrs. Russell's liking. "Mamma visited it and was greatly attracted to dear Mother M. Bridgeman and the Community, and delighted with the amount of good they were doing for the poor, in their fine, well-appointed literary and work schools. The sale of the produce of the latter from that time out was one of the many works of charity to which dear Mother devoted herself. She spared neither labor, time nor money if she could effect sales for this school."[12]

In the days of King Charles I and King James II, Kinsale had been an important and thriving town, but by 1844 the larger port at Cork City had taken its business and the dockyard was closed. Kinsale, as a result, experienced severe economic hardship. Father Justin McNamara, parish priest of Kinsale, worked tirelessly for the poor of his parish. He was especially concerned for the well-being of its uneducated and unemployed young women. This concern was amplified by the fact that troops were billeted in the town.

Father McNamara's sister, Mary Ann Burke, a wealthy heiress, indicated a desire to join a religious community and use her wealth for the poor. Father Justin convinced her to use it for the poor of Kinsale. Mary Ann entered the Mercy foundation in Limerick with this intent and returned to Kinsale as foundress and benefactress in 1844. Mother M. Francis Bridgeman was appointed the first superior.[13]

The works of mercy began immediately. While waiting for their school to be built, the Sisters taught in the National School and conducted religious education for those in need. It was apparent to the Sisters that one of the most urgent needs was employment. Taking example from the Limerick foundation, Mother Francis Bridgeman sent teachers to Limerick to learn the art of lace making. To this craft was added muslin embroidery. The following year the Sisters established an industrial school to help poor women and girls support themselves.

The industrial school taught students all sorts of fine needlework, and the sale of these products provided them with needed income. The Kinsale annals describe what went on in the school: "Employment was given to numbers in various kinds of needlework. Flower-making also taught—knitting, carding, both hemp and wool—net-making were all carried on, so that the establishment was called a *factory.*"[14] Monies were provided by the Sisters to supply materials. From this undertaking Katherine Russell learned the importance of providing women with employment skills; later she would include job training as part of her work in San Francisco.

Mother Francis Bridgeman's intent in establishing the industrial school was two-fold. The school provided needed employment for women and children, but it also freed them from what were called "soupers." Persons having no means of paying for food were attracted to soup lines set up by Protestant religious societies. Sometimes the price of the food was conversion to the religious group that offered the aid. Mother Francis Bridgeman found this practice most distressing and wished to free poor Catholics from having to choose between food and faith. The Sisters themselves gave out food to 600 children twice a day. The Kinsale annals report that "with few exceptions [the children] were actually starving."[15]

The impressive work of the Sisters in Kinsale proved to Katherine that the community was committed to working with persons who were most in need. Her mother quickly and willingly gave permission for her to enter the Kinsale foundation. It was hard to break the news of her decision to the younger Russells. The summer before Katherine's entry into the Sisters of Mercy was spent in Killowen with all its memories. Sarah poignantly recalls climbing Slieve Ban Mountain for the last time with Katherine and Matthew. On that early morning the Angelus bell was rang out as the three siblings prayed together for the last time.[16]

Katherine was much loved and her departure was greatly felt in the family. Sarah says, "There was always something so restful, genial and bright about her, that no one in her company could keep dull or anxious long. She was thoroughly sensible, practical and energetic, and she never understood nursing sensibilities or humours; yet she was forbearing, patient, and reasonable, so that you could always talk of your little difficulties with her when they would be sure to fade away of themselves."[17]

Convent life in Kinsale could not have been significantly different from the pattern of Russell family life. Both were liberally graced with prayer, service, love for the poor and a strict discipline of life. This grounding allowed the Kinsale Sisters to give themselves wholeheartedly to the service of the poor. By the time of Katherine's entry into St. Joseph's Convent, Kinsale, the works of mercy were well established. The ministry carried on by the Sisters—a House of Mercy, the instruction of children, an industrial school, an orphanage, and, of course, visitation of the sick poor—followed the same pattern as Katherine, the future Mary Baptist, would implement in California.[18] It was the belief of Mother Francis Bridgeman that, once the essentials had been provided for the Sisters, first priority should be given to the works of mercy. Schools should be established before convents were built.[19] This pattern replicated itself in the early Mercy foundations throughout the United States. In story after story, Sisters arrive and immediately begin whatever works of mercy are called forth by the needs of the area.

According to the records of the community, Mother Mary Teresa Maher, later to become the foundress of the Cincinnati foundation, was appointed Mistress of Novices in August 1849.[20] Katherine received her habit just the month prior on July 7, 1849. Upon her reception, Katherine took the name

Sister Mary Baptist. It is the name we shall use for her from this point on.

Mary Baptist's educational training and natural talent were put to immediate use in the community. Sister Mary Howley, one of the original members of the San Francisco foundation, tells us that Mary Baptist, then a postulant, was given the task of teaching the novices.[21] This unusual circumstance could have caused the new postulant to take a superior attitude, but Sister Mary notes, "She was always very humble and made nothing of it."[22] Mary Baptist loved learning and soon used her skills in the schools of Kinsale. Given a choice, she might happily have devoted all her energies to teaching. Circumstances were to prove otherwise.

In May 1849, cholera broke out in Kinsale. The Protestant Guardians[23] of the workhouse had previously barred the Sisters from visiting the Catholic inmates of the facility. The critical need for nursing skills changed that stance, and the Sisters were accepted for duty in the workhouse hospital. Mother Francis Bridgeman and the professed members of the community served in the hospital and provided both physical and spiritual comfort for the ill. The Sisters worked night and day while the cholera epidemic lasted and actually lived at the hospital.[24]

The victims of the fever experienced constant pain, relieved only by rubbing and other remedies.[25] In one week alone, there were 150 fever patients and another 164 with other illnesses. With such great numbers, the energies and skills of the Sisters were sorely stretched. Novices, like Mary Baptist, were called upon to assist in the work because there were only ten professed Sisters.[26] This episode could be called a prelude to the later nursing story of Mother Francis Bridgeman, who would be asked to lead a delegation of Irish Sisters of Mercy to the battlefields of the Crimea. The Sisters of Mercy would be particularly suited to this mission, as only they and the Poor Servants of the Mother of God had been allowed to serve in the workhouses of Ireland where they gained in-depth experience with both cholera and fever patients.[27]

The reward for the services rendered by the Sisters in Kinsale was a change in policy by the workhouse Guardians. From that time onward the Sisters had free access to the workhouse for the purpose of visiting and instructing the sick and other inmates. The Sisters learned to do what they could do in very restrictive situations. Access carried with it the condition of not interfering with the temporal matters of the institution. This training in the ways of political systems was instructive for Mary Baptist, who would later have to maneuver her way through the currents of political whimsy in the California mission.

The year 1849 was one of intense activity for the Kinsale community. Not only did the Sisters work to contain the cholera epidemic, but 1849 also marked the first of the Kinsale foundations: Derby. This foundation faced east to England. The famine had driven many Irish emigrants to look for survival in England, Canada, the United States, and Australia. Now, Father Sing, the Pastor of Derby, was referred to Kinsale by the Sisters of Baggot Street. He sought a community of Sisters to serve the poor people of his city. Sister Mary Evangelist Benson was selected as superior for this new foundation and, in 1849, she left with six other Sisters to begin this new venture. This English foundation proved to be a type of pilot model for adaptation of the Mercy mission in cultural contexts far different than that of Ireland. It would provide further endeavors with lessons on what to avoid and what to embrace.

At first the Derby foundation seemed to be off to a great start, but what was a promising beginning proved to bring abundant suffering. First, the Sisters had to contend with the prejudice and bigotry of the time. Animosity between Catholics and Protestants was a sad reality in nineteenth-century England and Ireland. While the good works of the Sisters won over many of their Protestant neighbors, nothing could prepare them for their second cross—sickness among the Sisters.

Mother Mary Evangelist quickly became ill, requiring that Mother Bridgeman remain six months at the new foundation. Others within the community also became ill. A typescript memoir on the life of Mother Bridgeman found in the Kinsale archives notes: "Not only did M.M. Evangelist's own health continue delicate, but so many of the other members of the Community got ill that friends became seriously alarmed."[28] The cause of all this suffering turned out to be the convent itself. It proved to be situated in an unhealthy area and had to be abandoned.

Having moved through prejudice and illness, the new foundation was hit by a third woe, lack of money. While the initial foundation had been well endowed, the necessity of giving up their convent and finding other suitable quarters, as well as the death of benefactors, left the Sisters in need. For a period of time it was thought that the foundation would have to be abandoned. Some members received extended hospitality with other groups while financial affairs were put in order. As the situation improved, the dispersed members began to return to Derby until, finally, all were reunited.

This was not the end of their troubles, however. A serious challenge arose from the issue of certification of teachers. All Sisters were required to obtain a first class certificate in order to teach. Without such a document no one could be assigned to a Board School.[29] Such a requirement narrowed the selection of applicants that the Sisters could accept into their community because uncertified sister-teachers were unable to undertake the key ministry of the group. The Sisters learned, first hand, the difficulties of being dependent upon the state for licensing.[30]

These four struggles of the Derby community were well known to Sister Mary Baptist, since communication between Kinsale and Derby was frequent. Mother Mary Evangelist, superior of Derby, was the sister of Sister Mary Francis Benson, later one of the founding Sisters in California. Vicariously, Mary Baptist learned from the Derby experience three important lessons. She learned the need for great skill in working with governmental agencies, the wisdom of avoiding unnecessary entanglements with state educational policy, and the importance of selecting healthy locations for new convents.

Her six years in Kinsale provided Mary Baptist with practical training and experience which would be needed in her future work in California, but this time also provided something even more precious. At Kinsale Mary Baptist apparently absorbed from Mother Mary Francis Bridgeman an interpretation of Mercy life that she would make her own. The extent of the influence of Mother Mary Francis is hard to calculate, however, since Mary Baptist brought a kindred vision with her to religious life. She already had a passion to serve those who were poor and in need. She was raised with a discipline of life and a religious fervor that mirrored the life of her religious community. Love for learning and a belief that education was the way to escape misery was deeply inculcated in her spirit long before she took up her life's vocation. All these same elements were part of Mother Bridgeman's vision. Perhaps this is the reason she had such respect and affection for Mary Baptist and trusted her so much—she saw in the younger woman a kindred spirit.

Like Mary Baptist, Mother Bridgeman was of Norman descent. Orphaned early in life, she was raised by her aunt Joanna Reddan after whom she was named. Like Mary Baptist, Mother Bridgeman had absorbed from her family a great love of her faith and her country. "On his [her grandfather's] knee she learned the history of her own country—Religion and politics always going hand in hand."[31] Joanna Reddan provided home tutoring for her niece. Literary pursuits were particularly favored, and Joanna Reddan often hosted gatherings to discuss literary works.

Joanna Bridgeman learned the works of mercy from her aunt. Touched by the plight of poor outcast women, Miss Reddan used her fortune to provide a home for them. Since many were abused and used, she helped them to reform their lives and return to normal society. As a young girl, Joanna Bridgeman was exposed to this unconditional mercy on the part of her aunt. When cholera struck Limerick in 1832, Miss Reddan organized her penitents into a nursing corps to wait on the sick and dying.

Although young, Joanna Bridgeman showed her great nursing ability during this crisis. One description of her says:

> Miss Bridgeman was attractive and noble in her bearing, dignified in her address and manners. It was a charming sight to watch her as she passed from bed to bed with the smile of heavenly hope in her face. For every one she had a kind word, and her look was even more eloquent than her language in consoling the wretched. In their direst extremity, the sufferers felt the balm of the new consolation when the young girl stood by their side.[32]

Relatives and friends of the Reddans worried that young Joanna was engaging in a life that was unsuitable for such a vivacious girl. They prevailed upon her aunt to allow them to introduce her to the social life of the city. Miss Reddan agreed and friends went about arranging visits and entertainments for Joanna. It was not very long before she realized that this was not the life she desired. She withdrew from the social circuit and, like her aunt, devoted herself to works of mercy.

One curious insight into Mother Bridgeman is contained in the Kinsale memoir. The author tells us that Mother Bridgeman had what she called "the curious gift" of seeing the consequences of actions long in advance. Her decision to withdraw from the social activities of her time was based on her perception that it would lead her to neglect of her spiritual life and ultimately to disaster. Likewise, Mother Bridgeman said that had she not entered religious life, "she thought she would be a gipsey." [sic][33]

In September 1838 the Sisters of Mercy came to Limerick. Mother Catherine McAuley, foundress of the Sisters of Mercy, accompanied them and stayed with them for three months.

Joanna, later known as Mother Francis Bridgeman, entered this community the following November. It was Mother McAuley who instructed the aspirant as she prepared for her reception. "This she always looked on as a very special privilege, not only for the sake of the instructions received, but because it afforded her such ample opportunities of learning the Foundress' views and opinions on religious life in general, and on the duties and spirit of our own Order in particular."[34] For the rest of her life, Mother Mary Francis would always believe that she understood the vision of Catherine and would work to see that vision regularized in customs and policies. Deviation from the exact manner in which Mother Catherine did things was not acceptable in Mother Francis' eyes.

From today's perspective it seems that Mother Bridgeman exercised a strict asceticism in her own life. Spiritual darkness surrounded her year as a novice, and only engagement in work and the mortification of her own desires allowed her to move through that night. After a year of self-discipline, Mother Francis Bridgeman found that her darkness gave way to the brightness of a new dawn the day she made her profession of vows. Seen in this light, her strict adherence to the rule and to religious discipline was most likely rooted in the belief that only authenticity and fidelity could sustain one in darkness and preserve one from straying from the right path.

Mother Mary Francis remained fully engaged in the works of the Sisters in Limerick until she was called to be superior of the new Kinsale foundation. For Mother Francis Bridgeman it was a new chapter in a continuing story. The works that she pursued with such vigor in Limerick were established in Kinsale. One work was not established, however: a pension or a tuition-supported school. Mother Bridgeman was always strictly opposed to such an undertaking for she believed that it took energies and resources away from service to the poor. She believed that Sisters who taught students with means would later find teaching those without monies less congenial. This discussion would surface again in the American mission.

One of the deep joys of Mother Bridgeman's life occurred in 1848. It was not the entry of Mary Baptist into the Kinsale community, but the entry of her own beloved aunt, Joanna Reddan. The woman who had nurtured her niece's love of God and her passion for service now became a postulant in Kinsale. Friends of the Reddans and Bridgemans were delighted that Joanna Reddan, having spent so much of her life for others, would now live out the rest of her life in her niece's care. Little did they anticipate the course of events that would evolve in 1854.

III

To a Far Distant Shore

While Ireland was locked in a life-and-death struggle with famine and hopelessness, other parts of Europe were engaged in political and economic upheaval. Movements toward democracy caused political unrest culminating in the 1848 revolutions that swept across continental Europe. The underlying causes of the revolts were economic and political. People wanted more democratic systems of governance instead of the older autocratic ones. Economically, the gap between social classes grated upon people who saw no future for themselves or their children in such a system. Writers like Charles Dickens and Karl Marx gave expression to the plight of persons on the lower economic rungs of society.

Ireland was not exempt from the movement to have greater voice in self-governance. The Act of Union, which was opposed by the Russells, eliminated an Irish Parliament and provided only a minimal voice in the British Parliament for the Irish people. In the eyes of many, this structure of governance was useless. The needs of famine-struck Ireland were easily overlooked or ignored in favor of the economic theory of free trade that dominated the day.

In Ireland the political struggle for voice had another effect as well. It created an "if only" dynamic. "If only we had home rule we could take care of this problem." "If only we had the power to make our own laws and policy, everything would work

40

out." Energies were siphoned off into the political arena while people went hungry. English legislators funneled monies into an Irish Public Works program, which by design, served no useful purpose. In the name of free trade, Ireland's food supply continued to be exported while the food stores for people were radically rationed.

The revolutions that promised change were repressed. The only way to a new future seemed to be self-chosen exile. The scope of the desperation which led to massive emigration was caught by Thomas Carlyle: "The whole country figures in my mind like a ragged coat, one huge gabardine, not patched, or patchable any longer."[1] Persons were reduced to begging or selling all their personal possessions for food. Famine silence descended upon the land as pigs and other animals were sold off or eaten. Disease took its toll. The act of visiting the sick in their homes took on heroic dimensions, for lack of basic hygiene made the homes of dysentery or cholera victims incubators of infection and death.

In the midst of this darkness, stories of America provided a beacon of hope. The United States was seen as a land where food and opportunity awaited. Letters came from relatives who had made the journey urging those remaining to come to a land of promise. "I wish to heaven all our countrymen were here," wrote one such emigrant from the Chicago area. "… the labourer can earn as much in one day as will support him for a week. The richest land in the world may be purchased here or in Wisconsin for $1.25 an acre—equal to 5s 3d sterling—pure alluvial soil, over 30 feet of surface."[2] And so they came, over a quarter million Irish emigrants in 1847 alone.

Leaving Ireland was not an easy undertaking. The people left behind were too poor to buy passage or too weak from hunger to reach the ports; some were too ill to board the vessels.

Among the people leaving Ireland in 1847 were many the country could ill afford to lose. It is estimated that at least 50,000 of the quarter million emigrants were from moderately successful farming families, families who hoped to give their children a chance for a better life in America. As much as these families wished to stay together or go "for the whole in a lump" on the same ship, most could not. Some simply didn't have enough money while others had to leave behind grandparents or elderly relatives too infirm to travel. While some lacked money, others simply lacked the heart to leave Ireland.[3]

The pain of such parting gave rise to "American wakes." For an Irish family to have one of its members leave for America was both hope and death. While successful passage would mean a better chance at survival and the hope of money sent home to those in need, most believed that they would never see their loved one again. On the eve of the passage, people gathered to mourn the departure in the same way that they mourned the death of a loved one. Music, story telling and tears were all part of the good-bye.

It took a great deal of courage to set out for America. The passage was beyond contemporary imagining. The emigrants took with them food for the passage, bedding, what few clothes they had, and animals when they could. Having little money, most were booked in steerage where they were limited to a small patch of space without dividers. Privacy was not included in the price of their ticket. Into the space they crowded all their possessions, but what they did not anticipate was the lack of sanitation facilities. If emigrants booked their ticket on an English ship, the only bathroom provided for them was located above deck, yet during storms the steerage passengers were locked below deck.[4] Without proper facilities for bathing and personal needs, passengers suffered from the resultant stench. Worse, steerage rapidly became a breeding ground for disease. Once fever hit, death spread quickly. Food was provided in the price of passage, but the steerage class was subject to the whims of the person who distributed the food. Cooking the allotted ration was not always possible. The weary passengers endured such conditions for the entire two-month journey. It is no wonder that some of the ships were later called "coffin ships." Ships' logs show that on some passages as many as one quarter of the passengers making the trip did not arrive. They were buried at sea.[5]

The conditions were different if one were lucky enough to book passage on an American ship, for American ships were designed differently. Unlike the temporary decks of English boats, which defied proper cleaning, the steerage decks were permanent and easily cleaned, thereby greatly reducing the rate of disease. Bathroom facilities were built into the ship's design, further providing for improved sanitary conditions. Due to this simple design element, passengers on American ships had a significantly better survival record. Whether leaving Ireland by British or American vessel, however, one thing remained constant for the exiles: they were leaving a land of no hope in quest of a better life. They were risking the journey even at the cost of their lives. The poorer and more desperate one was, the costlier the journey.

It was against this backdrop of massive emigration and poverty that Katherine Russell chose to dedicate her life to the service of the poor. She did not know when she entered the Kinsale foundation in 1848 that the needs of her countrymen halfway across the world would call her to a different country and a different life. A year after Mary Baptist entered the Kinsale foundation, gold was discovered in California. In the rush of excitement, many came to believe that anyone who had hands could simply pick gold up and become rich. The lure of instant wealth acted like a magnet drawing people to the gold fields. Nor did the appeal discriminate. Gold seekers came from all parts of the world from Ireland to China, to Chile, their port of arrival, San Francisco. The city would swell with persons from all faiths and economic brackets. With them would come the need to provide for their spiritual and material well-being.

At the beginning of the Gold Rush, San Francisco was still a sleepy tent city. That did not last long. The population of 1,000 in 1848 grew to 2,000 by February of '49. In July of the same year, the population more than doubled to 5,000. By the end of 1849 San Francisco was a town of 20,000 people. It is estimated that the population of California went from 15,000 to 250,000 during the Gold Rush years.[6]

Such enormous growth posed great difficulty to the Catholic Church in California. Many of the new Californians were Catholic emigrants in need of both sacramental and pastoral services. The number of clergy and religious to serve this community was minimal. Bishop Garcia Diego, the only bishop in California, had died prematurely in 1846. At the height of need, there was no Catholic bishop to minister to the faithful.

Letters during the intervening years (1846-1850) that referred to the state of Catholic religious life in California were unanimous in theme. In the opinion of some observers the Catholic Church was on the verge of extinction.[7] In 1850 Rome responded to the critical need in California by appointing Joseph Sadoc Alemany, O.P., Bishop of Monterey. Three years later, in 1853, he became archbishop of the newly created Archdiocese of San Francisco. Alemany's first order of business was finding clergy and religious to serve his vast diocese of which San Francisco was the largest town.

The extent of San Francisco's growth can be seen from a brief description of the city written in 1853. San Francisco boasted:

> 626 brick or stone buildings within the limits of Broadway and Bush street, Stockton street and the waterfront—350 of them two stories in height, 154 of three stories, 34 at four stories, 3 at five stories, and 1 at six; 160 hotels and public houses; 66 restaurants and coffee saloons; 63 bakeries; 13 foundries and iron works; 19 banking firms; 9 fire, life, and marine insurance companies; resident consuls for 27 foreign governments; 12 daily newspapers; and "regular lines of omnibuses on the plank roads, which run to the mission every half hour."[8]

Still, for all its growth and development, San Francisco
lacked an adequate legal system, medical facilities that were
prepared to deal with major health crises, and laws governing
public sanitation. Need abounded.

While the Dominican Sisters and the Sisters of Notre Dame
de Namur had come to the Bay area by 1851, San Francisco had
no sisters to serve its people. Archbishop Alemany acted quickly.
The first Sisters to make the long journey to San Francisco were
the Sisters of Charity from Emmitsburg, Maryland, arriving in
1852. Their original intent was to respond to three areas of need:
education, the care of orphans, and health care. The perils of
their trip provide a glimpse into the dangers that confronted the
traveler. The Sisters went by sea from New York to the Isthmus
of Panama. Upon their arrival they were lodged in a "hotel."
Actually it was a small shelter previously used as a stable for
mules. The proprietor scrubbed the place for three hours while
the Sisters waited in a barroom for the scrubbing to be done. The
wait was made worse because reaching the hotel had required a
three-quarter mile walk through ankle deep mud and water. The
accommodations included no mattresses and only a few pillows.[9]

Worse conditions were to come. First, the boat which was to
carry them on the next segment of the journey was too small,
and another had to be found. The captain refused to take them
as far as their destination. The natives were overheard planning
to drown them in the rapids. Not a good beginning. As things
worked out, the Sisters had to make the trip across the Isthmus
by horseback. Without protection from the elements, the weary
travelers then faced torrents of rain. Two of the Sister pioneers,
Sister Honorine and Sister Mary Ignatia, died before the company reached the Pacific where they would take the steamer
Golden Gate to San Francisco.[10]

Accommodations in San Francisco were not quite what was
expected either. Father John Maginnis, pastor of the Sisters' new
mission, provided housing for his new teachers as best he could.

The glamour of the Gold Rush had worn off and its hoped-for wealth proved elusive for most Californians. The new convent was barely more than a shanty. The looks of it would have caused the bravest heart to grow weak.

> Father Maginnis assured the Sisters that the soil on which they were about to labor would be well watered with their tears. The Sisters entered the house, to find the picture of desolation complete. Not a chair could be seen, only some wooden stools, the handiwork of Father Maginnis. A large wine barrel stood in the middle of the floor, and a few cans of preserved fruit were scattered here and there. Upstairs were seven cots with straw mattresses and little goats' hair pillows. There were neither sheets nor blankets.[11]

Given these experiences it is a wonder that others were willing to brave the journey, but they did.

By 1854 conditions had improved somewhat, and the stage was set for new companies of women religious to come to San Francisco in response to expanding need. Archbishop Alemany dispatched Father Hugh Gallagher to Ireland for the purpose of recruiting new workers for his growing community. Archbishop Alemany specifically wished to bring the Sisters of Mercy to his diocese because he felt they were well suited to serve its needs. While Father Gallagher advocated for Sisters from the Mercy foundation in Pittsburgh, Archbishop Alemany believed that the relatively new community would not be able to grant such a request. It was the Archbishop's desire that Gallagher recruit Sisters directly from the "fountainhead" of Mercy at Baggot Street. The Archbishop was very familiar with the works at Baggot Street and believed that Sisters near the original center of the Mercy Order would be most steeped in Mercy tradition. Mother Mary Vincent Whitty, superior at Baggot Street, was unable to spare Sisters and instead referred Father Gallagher to the thriving foundation at Kinsale.

When Father Gallagher made Archbishop Alemany's plea to Mother Francis Bridgeman, he believed that Mother Mary Vincent had forwarded his earlier request to Mother Francis and that the necessary arrangements were already in process. Such was not the case. Mother Mary Vincent had left Father Gallagher on his own with regard to negotiating the mission. When Archbishop Alemany's request was made to Mother Bridgeman on July 28, 1854, it was the first time she had heard of the proposal. The hoped-for departure date was September 13 of the same year. The Sisters immediately took the request under consideration. It was decided to put their response and conditions of acceptance in writing to avoid confusion.

Between July 28 and August 21, a series of letters passed between Mother Bridgeman and Father Gallagher. Mother Bridgeman could be classified as a strict constructionist when it came to interpreting the Mercy charism.[12] She voiced explicit concern that acceptance of the mission not compromise the commitment of the Sisters to serve persons who were economically poor. In a letter dated July 29, 1854, she required of Father Gallagher a guarantee that the Sisters "will not be required to undertake any duties but those which it [the Mercy Rule] prescribes, or which, if not expressly prescribed, are obviously in accordance with its spirit,—for example, tho' an hospital is not prescribed we would gladly devote ourselves to it."

The letter continues: "That the Sisters should not be, in any way dependent on their own exertions for support.—I believe you are aware that the real duties of our Institute are, the visitation of the Sick, Instruction of the poor, the protection of distressed young women. To these duties we are really devoted, in them we hope to find content [sic] and perfection, we could not hope for a blessing on duties (however good for others) to which we are not called by God, if we were to undertake such."[13]

Father Gallagher's response almost brought a quick end to the project. Mother Bridgeman felt he had indicated that the

Sisters would be engaged in teaching wealthy and middle class students as a main focus. She writes on August 11:

> Your letter has convinced us that the principal duty that awaits the Sisters in your mission is the education of the higher and middle classes, a holy and meritorious duty that is for those who are called by God to it, but it is not our vocation; no one in our Community has any attraction for it. We have vowed to 'serve the Sick, poor & ignorant,' and our Sisters would willingly go to the 'ends of the earth' to accomplish this vocation. If you know our Rule you must know that the whole spirit of it breathes devotedness to the poor.[14]

In her eyes such an educational focus on wealthy and middle class students was contrary to the Mercy Rule. Mother Bridgeman even went so far as to suggest other possible teaching orders that would be suitable for such a mission.

For Mother Bridgeman, the discussion was ended. That was not the view of Hugh Gallagher. He continued the conversation and assured the Sisters that the California mission was consistent with the Mercy Rule. Time was moving on. On August 21 a final letter was exchanged between Mother Bridgeman and Father Gallagher. Gallagher states categorically: "We have *all* the objects of your Institute in our mission—and these shall be the Sisters' primary duties.... No duties shall be pressed on the Sisters but such as they shall cordially approve."[15] With this assurance, the project moved forward. Departure time was less than a month away.

When the request to undertake service in California first came, the Kinsale Sisters began nine days of prayer asking for openness to God's desire. It was a novena to the Divine Will. At the end of the time of prayer, twenty-nine Sisters, almost the entire group, offered themselves for the Californian Mission. It was September 3 before the delegate of Bishop Delany, the Bishop of the diocese, could preside at the selection of the band for the mission.

It is hard to comprehend all the mixed feelings that must have stirred in Mother Bridgeman's heart. She knew that her daughters would face hardship and danger in their new mission. The trip itself was dangerous, but she had also heard that their appointed field of mission was equally dangerous. At first she did not approve of the undertaking. Sister Mary Howley tells us that Mother Bridgeman had heard some "strange stories" about California and feared the Sisters would be killed. The vastness of the geographical distances within the United States caused some confusion for Mother Bridgeman. She worried that her Sisters might be caught in the Indian uprisings of the period, which were occurring in places far distant from California. Only the reassurances of a traveling merchant from California attesting to the absence of warring Indians in San Francisco, freed her of her fears.[16] Now, only the selection of the members remained. That would be the joint task of Father Kellegher, the bishop's designee, and Mother Bridgeman. Five professed members were to be selected: Sister Mary Francis Benson, Sister Mary Baptist Russell, Sister Mary deSales Reddan, Sister Mary Bernard O'Dwyer, and Sister Mary Howley. Three novices begged to be added to the group and their request was granted: Sister Mary Gabriel Brown, Sister Mary Paul Beechinor and Sister Martha McCarthy.

The San Francisco annals simply list, without comment, the Sisters chosen. Such brevity fails to tell the whole story. Mother Francis Bridgeman had selected for the California mission one of her most promising members, Sister Mary Baptist. A Sister who lived with Mary Baptist at the time reflected upon Mother Bridgeman's decision:

> Mary Baptist was one of our loved old Mother's most highly esteemed and best beloved spiritual children. She often said of her that she seemed like one who had never sinned in Adam, and that she believed she never allowed self-love to argue for a moment with what she had reason to know was God's will or

good pleasure. This fidelity to grace, she thought, had much more to do with her remarkable calmness of manner than had her naturally sweet temper. She often watched her under trying circumstances, but could never detect a shade of disappointment or a ruffle of any kind.[17]

The calmness which Mother Francis admired in Mary Baptist was sorely tested when, without any warning, she heard her name announced as Superior of the California mission. The recollection goes on to describe the moment of the announcement.

When all the Sisters had been selected for the California mission, they were presented to the parish priest as the chosen missioners; and he casually asked which of them was to be Reverend Mother. Mother Mary Francis replied that it was Sister Mary Baptist; at which Sister M.B. got slightly pale, and the tears started to her eyes, but they were not allowed to fall, and when the Sisters surrounded her and offered their mingled congratulations and sympathy, she was as calm and cheerful as usual, and received all so cordially and simply that no one could form any opinion as to how the announcement affected her.[18]

It was a sign of Mother Bridgeman's generosity that she selected Mary Baptist, but she exhibited even greater courage in the selection of her own beloved aunt, Mary deSales Reddan, for the mission. At fifty-four years of age, Joanna Reddan would get her wish to serve in a mission country, but Mother Francis would forever be parted from the loving "mother" who raised her. No written memory records that moment, but, without a doubt, it was painful for both.

The members of the company were young, some as young as nineteen years. Mother Bridgeman wanted them to have the support of someone who was wise and experienced. Her desire for the well-being of the departing missionaries was greater than her own desire to spend the rest of her days with her aunt. Just how important Mother Mary deSales' experience would be was to unfold in the first three years of the San Francisco foundation.

Mary Baptist was always cryptic in describing anything that had to do with herself. The San Francisco *Annals* do not tell the reader what happened in those ten days before departure. Fortunately other sources fill in the gaps. Some would call it luck, others providence, that the time of the small band's departure coincided with an annual visit to Kinsale by Mary Baptist's mother and her youngest sister Sarah. Lily (Sister Mary Aquin) had already joined her Sister by entering the Kinsale community in 1850. Margaret Russell had made many sacrifices for her children throughout her life, but seeing her beloved Kate leave for America was almost too much. Mrs. Russell and Sarah were able to stay with Mary Baptist throughout the preparation period. In spite of her hesitation and grief at the parting, Margaret Russell poured her energies into helping prepare for the departure of her cherished daughter.

Sarah, writing to her brother, says:

> During all that time Kate was as calm and recollected as if leaving her convent home were a matter of every-day occurrence. Once only did her great self-control break down, and that was one day when the two Nuns, our mother and myself, were busy drawing out a quantity of tangled silk. I began to read for them some verses you [Matthew] had sent me from Maynooth, in which you recalled the old place in Killowen, and the family circle there, and since then the way that all were scattered, leaving me behind alone.... While I was reading, I saw Kate's head droop a little and a tear steal down her face—then, just for a moment she bent with her face on her hands on the table, and when she raised it again, her face, though wet with tears, wore its usual calm, sweet expression. None of us noticed her emotion, and the work we were at went on without a word about it.[19]

While the Sisters busied themselves with preparing for the journey, Father Gallagher was busy as well. His recruiting of new personnel for California had been very successful. He was returning to California with two new communities of women religious, the Sisters of Mercy and the Presentation Sisters. Several Jesuits were also to join them on the trip as well as Father Cassin, assistant pastor of St. Rose in Sacramento. The group, now eighteen in number, gathered in Dublin. Mother Francis Bridgeman and Sister Mary Aquin accompanied the Kinsale contingent. There was a slight mix-up in Dublin when carriages arrived intending to take the Mercy Sisters to Baggot Street and the Presentation Sisters to George's Hill. The passengers, however, simply got into the nearest coach, sending some Presentation Sisters to Baggot Street and some of the Mercy Sisters to George's Hill. The Mercy Sisters arrived at George's Hill to discover the Presentation Sisters celebrating the twenty-third anniversary of Mother McAuley's admission to their novitiate. After conversation and refreshment, the Sisters proceeded to Baggot Street.[20] An honored memento of this Sisterly connection and friendship between the Presentation and Mercy orders, the prayer book of Catherine McAuley's mistress of novices, Mother Teresa Higgins, is preserved today in the Auburn Regional Community archives.

In the evening Father Gallagher arrived with unfortunate news. He was unable to book passage for the large party of eighteen on the *Arctic*. Unwilling to separate the group, Gallagher elected to book passage on a later ship. What seemed to be a disappointment proved to be a blessing, for the *Arctic* and all on board were lost at sea. It was only when the group arrived safely in New York that they heard the news of the tragedy and their own near brush with death.

New plans were made and the group was now to depart from Liverpool. Since there were ten days until their departure, the Sisters of Mercy decided to visit the convent in Derby where Sister Mary Francis Benson's sister, Mother Mary Evangelist, was superior of the foundation. The visit provided an opportunity for family connection and for learning more about the challenges their Sisters faced in a different country.

By September 23 all the delays and preparations were over and the missionaries boarded the *Canada* for the first leg of their journey to California. Conditions were a definite contrast to the steerage quarters of the emigrants who fled the famine. Father Gallagher was an experienced traveler and had provided for needed contingencies. He saw to it that a temporary partition was erected in part of the ship's saloon and arranged for several staterooms to be given over for the exclusive use of the party. This arrangement allowed the Sisters privacy for personal modesty and the space to continue their religious devotions. During the voyage, preparations for their new life continued, including an intensive study of the Spanish language.[21]

The trip provided an unexpected opportunity to find out more about the life of Sisters in the United States. Mother Mary Agnes O'Connor, Superior of the New York Mercy community, and her companion Sister Mary Austin Horan joined the group in Dublin and traveled back to the States with them on the *Canada*. Mother Agnes was well versed in the suffering and hardship Irish emigrants faced when they arrived in the country. She knew about the religious prejudice that the Sisters would encounter as well as the scarcity of monetary and human resources common to American foundations. Her wisdom and practical suggestions, born of her lived experience, were of immense value to the new pioneers.

When the *Canada* docked in New York on October 6, the Sisters accepted the hospitality of the Mercy community in New York. Due to business in Philadelphia, Father Gallagher was unable to leave for California right away. The Sisters were reluctant to travel without his seasoned travel experience and therefore elected to stay with the Mother Mary Agnes and her Sisters until November when the second leg of their journey would begin. The Presentation Sisters, bound for the Sacramento mission, left with their assistant pastor Father Cassin. Meanwhile the time in New York provided the California pioneers with two important pieces of information: a realistic sense of what was to come and a heartfelt conviction that all the other Mercy foundations were joined with them in a common enterprise: putting a human face on the mercy of God. With this insight to guide them, on November 13, 1854, the Sisters began their final passage to California.

IV

Together on the Journey

Everything had brought them to this moment. As the company of Mercy women began the trip westward, their lives
were cast together in a common future. Each of the volunteers
had given up family and the familiar to respond to the challenges
of an emerging young land. Their destination, California, was a
place of many contrasts. Wrested from Mexico and admitted to
the United States in 1850, California had grown like Topsy
because of the lust for gold. It would now have to survive its own
myth and develop into a stable region. Mary Baptist and her
Sisters were to be an important part of that transition.

Ever since the discovery of gold in 1848, California had
lured the individualist. Men abandoned their families to seek
gold. Children were left behind in San Francisco as parents
sought their fortune in the Gold Country. By the mid-1850s,
things were beginning to change. California, and San Francisco
in particular, stood at a juncture. How would it move from the
freewheeling lawlessness of the gold rush times to the stability of
a major commercial city? How were such services as education,
good health care, safe havens for women, and care of abandoned
children or orphans to be provided? These were questions and
challenges that lay ahead, but first it was necessary to get there.

The Sisters stayed with the Mercy community in New York
until Father Gallagher completed his business and was able to
accompany them on the next stage of the journey. They bade

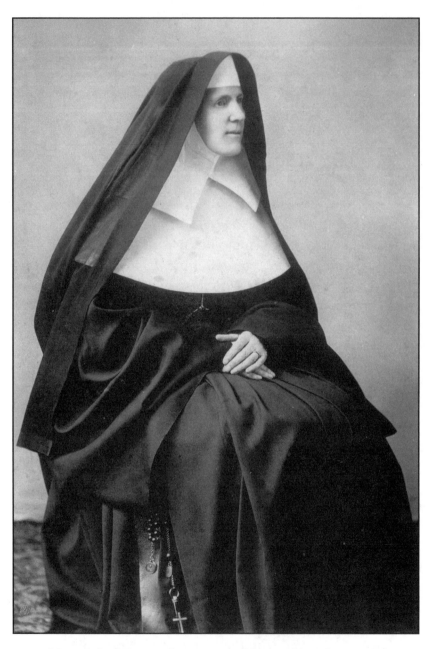

Mary Gabriel Brown, first superior of St. Joseph's in Sacramento,
Mary Baptist's companion and collaborator

farewell to the New York Sisters and began their trek to California on November 13, 1854. Along with Father Gallagher, some Jesuits, and the Sisters of Notre Dame, the eight Mercy women boarded the *Star of the West* destined for San Juan del Norte, Nicaragua. Mary Baptist notes in the *Annals* that they sighted the island of Inigua and Cuba as the ship made its way south.[1] Ten days later they landed at San Juan del Norte and made arrangements for the next leg of the journey. Unlike the religious women who went before them by way of Panama, they would go by a new route, crossing the Isthmus of Nicaragua. Mother Austin Carroll, Mercy historian and annalist, describes the trip in *Leaves from the Annals of the Sisters of Mercy:* "At Greytown the Sisters were transferred to river-boats and packed so close that no one thought of lying down, so great were the crowds going out in search of gold…. In the middle of the night they reached a point on the river that was impassable. All had to go ashore, and after walking some distance north they embarked in another boat."[2]

Housing along the way was another matter entirely. The "hotel" where they were to stay before crossing Lake Nicaragua lacked any kind of chairs, let alone beds. In the center of the room was a single table and tallow candle. Their respite at the hotel was short-lived, however, as they were soon summoned to the river where they boarded another river-boat. This craft would take them to the steamer that would cross Lake Nicaragua. The group boarded the *Virgen Maria* at 5 am on November 24. It would take a full day to cross the lake. So far in their journey, no major dangers had occurred and even the weather proved auspicious. Since space on the boat ruled out any possibility of a bed, the weary party leaned their heads on their bundles and dozed a bit.

Like other travelers, the company found that food was scarce and accommodations lacked furnishings and comfort. Father Gallagher had learned from prior experience and brought provisions with him on the journey. What food they had, they shared with those who found themselves without sufficient provisions to last the crossing.

Storytelling helped the company pass the time. Father Gallagher told stories of his travels in Europe and his experiences in what might be called the backwoods areas of the United States. All contributed to the night's conversations and the animated storytelling almost compensated for the lack of sleep they endured. The tropical environs of Nicaragua must have fascinated Mary Baptist. Always a lover of nature and beauty, the trip provided sights beyond her experience.

Lake Nicaragua covered about ninety by forty miles and was dotted by islands of volcanic origin, some still active at the time of their passage. Mother Austin Carroll, who gathered the stories of early Mercy missions from the pioneers, describes the scene:

> The full moon added to the beauty of the scene, but prevented the fireflies from showing off to advantage. When the party reached their destination they expected to be obliged to mount mules, but to their great delight large, double-seated wagons, each drawn by six beasts, awaited them. From the lake to the sea-coast, about fifteen miles, the drive was delightful.[3]

The beauty of the ride was interrupted by the dangers of travel. Roads over the passes were steep and treacherous. At one point the mules pulling the wagon carrying the Notre Dame Sisters became unmanageable as the animals pulled the wagon to the edge of the precipice. Fortunately, a member of the party, Mr. James Kelly, was quick to the rescue. He ran along side the wagon and guided the lead animal away from danger. Mr. Kelly must have summoned up extraordinary strength, for it is recorded that the wagon raced a full mile before he was able to bring the crisis to resolution.[4]

Without further mishap, the party reached San Juan del Sur about 5 pm. Accommodations were slightly improved over their first "hotel," as this time the establishment had cots and sheets. The Sisters had barely improvised dividers and settled into their quarters when Father Gallagher came to bring them to the *Cortes*, the ship that would carry them up the Pacific coast. Father Gallagher believed that it was better for them to spend their night on the ship than to stay ashore.

Getting to the boat was quite a surprise for the Sisters. The ship docked in deep waters off shore. Mother Austin describes the adventure.

> When they came to the beach they were bewildered at the sight that greeted their eyes. Men almost naked were carrying ladies and gentlemen about fifty yards into the sea to a point at which small boats were stationed to take them to the steamer that stood far out in deep water. There was not the least semblance of a wharf, and in that shallow water not even the smallest *pirogue*[5] could reach the shore. Presently their escort appeared with four "natives," whom he had induced to dress in linen shirts and pantaloons. By these the Sisters were carried in "My Lady to London" style to the skiffs.[6]

By this point the Sisters must have wondered what they had gotten themselves into. The saga continued once they reached the *Cortes*. Unlike the other boats of the passage, the *Cortes* had one large dinner table for the passengers. Normally, each person was assigned to a numbered place. On the night of their boarding, however, both the Captain and the purser were absent and the hungry passengers nearly rioted getting to the food first. When those in charge arrived later in the evening, they distributed the dinner assignments to the passengers. Father Gallagher and his party were seated in the places nearest the Captain. This small courtesy on the part of their Captain aroused bad feelings among some of the other guests. The cost for the Captain's courtesy would be paid for by a public press attack on the Sisters immediately after their arrival in San Francisco.

Newspaper accounts in the *Daily Alta California* tell us that the *Cortes* carried 222 packets of express freight and 245 passengers. Of the passengers 100 were ladies and 33 were children.

The names of 132 were listed and the other 112 passengers remained anonymous.[7] The character of the guest list reflected the changes coming to San Francisco. Women and children were arriving, and in their wake stability and civility would begin to replace the instability and lawlessness of the Gold Rush period.

The *Annals* of the Sisters tell us that the *Cortes* anchored in San Francisco Bay at 2 a.m. on December 8, 1854, the Feast of the Immaculate Conception. With precision the story notes that it was 5 a.m. when the eight Sisters of Mercy arrived at the Orphan Asylum run by the Sisters of Charity where hospitality was arranged for them until they could move into their own residence.[8] Such hospitality would be welcome in the face of unexpected attacks by the San Francisco version of the "Know-Nothing" movement.[9]

The day after their arrival, the *Christian Advocate* carried the following article:

Carried Past Their Port

The large company of European priests and nuns, who arrived yesterday morning by the *Cortes* should obtain heavy damages from the Nicaragua Steamship Co. for bringing them past *their port*. The ignorance, debasement, licentiousness, and bigotry of the people of Acapulco is certainly not more than paralleled in any other part of Mexico, or in any quarter of the city of Rome. Though it has been for so many years the metropolis of the Roman Catholic possessions on the Pacific, it *still* needs their ecclesiastical labors. That port opens up also a wide field, that they have hitherto cultivated with great success—we refer to Mexico and the regions south of it, extending from Guaymas to Chagres. We trust these ladies and gentlemen may be able to return without delay to their proper destinations particularly as the institutions of our Protestant and Republican country are known to be obnoxious to their sentiments and tastes. In case they do not commence suit against the Nicaragua Company for damages in bringing them here, we think it the duty of the

Attorney General of California at once to institute proceedings *in behalf of the state.*   *NO SABE*[10]

Other articles followed, charging the Sisters with neglect of the Sabbath and a tendency to indulge too freely in alcoholic beverages. Always the writer was anonymous. During this period of public attack Captain Cropper, Commander of the *Cortes,* was absent from the city due to illness. When he returned in mid-January, and was informed of the articles, the Captain took it upon himself to set the record straight. Writing to the *Herald* on January 18, 1855, he says:

Editor of the Herald:
  Owing to ill health, I have been absent from this city for several weeks, and it was only today that my attention was directed to an article signed "Observer," which appeared in the *Christian Advocate* of December 15th. Said article charges certain Reverend Fathers and Sisters of Mercy of Notre Dame (who were my passengers from San Juan on the Steamer *Cortes,*) with a neglect of a proper observance of the Sabbath, and with a disposition to indulge too freely in the use of intoxicating drinks. My position, as the commander of a passenger steamer, makes me a servant of the public in general, and especially so to those who come under my care and protection as wayfarers; and I feel myself called upon to notice the article alluded to, and to pronounce it the most disgusting, detestable calumny I have ever known or heard of. The Fathers and Sisters in question are Catholics, and on board the *Cortes* their seats at table were next to me, and I may say that at all times they were constantly under my eye and observation.
  Their religious exercises were performed not only on Sunday, but every day by themselves, without intruding on others; and in regard to "hard drinking," I cannot imagine how any person could be so very base a slanderer as to prefer such a charge against them. The extreme propriety of their deportment, their unobtrusiveness, and the gentle ladylike manners of the Sisters, and

perfect correctness of the Fathers, should have shielded them from so gross an outrage.

Thomas B. Cropper,
Commander of Steamer *Cortes.*
San Francisco, January 18, 1855[11]

The articles were more than just inhospitable. They must be seen within the larger horizon of San Francisco life in the 1850s. This was a time of both racial and religious intolerance. The Gold Rush had attracted persons from all nations to California, both the lawless and the law-abiding. The wide diversity of languages, customs and religious traditions in San Francisco led to ethnic clustering in the city. Among the ethnic clusters were Chilean, Chinese, Irish, and other communities.

While many of the new immigrants were persons looking for a new way of life, some were outlaws from their own lands. One of the groups that proved particularly lawless was the Australian "hounds" who took it upon themselves to drive the Chilean community from San Francisco. They were soon replaced by a group called the "Ducks."[12] It was the violence and lawlessness of this group that gave birth to the first vigilante committee. The committee took it upon itself to enforce its vision of law but often without paying attention to either rights or due process.

One person who fed the flames of intolerance was James King, editor of the *San Francisco Bulletin.* This newspaper was known for its journalistic attacks upon individuals. Catholics were particularly vulnerable because Mr. King had a strong dislike for them.[13] John B. McGloin, S. J., a noted California historian, described Mr. King's writing this way:

Fair (or unfair) game for his pointed and even poisonous pen was furnished by various persons whom he decided to attack and whom he did attack viciously and, at times, without proof of their being guilty of what he accused them. It quickly became apparent that King was at his best when heaping personal abuse on those persons or conditions or institutions that he disliked. Included were priests and nuns, for he entertained a special malevolence toward the Catholic Church.[14]

The Sisters of Mercy found themselves among Mr. King's targets not only in areas of their mission but also concerning their holiness of life. Mr. King went so far as to demand an investigation into whether the Sisters were holding their members in the convent against their will. Perhaps some of Mr. King's hostility was occasioned by the growth of the Catholic community in San Francisco. The timing of the Sisters' arrival coincided with significant improvements in the fortunes of Roman Catholicism in San Francisco. While the Sisters of Charity had found meager accommodations when they arrived in 1852, this first pioneer group was able to move into a newly built orphan asylum on the very day the Mercy company came to share the Western mission with them. The new facility allowed the Sisters of Charity to extend hospitality and shelter to Mary Baptist and her Sisters until housing could be secured. Little by little the services provided to the poor and needy were moving from makeshift buildings to more permanent structures.

At this same time, Archbishop Alemany turned his attention to the erection of St. Mary's Cathedral. The building was to be a concrete symbol of permanence. Many of the churches of the times were simple wooden structures vulnerable to the ever-present danger of fire. The courage it took to undertake such a task can only be seen when placed within the context of economic history. San Francisco in the early 1850s was constantly hit by severe economic depressions, business failures and unemployment. Archbishop Alemany was convinced that the erection of the Cathedral was necessary for the growth of his community. He and Father Gallagher went door to door collecting funds for the project. Only their hard work and perseverance brought success. Acquiring needed monies would always be a problem for the young Church in California.

On December 25, 1854, Archbishop Alemany formally dedicated the Cathedral during midnight Mass. Accounts of the dedication tell us that the Cathedral was almost devoid of decoration. Its primary decoration was the capacity crowd of believers who attended and the 1,000 persons who had to be turned away.[15] These were the people the Sisters came to serve, these and all others in need who came their way. The women would soon be known to them as "angels of mercy."[16] The power of their witness, expressed in service to the people, caused the San Franciscans of their time to ask: "Who are these women and what are they like?"

The Sisters of Mercy who arrived in San Francisco that December morning were eight in number. The eldest of the group, Mother Mary deSales Reddan,[17] was fifty-four. The youngest, Sister Mary Paul Beechinor, was only nineteen. The majority of the Sisters were in their twenties, including Mary Baptist who was twenty-five. Each had a different story.

Some of the circumstances and characteristics of Mary Baptist's early life have already been noted but much can still be said. Sister Mary Howley, one of the original seven companions of Mary Baptist, describes her this way:

> When I entered the convent, Reverend Mother [Mary Baptist] was in her nineteenth year. She had entered in November 1848, and I in the following May. When I saw her first, she had fair hair, dark eyebrows and rosy cheeks, and looked beautiful. While she was a postulant, she taught the novices, but she was always very humble and made nothing of it. She was ten months a postulant, Mother Francis Bridgeman having been called away to Limerick on account of the cholera.
>
> Mother had always great confidence in her. Even in the noviceship she [Mary Baptist] used to try to excuse the Sisters, and Mother Francis pretended not to like it, though she afterwards acknowledged that she admired her for it. She would say in such a nice, sweet way, "Now, Mother, Sister did not mean it that

way, etc." Charity was her favorite virtue. She could never see a fault in anyone. She could never blame anyone.[18]

Sister Mary goes on to speak of her experience of Mary Baptist's tender acceptance of each person's strength and weakness:

> I am sure I gave her a great deal of trouble, but she was so patient with me. When I would commit an imperfection, she would say, "Well, dear, if you did not commit that, there would be no imperfection, and then we might become proud." She was a religious according to God's own heart, and all that a Sister of Mercy should be. That is the reason Mother Francis sent her out here. I saw Mother McAuley, and she [Mary Baptist] always reminded me of her. She had a practice of always invoking the Holy Ghost in everything she undertook, and I am sure was always guided by His Spirit.[19]

Mary Baptist taught more by deed than by word. She was the first to take upon herself the hard tasks of cleaning, cooking, and scrubbing and reserved for herself the poorest accommodations. Her love for the poor exhibited itself in a variety of ways. She not only befriended them with food, resources, and the tender word, but she also took great pains to preserve their dignity when circumstances forced them to accept help. Two examples preserved through Sister Mary reveals Mary Baptist's love for those who were most needy:

> When we were really poor in the hospital, we did not have very many fine beds, and Rev. Mother used to sleep in a little place at the head of the stairs. She waited one day until we were at recreation, and went and hauled the hair mattress which she had downstairs, and gave it to a poor man who had only a straw bed. She arranged his bed with her own mattress. I found that she did this, and I told Bridget Kennedy, and she went to Rev. Mother's cell, and found a piece of carpet stretched on the cot to take the

place of the mattress. She then got her another mattress, and wrote, "Rev. Mother" in big letters, so that she could not give it away again.[20]

Mary Baptist's generosity was not confined to things she used herself. She would raid hospital supplies to meet the needs of the poor families whom she visited.

> She was kindness itself in her visitations to the sick. One time she heard of a poor family, and when she went there she found the poor woman lying in bed in consumption. Her husband was away. When Rev. Mother saw the distress, she came back, and went over to the Home, and took all the dresses, shirts, etc., she could get and also went to the Infirmary drawers and took sheets and tunics, etc. She did this so often that they had to lock the Infirmary drawers on her. They used to tell her she would never make a poor man's wife, as she would have him robbed, at which she always laughed.[21]

Mary Baptist was a blend of practicality and vision. Sisters who accompanied her on the visitation of the sick found her improvising clothes for the children out of whatever materials were at hand. When food needed to be prepared, she went in search of firewood among the sticks and scraps that she found around the yard. She sometimes made a nourishing stew or soup from scraps of food others would discard.

No one seemed exempt from Mary Baptist's care. She visited prisoners in San Quentin, the California State Prison; nursed at the bedside of smallpox victims, and possessed a natural gift for teaching both children and adults. Beyond this she had a knack for building lasting friendships and encouraging others to give generously of themselves. In a letter from California describing Mary Baptist, the correspondent says: "Kate is a grand creature ... the Martha and Mary elements are mingled in Kate in immense quantities and in most harmonious proportions.[22] She has chosen the better part, but at the same time she manages to have the tea-table pretty comfortable. That was always her way."[23]

Mary Baptist with her gracious manner, astute business sense, teaching and nursing skills, and utter faith in providence, still needed an equally dedicated circle of Mercy Sisters to face with her the rigors of life in California. Mother Francis Bridgeman, in selecting the women for the California mission, knew this and sent with Mary Baptist women of courage, accomplishment and faith. None of Mary Baptist's companions possessed these qualities in greater measure than Sister Mary deSales Reddan, who might be considered the "grandmother" of the group. Wise and experienced, she provided the young community an ever-ready source of serenity and compassion.

Sister Mary deSales had known her own share of hardship. Her desire to enter a religious community was twice thwarted, first by family death and then by a bishop unwilling to let her go. The death of her sister and brother-in-law left to her the care of her five nieces and nephews. One nephew, Richard, became a priest and missionary while her youngest niece, Joanna, later became Mother Francis Bridgeman. Mary deSales, then Joanna Reddan, poured out her energies in raising her young charges but she also spent her money and talent in relieving the misery of Limerick's poor.

Joanna Reddan was one of a group of wealthy women who committed their lives to social ministry. Even before coming to California she, like Catherine McAuley, had used her money to build a refuge for women. In her case it was for women who were prostitutes in the garrison town of Limerick. When Catherine McAuley came to establish the Mercy community in Limerick, the two women met and became friends and correspondents. Only one piece of that correspondence survives, quoted in *The Irish Monthly* in May of 1892. Mother McAuley writes:

My Dear Miss Reddan—I had great pleasure in receiving your kind letter; the friendship and regard you express are very acceptable to me. I have not known many whose esteem and friendship I should be more desirous to possess.... I have great reason to rejoice in our visit to Limerick. Every report is animating and delightful. The institution will be very valuable to the afflicted poor, and very edifying to all. I trust you will soon be added to their number—more than in spirit. And I shall never be surprised to hear that you are an obedient, humble sister. For, being so capable of fully understanding the nature of the state, its obligations and recompenses, you could not feel satisfied to lessen its value in your regard. And as God inclines you to desire ardently, a more perfect separation from the world, He will not permit any unfavorable results to follow, but will render you more instrumental in perpetuating the establishment over which you have so meritoriously and efficiently presided, and for which you feel so deeply interested.... I shall not omit to pray as you desire, with all the sincerity and fervor I am capable of, that God may guide you safely to the fulfillment of His adorable will.[24]

Mother Catherine never lived to see her friend become a Sister of Mercy because Bishop Ryan, bishop of the Limerick diocese, refused to release Joanna from the benevolent work she had established. Only in 1847 did Bishop Ryan allow her to find another religious community to carry on her ministry with women. Joanna sought out the assistance of the Good Shepherd Sisters and entrusted her work to them. Joanna now thought she could pursue her own heart's longing to join the Mercy Order. Mother Austin tells us "But Bishop Ryan put what he called a full stop to her proceedings, and desired her to join the new Sisters. 'If you do not,' said he, 'I shall send them all back to France.'"[25] Joanna followed Bishop Ryan's wishes. She was aware that Bishop Ryan was rather set in his opinions, yet she did not see how she could be professed in an order for which she had no inclination. In 1849 Bishop Ryan unexpectedly relented and released her to join the Mercy Sisters.

Sister Mary deSales brought this history and this faith with her to San Francisco. In addition to the skills she gained nursing cholera victims in Ireland and the years of experience in ministry with women caught up in prostitution, she brought with her the experience of living in darkness and uncertainty. Confidence in Providence was more than a concept for her; it was her history.

Sister Mary deSales was elected Mother Assistant to Mary Baptist. In this capacity she shared in the planning for and care of the community. Sadly, she died after only three years on the mission. Her death was the result of an arduous trip up the Sacramento River to prepare for the extension of Mercy to the Sacramento area. The conditions and crowding on the boat caused both Mary Baptist and Mary deSales to sit up on deck throughout a cold and damp night. Both were ill when they arrived back in San Francisco but the cold proved deadly for Mary deSales. On July 28, 1857 she became the first Sister of Mercy to die on the California mission. It was a major loss for the small community and especially for Mary Baptist, who had always looked to her for support and wisdom. Mary Baptist said of her:

> I never met anyone more forgetful of self or more zealous for souls. I have seen her with clasped hands, and tears coursing down her cheeks, praying for some poor hardened sinner. She felt we had a grand field for our labors in this country, and her gratitude for being assigned such a mission was unbounded.
>
> I never could tell you what she was, or describe the impression she made on all whom she came in contact; she is remembered and spoken of still after the lapse of so many years, and you know how short her career in California was—not quite three years. I did not mind so much the feeling manifested at the time of her death. It was so sudden that it created a sensation by that circumstance alone. Besides, she was the first Religious that died in San Francisco, or even in California. But I do really feel astonished when some circumstance causes her to be mentioned, and I see how vivid is the remembrance of her words and actions. Even Archbishop Alemany, who seemed a regular stoic in his way, more than once alluded to her with real feeling.[26]

Mary Baptist was not the only person to think well of her. One of the Sisters, Mary Howley, knew Mary deSales when she was still Miss Reddan. Remembering her, she said: "Mother de Sales Reddan is not easily described. She was a noble, motherly person.... There was an unction in her words that moved the erring to tears. Her benevolence and large-heartedness took in the whole world as it were. For all she had a kindly word and a smile."[27]

The story of Mary Baptist was well documented by her brother Matthew but less is known of the remaining Mercy pioneers. There is a stark brevity to entries in community annals. Mary Baptist herself retained the role of community historian until the 1880s when she finally gave it up. The pressure of duties and a natural reticence to praise what she considered the normal life of a Sister of Mercy combined to reduce details to a minimum. What is known is that Mary Baptist never governed alone. She relied upon her Mother Assistant and other elected advisors called the "Discreets." After the death of Mary deSales, no one was more a partner with Mary Baptist than Mother Mary Gabriel Brown, elected to replace Mary deSales as Mother Assistant in 1857.

Mary Gabriel was one of the three novices who volunteered for the California mission. She was twenty-six when she came to San Francisco, born the same year as Mary Baptist. Her novitiate was not ordinary. It was spent in nursing cholera victims, transforming the Marine State Hospital into Mercy's first health-care facility, and learning the ways of Mercy life. During her sixteen-month novitiate, she got a good look at what the future would ask of her. All the novices tasted bigotry, hardship, and need beyond anything they had expected. Still, each of the three novices accompanying Mary Baptist chose to commit her life to the California mission. Mary Gabriel was professed in 1856. The following year she was elected Mother Assistant and partner of Mary Baptist in shaping the Mercy mission. She served an unbroken period in community leadership from 1857 through 1882.

In a sense Mary Baptist and Mary Gabriel, while kindred spirits, were shadow personalities. Mary Baptist was more extroverted, a woman of action and a natural "people person." Mary Gabriel was reflective, introverted, and more drawn to the hidden life. She was a natural listener best described in the writings of Catherine McAuley, as one who speaks the gentle word, gives the tender, compassionate look, and patiently listens to another's sorrows. Together these two women gave the community its balance, depth, and passion for service. Working as a team, Mothers Baptist and Gabriel consulted with each other concerning the major crises that faced the young community. This type of communication was not always easy. The geographical distance between San Francisco and Sacramento was what prompted the decision to have the Mother Assistant act as superior of the Sacramento foundation. Mary Baptist believed that someone should be there who had the ability and authority to act quickly when the need arose; thus, Mary Gabriel served as superior of Saint Joseph Convent, the branch community in Sacramento. She was to spend fifteen years in Sacramento between the years 1857 and 1887.

After Mary Baptist served as superior of the Sisters for the first twelve years of the mission, Church law required that she have a break from leadership, Mary Gabriel was elected to succeed her. It was during this six-year period that a clear picture of Mary Gabriel emerges. She never asked anyone to do anything she would not do herself. In 1868 smallpox broke out in San Francisco. Mary Gabriel immediately went with Sister Francis Benson to serve in the "pest house." This ministry was short-lived, for Archbishop Alemany quickly ordered her home, saying that a general's place was at headquarters directing operations, not exposing herself as a common soldier.[28] Mary Gabriel's diplomacy was tested in another way when dealing with Bishop Eugene O'Connell who was in charge of the Vicariate of Marysville, California. Like Mary Baptist before her, she had to soothe the stirred waters of his episcopal ire when the Sisters assigned to the Grass Valley foundation failed to meet O'Connell's expectations.[29]

When her term as major superior was over, Mary Gabriel once more became Mother Assistant and later served for many years as Mistress of Novices, training the new generation of Mercy women. All this activity, this going up and down the Sacramento River, the strenuous labors needed to maintain the community, was done with a weak body. Mary Gabriel was tubercular and often struggled with periods of illness, a condition further aggravated by the damp and unhealthy conditions of the Sacramento convent. Still, her fortitude and her trust in Providence worked together in her to make the impossible become possible. After twenty- five years of community service, she was finally relieved of administrative ministry but went on to spend the last fifteen years of her life as Superior and guide of the Magdalen Asylum in San Francisco.

Two other Mercy pioneers, Sister Mary Bernard O'Dwyer and Sister Mary Francis Benson, were typical of the women of Mercy who came to America in the mid-nineteenth century. Sister Mary Bernard was twenty-seven when she arrived in San Francisco, Sister Mary Francis almost forty. Like Mary Baptist, both had Sisters in the Mercy Order.[30]

Sister Mary Bernard was "plain in appearance and manner" according to the *Annals*. This was an unusual entry for the document so her plainness must have been notable. According to Mercy historian Sister Mary Aurelia McArdle, Sister Mary Bernard had a special gift for comforting the dying.[31] Her commitment to the care of the sick was evidenced in her unceasing labors during the cholera epidemic of 1855.

If one tried to find a word to describe this early pioneer, it would be "solid." Sister Mary Bernard provided a no-frills stability and calm within the community. When the Grass

Valley foundation was struggling, she volunteered to be loaned there in order to provide an anchor in its stormy sea. Yet in spite of such stability and generosity, Sister Mary Bernard was not called to the ministry of leadership. She was more a model of day-to-day service.

Again the *Annals* tell us that Sister Mary Bernard was "neither talented nor educated tho' by dint of perseverance she had acquired considerable information of which she knew how to make the most."[32] Her fondness for discussing dogma at recreation, caused her to be nicknamed the "Mystical Theologian" by her Sisters.

Sister's death came quickly. On Monday, March 3, 1869, she thought she was getting "rheumatism in her chin."[33] The rheumatism proved to be an aneurysm. By the following Monday, she asked to see Mary Baptist. This was not easy because Mary Baptist was ministering in the small pox hospital, which was under quarantine. She had to be secretly brought to St. Mary's Hospital lest her visit create fear of contagion in patients and staff.[34]

Sister Mary Bernard quietly died after saying good-bye to each Sister. She was only forty-two. The *Annals* tell us: "About 10 o'clock the remains were conveyed to the cemetery followed by quite a number of carriages provided not by the rich and influential but by the humble and poor among whom are always found the *friends* of a Sister of Mercy."[35]

Sister Mary Francis Benson, with an impulsive streak to her temperament, provided a real contrast in personality to Sister Mary Bernard. More than once she received letters from her mentor Mother Francis Bridgeman, cautioning her to subdue her "anxious impetuous spirit against which I used to fight so desperately."[36] The fact that her impulsiveness was wedded to a great and generous spirit made her lapses in prudence most forgivable.

Education was the sphere where Sister Mary Francis excelled. Her gifts of imagination and openness led her to develop ways of reaching the many immigrant women who were in need of education and friendship. It was through her efforts that the St. Mary's Society was formed. This society provided a combination of learning, prayer, and community action. It had its own officers, funds, and policies. Within ten years it grew to include over 1,000 members.

Like her companions, Sister Mary Francis gave her energies to nursing when needed. During the smallpox outbreak in 1868, it was she who convinced Mary Gabriel to offer the services of the Sisters to the City. Sister Mary Francis worked night and day in the "pest house," transforming it into a place of hope rather than a place of fear.

The ease with which Mary Baptist excused the faults of another was needed at times to smooth ruffled feathers in the wake of Sister Mary Francis' activities. In her zeal to help Mary Baptist establish a home for the aged, Sister Mary Francis forgot to get formal approval from Archbishop Alemany. Work on the home was already underway before the annoyed Archbishop caught up with the project. With her customary tact and gentleness, Mary Baptist convinced the Archbishop that Sister had acted in good faith. The project went on.

Sister Mary Francis carried her vibrant and lively spirit into old age even as her body failed her. She was assigned to the Magdalen Asylum for the last years of her life. Always a woman of action and dynamism, she became like a young child in her senescence. Independence gave way to total dependence. Archbishop Riordan, who had succeeded Archbishop Alemany as Bishop of San Francisco, said of her:

> She was not an ordinary woman but a woman of high culture, great refinement, splendid education and yet all those qualities were spiritualized and sanctified, because they were used in the great service to which Almighty God called her. You will remember, those of you who have been long enough here that in the days of pestilence, when the call came to her and her Sisters to go out

of their Convent home and wait on the stricken with the terrible disease of small-pox, she was only too glad to devote her life to the service of the afflicted. She loved the poor and especially the aged. It was the dream and prayer of her whole life not to pass away until some large and beautifully equipped home might be erected in this city, within the walls of which the poor and aged might pass to their eternity. For this she lived and toiled and prayed. So Almighty God led her from one heroism to another, from one year of preparation to another, until at last, after over three quarters of a century passed in His service, she quietly and gently passed away as a child goes to sleep in the arms of his mother.[37]

Sister Mary Francis had a long and rich life ministering in California. Her companion in Mercy, Sister Mary Paul Beechinor, did not. She lived only eight years after her arrival in San Francisco, dying at the age of twenty-seven. Like many of her companions, Sister Mary Paul had a quality education that was complemented by a thoughtful, serene personality. Coming from a protective family and sheltered educational experience, the nineteen-year-old novice must have been shocked by the realities of California life.

During her novitiate she found herself sharing the cramped quarters of their six-room cottage with sixteen Sisters, serving in the cholera hospital, and listening to the Vigilance Committee drill under the hospital windows. Since the troops of the Vigilance Committee had surrounded the hospital, her profession ceremony was private. Making a decision to give one's whole life to serve in such circumstances demanded both a stout heart and deep faith. Sister Mary Paul had both.

Both Sister Mary Paul and Sister Mary Francis were part of the founding mission for Sacramento in 1857. Mary Gabriel went as superior for the new community. Separated from their Sisters in San Francisco, they had to find a way to respond to the needs of the city in a way different from the demands of San Francisco. In Sacramento, education was the primary need, and it is this ministry that demanded all of Sister Mary Paul's skill and stamina. By 1859 she was made superior of the branch community. She remained in Sacramento for five years before being recalled to San Francisco to serve as Mistress of Novices.

By 1861, the Mercy foundation had almost thirty Sisters in formation. Many of the new members had limited education but served in a variety of works. Sister Mary Paul's task was challenging. It was to impart the spirit and ways of Mercy to the new generation of Mercy Sisters. She did not remain long in this service, as death made a premature visit. Almost without warning, in December 1862, Sister Mary Paul had a premonition of impending death. No one took her seriously. It seemed beyond her Sisters' imagination that one so young and vital, only twenty-seven, would be taken from them, even though the *Annals* tell us that she had been delicate for some time. The certitude of her intuition is remarkable. The *Annals* report:

> She seemed to herself to have had more than a presentiment of death for on the preceding Retreat Sunday at evening Recreation when the conversation turned on the exercises of the day, she held up her hands saying, "I am all ready now for death if I were only anointed" and two days before her death one of the Sisters asked her (she had at the time the charge of the singing choir), what new hymn they would learn for Christmas to which she answered, "You may learn what you please, I will sing my Adeste in Heaven." One of the Sisters hearing this said in an undertone to her companion, "Certainly now *this* Christmas" but Sister Mary Paul overheard her and said at once in a gay but emphatic manner, "Yes, Sister, *this* Christmas."[38]

History proved Sister Mary Paul correct. She died December 15, 1862.

The last two members of the pioneer community were Sisters Martha McCarthy and Mary Howley both of whom were lay sisters. The story of these two early Sisters is intertwined with the realities of religious life in the nineteenth century. At the time of their entry into the Sisters of Mercy, religious life in general had two distinct levels of membership, choir Sisters and lay Sisters. The distinction was a vestige of the medieval European class system where social status was determined by birth, wealth and education.

Choir Sisters brought to their religious community a dowry and were generally well educated. Dowries were important because the religious women of the early nineteenth century received no payment for their service. Communities were dependent upon a member's dowry for all communal needs: food, housing, clothing, personal care of the members. It was not until later in the nineteenth century that it was considered legitimate to use some of the proceeds of ministries to support the community.

Lay Sisters came to the community without dowry and often with minimal education. Their dowry was their physical and domestic work in support of the community's mission. As a result they normally did not teach but did the hard manual labor of the community. For communities which had orphanages or asylums, like the Sisters of Mercy, they played a key role in the care of children and of women who received shelter from the Sisters. Because of their lack of education, the lay Sisters did not take part in praying the Office[39] of the community, which was sung or recited in Latin.

Practices existed which established a two-tier membership. Lay Sisters did not have "Mary" as part of their name; choir Sisters did. The lay Sisters were not given governing voice; they could not vote in elections nor could they be elected to leadership. Even their mode of dress was different. They had no train on their habits and wore white aprons. Today such a class distinction within a religious community would be unthinkable, and, indeed, has long been forbidden by the Catholic Church; but in 1850 it was the norm. Whatever the distinctions of class, education, or personal history, one fact is certain: the work of the community was dependent upon the contributions of both choir and lay Sisters.

Sister Martha was one of the first lay Sisters to break the mold. Her story is an example of how Mary Baptist was willing to leave behind practices that did not help the mission. It seems that Sister Martha had a gift for working with young boys. Mary Baptist recognized this gift in her and put her in charge of a class of small boys. While this was a risk for both women, Sister Martha proved more than able. She was a natural teacher. Sister Mary Aurelia tells us that "she won a reputation through the parish as a remarkable teacher of religion and the other basic "R's." The parish priest boasted that she could teach anything to any boy even if he had his eyes closed."[40]

Sister Martha's teaching career lasted until the Christian Brothers assumed responsibility for teaching the boys. She was then transferred to the Magdalen Asylum where she gave her energy and care to the inmates of that institution. The *Annals* have only a brief entry marking her death. Had Mary Baptist still been recording community history, more might have been added, but the brevity of the entry is symbolic of the way of life embraced by the lay Sisters. It was the way of hidden service, humble and unsung.

Sister Mary Howley was Sister Martha's companion from Kinsale. More is known of her because she was the last survivor of the original company, dying in 1907. She carried the living history of the foundation in her heart and in her storytelling. It was her memory that provided the animating story of the pioneer Sisters. Over and over again, Matthew Russell quotes Sister Mary's accounts of the foundation as he recorded the life of his sister Mary Baptist.

As a woman, Sister Mary was outgoing, loved celebrations, and was the soul of hospitality. Not a great deal is known about her own life. It is recorded that she was orphaned at an early age and taken under the protection of Joanna Reddan before Joanna entered Mercy. Through the later Mary deSales, she was introduced to Catherine McAuley. Mary's training in Mercy was received through the example and teaching of three remarkable women, Mary deSales, Mary Francis Bridgeman and Mary Baptist. It is no wonder that her story-telling was so vivid.

These eight women were the company of Mercy. Together they would bring healthcare, education and pastoral care for women to San Francisco and Sacramento. They needed every talent and gift among them to succeed in the task, for the task was formidable. They had to create structures that did not exist and adapt to an ever- changing society. How they did what they did challenges the imagination.

St. Mary's Hospital on Rincon Hill, San Francisco. First Catholic Hospital in California

V

Hearts for Healing

When Mary Baptist and her Sisters left Ireland, they thought they were coming to San Francisco to provide for the educational needs of children but by the time the pioneer community reached their destination, this situation had changed. The Presentation Sisters, who accompanied Mary Baptist and her Sisters on the voyage across the Atlantic, went directly to California in the company of Father Cassin, then associate pastor in Sacramento. The group arrived in San Francisco in late November 1854. The original intent was for the Presentation missionaries to proceed to Sacramento where they would open a school for children. Upon their arrival, however, the Sisters were deterred from setting out for Sacramento by stories of its unhealthy climate and physical hardships.[1] They remained in San Francisco and opened a school for children on December 1, 1854, just one week before the arrival of the Mercy contingent.

Finding little need for a school when they arrived, Mary Baptist looked to other pressing needs of the population. None was more pressing than care of the sick and infirm. The Sisters lost no time in beginning their work. By December 20 Archbishop Alemany had applied for permission for the Sisters to visit the County Hospital. On January 1, the Sisters went to the facility to visit patients for the first time. Visitation of the sick and the poor in their homes began just a few weeks later.

During this period, Mary Baptist sought a suitable residence for the Sisters, eventually renting a six-room house on Vallejo Street. The new convent was named Convent of Divine Providence. The community moved into the convent during the first week of January, and Archbishop Alemany confirmed the appointment of Mary Baptist as superior of the community on January 19, 1855. Mary Baptist had rented the new convent with the County Hospital in mind. Each day two or more members of the community walked to the hospital to provide spiritual comfort to its patients. It was the beginning of a work that would provide the Sisters with opportunities to do great good. It would also be the source of great heartache.

Visitation of the sick in their homes was a major work of mercy during the latter half of the nineteenth century. Catherine McAuley, foundress of the Sisters of Mercy, was particularly devoted to this kind of ministry. Mary Sullivan, RSM, comments:

> The "visitation of the sick poor" was one of three central elements in Catherine McAuley's vision of the merciful work to which she and, later, her companions in the Sisters of Mercy were called. She conceived of this "visitation" as affording to the desperately ill and dying both material comfort and religious consolation. What is especially striking about her service and advocacy of the sick poor is not only her willingness to care for people with extremely dangerous infectious diseases (cholera and typhus, for example), with consequent risk to her own life, but her overwhelming desire to offer these neglected and shunned people the dignity and Christian solace that she felt was rightly theirs, as human beings with whom Jesus Christ himself was intimately identified.[2]

For Catherine, this ministry was rooted in her understanding that the suffering poor were Christ in our midst. The Gospel admonition, "Whatever you do to the least of these, you do unto me" (Matt. 25:40) shaped and animated her dedication to this work of mercy.

Sisters, following in the footsteps of Catherine, undertook the same service with that conviction. Sister Mary Sullivan explains their intent: "Therefore the primary purpose of the visitation of the sick poor, as Catherine envisioned and described it, was to bring to the poor the comfort and consolation of God: to make known to them—by one's words, presence, prayer, and tenderness—that God in Christ was indeed present to them and in them, and that though they suffered grievously, God was indeed at work in them bringing lasting joy out of their affliction."[3]

The consistency with which Catherine's vision inspired and strengthened the California pioneers is seen in their letters, where little is told of medical interventions or discoveries; few contain information about changing medical techniques. What is always in focus is God's work in the life of the patient and the spiritual consolation the Sisters were able to bring.

The initiation of the visitation of the sick in San Francisco came none too soon for one poor woman. On January 4, the Sisters were called to pray for a newly deceased woman. As they knelt to offer the prayer, the Sisters noticed signs of life. Practicing the skills they had learned in Ireland, they revived the woman and had her taken to the County Hospital where her life continued for several months.[4] This was not an exceptional case, however, since the state of medicine in the 1850s was such that critically ill patients were sometimes mistaken for dead and were buried prematurely.

The Sisters began their nursing at the end of the "Dark Ages of Nursing." Medical practice was just on the verge of vast change. In 1856, two years after the Sisters began their work in California, the source for the spread of typhoid fever was identified. It took another two years for health officials to determine that contaminated water was responsible for cholera epidemics. Germ theory was not accepted until the mid-60s,[5] but long before germ theory was accepted by the medical profession, the Sisters approached nursing with two great healers—cleanliness and fresh air. Their approach to care of the sick provided a startling contrast to the model sometimes found. A description of a contemporary hospital given by Methodist minister, William Taylor, around 1858 put it this way:

> I thought the private rooms upstairs were filthy enough to kill any well man who would there confine himself, but in comparison with the others (public), they were entitled to be called choice rooms. The "lower wards" were so offensive to the eyes and especially to the olfactories that it was with great difficllty [sic] that I could remain long enough to do what I deemed my duty.[6]

The Rev. Taylor was equally critical of the caregivers for he continues, saying:

> The nurses were generally low men devoid of sympathy, careless, rude in the care of the sick, and exceedingly vulgar and profane. One hundred dollars a month was about as low as anything in the shape of a man could be hired, and hence hospital nurses were not only the most worthless of men, but insufficient in number to attend adequately to their duties.[7]

Rev. Taylor illustrates the deficiencies of the system through the story of one patient by the name of Switzer. It is easy to see from his story why people tried, at all costs, to avoid the hospitals of the day.

> I remember a poor fellow by the name of Switzer died in one of these wards; he told me he lay whole nights suffering, in addition to the pains of mortal disease, the ragings of thirst without a drop of water to wet his lips. A cup of tea was set in the evening upon a shelf over his head, but his strength was gone, and he had no more power to reach it than a man on a gibbet.... I have seen men enter these horrible wards with appar-

ently very slight indispositions who within a few days would wilt down and die.[8]

The Gold Rush had drawn many good and dedicated doctors to California, but it also provided tremendous opportunities for charging exorbitant rates and medical quackery. In his book *Memories, Men and Medicine*, Dr. J. Roy Jones quotes from a letter written by Dr. Thomas M. Logan to his brother-in-law in 1850:

> I am sorry to inform you that, like many articles of merchandise with which our country has been flooded, we physicians are at the most ruinous discount, and the ancient and time honored doctorate is in most cases held in so low repute that many a worthy physician studiously conceals his title. I have seen M.D.s driving ox-teams through our highways—laboring in our streets like good fellows—serving at bar-rooms, monte tables, boarding houses, etc., and digging and delving among the rocks and stones, to gather together their allotment of California's produce, the precious gold. Labor, however, is honorable to man, and it is not because some are obliged to put their shoulder to the wheel that the profession is rated at so low a standard. It is because many, and among them those who assume without any moral or legal right the title of Doctor, in their grasping cupidity, and impatience to amass in the shortest possible time their "pile" have, while taking advantage of the necessities of their sick and dependent fellow creature, drained the poor miner of all his hard-earned dust, be it more or less, for a few professional visits. These incidents of medical rapacity have become so numerous and aggravated as to create a distrust on the part of the community toward the profession generally and to bring odium on its practitioners.[9]

Such was the state of medicine when the Sisters offered their services to the County of San Francisco in April 1855. At this time in California's story, the State Marine Hospital was a shared undertaking of the County of San Francisco and the newly formed State of California. Economic conditions were poor and money scarce. A policy of bidding out the care of the sick was instituted. The Sisters submitted a bid to care for the sick to the County of San Francisco. The bid was rejected even though, as the *Alta California* pointed out, "On its face, the bid of the 'Sisters of Mercy' seems more favorable, in point of economy, than that which was accepted."[10] The Sisters had two strikes against them. They were Catholic in a period of intense nativism and they were women.

In the days following, public discourse concerning the rejection of Mary Baptist's bid continued. On April 6 a letter appeared in the *Alta California*. The writer clearly asserts that entrustment of the State Marine Hospital to the Sisters would constitute support of a religious sect. Such an action, in the writer's opinion, should have been rejected.[11] Three days later, another interpretation of the decision was published. The letter provides revealing insight into the cultural norms of the period. The author acknowledges the rejection of the Sisters' bid but wishes to give what he considers to be the real reason:

> This [description] was doubtless true. But it was not because of any disinclination to give the care of the sick to the Sisters of Mercy, that this was done. It was from no prejudice toward them. On the contrary, the Committee were disposed to give them the preference, and the person who spoke in their behalf, was distinctly told that if he would put in a bid in his own name, or in the name of any other, responsible man, it should certainly be adopted. But those of the Committee who were members of the Legislature, were disinclined to go back and report that they had contracted with some women to take care of sick men and sick women, and so the bid of the Sisters of Mercy, made through Mr. Roach, was not accepted.[12]

While the writers may not have agreed on the reasons for awarding the contract to other health providers, they all agreed on one point. "Farming out the sick" was prone to abuse.

Mary Baptist was not to be deterred in her efforts to assist the sick of San Francisco. The work went on with or without the contract. The following September events occurred that changed the mind and vision of San Francisco's political leaders. On September 5, 1855, a vessel owned by the Nicaragua Company, the *S.S. Uncle Sam*, arrived in port. Among its passengers was a most unwelcome guest, Asiatic cholera. Civil authorities were unprepared to deal with the illness that soon reached epidemic proportions. San Francisco at the time had no public health regulations, and few in the city were experienced in treating the disease. The Sisters, with their nursing experience gained from the 1849 cholera epidemic in Ireland, filled the void. Mary Baptist quickly offered the services of her Sisters to the city. It was no longer a question of the sick being placed in the care of "some women."

The Sisters labored in the State Marine Hospital around the clock, the members of the community rotating day and night shifts. The selflessness with which the group went about its work made a lasting impression on observers. The *Daily Times* on September 15 carried the following description:

> We visited yesterday the patients in the State Marine Hospital; a more horrible and ghastly sight we have seldom witnessed. In the midst of the scene of sorrow, pain, anguish, and danger were some four or five nuns who disregarded everything to render aid to their distressed fellow creatures. The Sisters of Mercy, (rightly named), whose convent is opposite the hospital, as soon as they learned of the state of matters, hurried to offer their services. They did not stop to inquire whether the poor sufferers were Protestants or Catholics, Americans or foreigners, but applied themselves to their relief. One nun would be seen bathing the limbs of a sufferer, another chafing the extremities, another applying remedies for the disease, while still another, with a pitying face, was calming the fears of the dying. The idea of danger never seemed to occur to these women. In the perfor- mance of the vows of their Order, they heeded nothing of the

kind. If any of the stricken are saved, they will in great measure owe their lives to these ladies.[13]

Mary Baptist could not have predicted the impact this act of mercy would have upon those who possessed no first-hand knowledge of the Sisters. The widespread respect and admiration the Sisters received because of their work was sorely needed to counteract the next wave of public censure.

Concurrent with the end of the cholera epidemic in San Francisco, the State Legislature decided to make the counties responsible for their own sick. As a result of this decision, the State Marine Hospital was put up for sale. Although aware of the dangers of going into debt, Mary Baptist borrowed funds, and on August 17, 1855, purchased the building for $14,000. The next step in the process was negotiating a contract with the County for the care of its indigent sick. The County was to pay the Sisters $400.00 per month for rent and to reimburse the community for the expenses involved in the care of the infirm. This remuneration would include food, clothing, bedding, fuel, medicine, medical and surgical treatment and anything else deemed necessary for their care. It did not include payment for the nursing services of the Sisters.[14]

The Sisters assumed management of the hospital on October 24. Change was immediate. Mary Baptist dismissed the former staff and hired new caregivers that matched the manner of nursing care the Sisters envisioned. The whole building was scrubbed, and three new wards were made from rooms formerly used by the staff. One other significant change was made: Mary Baptist converted a small upstairs room into a chapel.

From October until March all went well. In March, however, the Sisters were caught in a political minefield which centered upon three issues: the establishment of the chapel in the hospital, the quality of care given to patients, and the use of public funds. To understand the seriousness of the situation, it is important to note two elements in the life of the city: economic depression and the political vision of the Know-Nothing partisans. In the fall of 1855, the mayor of San Francisco announced a budget deficit of $840,000. As a result of this deficit, public officials proceeded to repudiate 1.5 million dollars of public indebtedness.[15] In the same year there was a statewide sweep of political offices by members of the Know-Nothing Party. This society was avidly anti-foreign in its stance. Historian Kevin Starr puts it this way:

> Anti-Catholic and anti-Irish feeling seethed through the Vigilance committees of 1851 and 1856. Irish immigrants from Australia and New York were branded wholesale as a criminal class. Yankees and Southerners put aside their quarrels, including the slavery issue, to unite behind the Know-Nothing Party and the Vigilance Committee of 1856 (an organization redolent of Masonry) in the fight against growing Irish political power....
>
> Anti-foreign reformism on the part of outraged businessmen accounted for both Know-Nothing and Vigilance movements.[16]

While the work of the Sisters was extolled by attending physicians, James King, editor of the *San Francisco Daily Evening Bulletin,* chose to use their public service as the focus for a virulent and unexpected attack. For eight weeks during the spring of 1856, a steady stream of public accusations was brought against Mary Baptist and the hospital. The substance of the complaints was inflammatory and unsubstantiated. The first target was the small chapel installed by the Sisters when they purchased the hospital. Mr. King charged that it not only violated the principle of separation of church and state but that it resulted in patients being "crowded into a lower portion of the building in an unhealthy and less comfortable condition in order to furnish better recruiting quarters for our Catholic friends."[17] This initial complaint was nothing compared to the next stream of accusations. Among the list of grievances were inhumane treatment of an "idiot," starvation of patients, filth, robbery and downright unwholesome food. Mr. King reported:

> The bread furnished the patients is generally stale. A patient informed us that in two-and-a-half months he had tasted fresh bread but twice; it is always sour; the corn meal from which the mush is made, often sour and lumpy; the lumps are hard and plenty enough as our informant said, to use as shot to bombard Sebastopol, and also full of impurities. For breakfast the patients had mush and molasses, bread and tea. For dinner, beef and potatoes, with soup thickened by the remains of the mush, and bread left at breakfast, and three times during two-and-a-half months cabbage substituted for potatoes. For supper bread and tea only. "The Sisters," after dinner, go around and pick up all the little scraps of meat and gristle left by the patients, which they put into the soup for the next day's dinner.[18]

The exposé asserted that patients were not given clean bedding and that Protestant patients received less care than their Catholic counterparts. More shocking was the claim that patients were beaten, sometimes upon their wounds, or threatened with such beatings. One assertion even claimed that a patient was hit with the end of a hammer.[19]

The vehemence of the charges is hard to comprehend. The *Annals* tell us that the stories originated with a young man by the name of Woodruff. The management of the hospital provoked his ire when it stopped the passage of letters between himself and a "depraved character in the Female Ward."[20] Mr. King used Mr. Woodruff's stories for his own purposes, involving the Sisters in a power struggle between Irish politicians and his own fellow-thinkers. The nature of the struggle is clearly seen when subsequent articles condemning Father Gallagher and corrupt politicians are examined.[21]

Mr. King did not limit his attack to the hospital. He took on the whole question of religious life itself. In his article of April 8,

1856, he requests that an investigation be made to see that no woman is held in the convent against her will. He says:

> You say—"If these women are foolish enough to enter these cells, let them do so." Certainly, let them suffer for a season for their folly; but let one little ray of hope illumine even the darkness of these dens of Papal superstition. Do not permit any citizen to be controlled by a power unknown to the State, or placed beyond the protection of our laws; and such parties must have an opportunity of claiming such protection. It should be made the duty of every Grand Jury to visit each convent or monastery and privately inquire of each person in durance whether she desires longer to remain, and if not, to compel her immediate release.[22]

In the mind of Mr. King, the Sisters were lambs being led about by a wolf, Father Hugh Gallagher.

When both Protestant and Catholic patients and other citizens came forth to defend the Sisters, Mr. King refocused the attack on the "wolf." In his article of April 17, he states:

> The reputation here of the lady at the head of the "Sisters of Mercy" stands equally fair. That lady did not know of the cruel practices on the patients. But Father Gallagher rules at the Hospital, and two of the patients, in evidence not yet published by us, say: "Father Gallagher leads the Rev. Mother just as he pleases. She is keen as a briar, but stands no chance with him: when she sees him coming she wilts like a leaf."[23]

Eight days later, by the 25th, the Sisters have become faultless in the eyes of Mr. King:

> The Protestant patients at the Hospital should surely be good evidence in this case, and they are unanimous in exculpating the ladies of any blame, and speak highly of their kindness to the sick, without regard to creed or nativity. They all speak in respectful terms of the Reverend Mother, and with that prejudice that is

natural to be expected of them, and equally to the credit of the lady Superior, they "regret that so estimable a lady should be a nun." With such expressions before us, how can we doubt that the Sisters are wholly blameless and Father Gallagher solely guilty.[24]

The whole hospital situation must have been a great burden on Mary Baptist. She had to choose between mounting a public defense or allowing the quality of the work to speak for itself. After conferring with Archbishop Alemany, Mary Baptist chose silence. Others would speak for her out of their experience. When James King had demanded an investigation of the hospital by the Grand Jury, Mary Baptist welcomed the opportunity. In fact, the investigation allowed the true realities of the relationship between the Sisters and the county government to be made known. The report of the Grand Jury was published in the *San Francisco Herald* on April 1, 1856. The report served to completely exonerate the Sisters. The article read as follows:

> The Grand Jury made a thorough investigation of the condition and management of the Hospital in charge of the Sisters of Mercy, with a determination to inquire into the causes which have led to the unfavorable reports in circulation.
>
> We are enabled to lay before the public a Report which will be read with much interest, having been carefully compiled from the books and vouchers of the Institution, from conversation with the patients, and from personal inspection of the premises. We find that there have been three new Wards established by the Sisters of Mercy, which had been formerly used by the attachés of the Hospital, thereby securing increased accommodation to the patients. We also found a room fitted up for religious exercises for the use of the Sisters, which they had done at their own expenses: this room had been condemned by the Medical Staff as unfit for the purposes of a ward for the Sick.
>
> We also made a thorough investigation into the expenses of the Hospital. After critically examining the vouchers, we find

that the average amount of monthly expenditures is ($5,747) five thousand seven hundred and forty-seven dollars; this includes many expenses which will not be required monthly—such as beds and bedding, altering Wards, crockery, and hardware— these articles are comprehended in the seven hundred and forty seven dollars expended monthly, over and above the amount paid them by the County—so that the County have paid but a small amount, if any, towards the purchase of the above articles. We are of the opinion that five thousand dollars will hereafter meet all the expenses of the Hospital.

There has been admitted to the Hospital in five months ending 24th of March, 527 patients, besides 254 out-door patients treated at the Hospital by the Resident Physician. There are at present 167 patients in the Hospital; of the 527 admitted, 174 belong to other Counties, in most cases having contracted disease out of this County, to be provided for by the tax-payers, amounting to the sum of $8,352 for the five months just past, or to the large sum of $20,040 per annum.

We respectfully call the attention of our Delegation at Sacramento to the law on this subject, suggested by the Board of Supervisors.

The Sisters have received the sum of $312.50 from private patients, which they assure us has been expended in assisting the convalescent to reach the mines, and for otherwise providing for their necessities.

We cannot dismiss this subject without congratulating the public that we possess three Departments which reflect credit upon us. We allude to the Common Schools, the Fire Department, and the Hospital under the management of the Sisters of Mercy.

The patients in the Hospital are unanimous in their praises of the present management of the Institution. We are of the opinion that any change would be impolitic at this time. The Grand Jury approve of the resolution passed by the Board of Supervisors to afford accommodation for the religious exercises of the patients.[25]

The report of the Grand Jury should have ended the attack, for the charges leveled against the Sisters were all addressed in the report which also indicated that for the seven months proceeding, the Sisters had received no cash payments for their services. The hospital subsisted on loans taken on by the Sisters, a dangerous practice for those with no means of acquiring large sums of money. Still, Mr. King kept up the attacks on the quality of care given by the Sisters. In response, physicians and lay Catholics as well as patients served by the Sisters came forward to attest to the excellent quality of care received by the sick.

Nothing speaks like personal experience. A writer identified only by the initials A.P.S. writes to the *Herald:* "Every kindness at first shown me was viewed with suspicion, and treated so, and only until repeated acts of kindness were heaped upon me could I divest myself of the first false impressions, and until my entire recovery and departure, which took place within a week, it seemed to me a mystery how persons to whom I was a complete stranger could take so deep an interest in my welfare."[26]

Doctor A. F. Sawyer gives another interesting perspective on the workings of the hospital in a letter he wrote in defense of the institution. The doctor tells us that patients were under the care of six physicians and surgeons, three of whom were on rotating duty every two months. Each doctor was in charge of one third of the patients. Reflecting on his practice the doctor says: "… the Sisters of Mercy have placed in my hands every facility for the management of my patients that I could reasonably ask for…."[27]

While the report of the Grand Jury and the plaudits of peers did not deter Mr. King from continuing attacks on the hospital, something else did: the violence of the day. As editor of the *Evening Bulletin,* Mr. King delighted in sensationalism. He chose James Casey, a prominent local politician, to attack in print. King published a story alluding to Mr. Casey's prison stay in New York's Sing Sing Penitentiary. Since Casey was among the men who came to San Francisco to leave their past behind them, it is not surprising that he took great exception to the story. His indignation resulted in violence: Mr. Casey murdered Mr. King. This murder reignited the fires of the Vigilance Committee.

The Vigilance Committee that emerged after the death of James King lasted for three long months. Casey and another gentleman, Charles Cora, were the first to stand judgment. After secret proceedings both were condemned to hang. The self-appointed enforcers of law were arbitrary in their ways. The then-Governor of California, Peter Burnett, considered their actions "incipient rebellion and a fatal precedent."[28] Members of the group carried on paramilitary marches, and an atmosphere of summary justice pervaded the city. It is remarkable that in the midst of this environment, Mary Baptist sought permission to give spiritual comfort to Mr. Casey before his death. It was a dangerous request given the times and the type of public attacks the Sisters had experienced. Exhibiting great hardness of heart, the Vigilance Committee refused to extend Mr. Casey this comfort.

In spite of the Vigilance Committee, the Sisters continued to go about their work as usual. Mary Baptist must have shared with the Kinsale community her concerns about the tenuous nature of the mission, however, for Mother Mary Francis Bridgeman makes allusion to their situation in one of her letters:

> It is pleasant to know that the supervisors cannot *turn you out* of the hospital—if they withdraw the sick from you, it will but stimulate the people to get up and endow your own hospital—of course you would, I suppose, take in sick to your present hospital and depend on Divine Providence for support—I have no fears for you—God who has done so much for you will do the rest— I rejoice to hear you are all so tranquil and confiding *in Him.*[29]

The failure of the County to live up to its monetary commitments was a serious challenge for the young community. Mary

Baptist used up her own resources and borrowed more money to continue to run the hospital. By February 28, 1857, the County was again nine months in arrears in its payments. Seeing no other course of action, Mary Baptist made a choice which would alter the horizon of Mercy ministry for the next century. She notified the Board of Supervisors for the County of San Francisco that she would terminate the contract on April 1, 1857, if they continued to ignore the obligations outlined in their contract for care of the sick. To put it succinctly, Mary Baptist said: "It is utterly impossible to hold out any longer."[30]

When April 1 came and went with no response from the County, Mary Baptist was true to her word, despite the pain it caused her. All ambulatory patients were dismissed from the hospital, and no new county patients were admitted. Those who could not manage on their own were cared for by the Sisters at the rate of one dollar per day. The *Bulletin* for April 3, 1857 describes the result:

> All the patients in the County Hospital able to walk were required to leave yesterday afternoon. The reason for this is that the Sisters of Mercy have declined taking further charge of the county sick unless their bills upon the city should be paid which has not been done and for which the prospects seem unfavorable.... An asylum for the patients will be provided by the Board of Supervisors which will take the matter into consideration tomorrow evening. It is difficult to tell how the persons discharged from the Hospital yesterday afternoon managed to find lodgings and provisions; one of them on crutches was seen seeking a place late last evening. Happily the weather was fine though a little cold during the night.[31]

From our distance in time, it is hard to understand the mindset of the Board of Supervisors that justified their neglect of contractual obligations. While economic times were difficult, the county never sought any renegotiation of the contract nor did it move to pay what it could. The replacement facility at North Beach for indigent patients was a barometer for how the county cared for its sick. Doctor Harris, a physician of the time, wrote of it in 1857 that the city "inflicted an economy upon the impoverished sick just short of murder.... The personnel was cheap, with medical men paid less than steam-boat officers. Cheap coffins furnished the finale."[32]

For Mary Baptist what seemed like a disaster became an opportunity. As soon as the city transferred its indigent sick to the facility in North Beach, Mary Baptist took down the legend "State Marine and County Hospital" and put up a new sign, "St. Mary's Hospital." San Francisco would finally have what it lacked, a private hospital serving the general public, and California's first Catholic hospital. It would be a place organized and managed according to the values of mercy, excellence and compassion. St. Mary's was to become the center for new outreach and undertakings by the Sisters. A new chapter was opening.

St. Mary's Hospital, San Francisco and Mater Misericordiae in Sacramento became centers for training nurses

VI

Outward from the Center

From the time of their arrival in San Francisco, the Sisters had partnered with the County of San Francisco in providing care for the indigent sick of the area; however that was only part of their work. San Francisco had grown without planning or preparation. Since the County Hospital accommodated only the indigent, other sick persons had no place to go. Recognizing the need for the poor and aged to be assisted, the Sisters had attended many sick San Franciscans by providing care for them in their homes. Ironically, the strange turn of events that forced the Sisters to give up caring for the county's indigent sick provided an opportunity to find new ways for San Francisco's sick to receive care.

Mary Baptist decided to transform the former county hospital into a private hospital. Prior to its purchase by the State Legislature in 1850, the hospital had been used as a hotel. Renamed three times by successive owners, it was old and limited. The state did nothing to improve the physical condition of its one and only hospital. In order to partner with the county, the Sisters had been required to purchase the property and were free, therefore, to determine its future use. Such a purchase was a great leap of faith. The need was evident, but whether a privately owned hospital would prosper remained to be seen. On July 27, 1857, Mary Baptist opened St. Mary's Hospital, the first Catholic hospital in California.

The woeful history of the state's and county's failures to comply with their contracts left Mary Baptist in serious fiscal difficulty. By the time St. Mary's Hospital opened in 1856, the monies expended for the purchase of the building and the loss sustained in unpaid bills, caused the Sisters' debt to climb to approximately $13,000. This debt was significant for a community that accepted no pay for its services, only reimbursement of costs. It was a time before salaries or stipends were provided for services rendered by the Sisters. With the encouragement of Archbishop Alemany, a number of Catholic gentlemen came to the assistance of the Sisters in July 1856. Their intent was to clear the large debt that had accumulated. The gentlemen placed the following advertisement in *The San Francisco Evening Bulletin* on August 4, 1856, outlining the Sisters' works in detail and appealing to the public for assistance:

Sisters of Mercy, San Francisco

The Sisters of Mercy now appealing, for the first time, to the benevolent inhabitants of California, consider it due to the public to state briefly the various works of mercy contemplated by their Holy Institute.

The first object to which the religious of this Order are solemnly devoted, is The Instruction and education of the Ignorant, rich and poor, young and old, without distinction of creed, country, age, or condition.

2nd The Care of the Sick, whether in their own houses or in hospitals.

3rd The Protection of unemployed women of irreproachable character.

4th The Care of helpless Orphans.

5th The Protection of the poor Outcast—the Penitent Magdalen.

As San Francisco has been provided to some extent with the means of education, the Community are of the opinion that the care of the sick has at present more claims on their attention. For the last six months the Sisters have had charge of the County

Hospital, which they undertook only in default of means to establish one of their own. Many circumstances combine to render the care of the sick an object of especial importance in this State; and the Sisters in acting as the almoners of those who cannot themselves come into actual contact with poverty and disease, rely on the affluent members of society for their co-operation. Every human creature is but the steward of his Creator, and if he shares with the unfortunate or afflicted the means entrusted to his stewardship, a rich reward may be expected from Him who said "I was hungry and you gave me to eat, I was thirsty and you gave me to drink; I was a stranger and you took me in; naked and you covered me; sick and in prison and you visited me."

The object of the Sisters of Mercy, is one which should elicit the sympathy of the benevolent—a House of Mercy for servants of good character while out of place. In affording them temporary protection, it is intended to shelter them from evil, and to train them in orderly and industrious habits thereby qualifying them for suitable situations. The public must be aware that many of them are *thrown out of employment not for any glaring misconduct, but on account of their incapacity* to discharge the duties they undertake. With limited means within their reach, the Sisters have already given protection and gratuitous support to upwards of five hundred persons, many of whom were children on their way to their parents, or married women in search of their husbands. Indeed, viewed in this light alone, a House of Mercy is particularly required in this country, as many wives, mothers of families, and friendless females are daily arriving here and are often under the necessity of waiting a considerable time amidst innumerable snares, the arrival of their husbands or relatives.

Attached to the House of Mercy is a Registry Office for servants. Upwards of eleven hundred have already, by means of it, been placed in situations without expense to them or their employers.

The House of Mercy is intended to be in some measure self-supporting, as the inmates are employed at washing, plain work, etc. The same remark will apply to the Magdalen Asylum.

On the fourth object of the Order of Mercy—the care of the HELPLESS ORPHAN—it would be needless to dwell at any length. It is the glory of San Francisco that institutions for the protection of this class have been and still are well supported, and the Sisters of Mercy do not feel called upon to undertake this duty until their other and more pressing objects are attended to.

The fifth and last object of the Order of Mercy—a MAGDALEN ASYLUM—has a particular claim on public attention. Is it necessary to use feeling language in making an appeal on behalf of the poor, wretched, broken-hearted victims of crime and credulity? Alas! They are friendless and abandoned. Many of them would willingly rise from their degradation and return to paths of morality, but they are shunned and mistrusted; they have no friends to encourage them to repentance, no one to strengthen their good resolutions, to protect them during the ordeal of their conversion. They require a home where they may be sheltered from sneers and ridicule, which is often sufficient to overwhelm the strongest mind. May not the Sisters appeal with confidence on their behalf, reminding all of the Divine Assurance, "that he who causeth a sinner to be converted from the error of his ways, shall save his soul from death, and shall cover a multitude of sins." May He who came not to call the just, but sinners, reward all who take a part in this good work!

The Sisters must look to a benevolent public for funds to carry out these views and objects, as all they have to give is their time, labor, and energies of mind and body. It may be well to mention that to purchase the premises at present occupied by the county sick, the Sisters were obliged to borrow at heavy interest, $14,000, secured by a mortgage on the property, which indebtedness is still pressing as a heavy incubus on their operations.

All persons charitably disposed towards the above object, can leave their donations or subscriptions with any of the following persons:[1]

Over a dozen individuals and business representatives signed the document, including representatives of Wells Fargo. The proceeds of this appeal were significant. In three months

$6,670.00 was raised to assist the Sisters. In August and September, two other groups, the managers of the Metropolitan Theatre and the Ladies Fair at Musical Hall, added to the amount. Combined, the proceeds erased the debt and allowed the works of the Sisters to continue.

At first glance the public drive to raise money for the Sisters might simply look like any other charitable appeal, but it was more than that. It was a public expression of Catherine McAuley's belief that her Sisters were to connect those with resources to those in need. The drive achieved three purposes. First, it defined the scope of services provided to the community through the works of the Sisters and presented a rationale to why such works were everyone's concern. Second, it invited people to share in the work. Instead of the County Board of Supervisors being the partner, now the whole San Francisco civic community was the partner. Finally, it resulted in sufficient monies for mission. This was a pattern that would be repeated over and over in the history of Mercy.

Involving the public in the works of mercy set the stage for the next phase of the Mercy mission in California. First, Mary Baptist consulted with Sister Francis McEnnis, a Sister of Charity then in charge of the Orphan Asylum in San Francisco. Sister Francis had experience in administering hospitals in the United States, and Mary Baptist desired her advice before beginning her new undertaking. Next, Mary Baptist began to build a partnership with the physicians of the city. By July 27, 1857, she made arrangements with Doctors A.J. Bowie and J.P. Whitney to staff the new hospital. They were to take turns attending the sick. For each full-pay patient, the doctors received 25 cents. For half-pay patients the fee was reduced to 15 cents. Mary deSales Redden, confined to bed as the result of a serious illness caused by a trip to Sacramento, did not attend the meeting but eagerly awaited its conclusion. When Mary Baptist returned to share with her the outcome of her negotiations, she found her sitting up in bed with clasped hands. Mary deSales said: "I have been praying the whole time that God would enlighten you and direct you."[2] The two guides of the community conversed about the proposed hospital and their plans to establish a branch house for Sacramento. Mary Baptist had no idea that her trusted advisor, friend, and partner would die of her illness before another day went by.

Mary deSales died as a result of complications from a case of influenza on July 28, 1857. The ten physicians on St. Mary's staff wrote in tribute that "the cause of Mercy and Charity has lost a devoted and ardent minister, the Order to which she was attached an indefatigable servant, and the world's great office of Universal Benevolence for which she sacrificed fortune and life, a pure and pious martyr."[3] The death of Mary deSales was a heavy loss coming at a time when two new missions were just beginning.

The path that lay before Mary Baptist must have looked very rocky during that summer of '57. She not only had the responsibility of establishing the hospital on a solid foundation, but she was now without her rock of support, Mary deSales. To add to her difficulties she was in the process of sending Sisters to Sacramento in response to Archbishop Alemany's urgent request. At this point another companion in Mercy came forward to be her partner in mission for the next two decades, Mary Gabriel Brown. Together they would expand the ministry in San Francisco, establish a foundation in Sacramento, send an affiliate community to Grass Valley, and set the course of Mercy life in California for the next century. In order to accomplish all this, the ministry had to be solid at the center. Saint Mary's Hospital would be that center for the next thirty years.

The first St. Mary's on Stockton Street began to build a reputation for medical excellence. Mary Baptist gathered a highly skilled core of medical professionals for its charter staff of twelve. Joining Doctors Bowie and Whitney was Dr. Beverly Cole, a founder of the University of California College of Medicine and president of the American Medical Association;

Dr. Levi Cooper Lane, considered one of the leading surgeons in the West; and Dr. Henry Gibbons, founder and editor of the *Pacific Medical and Surgical Journal.* The expertise of the physicians joined with the high standards of care demanded by the Sister nurses, thus guaranteeing a commitment to excellence.

As the patient enrollment grew and the building deteriorated, Mary Baptist knew that she would have to find a new location for St. Mary's. Money was once more a problem. To purchase new land and build a modern facility would mean raising funds since the resources of the Sisters could not cover the cost. Archbishop Alemany supported the idea of building a new hospital but did not take responsibility for funding the project. This burden rested on Mary Baptist. In May 1857 she had purchased a lot on Rincon Hill to meet the expanding needs but could not proceed.

Once more philanthropy was essential to the realization of the vision. Archbishop Alemany deputed the Rev. Michael King to visit the gold mining areas to solicit assistance. Writing a letter of solicitation the Archbishop noted:

> In order to carry out the charitable objects of their Institute, the Sisters have already purchased a hundred *vara* lot in a good location in this City where they purpose to erect a large, well constructed Hospital built in the most solid and permanent manner with airy wards and corridors, adapted in every way to the comfort of the Sick and provided with every means that the best medical skill can supply to alleviate disease.
>
> Such an Hospital attended by the Sisters and placed entirely in their hands it is manifest, must prove a likely Institute of great practical utility and efficient charity to the whole Community of the State but in a peculiar manner to those in the mines who are so often exposed to the danger of falling victims to some sad accident or disease and who having perhaps no friends or relatives in this country from whom they might receive aid and assistance would find in such an Institution relief and comfort in their distress.

The Sisters are ready and willing to do their part, but they cannot raise the building without the material aid of the arm of charity. The help of all charitably disposed is required. An effort made now will secure a permanent and lasting monument of public beneficence and Christian charity. Let us then make the effort now—generous—a general effort—let us all contribute something—let each one put a stone in the building, and it will be soon completed—and in doing this we will be bearing a part in one of the greatest and most enduring works of charity ever accomplished on the shores of the Pacific.[4]

Father King set about his mission and in about four weeks raised almost $3,000.00 for the new building. Unfortunately, ill health brought his efforts to a close. What resulted, however, was important, for it highlighted the interdependency of settlements in northern California. The fortunes of Sacramento, the gold country, and, indeed, all of northern California were linked together. A need addressed in Sacramento impacted San Francisco. Mining disasters in Grass Valley and the Mother Lode rippled out beyond their locales to the whole north state. Overnight, silver or gold strikes could empty San Francisco of its male population.

For the Sisters, the cities were linked together by the depth of their needs. San Francisco lacked health care, but the greatest need in Sacramento and Grass Valley was for education and the care of orphans. By the time the new St. Mary's opened its doors, Mary Baptist would be opening new fields of ministry in Sacramento, and St. Mary's would play a part in that ministry. A review of early records shows that Sisters moved among the three foundations as needed. Due to its favorable climate, Mary Baptist sometimes sent Sisters to Grass Valley for a "change in air." Communication between Sacramento and San Francisco was frequent. By the early sixties a trip by railroad would take just four hours, allowing for easier interchange.

The hospital had become for the Sisters the hub of their works. Sister Mary Francis Benson writes to Sister M. Vincent Harnett in July 1859 saying:

> Within the precincts of our Hospital are included Convent, House of Mercy, Orphanage, Magdalen Asylum, and an office for procuring situations for servants, here called "help." To describe the multitudes that have found shelter under St. Mary's roof would be a difficult task. I do not know any country unrepresented. Of all religions, we have had members. We have had perpetrators of every crime, under advise, [sic] instruction, or care: in truth, the hospital is a world in itself.[5]

Within a two-year period of time, the tightly controlled environment of the county hospital had been transformed into a center for a variety of works of mercy. It is not an understatement to say that Mary Baptist's vision included the healing of the whole fabric of society.

The growth of the various social services attached to the hospital was not planned but rather happened in response to emerging need. Each new work had a story attached to it. The House of Mercy provided a home for destitute women of good character while the Magdalen Asylum focused upon the rehabilitation of women drawn into addiction or prostitution. Mary Baptist was always conscious of the needs of the aged, and one wing of the hospital was given over to this work. In times of great crisis, such as the Sacramento floods of 1861, St. Mary's provided food and shelter for its fleeing victims. None of these developments were on the horizon when Mary Baptist began the work of establishing the new St. Mary's. All she knew was that the old State Marine Hospital building was now leaking and was not worth the cost of repair. It was time to move.

The cornerstone of the new St. Mary's Hospital, relocated to Rincon Hill, was laid on September 3, 1861. It took only two months for the new building to be completed. *The San Francisco Herald* described the new facility:

> St. Mary's occupies a beautiful and healthful position on the corner of First and Bryant Streets, having a frontage of seventy-two feet on Rincon Place. The building which is four stories high with a spacious attic occupying the entire length of the building, is one of the most substantial public buildings in the State. It was erected under the personal supervision of Mr. D. Jordan, a well-known contractor of our city.
>
> On the second floor for male patients and on the third floor for female patients, there are four wards, four private rooms, laboratories, wash and bath rooms. The Chapel is on the east side fronting First Street. Each floor is well provided with adequate water and hose connections in case of fire. The building is airy, well-ventilated, and commands a fine view of the Bay of San Francisco, Oakland, Alviso, and surrounding country. The arrangements throughout the entire edifice are of the finest order.... One of the most elegant and useful buildings in San Francisco, it is an institution whose benefits are daily felt by the poor in our midst.[6]

During November the Sisters busied themselves with arranging the hospital furnishings. Patients were then moved from the old building to the new. The excellence of the hospital medical staff resulted in St. Mary's becoming a training center for new physicians. Beginning in January 1862, students from the Medical Department of the University of the Pacific received clinical instruction at the facility. Costs were reasonable for the period; a ward bed cost $10.00 per week, while private rooms were $20.00 for the same length of time. Given the frequency of serious mining injuries, St. Mary's became a leader in orthopedic surgeries.

The expansion of St. Mary's was not without personal sacrifice for Mary Baptist. Margaret Russell had contacted her daughter about monies she wished to divide among her children. When Mary Baptist asked that her portion of her future inheritance be used to purchase hospital equipment not easily obtainable in San Francisco, Mrs. Russell set herself to the task of getting the most for the money. Sarah Russell tells of her mother's efforts:

> This duty dear Mother undertook with her accustomed zeal and energy, and in order to lay out the money to the best advantage she spared no fatigue or expense. As the list of things necessary for the equipment of an Hospital included feather beds, pillows, mattresses, sheeting, delf, [sic] glass, silver, blankets, flannels, my Mother went to the towns in England where these various articles were manufactured. She was so clever and so accustomed to business that she got all this immense work completed and packed in enormous bales and crated and finally shipped at the beginning of 1861, and all went safely.
>
> But it cost dear Mother too much. Just after this great work was over she was seized with apoplexy and became unconscious in Arthur's house in Eccles Street, Dublin. She was some days in this state and believed to be dying, but thank God she recovered and lived for six years. However, she was never the same again, as she was partially paralysed, so that she was an invalid all those years.[7]

Mary Baptist, an avid correspondent with family, must have written of her mother's death but no such letters remain to give insight into her heart. We do know that mother and daughter were kindred spirits. Mary Baptist inherited her mother's sense of duty, her business acumen, and her love for those who were poor. It must have been a bittersweet joy for Mary Baptist to know that her mother's death resulted from Mrs. Russell's zeal for those in need and her devoted love for her daughter.

During the 1860s San Francisco was transformed from a lawless port settlement to the largest city on the Pacific Coast. During this same time Mary Baptist's activities were like a round dance. One moment she was moving to the music of medicine, the next to the rhythms of education or care for the poor. After the opening of the second St. Mary's on Rincon Hill, her attention moved to challenges in Sacramento and Grass Valley. A sudden outbreak of black small-pox in San Francisco rapidly brought the focus back to healthcare. The political intrigues and manipulations to control wealth and power in the growing city had resulted in a lack of attention to the needs of public welfare. No State Board of Health had been established even though California had been a state since 1850. Public sanitation in San Francisco was an open invitation to disease, especially in the Chinese sector of the city.

Smallpox first revealed its deadly presence in March 1868. By June, 153 cases were reported, but the plague had only begun its destruction. The death ratio in the city reached one for each forty-eight residents, two persons died for every five infected.[8] The disease seemed to strike especially in hard those of Mexican, South American or Asian descent. Doctor I. Rowell reported to the San Francisco Board of Supervisors on the severity of the epidemic:

> The like of this epidemic has never been known. Previously, small-pox was much more dreaded for the deformity likely to result than from a fear of a fatal termination. But not so from this epidemic as may be inferred by comparing the mortuary record with the number of cases reported. Marked peculiarities characterize this plague. Death often follows before any well-defined variolous eruptions made their appearance. The cases that result fatally in the primary or secondary stage are generally accompanied by delirium, sometimes with maniacal ravings to the extent that require restraint.... Remedies previously demonstrated as proper and efficacious in certain stages of this disease have proved of little avail; and as the fury of the epidemic increases, many of them are found to be entirely worthless.[9]

The situation was enough to put fear in the hearts of San Franciscans. The Board of Supervisors set up a Variola Hospital in May 1868. The people called it the "pest house." The conditions at the Variola Hospital fit its popular name. It was six miles from the city in an area given to heavy winds and damp fog. It had four rooms that were meant for six patients, but during the epidemic twelve sick persons were often crowded into the space. To make matters worse, there were no bathroom facilities in the hospital. Carpet covered the windows to keep out the winds. The conditions were so bad that victims preferred to die in friendless desolation rather than be transferred to the "pest house."

The San Francisco Call provides an insight into the terror surrounding the facility. In an article published in July 1868 we find the following description:

> At ten o'clock every night the lights are extinguished, and the patients left in darkness. The nurses retire and are not seen again until morning. In the meantime the sick are without attendance, and their sufferings present a picture too terrible for contemplation. Their piteous cries for water and attentions they are too weak to procure for themselves are heart-rending. There in the dark, close room where nothing is visible and where the ears hear only cries of distress, pleadings for succor, or the ravings of the insane, they are locked in to pass the long hours of the night…. The few nurses who are employed are negligent or incompetent.[10]

Public outcry demanded improved conditions at the hospital, but Dr. Beverly Cole reported that the main problem was the absence of suitable nurses.

In 1867, having declined to allow the community to ask for an exemption from Church law to allow her re-election as superior, Mary Baptist enjoyed a respite from that role.[11] Her partner in mercy, Mary Gabriel Brown, was elected superior of the community, with Mary Baptist selected as her assistant. It was to Mary Gabriel that Sister Mary Francis Benson brought the plight of the smallpox victims in San Francisco. In the face of such suffering and need, Sister Mary Francis prevailed upon

Mary Gabriel to offer the services of the Sisters to the city. Sister Mary Francis even wrote the letter to Archbishop Alemany requesting permission to serve in the "pest house." The permission was readily given providing two Sisters remained together on night duty.

Mary Gabriel wrote to Dr. Cole on August 10, 1868:

Sir:

It is one of the privileges of our Order of Mercy that we attend our poor fellow creatures in whatever form of disease it is the Divine Will to afflict them. Therefore, if the City Authorities are willing to accept our services two of our Sisters will, D.V., go to the "Pest House" and take up their residence there until such time as the Almighty wills to deliver the city from this terrible malady. If the Authorities are willing to accept our services, we shall go on Monday, August 17. One small room is all we require; the accommodations of a Sister of Mercy are very simple. We have been vaccinated lately.

    Wishing you every success in your work, I am,
    Faithfully yours in J. C.
    Sister Mary G. Brown, Superior of the Sisters of Mercy.[12]

The city authorities were more than willing to accept the services of the Sisters. Mary Gabriel decided to assign herself to the work for the first week in order to see what the needs were. When Archbishop Alemany discovered that she was at the "pest house," he immediately ordered her back. Sisters Mary Francis Benson and Mary Bernard O'Dwyer were then placed in charge.

Sister Mary Francis gives us a look at what their service entailed. Writing to Kinsale she says:

It is a truly horrible disease, so loathsome, so pitiable. Twice the number of patients with any other disease would not require the care and attendance those afflicted with small-pox required. Not one spot from the crown of the head to the sole of the foot is sound. The eyes of the greater number are closed, pus running down from them to their cheeks. Their throats are so sore that to take a drink almost chokes them; the tongue in some instances so swollen that one drop cannot pass down; their hands so sore they are helpless, and the mal-odeur [sic] so terrible that they themselves cry out: "O Sister, I cannot stand the smell." The doctors say it has assumed a more malignant form than smallpox usually does.... We take the greatest precaution to prevent the spread of the disease ... burning beds, stacks of bedding, and clothing.[13]

Sister Mary Francis worked for five months in the pest house, but the intensity of the service and the arduous nature of the work caused her health to deteriorate. In January 1869, Mary Baptist took her place as supervisor of the hospital. Once more an official report reveals the excellence of care for which the Sisters were noted. A committee of three physicians reported the following to the San Francisco Medical Society:

Indeed it is wonderful that an institution so unmercifully crowded with small pox patients in all stages of putrefaction and exfoliation could be kept so free from a sickening and disagreeable odor so common to all cases in private practice. Had we gone through the hospital blind-folded, we would not be able to ascertain that it was a small pox establishment. This was one of the most striking facts and speaks volumes of praise to the medical management and those devoted Sisters whose sublime charity shrinks not from such repulsive and perilous labors.[14]

The sacrifices made by Sisters serving in the pest-house were many. They were under constant quarantine and therefore cut off from the normal life of the community. They could attend Mass only by secretly coming to the Magdalen Asylum where their presence would not be a cause for alarm. In the midst of this time, one of the California pioneers, Sister Mary Bernard O'Dwyer, became seriously ill. In her final days she had one request, to see Mary Baptist. Her long-time friend and leader came secretly to be with her, to share their common memories, and to say good-bye.

The Sisters remained at the pest-house until May 1869. In tribute to their service, the County gave the community $5,000. In addition the Sisters were granted the right to ride San Francisco public transit for free.

The progress of St. Mary's followed the pattern of other hospitals across the country. It was in a constant state of responding to medical discoveries and expanding medical needs. A small addition to the hospital, needed as early as 1879, was followed by a larger expansion in 1891. The pride that Mary Baptist took in the hospital is seen in a letter written that year:

> Everyone says the Hospital is now perfect. There is every convenience that could be imagined: electric bells and lights, speaking tubes, a passenger elevator, chutes for soiled linen, letters, dust, etc. The three principal corridors are 200 feet long with large triple windows at each end; there are thirty-five private rooms, about a dozen of which are double, and there are eighteen wards, but none large—the largest accommodating only twelve. The bathrooms, water-closets, and lavatories are all nicely tiled, both floors and walls to the height of six feet and the basins, slabs, etc., are of marble. The house is heated throughout by steam.
>
> But the grandest part of all is the mansard story, in which the operating rooms are situated. There are two antiseptic rooms, the ceilings, walls and floor are tiled, and they are so constructed that the whole can be hosed out, the water flowing off and down a marble gutter. The operating tables are heavy plate glass with nickel frames. The ophthalmic and electric rooms are furnished with hard wood with oilcloth on the floor. There is a large waiting room off which all these rooms open. We have got the attic hard-finished, one end is for the female employees; the other for the male. The operating rooms are placed between them and only reached by the elevator.... All this, of course, has greatly increased our debt, but I have no doubt that with the blessing of God, we shall pay it off in due time.[15]

The description of the hospital given by Mary Baptist reflects her attention to detail. Much research went into the planning and shortcuts that would reduce the quality of care were never allowed.

It was not the bricks and mortar which gave the most satisfaction, however. For Mary Baptist and all the early Sisters, the buildings were a bridge to people. These Sisters were not concerned just with the bodies of those served but with their spiritual welfare. Letters to their Sisters in Ireland reveal that central focus repeatedly. One letter from Mary Baptist shows the extent to which they sometimes went to make sure that no one went to God unprepared. Writing to Sister Mary Evangelist Fallon in 1894, she shares the following story:

> A man named Edward Worton in the last stage of consumption was brought yesterday about noon; between the journey and excitement, when Sister went in she found him evidently dying. She raised the eye lid: no sight, no feeling of breath from his nostril or mouth and the faintest pulse. She instantly called the Resident Physician, but he shook his head, too far gone, dying. Sister begged him to inject Brandy sometime [sic] to rouse as she did not know if he was a Catholic or not. Accordingly the Doctor worked over him injected strychnine, ether and fully a wineglass of Brandy in the arms, around the heart and limbs, Sister at the same time giving all the whiskey and water she could get him to swallow and hot applications at his feet. At last to their great delight he opened his eyes and Sister saw he was conscious so she asked at once if he was a Catholic. "Yes, Sister and for God's sake bring me a Priest."[16]

The gentleman lived to make his confession and receive the anointing of the sick according to Catholic custom. He then died.

Stories of conversions, remarkable recoveries, and sadness dot the correspondence of Mary Baptist and other early Sisters. To them, healing was a holy and sacred task, a time when the sick should most experience the mercy and compassion of God. It was this conviction that caused them to demand the very best from their staff, the physicians, and themselves. It was not always easy. In one letter Mary Baptist even laments that "doctors don't like to take in hopeless cases because it runs up the death rate."[17] Such considerations did not enter into the concept of service held by the Sisters.

From the "Hospital on the Hill," as many San Franciscans called St. Mary's, Mary Baptist extended the mercy ministry in multiple directions. No one was outside the boundaries of her compassion.

VII

Befriending the Social Outcast

The Sisters of Mercy did not specialize in any one area of service. While caring for the sick was enough to keep Mary Baptist and her Sisters fully occupied, they also responded with their time and compassion to other needs pressing for attention. In San Francisco the needs were shaped by the character of the times and city. The wild and lawless nature of San Francisco in the 1850s and early '60s created two groups in dire need of their compassionate service: the prostitute and the prisoner.

Unmarried women were highly vulnerable in early San Francisco. Young women sometimes journeyed to the city on the strength of a promise of marriage. Upon their arrival some discovered that their promised husbands had abandoned the city in favor of the gold or silver fields. The diary of B. Vicuna Mackenna provides clear perspective on the plight of women who depended on the promises of husbands they had yet to meet.

In the winter of 1853, Mackenna arrived in San Francisco from South America. Soon after, the frigate *Magellan* arrived in port with three hundred French citizens deported by Louis Napoleon. Mackenna describes the lot of the immigrant groups populating the city. "They [French refugees] had only recently arrived, bringing with them the lightest baggage possible. That had been all that was allowed each in his exile. Many of these unfortunates I later recognized shining shoes on the city streets. For two *reales* a pair."[1]

The diary tells of a city that merged the peoples of the world, a variety of national dress being evident everywhere. In truth, San Francisco was an ethnically defined city. Its environs were segregated according to nationality: Chinese, Chilean, French, Irish, and so on. Each community tended to enforce its own norms and practices on its residents. In such a context, women were socially vulnerable, having little or no recourse when abused or exploited. Mackenna includes an incident, which vividly illustrates the point:

> The most extravagantly strange transactions have been made in San Francisco that the imagination fairly reels. One of these was the auction of women in the public square. I have undoubtedly arrived at a time of great social unstability. However, there was the occasion when a ship with more than sixty Frenchwomen aboard arrived in this harbor. It was said that none of them had paid their passage but that anyone who would cancel their respective accounts would receive a woman in exchange. On the following day not one of those passengers remained aboard the ship.[2]

Lacking resources, sometimes not speaking English, these "brides" were left to make their own way when no husband was forthcoming. In a city where many men had left their families behind to seek their fortune and were hungry for feminine companionship, prostitution became a way of life for many unfortunate women. Once set upon that path, some of the women eased their pain with alcohol or opium. To break out of this destructive cycle and re-enter normal family and civic life was almost impossible without assistance.

No group of women was more exploited and abused than young Chinese girls, sold by their parents or kidnapped to serve as comfort women for the men of San Francisco. Anne Seagraves gives a harrowing account of the lives of these young women in her book *Soiled Doves*. She points out that young girls were shipped to San Francisco in large padded crates, abused, forced into prostitution, sold, and, when diseased and used, discarded. The fate of these girls, really just children, was further sealed by a legal contract. Such contracts included stipulations which added time to the term of prostitution for any days of illness or incapacity. If the girl tried to escape, the contract bound her to her "owner" for life.[3] Drugs, torture, and forced suicide were all part of the landscape for the Chinese prostitute. Attempts to break the cycle of bondage that enslaved them did not emerge until the latter years of the century.[4]

It is hard to know just how much Mary Baptist and her Sisters knew about the girls locked in the Chinese cribs. *The Leaves from the Annals of the Sisters of Mercy* tells us that a few young Chinese girls found refuge with the Sisters. One was included among the numbers of sick Chinese transferred directly from their passage ship to the hospital. This young girl, around the age of ten, immediately threw herself into the arms of an Irishwoman who stood by. When she was able to speak a little English, she kept saying, "The Chinese are bad, bad, bad!"[5] Later, when a Chinese priest attempted to minister to her during a typhoid fever attack, she steadfastly refused to have anything to do with him. It was learned that Nora, as she was then called, was stolen from her family and had suffered the same cruelties that other enslaved girls endured during her passage on the ship. Nora did not live many years longer but before her death she became a fervent Christian, asking to have the Carmelite habit in which she would be buried pinned to her curtain. She died at the age of eighteen.[6]

Mary deSales Reddan was familiar with both the pattern and the circumstances that led young women into lives of prostitution. In Limerick, a garrison town, girls without protection had been subject to the same danger. There she had established a

Magdalen Asylum, a refuge where women could be protected from the lure of such a life and learn the disciplines and practices needed to re-establish themselves in society.

Mary Baptist listed ministry to women wishing to escape the cycle of prostitution, as one of the works of mercy to which her Sisters were committed. Nowhere was such a ministry more needed than in San Francisco at mid-century. Meeting with benefactors on July 4, 1856, Mary Baptist described the situation:

> The fifth and last object of the Order of Mercy—a Magdalen Asylum—has a particular claim to public attention—. Is it necessary to seek for forcible terms when making an appeal in behalf of the poor, wretched, broken hearted victims of crime and credulity? Alas! They are friendless and abandoned. Many of them would cheerfully return from their wickedness to paths of purest morality, but they are shunned and mistrusted; they have no friends to encourage them to repentance, no one to strengthen their good resolutions, or protect them during the ordeal of their conversion. They require a home where they may be sheltered from the sneers and ridicule of the scoffer, which is often sufficient to overwhelm the strongest mind. May not the Sisters appeal with unhesitating confidence, in their behalf....[7]

To understand the plight of the prostitutes of Mary Baptist's time, it is important to remember that Victorian mores dominated the period. A double standard was the norm when it came to sexual matters. While the infidelity of men was overlooked, women who were considered "fallen" were outcasts from family and society. Anne Seagraves notes that most American frontier prostitutes embarked upon this life because they had no control over their situations. Since the job market was geared primarily to a male work force, "regardless of their education, the majority of women were offered only the most menial and lowest paid work."[8] Prostitution, especially in the upscale parlors, provided needed income. A madam provided good clothes, shelter, food and drink. The cost: long-term disaster. The majority of women caught up in prostitution wound up isolated, diseased, and thrown away.

To reclaim one of these young girls, many of whom began their service in the mid-to-later teens, was a demanding task even when she asked for aid. Mary Baptist's description of the Sisters' work with prostitutes brought a quick response from a prostitute called Amanda Taylor. Amanda, from New Orleans, was unhappy with her plight but could see no way out. After seeing the description of the works of mercy published in the paper, Miss Taylor sought refuge with the Sisters. She begged Mary Baptist to find some place for her to stay, even a "coal hole" if necessary. Such a plea for help could not go unheeded by the Sisters. Miss Taylor was assigned to a room in the hospital building and the long process of healing began.

For eight months the Sisters supported Amanda with kindness and patience. At first she expected them to do all the normal chores of life for her, making her bed and cleaning her room. Their kindness was not without profit. Within a year Amanda became a changed person and began to assist in caring for young girls brought within the shelter and protection of the Sisters. By 1859 the Sisters had helped twenty-nine women regain their self-respect and their lives.[9] As time passed, the growing numbers of women seeking assistance caused an entire wing of the Stockton Street hospital to be allotted to them. In 1868 the *Monitor* reported that only nine of 187 women confined to the Magdalen Asylum had to be sent away as incorrigible that year. A review of the Sisters' records shows this to be typical of the proportion of women who profited from the Sisters' care.[10]

The way in which the women were assisted is important to note. No resident was forced to stay in the institution. When a woman felt she was ready to return to normal society, she was free to leave. From the time of her entry into the Asylum until her departure, no mention was ever made of the reason for her residency. That part of the penitent's past was left behind, not to be revisited.[11] During her stay all the supports that could be provided were available. The women had their own chapel and devotions, and a program of studies, work, and recreation. The most powerful element of the program was the role of older inmates to tend and mentor the younger girls.

Some of the Children of Preservation, as the youngest charges were called by the Sisters, were really toddlers of three or four years of age.[12] The children needed attention, mothering and love. This involvement of the penitents not only provided tender care for the younger victims of such a life but provided the older residents with responsibility and the motivation to move beyond their own needs. While many of the residents of the Magdalen Asylum found jobs, married well, and raised their own families, others chose to embrace the way of the consecrate.

The consecrate's way of life was familiar to Mary deSales. Prior to her entry into Mercy, she had established the first institution within an English-speaking country to minister to the prostitute. During part of this time, Mary deSales had lived with the Good Shepherd Sisters; later she entrusted her work in Limerick to their care. From Sister Mary Euphrasia, R.G.S, she learned about the practice of "consecrates." Consecrates were a group, formerly Magdalens, who gave themselves to God and who assisted in helping other women. Each had experienced her own journey of transformation within the Magdalen Asylum and wished to pass on what she had gained.

The consecrates formed a community among themselves, adopting a practice of prayer, work and recreation. Stages in their journey were marked by external symbols. Some wore the characteristic habit or garb of a consecrate, others wore a badge denoting their stage of healing. The women [penitents] took upon themselves the recitation of the Little Office of Our Lady of the Seven Dolors, the Rosary, spiritual reading, and visits to the Blessed Sacrament.[13] It was a penitential way of life. To put it bluntly, it was a total change from the way of life each experienced prior to her entry into the Asylum. Two consecrates from the Magdalen Asylum in San Francisco transferred to St. Louis to join a larger group of their peers, associated with the Good Shepherd Sisters, in 1859. The link between the Good Shepherd Sisters and the San Francisco Mercys was strong and enduring. Like the earlier establishment in Limerick, the Magdalen Asylum was eventually placed under the supervision and care of the Good Shepherd Sisters, but that would not happen until after the turn of the century.

Mary Baptist did all she could to provide for the needs of the penitents. Housing was a major concern. When Amanda Taylor arrived, Mary Baptist improvised housing in the hospital itself. As time went by, this arrangement proved insufficient for the numbers of women served. Between 1857 and 1862 the hunt was under way for a more permanent residence. The Archbishop loaned the Sisters a lot on the corner of Van Ness and Grove Streets, but this residence also proved inadequate. By 1865, when the Magdalen Asylum came to its permanent home on Potrero Avenue, over 100 women had been cared for by the Sisters.

Funding the work of the Magdalen Asylum was challenging. As with the County Hospital appropriations, government monies were a vital part of the picture to insure continuance of the work. Every two years the Sisters approached the Legislature to ask for money to house and feed the women of the Asylum. Sometimes the funds were provided, sometimes not. In each report there is an appeal that compassion be shown to the Magdalens. Writing in January 1864, Mary Baptist says:

> In presenting the above Report of the state of the Magdalen Asylum, the Sisters of Mercy beg to return thanks for the past Liberality of the Legislature by which they have been mainly enabled to undertake this work of Mercy. In behalf of their charge they again throw themselves on the charity of the State of the persons of it's Representatives, and they feel it is unnecessary to seek for forcible terms, when making an appeal on behalf of the unhappy victims of crime or credulity, as every one feels the

necessity of an Institute in which they can be sheltered and encouraged in their repentance, strengthened in their good resolution and protected during the ordeal of their conversion.[14]

Mary Baptist did not rely solely on state funding, however. In December 1863, she formed a society to assist in the work through fundraising, advocating for the ministry and its clients, and praying for its success. It was called the Society of the Good Shepherd for the Reformation of Penitents and the Support of the Magdalen Asylum. The duties of the members were four-fold. They were to contribute twenty-five cents a month or make a one-time donation of fifteen dollars. They were to pray daily for the prosperity of the work and offer up Mass and Holy Communion for that intention monthly. They were also to assist the Sisters in procuring suitable employment for the inmates of the Asylum and to market the goods made by them. This aspect of the Society helped make the work more self-sustaining. Finally, a complete report on the ministry was given to the Society four times a year.[15]

In publishing the appeal, and, in the establishment of the Society, Mary Baptist made her case that the institution was in great need. First, she reminded the group that not all the residents of the Asylum were able to support themselves. "It must be remembered that the Asylum contains a class of Children of Preservation who are too young to contribute in any way to their support."[16] The Sisters supplied what they could, but Mary Baptist points out that the furniture was "poor and insufficient, and the clothing and comforts of the Inmates but scantily provided for."[17] In spite of the hardships of providing for their charges, the Sisters never turned away anyone who applied for admission.

A review of the reports submitted to the State Legislature by the Sisters does provide a good idea of the women who were given assistance. The report of 1863 lists fifty-nine residents in the Asylum. Among those noted are representatives of New

Orleans, New York, Germany, Australia, Ireland, Maine and California. Comments in the reports speak of some residents finding work, others returning to their families, and some running away. By 1868 the total number of women who had been served by the Magdalen Asylum was 417.

The following year a major change occurred at the Magdalen Asylum. The *Annals* tell us that serious difficulties arose at the County Industrial School housing delinquent boys and girls. The *Annals* do not describe the problem, but the gravity of the situation caused the county to look for another way to address its wards. As a result, arrangements were made to have the girls placed at the Magdalen Asylum. The young female delinquents were to be under the Board of Managers, who would assume the cost for the care which would be provided by the Sisters. Seven girls formed the first group.[18] By July of the same year, the Female Department of the County Industrial School was completely disbanded and the girls left to the care of the Sisters. Within a year, the number of girls at the Magdalen Asylum grew to sixty.

These "delinquent" young girls were usually the victims of their environments. The majority responded to a program of work, education, recreation, and the affection of those who cared for them. Sister Consecrates, who had committed their lives to prayer and service, cared for the younger charges. The education program was geared to the abilities of the girls. For some it meant training in domestic arts in order to prepare them for future employment; for others it meant a regular high school curriculum. Music and the arts were a standard component of the overall program. The physical well-being of the girls and opportunities for exercise were also addressed.

A reporter visiting the Industrial school at the Asylum left to us this description:

> The Industrial school is large, airy and exquisitely neat. On the walls are maps, charts, and everything necessary for school work.

There is a large handsome piano, at which any girl who pleases can practice. All were neat and clean, some nice-looking, others repulsive. They were of various ages.[19]

The writer goes on to describe the differences between the environment provided by the Sisters for their charges and the conditions of contemporary jails. Throughout the narrative the qualities of order, harmony, and beauty are noted repeatedly. To the Sisters, these were an essential part of healing the human spirit. Mary Baptist and her Sisters believed that the degradation of women resulted in the worse possible end. Reclaiming one from such a fate demanded utter patience, kindness, order, and prayer.[20]

For the Sisters, an ounce of prevention was worth pounds of cure. Like Catherine McAuley, Mary Baptist knew that education, housing, and employment were the best tools to prevent a woman's decline into destitution and/or crime. Even before the Magdalen Asylum was opened, Mary Baptist rented a house to shelter young women looking for work. Opening a House of Mercy was one of the first services undertaken by the Sisters. A small house next to the convent was rented by Mary Baptist in January 1855 and opened the following month.

The work of the House of Mercy was significant in both its scope and its results, but the initial years were not solely focused on the needs of women needing shelter and employment. The first house was small in size and offered shelter to many children who came to California to join their parents. It was often the custom for parents to come to the mining fields and then send for their children. The Sisters cared for these children as they waited for their parents to arrive in San Francisco. Travel was a risky undertaking for parent and child alike. Children would arrive by ship and be left without any support until their parents could be notified of their presence in the City. Unfortunately for some of the children, death, illness, or other circumstances claimed their parents before they were able to come from the mining fields. Such orphans or half orphans were left to fend for themselves. The importance of a refuge for these children is highlighted by the recorded ages of "delinquent" children found at the County Industrial School. There, children ranged in age from three to thirteen years of age.

However, the House of Mercy was not meant to serve children. Like the House of Mercy established by Mother Catherine McAuley, its primary intent was to provide safe housing for destitute women of good character. The history of the work is provided by Sister Mary Joseph O'Rourke in a letter to Archbishop Alemany:

> The House of Mercy and Intelligence Office[21] were opened simultaneously on the second of February 1855. We have always been more anxious to do good than to keep an accurate record of the same, so that the subjoined figures are much below the reality, but they are what is to be found on the Register.
>
> From the date given above to the present time [1874] one thousand, six hundred and sixty four persons have been lodged and fed for a longer or shorter term in the House of Mercy. The present average number in that Institution is forty five of whom about fifteen are employed at needle work, as are also about the same number of out door apprentices....
>
> From the opening of the Intelligence Office until our removal to this Building, a period of nearly seven years, over nine thousand were supplied with situations; but after our removal to this locality the number fell away considerably....[22]

Residents of the House of Mercy, Mater Misericordiae, were to be of upright character. Training for domestic service was offered in order to assist young women to become self-supporting.

Economic hardship hit San Francisco in the 1870s and at the prompting of Archbishop Alemany and Fr. John Prendergast, the Sisters renewed their efforts to find appropriate employment for those seeking their assistance. Notes in the archives of the

Sisters of Mercy in Burlingame, California, indicate that the employment office was open about four hours a day. It was designed to provide space for registration of applicants as well as a room where they could wait to be called for work. Father Prendergast proposed that the target population served by the office be girls fourteen to seventeen years of age. Mary Baptist chose not to restrict the age of those assisted but opened the service to women of all ages.

The increasing numbers of those in need caused the Sisters to relocate the House of Mercy once more. The new location brought together the Industrial School, the employment office and a shelter for women who had no place to go. An announcement of the home appeared in the *San Francisco Post* in 1874:

> The Sisters of Mercy who have charge of St. Mary's Hospital have established a Home for working women. Girls who come to the City from all parts of the United States and are unable to procure employment, find in the home a stopping place until they can get employment. If they are able they pay a small board. If not they earn it in the sewing room and laundry.[23]

The *Post* reporter indicates that the youngest worker was thirteen. Some of the girls were orphans and followed a program of a half day's instruction and a half day's work. As soon as they were well taught, employment was found for them.[24] The article continues, describing the sewing industry undertaken by the boarders. All in all, eighteen machines were in use. Some of the girls worked on an order from Murphy, Grant and Co. while others engaged in quilting. The Industrial School was indicative of the practical nature of the Sisters' ministry. They organized the ministry along the lines of a modern cooperative, with a percentage of earnings going to the women who produced the work and the other portion to the support of the residence and school. The focus was on providing needed help for today and practical training for tomorrow.

In addition to their service in the hospital, House of Mercy, Industrial School, and Magdalen Asylum, the Sisters were dedicated to another work of mercy—visiting the prisoner. From the time of their arrival, the Sisters began to visit men who were incarcerated for a wide variety of crimes. Crime and violence were permanent residents of early San Francisco. From 1849 to 1856 there were an estimated 1,000 homicides in the City, most of which went unpunished.[25] Ethnic, religious, and social rivalries fed the violence. Duels were frequent prior to the 1860s. Out of this lawlessness, as previously noted, came the vigilante movement.

Many of the Vigilance Committee were nativists opposed to Catholicism and its immigrant community. The number of conversions to the Catholic faith that took place in the hospital stirred deeper resentment among those who were already avidly opposed to the Catholic Church. The controversy over the management of the County Hospital only added fuel to the fire. Mother Mary Austin Carroll asserts: "the 'vigilants' often sought to terrify the Sisters. They chose to drill under the convent windows, and the inmates were expecting some terrible catastrophe every moment. But they [the vigilantes] never injured them."[26]

Just when the risk was the greatest, the Sisters sought leave from the Vigilance Committee to visit the men who were victims of the group itself. In particular, the Sisters sought permission to minister to James Casey before he was hanged for shooting James King. It must have taken great courage and compassion to seek this permission, since Mr. King had been unremitting in public condemnation of the Sisters in his paper. While permission was denied, the rejection did not dissuade the Sisters from the work. Throughout their ministry in San Francisco they constantly visited the country jail and later San Quentin, the state penitentiary.

The *Annals* carry many remarkable stories of the impact the Sisters had upon the prisoners, but none is more notable than the story of Tipperary Bill. Sister Francis Benson relates the story in a letter to her Sisters in Kinsale:

> We visit the jails continually and find there many sad cases. We prepared two Prisoners for execution; the last was hanged three weeks ago. He was a well-known robber, the terror of the country. He was called "Tipperary Bill," but his real name was William Morris. For many years the authorities had been endeavoring to capture him, but woe to the man who came near Bill; he would shoot him down and be off, no one knew where. At last came the time when Providence decreed he should be taken, and he was lodged the County Jail. He was not there long when he was detected cutting his chains. He was then heavily chained both hands and feet, and an immense thick chain around his ankle was attached to a ring in the ground. He was like a wild beast and men were afraid to approach him.
>
> When the Sisters went to visit him, the jailor would not open the door unless he had two men with him, so great was the terror of Bill. They seemed astonished that we were not afraid of being admitted to so desperate a character. At first we thought him very hardened, and so he was. It was very difficult to bring him to any idea of repentance until the trial was over and the death sentence passed. Even then, he said he would never give in to the Yankees to laugh at him hanging in the air. The poor creature was terribly tempted to destroy himself, and for some time we did not dare to leave a holy water bottle with him for fear he might use the glass as a knife to cut his throat. During the trial Mother Gabriel's brother was near him in court; he described the prisoner as being a most ferocious looking man with the fire of anger and desperation flashing from his eyes.[27]
>
> Well, we visited him frequently; we were locked in the cell with him, and though still savage to all others, the poor fellow was gentle with us."[28]

Sister Mary Francis goes on to say that little by little, the gentleness and patience of the Sisters brought about a change in this hardened criminal. They brought him books to read and prepared him for his First Communion, Confession, and Confirmation. Bill was full of remorse and filled with peace at the time of his execution. Sister Mary Francis comments: "On the scaffold his demeanor surprised everyone, and the change in 'Tipperary Bill' was the subject of conversation among all classes and parties. The anti-Catholic newspapers expressed their astonishment, and there was quite an excitement in the city about it."[29]

Bill was only one of the many prisoners who experienced the comfort and compassion of the Sisters. For some of the incarcerated, visits from the Sisters were the only solace in a life of utter desperation. The jails of the period were extremely austere, even crude. The environment was meant to punish. What was worse was the corruption and instability of the social climate that allowed innocent victims to be incarcerated. Writing in 1876, B.E. Lloyd attests:

> Were it only the guilty that suffer abuse, it would be a matter of less moment, although even such treatment of criminals is inhuman. It is a fact, however, that innocent persons alike are forced to submit to such usage, and they have no recourse. Once in the City Prison, a person merely under the ban of suspicion is thrust into a cell among a mob of low and vulgar criminals, and must there await the "law's delay" and bear the "insolence of office." It is not a difficult matter to get *in jail*, but to get *out* of a San Francisco prison, some strategy as well as considerable coin is needed.[30]

The jails were breeding places for disease, despair and human degradation. Into this darkness the Sisters came. While they were present, the humanity and dignity of these forgotten prisoners were honored. Mary Baptist and her Sisters carried on the jail visitation three times a week. Sometimes they taught the prisoners the basics of religious belief; at other times they simply offered gentle kindness ... writing a letter to a prisoner's mother, speaking a tender word.

In 1871, Mary Baptist turned her attention to the state penitentiary at San Quentin. Prison regulations barred women visitors, but that did not stop a determined Mary Baptist. She wrote to Governor H.H. Haight, requesting permission for the Sisters to visit the prison. This he granted. For forty years the Sisters continued the ministry until government rules revoked the permission. Mary Baptist herself visited death row. Her compassion caused her to intervene for two dying prisoners, John Moore and Alexander Walker. For the former, Mr. Moore, she sought and received a pardon from Governor Markham. The dying prisoner was then transferred to St. Mary's Hospital where he died just days later. Mr. Walker was not so fortunate. He died before the pardon arrived. To avoid causing pain to his mother, Mary Baptist had his body taken to St. Mary's and buried from the mortuary chapel there. His bereaved mother never knew her son died in prison.[31]

The full significance of the work of visiting the prisoner may never be known. Its fruit was the transformation that occurred within the hearts of the prisoners. In 1894, the inmates at San Quentin sought an unusual permission. They wanted their gratitude to Mary Baptist and her Sisters publicly expressed in the press. A letter was sent at their request to the *Monitor*, the Archdiocesan newspaper of San Francisco. After affirming the soothing and beneficial effect the Sisters had upon the prisoners, the letter says:

> Such, Mr. Editor, is the character of the work engaged in by the Sisters of Mercy amongst the prisoners at San Quentin—a work that is not merely confined to the inmates of the prison, but which reaches beyond, to the blighted homes and aching hearts of our friends and relatives. Nor does the work stop at this point. Many a discharged prisoner has been made the object of their Christian zeal and has been given such aid as would enable him to

turn his back upon evil paths and lead a correct, honorable and Christian life in the future. As an apt illustration of the earnestness of purpose and Christian charity of these noble women, we cannot refrain from citing a particular incident which occurred here not many months ago.

A prisoner lying in the last stages of consumption was pardoned by the Governor upon condition that his relations should care for him. His Sister, residing in the southern part of the State, was notified of the Governor's action, but being very poor found it impossible to raise the necessary means to cause his removal. The poor sufferer eager to die beyond the precincts of dishonor and shame was overcome with grief when this state of affairs was made known to him and the matter was in some manner communicated to Mother M. B. Russell. The picture of that poor man's despair touched her heart; she could not let him pass from earth with those shadows of grief upon his dying bed and she at once caused his removal to St. Mary's Hospital, where he received every care within her power to bestow until the grim messenger at last claimed him.

It is such instances of Christian charity as this—and they are by no means rare—that move us to deeply love and revere the Sisters of Mercy. The work undertaken by the Sisters in this prison is so fraught with discouragements, so tedious and arduous in its nature that the prisoners desire by these means to make known their high appreciation of their untiring zeal and to offer a warm and hearty tribute of gratitude for their manifold services in their behalf. A noble work to which Mother Mogan [Mary Baptist Mogan] has given much time and care has been to increase the number of good books in the library here. Through her energy fully three hundred volumes have found their way upon our shelves during the past two years.[32]

And so it was. No woman or man, however, broken and outcast, was beyond the ken of the Sisters' compassion. It was this quality of heart and spirit that helped San Francisco associate the Sisters of Mercy with those who were most in need.

St. Joseph's Academy, Sacramento

VIII

No Greater Work

In the mind of Mary Baptist and her Sisters, there was, perhaps, no greater work than education. Coming out of post-penal Ireland, Mary Baptist knew from her own experience the consequences of educational deprivation: poverty, oppression, and lack of social opportunities. She was in total agreement with Mother Catherine McAuley, who wrote in the Original Rule of the Order:

> The Sisters shall feel convinced that no work of charity can be more productive of good to society, or more conducive to the happiness of the poor than the careful instruction of women, since whatever be the station they are destined to fill, their example and advice will always possess influence, and where ever a religious woman presides, peace and good order are generally to be found.[1]

When the contingent of Mercy Sisters from Kinsale started out on their mission to California, their original intent was to meet the need for basic and religious education for the Catholic community in San Francisco. In February 1855, the Sisters opened a night school for adults. The following September saw the opening of a school for children in the basement of the Cathedral. The latter endeavor existed only a month. Its premature closure was due to a decision by church leadership to place

135

the Catholic schools under the Education Board in order to obtain public funding for them. In establishing the school, Mary Baptist had indicated that if such a decision came to pass, the Sisters would withdraw, and withdraw they did.

Father Gallagher pressed the Sisters to accept the supervision of government authorities; but having learned from the experience of their Sisters in Derby that such an arrangement has a shadow side, Mary Baptist declined to have her Sisters caught up in such a system. Father Gallagher feared that if the Mercy Sisters did not accept the supervision of the Board, the other teaching orders would follow suit. Time proved Mary Baptist correct in her assessment that board control would bring difficulties. Teaching orders working under the supervision of the Education Board found that the yearly examination of teachers was sometimes carried out in arbitrary ways. All teachers had to reapply for their positions each year. In San Francisco, the one-hour exams included questions like, "Name all the rivers of the globe," and "Name all the bays, gulfs, seas, lakes and other bodies of water on the globe."[2] The other orders of teaching Sisters soon followed in Mary Baptist's path and refused to work under the Education Board. If the schools were to succeed, they would have to do so without governmental funding.

In Sacramento, the educational scene was different from that in San Francisco. Schools, private and common, were established, but there was no opportunity for Catholic education. Archbishop Alemany had originally sought the services of the Presentation Sisters for the growing Sacramento population. Due to circumstances already noted, that did not happen. By 1857, Archbishop Alemany had still been unable to obtain a Religious Order to minister in the "doorway" to the mines. On the feast of St. Joseph, March 19, 1857, Archbishop Alemany asked Mary Baptist to take on this task. With the Sisters already engaged in building the new St. Mary's Hospital, working in the Magdalen Asylum, and providing shelter for women and children in the House of Mercy, it is hard to imagine how Mary

Baptist could say yes to this request. It would mean that four or five of her Sisters would be sacrificed to the needs and mission of this new branch house. At the time there were barely twenty Sisters in the community. The stretch would be great.

In April 1857, Mary Baptist and her assistant Mary deSales Reddan journeyed to Sacramento and to Shasta County to see if either area was suitable for a foundation. The journey to Sacramento was by steamer up the Sacramento River. Unlike trips made later by train, this first journey to Sacramento took a night and a day. The crowded cabin full of miners heading to the gold fields led the Sisters to make a bad decision; they elected to spend the night outside on the deck of the streamer. Both caught severe colds as a result of the damp and chill. While the *Annals* are silent about the trip, a contemporary description of a similar journey in *Dreadful California* gives a hint of what the Sisters must have experienced:

> We left San Francisco in a stern wheel steamboat so crowded with passengers that berths were entirely out of the question. We were doomed to get through the night as best we could. And such a night! I solemnly assert that almost every winged insect and creeping thing within a circuit of five leagues paid their respects to me on board that miserable river steamer.[3]

After completing the visit to Sacramento, the Sisters journeyed on to Shasta. This trip was also physically challenging, as the only mode of transportation up to the Shasta area was by stagecoach or horse. It is not surprising that Mary Baptist decided to delay any foundation to Shasta until a later time, but for Sacramento, she promised a foundation. This promise was made despite her realization that the Sacramento Sisters would have to struggle with an unhealthy climate, limited accommodations, and lack of ready access to the spiritual resources provided to them by the Jesuits in San Francisco.

The exploratory trip had taken from April 20 to May 7. Upon her return to San Francisco, Mary Baptist began preparations for the new foundation. This involved a second trip to Sacramento in July. Again the Sisters spent time out in the open balcony of the steamer, and once more the cost was catching cold, a cold which proved fatal for Mary deSales, her life sacrificed for the Sacramento mission. Mary Baptist now found herself immersed in opening the new St. Mary's Hospital and preparing for the new undertaking in Sacramento. She needed a partner with whom she could share the responsibility for the multiple tasks before her. Sister Mary Gabriel Brown, elected Mother Assistant on August 9, 1857, became that partner. On that same day Sisters were selected for the Sacramento mission. They were Mary Gabriel Brown (Superior), Sister Mary Paul Beechinor, Sister Mary Agnes Stokes, Sister Martha McCarthy, and Sister Madeline Murray.[4]

While the Sisters prepared, so did Sacramento. The coming of the Sisters was quickly announced to the civic community. The ladies of the city held a fair on May 11, 1857, to raise funds for the convent and school. One contributor to the cause was Peter H. Burnett, then serving as Judge of the State Supreme Court. The Sacramento press kept the community informed of the impending arrival of the Sisters. On September 30, the *Sacramento Bee* carried the following item:

> We learn that a number of Sisters of Mercy will arrive in this city on Friday, and will commence the foundation of an institution similar to those found in almost every city of the world. For the present they will occupy the old frame building in the rear of St. Rose's Church, corner of K and 7th, but so soon as the necessary means are obtained, a substantial building will be erected, such as will render them ample room to accommodate day, weekly and quarterly pupils."[5]

On October 9 the same paper carried a follow-up article.

A few days since, several "Sisters of Mercy" arrived in our city with the determination of making it their future home. It is determined to purchase a lot in a central locality, and erect, speedily as possible, an Orphan Asylum, provided the necessary funds can be obtained: consequently, those of our citizens who would like to see such an institution in Sacramento, must step forward immediately and subscribe liberally. It is proposed to erect a building sufficiently commodious to accommodate about one hundred orphans, as well as a large number of day scholars who will be taught, for a small consideration, the higher branches such as are not taught in the Public schools, including French, music, painting, needlework, etc. As orphans whose parents are Protestants, as well as Catholics are to be cared for alike, the project is one of Christian Charity in the largest and truest sense, and should appeal in the most efficacious manner, to all classes who may be able to contribute towards the accomplishment of the end in view."[6]

At first glance the above article seems quite ordinary, but behind it lay an animated debate among Mercy educators over the nature of Mercy education. In the United States, Mother Mary Francis Xavier Warde, foundress of the first Mercy house in the country, had gone about the task of education by establishing academies which included boarding schools. For the most part, attendees came not from the economically poor but from families who could pay partial or full tuition. With a bias that originated in her youth, Mary Baptist felt that such academies were contrary to the Mercy spirit. In this opinion she was encouraged by Mother Mary Francis Bridgeman back in Kinsale. Mother Bridgeman looked upon Mother Warde as an innovator who had strayed from faithful observance of what Mother McAuley taught.

Writing to Mary Baptist in February 1856, Mother Bridgeman says:

Open your *free* school as soon as possible—classify as you please—ask nothing—refuse nothing—God will send sufficient.... You have no Sister that can really teach the languages respectably, besides they have not time, but if respectable children come I see no objection to your engaging teachers for any thing in the way of accomplishments you wish them to learn and let them pay, of course they should provide their books, stationary &c. [sic] To supply maps or general requisites, raffles amongst the children & their friends might succeed.

If you once begin to require payment for any service to any class, I firmly believe you shall have reason to regret it in more ways than one.... Pray then *keep free* while you are so & believe me if you once involve yourself in a *pension* school, or any other *pension* you will never be able to burst your bands. I never consented to your opening a *pension* school still less did I contemplate your doing it as a means of getting up funds for any other purpose. When assured the children of the rich were in pressing need of Instruction of all kinds and that they would *never come* to you unless permitted to pay—I suggested voluntary payment as I do now which you might use as you please.[7]

The environment of Sacramento presented a dilemma for Mary Baptist. She strongly believed in free schools, seeing them as an authentic expression of the Mercy charism. Rural families in Sacramento wanted their daughters to be educated by the Sisters. To do this would necessitate opening a boarding department. Writing to Mother Warde in 1859, Mary Baptist explains her position:

Now dear M.M. Xavier, the difference between Sisters of Mercy in *Ireland* and Sisters of Mercy in *America* that strikes *me most* is that in the former we are devoted to the *poor suffering,* members of J. Christ, whereas in America with the exception of ourselves here, in California, and those in St. Louis, New York, Brooklyn & Cincinnati, our Sisters are employed in conducting *Boarding Schools,* and now for the first proof of my frankness, *you* get the credit—deservedly or not I can't say—of introducing this change first. I know Londonderry and Down Patrick are exceptions to what I have said in Ireland.

> I have always been taught to consider Boarding School as entirely contrary to the Spirit of our Holy Rule every line of which breathes devotedness to the Poor and which even expressly forbids our receiving Boarders. Even day Academies for the children of wealthier classes seems to me not in accordance with its Spirit.[8]

Mary Baptist goes on to press her point. Although she knows that in Ireland, day schools for the wealthy existed in Cork and Carlow during Mother McAuley's lifetime, she points out that they were balanced by intense service of the materially poor. In her estimation the degree of attention and resources needed to run academies changed the focus of those involved from the economically poor to the "educationally needy." Even necessity was not a strong enough justification for Mary Baptist. She felt that in such cases an order with a different charism should more suitably take up the work of educating the well-to-do. In a comment bordering on boastfulness, Mary Baptist tells Mother Mary Francis:

> Our Convent is small and we are much inconvenienced in it as well as in the House of Mercy, still I would not have recourse to such means but wait on Divine Providence; tho' our works may be more limited still I believe more real good will be effected for the glory of God, our own sanctification, and the Salvation of Souls so long as the true spirit of the Institute is carried out; this is my *pride* and not extensive works at the expense of the *end* for which our Holy Rule was instituted. Our Schools are entirely free, no child has, up to this, paid us one cent. A great deal will be done for Religion by good free Schools taught by Religious. I hope you will never have any other but for the Poor[9]

Mary Baptist went so far as to assert: "For my part I am altogether against both Boarding & Day especially the former, and in fact, I would never have joined the Order had I thought they were a duty of the Institute."[10]

Mother Warde lost no time in responding to Mary Baptist's concerns. While her response has not been preserved, a third letter from Mary Baptist indicates that Mother Warde shared with her that Catherine McAuley herself had been in favor of boarding schools. As Mary Baptist points out, "Many things you say are rather startling to me. I was quite unprepared to find our holy Foundress quoted in support of Boarding Schools which I was always led to consider a sort of innovation."[11]

In spite of Mother Warde's assurances that Mother McAuley had thought favorably about boarding schools, Mary Baptist remained skeptical. This skepticism was rooted in a belief that the Mercy Rule's silence concerning teaching members of the middle or wealthier classes meant disapproval. The emphasis in the Rule was placed upon service to the economically poor. Mary Baptist believed that since nothing was stated about serving other social classes, such service was not part of the charism. It is interesting, however, to compare the experience of the hospital with that of the schools. No controversy emerged concerning the hospital's care for persons of means. The healing ministry simply embraced all those in need. The debate over who should be served was strictly confined to the educational sphere. Time would resolve the question in favor of serving all in need.

A second point of concern about the establishment of boarding schools involved their focus on more than the basic education. The types of training and education needed to prepare Sisters for teaching removed them from the immediacy of poverty. Teaching fine arts and spending hours in study and preparation would, it was feared, dampen the desire of the Sisters to be among the poorest of the poor. This concern was coupled with the fear that commitment to boarding schools could subtly move the focus of the Sisters away from those in most need of assistance. In spite of all this, however, Mary Baptist acknowledged that if the majority of Mercy leaders believed such a ministry to be consistent with the charism, she would accept that interpretation.[12]

The *Sacramento Bee's* description of a curriculum including painting and music is all the more surprising in light of Mary Baptist's letter to Bishop O'Connell in 1862. Bishop O'Connell, urged on by Father Thomas Dalton, besieged her with requests to open a Mercy foundation in Grass Valley. The Sisters were badly needed to care for orphans and to establish a Catholic school there. Mary Baptist tells Bishop O'Connell:

> We do not charge the children who attend our schools but we take from their parents any voluntary offerings they make us. Our primary duties are the instruction of poor Girls, the protection of unemployed Women of good character, and the visitation of the sick. We do not exclude the Rich from our Schools. We endeavor to give all a thorough education, but we do not teach Music, Drawing, or any of those accomplishments that consume time, and are unsuited to the class to which we principally devote ourselves. We are willing to conduct a school for Infant Boys.[13]

While Mary Baptist was flexible in her approach to the challenges of ministry in the gold fields of California, she never deviated from her commitment to serve the poor first, last and always. The Sisters in the schools tailored the curriculum to the needs of the students and by the mid 1870s, music and drawing made their way into St. Joseph's Academy in Sacramento. This was not the only change. At a gathering of Mercy leaders held in Ireland in 1868, boarding schools were accepted as compatible with the Mercy mission. This led to the inclusion of a boarding department at St. Joseph's in Sacramento where many of the boarders were not young women from wealthy families but the daughters of rural farmers living in the far-flung Sacramento Valley.

Time given to philosophical discussion was important to the Sisters, but a readiness to respond to the need of the moment was moreso. When the Sisters arrived in Sacramento, they opened a school in the basement of old St. Rose's Church. They enrolled sixty-five pupils on the first day, and by the end of the term that number had nearly doubled to 115. The sheer numbers must have been daunting given the small space used by the school. A more advantageous site needed to be found. Mary Baptist located what she believed to be a perfect location, a half-block on M Street between Tenth and Eleventh Streets. This site was located in one of the most desirous areas in Sacramento. The city was subject to regular floods, leaving much of the riverfront land in marshy or swampy condition, but the site on M Street was elevated and protected from this dynamic. The Sisters hoped to build their convent and school at this location by the beginning of the fall term in 1858. With the help of benefactors and the civic community, the desired land was purchased. Unfortunately, sufficient funds to build the facility could not be raised in time and construction was delayed. By the following year, though, the Sisters' school had an enrollment of 120 students. In addition, the Sisters made sure that adults received religious instruction, and visitation of the sick was carried out throughout the city. The physical toll of all this work on the small community was significant. Dr. Roy Jones comments in *Men, Medicine and Memories,* that:

> These Sisters in their after-school hours and on Saturdays and Sundays administered to the sick. Mostly their rounds were made on foot; and as there were few sidewalks, during the rainy season passage was no small difficulty. They were the first visiting nurses in the City of Sacramento.[14]

Like her earlier experience with government in San Francisco, Mary Baptist once again had to change her direction in response to legislative action. In March 1860, the State Legislature passed the "Capitol Bill" designating the grounds between Tenth and Twelfth, L and M Streets, as the site of a new capitol building for the State. Exercising the right of eminent domain, the State condemned the property and forced the Sisters to relinquish their land. Reimbursement was set, not at the going rate for property, but at the lower amount paid for the land two years prior.

Mary Baptist was now dividing her time between her two foundations. Finally, in July 1860, a decision was made to purchase a half-block site at 9th and G Streets then owned by Col. Ferris Foreman. Contrary to reports in the *Sacramento Daily Union* stating that the land was purchased for $4,000,[15] the Sisters paid $8,000 for the new property and an additional $5,000 for the adjoining half block. Sister Mary Gertrude King, one of the first postulants to enter the Sacramento community, describes the property: "A pretty residence surrounded by a tasteful garden and fine orchard occupied the half-block near G Street. Other buildings were erected for school purposes."[16] The convent and school were placed under the patronage of St. Joseph. By 1861 the school had grown to serve 272 students and was divided into two departments, one for girls and one for boys. This is the first indication that the Sisters taught young boys. At the time it was not considered appropriate for older boys to be instructed by women, but Mary Baptist felt there was no difficulty in accepting the younger lads. Then disaster struck the city.

In December 1861 and again in January 1862, severe floods inundated Sacramento. The waters from these floods did not fully recede for six months. Mother Mary Austin Carroll, a Mercy historian who recorded the stories of all the early Mercy foundations in the United States, provides us with a graphic description of the experience:

> December 9, the weather was clear and bright, and the schools opened with a good attendance. About ten, a man rushed in for his daughter, saying there would be a flood. Another followed, and another, till the school was thinned, and the Sisters

dismissed all, though they saw no cause for apprehension. They looked from the balcony in the direction indicated by the men, but the landscape showed nothing unusual. One jocosely remarked: "If the flood really comes we can go see our new house in San Francisco." Twenty minutes later the Sister on watch perceived the water rolling over the roads on the north east, so rapidly that before noon the waves were gurgling under the convent walls.

They began to remove their stores from the cellar, but the whole lower story was soon under water. They raised their pianos, hoping to save them, but so quickly did the water rise that the idea of saving anything was abandoned.... The one-story houses in the neighborhood were covered before the water reached the convent. The Sisters gave a room to a family consisting of father, mother, and two children. The poor woman, a Mrs. Manning, spent hours on the balcony, gazing vacantly on the surging waters, and bewailing the loss of her hard-earned home. Her eight cows were floundering about seeking terra-firma.... Their faithful servant, Pat McCormick, was helping every one. As he had no way of feeding the fowls, he killed some every day, and boiled chicken was dished in the garret for breakfast, dinner and supper. As the Sisters had only a tiny grate, dinner was put on after breakfast. Wonderful to relate, they were never without Mass; a Chinese priest rowed in a skiff to the upper chamber every morning, and celebrated the Holy Sacrifice for them.[17]

When the first waters flooded Sacramento in December, leaving the convent under three feet of water, four Sisters took refuge in San Francisco. By the end of December, Father James Cassin, Pastor of St. Rose's, asked that the remainder of the Sisters go to San Francisco as well. Father felt that the Sisters were not able to do anything for the flood victims and were exposing themselves unnecessarily to the aftermath of the deluge. The Sisters had a different opinion. After completing their annual retreat in San Francisco at year's end, five professed Sisters were given permission to return to Sacramento. They arrived just before the second flood of January 9, 1862. School was not able to open until the following summer. In the interim the Sisters carried on their labors of visiting the sick and caring for the city's most needy. Mother Mary Austin explains how the Sisters went about their ministry:

> The Sisters went daily in a large boat to the Pavilion, an immense building thrown open to the poor. Naturally, there was a good deal of sickness, and several deaths occurred. Families that had upper lofts withdrew to them; those who had not, took posses-sion of deserted houses; the Sisters had ample scope for their zeal. As late as May, half the city was still under water. To minister to the sick and dying, the Sisters had to turn their prow towards windows on the second or third floor, and mount planks to enter. All the streets of Sacramento are lined with trees, and rowing between their tops in spring, when they are in full bloom, was like moving through a fairy scene.[18]

The impact of the floods was not limited to the immediate suffering of the victims; it extended to the whole region. Over time the city began to revive and normal commerce resumed; however, to prevent future disasters, it was decided that steps needed to be taken to protect the city. The solution of the city leaders was to raise the core streets in Sacramento's downtown area thereby transforming the Sisters' property at 9th and G Streets from an elevated part of the city to a runoff area. The prime property was no longer prime. Future population growth would now expand into the southern and eastern areas of the city, leaving St. Joseph's behind.

An unforeseen consequence of the flood in Sacramento was the establishment of another work of Mercy in the city, an orphanage. The floods had left many families unable to provide housing for their children. Suffering among the laboring classes was great. Mary Gertrude King, a member of the Sacramento community, tells us that the Sisters "made room" for some orphans and other destitute children, thereby taking the first step toward founding an Orphanage.[19] This had long been a hope of the Sisters, and by 1863 twenty-nine orphans were under their care. The number doubled the following year.

In some ways the ministry of education was especially demanding for the Sisters. Mary Baptist shared with Mother Warde that at least half of the Sisters in her foundation were lay Sisters. The lay Sisters did not possess the education needed for the teaching profession. Those accepted as choir Sisters were prepared to teach by earlier training and talent. In practice what this meant was that Mary Baptist had to send some of her most talented and educated members to the Sacramento mission. The *Annals* of the community report that many became ill due to the climate and conditions in Sacramento. In addition, the flood had left the Sacramento convent in ill repair. During the 1860s and '70s, concerns were raised about its leaking roof and overall dampness. While benefactors of the Sisters were willing to raise funds for a new building, church leaders refused permission. In their eyes the debts of the local church had to be paid off before monies were directed elsewhere. Meanwhile, more Sisters fell ill.

Arbitrary governmental regulations, economic depression, floods, illness, and bigotry had all been part of the California experience. In 1863, Mary Baptist faced another challenging situation, a determined and authoritarian bishop, Eugene O'Connell. In April 1863, Bishop O'Connell prevailed upon Mary Baptist to open a house in Grass Valley. This town was part of the Vicariate of Marysville and thus outside the immediate supervision of Bishop Alemany, whose jurisdiction extended only throughout the San Francisco diocese. Bishop O'Connell demanded strict obedience from his clergy and from all who worked for the church. He was strict with himself and held himself and others to the highest standards of commitment. Assured that the Sisters' spiritual and temporal needs would be supplied by Father Dalton, Mary Baptist had accepted the Grass Valley mission in 1863. She appointed to the mission Sister

Mary Teresa King (Superior), Sister Mary Joseph O'Rourke; lay Sisters Josephine Denis and Felix Carr, and a choir postulant who entered for the Grass Valley foundation. As in Sacramento, the focus would be on education and care of the orphans.

There was a significant difference between the branch house at Sacramento and this foundation. Because the new mission was located in the Vicariate of Marysville, it was considered an affiliate house. Mary Baptist would be responsible for it only until it had enough professed Sisters to have its own governance. In the interim Mary Baptist would have to apply all her skills to maintain peace and harmony between Bishop O'Connell and the Sisters in Grass Valley. Part of the problem revolved around Mary Teresa King, the first superior of the new foundation.

A series of letters between 1864 and 1865 reveal great distress in the Grass Valley mission. Through innocent misunderstanding, Mary Teresa left Grass Valley and returned to San Francisco for health reasons. Bishop O'Connell was quite incensed, seeing the move as a decision made without his knowledge or approval. Mary Baptist ended up writing to Bishop O'Connell in hopes of clearing up any misunderstanding. What was more significant, however, was that Mary Teresa did not feel that Grass Valley was a suitable location for a permanent Mercy foundation. Mary Baptist arranged to have Mary Teresa discuss the matter with Archbishop Alemany who disagreed with Mary Teresa's assessment. He felt that "everything regarding the foundation had been maturely and prudently considered and that he believed it to be the Will of God for them to be there, and that if a wife is bound to her Husband as long as he lives so are they till Grass [Valley] dies away."[20]

Since abandoning the foundation was out of the question, Mary Teresa now asked for a third professed choir Sister. She feared the responsibility for formation of new members when there were only two choir Sisters in the community.[21] Archbishop Alemany was not, at first, open to her request, but finally allowed Mary Baptist to loan a professed Sister to the Grass

Valley foundation for six months. This did not resolve the situation, which came to a crisis point in March 1865.

The situation was precipitated by a clash between need and charism. Bishop O'Connell seemed to have indicated to the Grass Valley Sisters that he wished them to open a boys' orphanage. The Sisters there felt this was outside the usual scope of their Rule. Writing to Father Thomas Dalton, Bishop O'Connell reveals displeasure and anger at the refusal of the Sisters to comply with his request:

> A positive refusal to receive the boys or have anything to do with them I look upon as disobedience to the Bishop of the Vicariate. If the Sisters persist in their refusal to take charge of the boys I will either transfer them or discharge them. Either alternative may be rather unpleasant so I request of you in my name to tell the good Sisters that I recognize no Sisterhood that won't obey me. I ask no more of your Sisters than Bishop Duggan does of the Sisters of Mercy of Chicago or than the Bishop of Pittsburg [sic] does of the same Order. I am sure the Sisters of Mercy in Grass Valley are not so uncharitable as to think that the Ladies of their Order in Chicago & Pittsburg [sic] are living in violation of their Holy Rule. I have been trying up to this time what virtue there was in tufts of grass, now I have resolved to try what virtue there is in stones. My ultimatum is then: Let the holy Sisters in Grass Valley either agree to take charge of little boys or repair without delay to Yreka where they shall have charge of little girls. May God direct them to the best.[22]

The Bishop's position posed several points of tension. First, it was not within his authority to determine where the Sisters would be assigned; only Mary Baptist could do that. Second, the Sisters were the interpreters of the Mercy Rule. No Bishop had the authority to override the constraints the Rule imposed. Mary Baptist herself could see no problem in taking the younger boys, but older boys were deemed inappropriate. As was her custom, Mary Baptist sought advice and counsel not only from Archbishop Alemany but from Mother Bridgeman as well. Mother Francis' words had been very direct: "My advice is, if possible, bring back the two heads and send a head with a better spirit, without this, all the qualifications they could have will not suffice to form good, happy practical Sisters."[23]

Mary Baptist also discussed the situation with Archbishop Alemany. After hearing all the details, Archbishop Alemany indicated that Mother Mary Teresa was "too pusillanimous, that you feared if you did this you could be required to do that, that you feared the place would not last &c so said I do not think she will ever get on, you had better recall her and send another."[24] It was the Archbishop's direction that both Mother Teresa and Sister Mary Joseph be recalled and two more compliant Sisters assigned to the mission. In the Alemany's words: "… but you have to see that she be pious, agreeable, willing to do anything she can that her Bishop would wish, a Sister should not thwart a poor Bishop when he is trying to do the best he can do for his flock."[25] Archbishop Alemany promised to smooth the way with Bishop O'Connell and write to apprise him of the change in leadership.

Writing to Mother Teresa and Sister Mary Joseph, Mary Baptist advises them not to "spend time pondering over the past or imagining what may be here after."[26] She also wrote to Father Dalton asking him to comfort the Sisters in their distress and to ease their departure. Sister Mary Baptista Synan was appointed to replace Mother Teresa but the Grass Valley troubles were not over yet, however.

Sister Mary Baptista did not have the governing skills of her mentor, Mary Baptist Russell. She was, most likely, too tolerant of the weaknesses in her Sisters. Bishop O'Connell writes to the newly elected Mary Gabriel Brown of his concern in a letter dated May, 1868. Referring to the contrition of a Sister who had no control of her temper, he fears that Mary Baptista [Synan] is unable to deal with the situation. "At the same time as the present Revd. Mother has had such forbearance with her it is to be feared without special graces, cooperated with more faithfully than she had done hitherto there may be another ebullition of temper, if so I must for the peace of the Community insist upon her leaving."[27] Mary Gabriel writes in response that the Sister in question has been without a sure guide. "I fear good Mother M. Baptista has been somewhat wanting in prudent determination with her, but as in all probability she will be (happily for herself) soon released from the burdens of Superiority. Let us hope her Successor will be better in this respect as in others."[28] In this observation Mary Gabriel was right.

The following week Sister Mary Baptist Mogan was appointed Superior of the community. The change marked the beginning of a new relationship between the Sisters and their Bishop as well as renewed vitality in the Grass Valley foundation. Now what remained was to nurture the educational mission in Sacramento and Grass Valley and plant new seeds for Mercy education in San Francisco.

IX

Opening Doors to the Future

For Mary Baptist Russell and her Sisters, education was the path out of economic hardship, oppression, and ignorance for those locked in poverty. The Sisters were practical educators with an eye to challenging the mind while providing the skills and training needed for self-sufficiency. Their understanding of education was forged by the experience of seeing the hardships wrought by educational deprivation. The Sisters were women of Ireland, a country where access to schools and learning was used religiously and politically to impose the will of one country upon another. As a result of their years of service to the economically poor, the Sisters knew that without education and practical skills, people were sentenced to hardship and poverty.

Mercy education is rooted in a vision of the human person. Mother Catherine McAuley placed her vision of service within the context of Matthew's Gospel, "Whatever you do to the least of these, you do to me." (Matt. 25:40) Because the Sisters believed in the value of each human person, they were dedicated to a mode of education that would reverence human dignity, provide access to all, regardless of economic circumstances, and promote the utilization of all one's gifts and abilities. The Sisters saw education as an essential element in bringing others to God and proclaiming the Gospel message.

In years when education was not universally accessible, teaching was difficult work. Mother Mary Francis Bridgeman reflected on that reality in a letter written to Sister Francis Benson:

> Until you have a School attached to your principal Noviceship and that your Novices are all perseveringly trained in it whether they like it or not, you will always have a scanty supply of teachers. It is real hard work to make good teachers of most of those who enter and often those who have had many advantages of education are in the end not at all equal to those who [had] few. Nearly all who enter would prefer the "run about" duties to the application, mental labor and restraint that must be encountered to become a good teacher, but when they have surmounted these difficulties they are generally fit for every other duty the rest of their lives....[1]

Within the Mercy communities, teachers came from among the choir Sisters, who came to the community with both education and dowry. Some, like Mother Mary Vincent Phelan, the first Superior of the Sacramento community after it became an independent foundation in 1887, had trained under masters in music and other fields. Mary Baptist herself possessed the advantages of private tutoring in academics and arts before she entered the Kinsale foundation. While the lay Sisters usually took charge of "mothering" the orphans, the choir Sisters "mothered" the mind.

Like educational policy in contemporary times, educational policy in the mid-1800s was not exempt from political considerations. When Mary Baptist opened her first school at the Cathedral in San Francisco, she was determined to steer clear of the ups and downs of political entanglement. In Sacramento that was not an issue. Common schools, known as public schools today, were established in the city in 1854. Prior to that time only private schools were available to the children of Sacramento and its environs. According to the Sacramento Directory of 1854-55, six schools were opened with an average daily attendance of 350 students.[2]

The common schools were not totally inclusive at this time, however. The experience of black Californians illustrates the point. Although public funds were appropriated for education, the thought that children of all races would be educated together was not in the popular imagination. For some, like State Superintendent of Public Instruction Paul K. Hubbs, such a practice would undermine the whole system. "... While I foster by all proper means the education of the colored races, I should deem it a death to our system to permit the mixture of races in the same school or to take any action, other than that prompted by benevolent feeling for the true benefit of the colored races."[3]

Asian students fared worse. A petition to admit a Chinese child into the public schools was denied in 1863. While separate schooling was made available for black children in the 1850s, such an institution for the Chinese community was not established until 1895.[4] Into this educational milieu the Sisters brought a different perspective. In her first appeal for public support in July 1856, Mary Baptist stated: "The first object to which the religious of this Order are solemnly devoted, is THE INSTRUCTION AND EDUCATION OF THE IGNO-RANT, rich or poor, young or old, without distinction of country or creed."[5] To this commitment she was always faithful.

While her first school in San Francisco was short-lived, St. Joseph's School in Sacramento was to be a center of Mercy education for over a century. When the Sisters arrived in Sacramento, approximately 950 students were enrolled in the common schools although the daily attendance was only a little more than half that number.[6] Three days after their arrival, the Sisters opened St. Rose School, the first Catholic school in the city. Accommodations provided for the initial 65 students were quite limited, two small rooms in the basement of St. Rose Church. The site proved to be inadequate and plans were made to move.

The *Annals* of the Sacramento Sisters tell us that daily enrollment reached 120 students by 1859. When the Sisters relocated to the newly purchased property at 9th and G Streets that year, one story of the building was constructed to meet the needs of the school which was placed under the patronage of St. Joseph. As student enrollment grew, so did the need for teachers. The lack of qualified teachers in the boys' department of the parish school led church leaders to ask that the Sisters take charge of them. This they did, adding an extension to the newly built facility. The boys' department of St. Joseph's served seventy-five to eighty boys until 1875, when the Christian Brothers arrived in Sacramento to take on this work. This new development sheds light upon the conflict over caring for orphaned boys in Grass Valley. Since the instruction of younger boys was no problem in Sacramento, it becomes clear that the housing and care of orphan boys was the focus of conflict. Teaching was not the issue.

The Mercy vision of education was broad in its scope. Unlike orders that devoted their full attention to academies or schools, the early Sisters of Mercy saw their educational mission as one that enfolded all those in need of instruction. Diversity was its hallmark. In Sacramento Mercy education took on a more traditional form at St. Joseph's Academy; however, in San Francisco the form was multi-dimensional, including industrial training and adult education. Nursing schools were established in both Sacramento and San Francisco in response to the pressing need for trained nurses.

Educational opportunities focusing on basic education and job training were key to the work done in the House of Mercy in San Francisco, as well as in the Magdalen Asylum. Training in needlework, tailoring, laundress skills, and practical arts were seen as essential in assisting women to obtain self-sufficiency. To some degree these trade schools were organized as cooperatives where the student work was sold. Sisters depended on their social contacts with wealthy benefactors to market the creations of the women. It was a total package of transformation. First, the women in need were identified. Next, they were given the basics of shelter, food, and safety. These basic needs were met in a manner that respected the dignity and value of each woman. Then, once the basics were addressed, education began—reading, writing, and math coupled with some form of job skills. The model was simple, direct, and highly effective.

For the adult population in Sacramento, the arrival of the Sisters brought a new opportunity for education as well. Since many pioneer members of the community lacked formal education, the Sisters coupled religious instruction for adults with other subjects such as reading, writing, spelling, arithmetic, and account-keeping. This endeavor was especially focused on providing women with basic education.[7]

The well-educated were not ignored. In mid-nineteenth century California, there was a hunger for literature, drama, and music. The populace that raced to California in search of its gold included representatives from the whole spectrum of social classes and educational backgrounds. In the emerging world of commerce everyone, including professional business leaders, lawyers, doctors and others, were in need of good reading materials. Subscription libraries developed in response to that need. Prior to the opening of the Public Library in Sacramento in 1879, the Sisters established a subscription library for the city's eager readers. Selections from English classics, poetry, philosophy, politics, and history were all available, as well as religious works. Over one thousand Sacramentans withdrew books from that collection on a regular basis. Income from the lending library was used to assist the school. Such creative fund raising was essential for the economic viability of St. Joseph's. No student was turned away for lack of funds, and only voluntary donations from students' families were accepted for the services provided. Fairs, raffles, charity sermons and all manner of benefits worked to make up the difference between income and costs.

The economic struggles of the Sacramento community were a hindrance to the accomplishment of one of the Sisters' key hopes, the establishment of an orphanage for those who were orphans or half-orphans. The plan had to be delayed several times and was only realized after the floods of 1861. Mary Baptist wrote to Mother Mary Francis Warde, "In time they expect to have a half-orphanage but it is pretty hard to raise the necessary funds even in this so-called golden country."[8] In spite of the difficulties, the Sisters elected to build a refuge for children left homeless after the floods. They hoped to provide shelter for forty to fifty children while their parents struggled to rebuild their homes and lives in the aftermath of the floods. The State promised to assist with the support of the residents but offered no aid in building the new home. By 1863 twenty-nine orphans were under the care of the Sacramento Sisters. That number grew to sixty-five by 1864. In 1865 an orphanage was established at the Grass Valley foundation. Both functioned until their futures were altered by legislative action. In 1878 the California Legislature decided to give state aid only to two Catholic orphanages—St. Joseph's in South San Francisco and St. Vincent's in Grass Valley. As a result, the Sacramento Sisters reluctantly gave up their ministry to orphans and entrusting the orphans to their Sisters at St. Vincent's.[9]

The decade of the '70s brought growth in the scope of Mercy education in both Sacramento and San Francisco. Children in the Rincon Hill area of San Francisco had to travel a significant distance to attend St. Vincent's, the closest Catholic elementary school. Mary Baptist, always an educator at heart, decided to provide a school closer to the Rincon Hill community. The building was funded through the proceeds of a raffle, some minor donations, and a generous bequest from Reverend John McCullough. Our Lady of Mercy School was opened on the feast of Corpus Christi, 1871. At the time it was considered a significant asset to the growing Catholic community. The *San Francisco Monitor* of May 27, 1871, provides a sense of the school:

It was with the greatest pleasure that we visited yesterday the new school building just erected by the Sisters of Mercy. It is thirty-six by one hundred and fifty feet and is divided into two large assembly rooms off each of which there are two classrooms with galleries for recreation. There are also two music rooms.

We saw cabinets containing a collection of specimens in natural historical setting for use of the classes. The whole building is lofty and well ventilated, supplied with very neat school furniture including a large expanse of blackboard. Along the entire south side runs a wide covered balcony with seats where the pupils can enjoy themselves during recess. The entrance is on First Street.

The good Sisters have not forgotten the interests of little boys; for them they are preparing a small school on Rincon Place in which boys under eight will be received. Both schools will commence operations on Monday, June twelfth, and no doubt will be an inestimable blessing to the children of the area.[10]

Like St. Joseph's Academy in Sacramento, Our Lady of Mercy School was highly successful. On its opening day, Mary Baptist welcomed thirty-nine girls to the school and another twenty-seven to St. Joseph's, the younger boys' school. Before month's end the enrollment grew to 178 girls and forty-one boys. Before a fire destroyed the buildings in 1887, the Sisters were teaching five hundred students in primary through secondary grades.

With a successful start in responding to the educational needs of the children around Rincon Hill, Mary Baptist began to look to other areas equally in need of educational facilities. She did not have to look far. The Sisters were the only religious educators in Sacramento, and the school there had outgrown its capacity. Plans were made to enlarge the school and in 1872, Mary Baptist laid the cornerstone for a new convent and school building. Four years later in 1876, St. Joseph's received a High School Charter. The expanded facilities, now called St. Joseph's

Academy, became the training ground for many of Sacramento's teachers and women of influence. In commenting on the importance of St. Joseph's Academy to the Sacramento community, historian Steven M Avella notes:

> Graduates of St. Joseph's received a high-quality education, and the school itself represented an important asset for the community at large. Even though the school was Irish-Catholic in its orientation, Catholics did not, and indeed for financial reasons, could not exclude others not of their faith. While the enrollment at St. Joseph's included a preponderance of Catholic girls, most of Irish extraction, a substantial portion of its pupils were from various other denominations—including the daughters of local Jewish Sacramentans. The attractiveness of the education for a wide diversity of Sacramento's young women redounded to the steady improvement of the city, and St. Joseph's Academy itself was one of the city's cultural symbols of the rising numbers of female citizens that brought stability and settlement to the community.[11]

While the Mercy education mission was flourishing in Sacramento, Mary Baptist's mission of education in the San Francisco Bay area was just beginning to bloom. In 1874, an industrial school for girls was opened in San Francisco. Another elementary and high school quickly followed when, in 1877, a plea from Reverend William Gleeson caused Mary Baptist to accept a mission in Oakland.

Oakland was readymade for Mary Baptist. It was unpretentious with an increasing number of poor families. Since resources were few, Father Gleeson, a prominent Catholic writer of the period, promised to dedicate the revenues from his literary works to the support of the school. His sincerity and commitment won the day. On July 5, 1877, Our Lady of Lourdes Academy was opened. Many of the first eighty children enrolled traveled long distances to the academy. Within a week of its opening, enrollment grew to 120 children, many without economic means. Still Mary Baptist's work was not finished.

In 1878, Father Thomas Gibney, pastor of St. Peter's Church in San Francisco, came to Mary Baptist with another plea for teachers. Girls in the Mission District did not have the same educational options as their counterparts in other areas of the city. Mary Baptist could not bring herself to refuse the request in spite of her recent foundations. With its premises unfinished and no convent, St. Peter's Academy opened on July 7, 1878.

During her lifetime, Mary Baptist had one more school to establish, St. Brendan's School in San Francisco. When fire destroyed Our Lady of Mercy School in 1887, discussion was held on whether or not to rebuild the facility. St. Peter's was flourishing; St. Joseph's Academy, Sacramento was full to capacity; and Our Lady of Lourdes was well established in the Oakland area. Both Our Lady of Lourdes, and St. Joseph's Academy now provided a day school, secondary program and boarding options. Ultimately, it was decided not to rebuild Our Lady of Mercy School, but to accept the invitation of Father John Nugent to staff a new parish school just a block away from St. Mary's Hospital. The school, St. Brendan's would be the last established by Mary Baptist.

Instruction at the Mercy elementary schools stressed the basics. A recollection written by Sister Mary Regis Wallace in 1944 describes the style of instruction. "The children were drilled in the fundamentals."[12] Mary Regis goes on to outline the various steps of learning to diagram sentences and identify parts of speech. She also remembers visits to the classroom by Mary Baptist herself. Sister tells us that such visits were a combination of encouragement and practical lessons on the subject at hand. Mary Baptist often reminded the students that the strict discipline they encountered was out of a sense of caring:

Remember children when you sometimes think the Sisters cross with you, they are only interested in you and want you to

Students and Sisters of Our Lady of Lourdes, Oakland

remember that there is nothing like doing the right thing and doing the best you can in school and out of school and always doing it for God.... Remember when the Sisters correct they are not cross with you but interested in you and want to fit you for what God has planned for you and in this way train you to help yourself and save your soul.[13]

For the Sisters, Mary Baptist had words on this same topic. Sensitive to the feelings and impressions of children, she felt that irreparable harm could be done by criticism or harshness on the part of her Sisters. Notes from one of her retreats make her feelings clear:

... let us win the young hearts to God by our gentle kindness and interest to all, carefully avoiding favorites. We can scarcely understand the serious and evil consequences of unkindness to children, especially when accompanied, as it generally is, by a display of temper. It embitters the young mind, and does not convince it of the wrong it has done; but rightly enough the child considers the religious at fault.[14]

Mary Baptist's animated, vivid teaching manner made students love to have her around them. Whether it was on an occasional visit to the classroom or when she took time out to instruct them, they were drawn into her teaching. As one Sister put it, "Reverend Mother was the children's best and dearest friend."[15] Sister Mary Monica Carroll recorded the recollections of Mrs. Fitzgerald, a student at Our Lady of Mercy School.

As a school girl I revered her [Mary Baptist] as a saint and I have never changed my opinion. I never knew any one who so closely portrayed the life of Our Lord. We loved to have her give our religious instruction and for many years she reserved this duty for herself although she had innumerable important calls on her time. She told Bible stories in such a fascinating way and so earnestly that we were deeply impressed. The Scriptural quotations were so often repeated in appropriate places in the course of her instructions that we learned them without any labor; in fact her classes were the ones we most loved.

Many of the early pupils of Our Lady of Mercy School became religious; I feel they would unite with me in attesting that they owe their vocation under God to the beautiful Gospel lessons she impressed on our young minds. All loved her; she was gentle and kind to us, and always so interested in our sodalities and entertainments; she gave us great encouragement.[16]

A review of the curriculum at Mercy schools in Sacramento and San Francisco shows that circumstances and needs had brought a change in Mary Baptist's thoughts about what should be taught in Mercy schools. While she initially wrote to Bishop O'Connell that her Sisters would not teach music, she quickly adapted that rule. Musical instruction became an important discipline at both Our Lady of Mercy School and St. Joseph's Academy. While nothing is said of the change in policy, it can be surmised that the cause was three-fold. Among the Sisters were talented musicians such as Sister Mary Lorenzo O'Malley, Sister M. Aloysius Reichart, and Sister Mary Vincent Phelan. Trained before their entry into the community, they were able to earn needed income through music lessons. Ready talent, economic need, and the knowledge of its power to foster appreciation for beauty and peace converged to justify adding music to the curriculum.

Sister Mary Lorenzo was gifted in teaching vocal music. Her technique began with instruction in the melody and then adding the words later. Students were not told what song they were learning. The suspense added to attention. Sister Mary Aloysius likewise excelled in teaching music and the San Francisco schools soon set four music rooms set aside for instruction. In Sacramento the same was true. Under Sister Mary Vincent a music conservatory was established at St. Joseph's, Sacramento. Piano lessons and instruction in other musical instruments was a chief source of income for the Sacramento community. Money earned through music lessons subsidized other works of charity.

The high school programs established at St. Joseph's Academy, Sacramento and at St. Peter's in San Francisco were geared toward the highest academic achievement. Among the curricular offerings were religion, English, history, Latin, Greek, algebra, geometry, botany, philosophy, physiology, astronomy, dramatic arts, drawing, instrumental and vocal music. It is not surprising that graduates of the high school frequently passed the State Normal Examination for teaching. This was particularly true in Sacramento where St. Joseph's would become "one of the main providers of teachers for Sacramento's growing school system."[17]

Mary Baptist took great pride in the accomplishments of Mercy students. She believed in promoting their work and encouraged participation in various public exhibitions of student achievement. Sister M. Leo Mahoney recalls that Mary Baptist always tried to be present at these student exhibitions. On one such occasion Mary Baptist had words of commendation and comfort for those who did well and those who did not:

> I think it was on the occasion of our first Public Exercises, she entered the room in which were assembled the children that had taken part; I was one of the number. I cannot remember her exact words but they were to this effect: My dear children,—I am well pleased with you all, and what is better still, I am sure you are all pleasing to Almighty God; and those who have not done so well have the same merit in God's sight. He looks to the intention and I am certain all tried to do their best.... These were cheerful words for the unfortunate ones like myself, who did not do so well.[18]

It is fortunate that some examples of student exhibits from this early period have been preserved. In the archives of the Sisters of Mercy in Burlingame, California, a collection of student work exhibited at the World's Columbian Exposition in 1893 testifies to the scope and excellence of student achievement. The collection was the contribution of the students and faculty of Our Lady of Lourdes Academy in East Oakland. Included in the work are detailed physiological and botanical drawings, biographical compositions on historical figures of national and church history, studies of Chopin and Pozanini, and other examples from various fields of study. The exhibit was subsequently sent to the Chicago World's Fair.

Mary Baptist's love of learning gave her a natural enthusiasm for natural history, literature, and history. Her letters echo with references to flowers, literature, politics, and, of course, religious issues. Stories of life in California, as well as the stories of the people, served stirred in sentiments of wonder experienced at the workings of God. For Mary Baptist, learning and God went hand in hand. She and her Sisters possessed an understanding of natural existence as a mirror of God. The phrase of Gerard Manley Hopkins, "The earth is charged with the grandeur of God," was the way she saw creation. In a four-volume science text, *God in His Works,* developed by Mother Mary Francis Bridgeman, this understanding is systematically developed.[19] In the texts, children are encouraged to look, to see, and to examine the life forms around them. Each area of natural science is explained according to the most up-to-date knowledge of the period. Out of the experience, the student is asked to look deeper and see the Creator God beyond creation. The wonder of plant physiology, workings of the human body, and other natural phenomena are presented as a source of praise and thanksgiving to God.

Mary Baptist's knowledge of and love for nature and natural history is also seen in a letter sent to Sister Mary Aloysius at St. Joseph's in Sacramento in 1895. She knew the Sisters wished to set up a natural history display, so she collected a wide variety of items for the museum, boxed them up in her trunk, and sent them off. It was a motley collection: corals, whale bone, marble from a broken table, a piece of a hundred-year-old pear tree, Irish turf, and shells. Included with the collection were exact directions on how to bleach the shells, background on whales to accompany the whale bone she sent, and essential data on biological classifications.[20]

Mary Baptist sought other opportunities to foster learning as well. She was instrumental in encouraging Mrs. Alice Toomey to seek diocesan support for the first Catholic school convention on the West Coast. The gathering welcomed 150 delegates to the first conference held in September 1894.

The history and lore of California were of special interest to Mary Baptist. She collected items, big and small, and set up a museum display at Rincon Hill. Among its treasures were gold from the Sierra Nevada and a cockle shell used for the baptism of Indian neophytes at Mission Santa Barbara. One treasure that has been preserved is a collection of original tiles from the California Missions. On each tile was painted a picture of the mission, its foundation date and the name of its founder. At the time two sets were made. One set was sent to the newly founded Catholic University in Washington D.C. where they are still exhibited; the second was destroyed in the earthquake of 1906.

The impact of Mercy education upon its recipients is hard to quantify. Both in San Francisco and in Sacramento, the educational efforts of the Sisters touched influential women of the times, shapers of society like Eleanor McClatchy whose family established the *Sacramento Bee*. Mercy schools, elementary and secondary, provided a way for newly arrived immigrants to move into the mainstream of their communities while preserving their religious and cultural identities. It was, from the beginning, a blend of academic excellence and practical wisdom. Mercy Education, as imparted by Mary Baptist and her Sisters, trained students for life. It was a three-fold education focused upon character formation, preparation for future careers, and, most of all, centering one's life in God. The formula was timeless: education for the spirit, the mind and the marketplace. Such an education was to be a doorway to the future.

Mary Baptist Russell: Mother of the Poor and a "Maker of California"

X

A Life That Speaks

In an age of specialization, it is difficult to comprehend the scope of Mary Baptist's expertise. Her story and the stories of the early Sisters of Mercy are ones of achievement, social influence and faith. Mary Baptist is the foundress of Catholic healthcare in Northern California, a pioneer in outreach to women in need, an inspired educator, a practical administrator, and a spiritual leader, animating women to give their total energies to the service of God and God's people. She was also a woman who worried about whether children were treated gently, whether the released prisoner had clothes to wear, and whether an old homeless woman had a bed to sleep in that night. For her, life and love were found in small things as well as in great. It was the small acts of tenderness and compassion which endeared her and her Sisters to the persons they served. These actions were not headline news. They were heart stories.

The depth of Mary Baptist's love and mercy is best captured in the anecdotal and "legend" stories passed down by word of mouth. Mary Baptist took upon herself the role of community archivist and chronicler, so the stories about her do not appear in the historical annals of the San Francisco foundation. They are revealed, instead, in the small details, echoed in her personal letters, and vividly depicted in the personal reminiscences of those who knew her.

One "legend" that has been passed on by her Sisters was Mary Baptist's practice of raiding the hospital linen supplies to provide for the needs of the sick poor visited in their homes. Since economic times were difficult, losing the linen was not always looked upon with favor. In the hopes of limiting her bounty, a lock was finally installed on the linen supply closet. This short, humorous anecdote provides a window into the generosity of heart that was characteristic of Mary Baptist.

Sister Mary Regis Wallace recounts her memories of accompanying Mary Baptist on her visitation rounds to the sick poor in their homes:

> The Sisters loved to go on visitation with Mother. When ill health was upon her and the Sisters wished to spare her carrying heavy baskets to the poor, she thought of a way to spare them anxiety. Under the cloak and habit she fastened sheets, towels, linen and dressings she would need, in the large pocket other articles would fit. Mother looked so dignified in the long cloak and with the light looking bag that the Sisters did not worry. The young Sister carried the bread, tea, meat and potatoes, etc. While on the visitation Mother's partner was often surprised; out of nowhere would appear all that was needed in the sick room of the poor.[1]

Sparing the Sisters the task of carrying heavy supplies was only one aspect of Mary Baptist's strategy. Wrapping sheets and linens around her under her skirts concealed from neighbors and public the full dimension of need in the families she visited. It was a way of respecting their dignity. That was what her mission was all about, honoring and reverencing God's people. She worked tirelessly to meet the needs of the suffering poor because they deserved nothing less. Whether it was feeding hundreds of hungry San Franciscans during economically depressed times, finding a wedding dress for a young girl too poor to purchase one, encouraging children to do their best and use their talents to the full, or negotiating for governmental contracts, in her eyes, it was all God's work.

For the majority of her days, Mary Baptist had enjoyed an active life of service, good health, and abundant energy. That reality began to change in the 1890s. First, in 1891, she experienced a small stroke. Although she recovered and resumed her work, her letters began to hint of the aches and pains of aging. To Mother Mary Evangelist Fallon of Kinsale she spoke of an attack of bilious fever that left her "not as strong."[2] In a later letter to Sister Helena O'Brien, Mary Baptist speaks of resting immediately after returning from home visitation.[3] The context of the letter seems to indicate that Mary Baptist suffered either from a type of digestive disorder or a heart problem. The strongest indicator of failing health is found in a letter written to her sister, Mother Mary Emmanuel, in 1898:

> Mother Austin Carroll says she has not one delicate Sister in her community of sixty! I envy her. We have many, and I head the list; but I am not suffering in any way. Yet, without any premonitory symptoms, I lose for an instant the power of my right side; and, as long as I am subject to such attacks I can't say I am *well.* Still I am stouter than ever, and no wonder for I sleep well, eat well, and cannot go around as much as formerly. These symptoms ceased for several months, but have returned of late, though I still follow the doctor's regimen.

By July 1898, Mary Baptist's illness was moving into its final stage. A progressive clogging of the arteries to her brain dulled her senses. Mary Columba O'Kelly, her Assistant, wrote to Mother Emmanuel on July 30:

> Our dear Mother is still with us but each day growing weaker. Her eyes are dark to this world. Ah, how much brightness she will gaze on for all eternity! She has not been able to see for the past few days. It is so sad not to hear her voice, and to know that she cannot hear us is inexpressibly sad.[4]

Letters written by the Sisters to Ireland during July and early August of 1898 reflect a sense of impending loss and resignation. One letter summed up what Mary Baptist meant to her Sisters:

> What shall we do if the good God takes her? I cannot imagine this House and Community without her: she is its heart and its life. She was always ready to help us and make everything light and pleasant: and oh! Her charity was really boundless. Her right hand did not know what her left hand did. No one ever saw her angry or impatient—always willing to forgive, no matter how often one had offended. Indeed, she was a faithful copy of our mild and loving Jesus. She lived and moved in and for God. Her charity and sympathy for the poor were unbounded. She always helped every one who applied to her. Her very last direction to me was to send some money to a leper settlement in Japan.[5]

Mary Baptist lingered until the morning of August 6, the feast of the Transfiguration. At twenty minutes past six in the morning, she died and was delivered into the hands of her God. Her death was a citywide moment. San Francisco newspapers gave daily updates on her illness as soon as it was evident that her death was near. The articles were, in tone, distinctly different from those that, upon their arrival in San Francisco, accused Mary Baptist and her Sisters of unseemly conduct on the *Cortes*. Now they spoke of her as one treasured and esteemed:

> From the *Bulletin* August 6, 1898:
> The best-known charitable worker on the Pacific Coast.... From the days of the Argonauts she had been a unique figure in the public view.... The energy, skill, and powerful will of Mother Russell have dominated in times of crises...

> From the *Call* August 6, 1898:
> No death in recent years has been heard of with more regret in this community than that of Mother Superior Mary Baptist Russell who watched over the destinies of various charitable

institutions in this city during the past half century.... Her constant aim in life has been to uplift the sick and the wounded, and in this she was most successful.

As the rituals of her funeral progressed, thousands came to St. Mary's to honor her. The hospital chapel proved too small to hold those who came to her Funeral Mass. The outpouring of public sentiment came from persons of all walks of society, the wealthy and the impoverished, persons of every ethnicity and religious creed. In describing the throngs of mourners, the *Chronicle* of August 10, 1898 reported:

No dead sovereign ever had prouder burial than Mary Baptist whose life of self-denial and good works has crowned her in a city's memory. The great crowd literally besieged St. Mary's Hospital where her body was lying yesterday morning and swelled to such immense proportions when the graveyard was reached that the utmost efforts of a band of policemen were hardly sufficient to hold it in restraint.

Father Matthew Russell, writing of his Sister's funeral, tells us that the size of the crowd was so large that it actually frightened the Sisters.[6]

When one reflects upon some of history's notable pioneers, it is sometimes said that they were "ahead of their times" or "born out of time." It is a way of saying that the patterns and paradigms of life bequeathed by that historical figure to succeeding generations contain important insights into the present. It is not accurate, however, to say that Mary Baptist was "ahead of her times." She was thoroughly a woman of her time and her culture. She was gifted with an inner vision that fully matched the needs of society during the latter half of the nineteenth century.

While it is important to acknowledge that Mary Baptist was immersed in her own time, it is also accurate to say that the patterns and paradigms revealed in her story are as important and significant today as they were 150 years ago. The urgent demands that called forth her attention and compassion have not lessened with time. The poor still struggle to find adequate food, shelter, employment, and hope. Those without health insurance still need someone to reach out and care for them in their suffering. Education is still the doorway to a better life.

Mary Baptist did not let the realities of bigotry, the failure of local and state governments to honor their commitments, the ever-present gap between the cost of providing for those in need and her limited financial resources deter her from her mission: providing for the poor, sick and uneducated. Mary Baptist knew the hardships of damp housing, scarce food and long hours as well as the heartache of burying her Sisters when the hardships and rigors of service brought them to early graves. She persevered and flourished only because she drew upon the deep resources of her soul and the strength of being in communion with others who held the same hope. Through good times and bad, she provided wise guidance and encouragement to the Sisters with whom she shared her life, animating them to spend their lives for God and God's poor.

It is one thing to tell her story. It is another matter to allow that story to speak its truth to us, to allow it to be a guide for our own journey. Through Mary Baptist's personal letters, the reminiscences of those who knew her well, the testimony of her deeds, and the lessons she taught, a portrait of her spirit emerges. It is the portrait of a life and ministry animated and rooted in five foundational characteristics. These characteristics are Mary Baptist's legacy to all who embrace lives of compassionate service.

The commitment to serve everyone, regardless of race, creed, or economic status is an abiding characteristic of the Mercy mission. This commitment to service was the hallmark of Mary Baptist's life and ministry. No one was excluded from the embrace of Mercy's service. Sister Mary Francis Benson described St. Mary's Hospital as a "world unto itself."[7] Indeed it was. As many as six languages were spoken within the facility. The Sisters didn't preach at the patients; they simply gave the witness of devoted service, especially during times when others recoiled from the task of caring for the sick.

Sister-nurses caring for victims of small pox, typhoid, cholera, and other diseases were constantly at risk. They put their lives on the line to take care of the infirm. The manner in which they served was characterized by tenderness, compassion, and medical expertise. When ministering to Catholic patients, the Sisters prayed with them, made sure they received the sacraments of the church, and sat with them during their death agonies. This type of devotion impressed staff and patients alike. Many in California had long given up their own religious practices; but seeing the love with which the Sisters cared for patients, some of the "unchurched" asked for instruction in the Catholic religion. The practice of caring first and sharing religious beliefs later was followed in other areas of service as well. It was based on the understanding that the quality of one's love and service was more important than words in bringing others to Christ.

Like Catherine McAuley, Mary Baptist had a particular love for the Gospel passage from Matthew, Chapter 25: "Truly I tell you, just as you did it to one of the least of these who are members of my family, you did it to me." In a letter written to Archbishop Alemany in 1867, Mary Baptist asks the bishop to intercede in obtaining this Gospel text for the Feast of Our Lady of Mercy on September 24:

> Whenever the Feast of Our Lady of Mercy occurs I feel a regret we have not a Mass more appropriate to the Day, and the Order. I always feel a regret the Gospel is not that where our Lord is represented at the Day of Judgment granting the Kingdom of Heaven to the Elect in reward for exercising the *works of Mercy.*[8]

In the eyes of Mary Baptist, no work of mercy was more important than caring for the poor. It is not an exaggeration to say that love for the poor was the consuming passion of her life. It was this characteristic that shaped her entire ministry and that of the California mission. No action was too great or too small when it came to responding to immediate need. Sometimes the depth of her generosity proved challenging to her Sisters, especially when it meant that her own mattress went out the door or supplies meant for the hospital found their way into the homes of the poor. Practicality and efficiency always gave way to the demands of love.

It was not just supplying the need but the manner in which Mary Baptist went about it that most touched her Sisters. The linen carried to the homes of the poor was always concealed either in a basket or underneath her petticoat, to preserve the dignity of the recipients. Visits to bring material supplies would often become occasions for cleaning the house, cooking the meal for a sick mother, and bathing the children. No tenderness was omitted.[9]

Little things were important, too. Sister Mary Regis Wallace relates that clothes worn by new community members on their entrance day were quickly recycled to women in need. Mary Baptist took time out of her busy schedule to write to friends to seek jobs for the unemployed. The hospital became a food distribution center during the various economic depressions that hit California. During the depression of 1894, St. Mary's Hospital served breakfast for crowds of unemployed men ... between 600 and 700 people daily.[10]

It was Mary Baptist's abiding commitment to serve the poor that caused her initially to reject the idea of academies or pension schools. She wanted her schools to be free for all to attend. Other works like the industrial school, the employment office, and the Magdalen Asylum were all geared to end the cycle of poverty and deprivation. Since Mary Baptist saw the life of Sisters of Mercy as devoted to the economically poor, she believed in accepting as future Sisters only those in whom she saw a deep love for such service.

In the mind of Mary Baptist, body and spirit were one. Caring for the physical needs of those served was coupled with a deep concern for their spiritual welfare. This theme is often found in her family letters, letters rich with indicators of her own deep love for God and her passion to bring others to God. At times, her expression of concern is both humorous and unsettling. The stories she told about the work of the Sisters seem to indicate that they went to great lengths to ensure the benefits of salvation for those they served. Mary Baptist lived in a period of deep sectarianism, a time when there was strong division among the various Christian churches. Converting persons to one's faith was a major focus for Catholics and Protestants alike. The placing of medals in pillows, baptizing infants in danger of death, and praying for conversions need to be seen within the context of the times. The ecumenism that characterizes today's relationships among the Christian churches had not yet emerged. What did emerge, however, was an ecumenism of service. Mary Baptist did not work in a Catholic ghetto; she labored in the neighborhood of need.

Mary Baptist was able to pour out her life in the service of others because she believed firmly in the providence and mercy of God. This stance of trust and confidence in her God sustained her in every difficulty, in every crisis. She wrote to her mother after the death of Mother Mary deSales saying: "Should we ever depend on an arm of flesh? If we do, how sadly are we deceived."[11] This theme was expanded in a letter written in 1882 to Sisters Mary Columba O'Kelly, Mary Carmel Pidgeon and Bernardine Ward:

Our Lord assures us, a hair does not fall without His permission. If we really believe this, how then can we be over-anxious or worried? Let us then leave ourselves humbly & confidently in the Hand of Divine Providence, do all we can to glorify Him, by living as true religious, real Sisters of Mercy—"gentle, patient, hard-working, humble, obedient, charitable and above all, simple and joyous."[12]

Leaving herself in the Hands of Divine Providence was not always easy. It meant trusting that God would protect her little community during the times of nativist opposition and public attack. It meant saying "Yes" to service when practicality said "No." Mary Baptist's steadfast trust in providence gave her courage to risk beginning new ministries even when no funding was available, ministries like the care of the aged. Her radical trust in God gave Mary Baptist daring in the face of overwhelming obstacles. That same trust enabled her to risk starting her own hospital when the County defaulted on their bills. It was not an accident that the first convent established by Mary Baptist was placed under the patronage of Divine Providence.

The trust in God's providence and mercy that was central to Mary Baptist's life instilled in her an ability to see all events, challenges and successes as the action of God in her life and in the lives of others. She saw God's presence in people, events, and creation and she fostered this type of sacramental vision in her Sisters.[13] Illness, misfortune, and difficulties were seen as moments when God's saving strength could break through. Her letters are peppered with anecdotes about attempts to help the suffering see that God was there with them in their time of need.

Mary Baptist reveled in the beauty of creation and saw it as an expression of God's tender providence. She reflected upon God's working in events and was moved to prayer by the tragedies of the day. Most of all, she saw God in people and inspired her Sisters to the same vision. This is clearly seen in a letter written by Sister Mary Francis Benson to the Sister who would replace her at the pest house during San Francisco's smallpox epidemic:

> Besides the real thing is to begin for God, and you will surely end
> for God, and in this way you do good for soul and body, and what

more is required? … I am astounded at myself, and what is doing it but prayer? My Mass is my morning visit to the afflicted victim personifying Our Divine Lord Himself. My Communion is the deep gratitude and consolation I feel in being allowed to comfort and console Him in their persons.[14]

The belief that any service given to persons in need was service to Jesus Christ translated into reaching out to those who were most ignored and neglected by society. In Mary Baptist's time this meant serving the prisoner, the prostitute, the neglected dying, the homeless. It was not just a case of people; it was also a question of place. Mary Baptist was willing to go wherever need was great. Her acceptance of the Sacramento mission in spite of its hardships is testimony to that devotion. The meager resources available to the church in California's capital meant that Sisters lived with the harsh reality of dampness, leaks and scarcity. Such a cost was willingly embraced in order to bring mercy to those in need.

Another characteristic reflected in the life of Mary Baptist was her quality of presence and ability to maintain strong personal relationships. This quality is seen over and over again in her letters. They are full of concern for persons who had been part of her life. She asks about neighbors, friends, and most of all, family members. Even though she was thousands of miles away, she was fully in touch with the personal and professional circumstances of those she loved.

This quality of relationship was not reserved for past friends and family. It was integral to her life within her religious community. In the midst of all her bubbling activity, Mary Baptist found time to mentor other Mercy leaders coming to serve in California. She could not answer every request for a foundation or respond to every pressing need; others would need to share in that task. One recipient of her guidance was Mother M. Bonaventure Fox, who, in 1888, had come to California during hard economic times. Her intent was to establish a foundation in Salinas. When that mission was unable to survive, she then focused on Los Angeles. Since Mary Baptist was no stranger to economic depressions, she supported and encouraged Mary Bonaventure as she struggled to establish the first Mercy foundation in Southern California.

Mother Mary Michael Cummings was another of the Mercy women who found in Mary Baptist a wise guide and loving Sister. Discouraged by the failure of the Salinas mission, Mary Michael had decided to return to her Denver Sisters. Instead, Mary Baptist encouraged her and Sister M. Alphonsus Fitzpatrick to accept a call to San Diego, California. Mary Baptist had been asked to take that mission but was unable to do so. She felt strongly that San Diego would prosper. Mary Michael took her advice, and the San Diego foundation was established in 1890.

A third Mercy leader befriended by Mary Baptist was Mother Mary Camillus McGarr, foundress of St. Gertrude Academy, Rio Vista on the Sacramento Delta. Rio Vista had been another foundation that Mary Baptist had to decline for lack of Sisters. Mary Camillus had originally come to California to serve the Catholic population of Yreka, California. Like the Salinas mission, the Yreka foundation also had fallen upon hard times and eventually disbanded. Half the group went to Red Bluff, California and Mary Camillus, along with three other Sisters accepted Archbishop Riordan's invitation to move to Rio Vista. Over the years Mary Camillus was a frequent visitor to the San Francisco Sisters, and in 1894, the Rio Vista mission was received into the San Francisco community. In 1922, the San Diego and Los Angeles foundations also became part of a newly formed Burlingame community.

Mary Baptist maintained an on-going correspondence with her Sisters throughout the United States and Ireland. She had for her correspondents, words of encouragement and inspiration for the weary, expressions of concern about their health, families and state of soul as well as spontaneous reflections upon the small blessings of life. It is one of the wonders of her life that

Mary Baptist could develop such strong relationships with Sisters whom she only met face to face once or twice in her life. One such relationship was her abiding friendship with Mother Mary Austin Carroll, then ministering in New Orleans. These two women of Mercy had a friendship that lasted over twenty years. Mary Baptist even sent money to Mary Austin when she needed it to help the poor newsboys of New Orleans. Perhaps it was their joint love for history that brought them together, or perhaps it was the common bond of love for the most oppressed that united them. Whatever it was, it was a lasting bond. Mother Austin wrote at the time of Mary Baptist's death:

> For myself, I have no words to describe my grief. Humanly speaking, I could not have a greater loss. For almost two score years we loved each other in God and interchanged thoughts and mutually sought of each other advice and direction in matters which all outsiders could not readily understand. I never knew a more generous, charitable soul.[15]

Mary Baptist also took time to correspond with those who really had no direct claim on her time or affection. One example is the correspondence between the young girl called Gussie and this busy pioneer.[16] In her letter Mary Baptist writes in a way that speaks to a child's heart. Taking time out of her overloaded schedule is indicative of the value she placed on human relationships.

A familial, direct, and humorous tone is found in Mary Baptist's letters written to her Sisters in Kinsale. In these letters, she takes time to chatter about the day-to-day matters that would interest Sisters far away. The letters are like snapshots of another world and leave the reader with a sense of being part of the activity. The tenderness and humor expressed in the letters is an echo of her interaction with the Sisters around her. Sister Martina, a member of the San Francisco community, recalled a time when, being late for daily lecture, she ran down the corridor only to collide with Mary Baptist. Such a mishap might well have earned a reproof, but Mary Baptist only suggested that since she was already late she might as well skip the lecture and return to her patients.[17]

Persons she served were also embraced with maternal affection. Sister Mary Howley, among the original Sisters who came to California with Mary Baptist, tells us that:

> [Mary Baptist] loved the poor. There used to be a crazy woman, and she use to go to her cell[18] and say, "I want to get into your bed." And Mother would get up and put her in, not thinking that any one knew it, and would stay with her. She loved to make her happy even for a couple of minutes.[19]

Nowhere was Mary Baptist's gift for nurturing relationships more evident than in her correspondence with her own family. Throughout her life Mary Baptist exhibited an abiding love for family, country, and community. This sense of identity, cultural roots, and bondedness was another of her characteristic qualities. Mary Baptist knew who she was as a woman, as a Russell, and as a Sister of Mercy. She was grounded in that sense of identity through her continuing ties to family and friends. She followed the progress of every niece and nephew, asked for family photos, and avidly read the newspapers of the day reporting on in Ireland. Matthew, as editor of the *Irish Monthly*, must have kept her supplied with reading material for she sometimes comments on items from that source.

The greater volume of extant family letters are those written to Mary and Arthur Hamill. Arthur, Mary Baptist's stepbrother, was like another father to her. Her letters to Arthur are filled with concern about his health, work schedule, and spiritual well-being. Letters to Mary, Arthur's wife, have a more chatty style with questions about who is doing what and about family events. It is in these letters that one senses the wide scope of Mary Baptist's interests. She keeps them abreast of all the activities in San Francisco and provides vivid descriptions of places and works. Sometimes her political views creep into the correspondence, making it clear that she retained a deep sense of Irish patriotism throughout her life.

Another important quality, flexibility, is seen in the life of Mary Baptist, a flexibility that allowed her to constantly adapt the Mercy charism to the changing circumstances of her time and situation. Time and again, Mary Baptist had to adapt her plans to effectively respond to changing realities. She came to San Francisco to teach and ended up responding to the health care crisis of the city. She bought land in Sacramento for her new foundation only to have the State claim it through the power of eminent domain. New land had to be found. She had to redefine who to teach in order to effectively meet the educational needs of the Catholic community.

Sometimes flexibility was demanded by immediate need. The arrival of Amanda Taylor at her door started the work done at the Magdalen Asylum; a few forgotten elderly finding refuge at St. Mary's led to the establishment of a home for the aged. When Sister Mary Columba Stokes had to return to Ireland on urgent family business, Mary Baptist used the opportunity to recruit new members for the mission. When a door closed, Mary Baptist looked for a window to open. Hers was a task of interpretation. How was the Mercy charism to be lived in a context very different from that of Catherine McAuley's Dublin? What could be changed and what was to remain constant?

Mary Baptist considered this process of adapting the Mercy charism to new circumstances to be one of the most serious tasks before her. In her efforts to find answers, she provided a pattern of communal searching. She wrote letters to other Mercy leaders seeking their advice and counsel. She looked at common practice and she searched the tradition itself, moving forward only when she was thoroughly satisfied that there was harmony between the Rule and the practice. When something was outdated or obstructive, she left it behind.

Finally, the life of Mary Baptist reflects a commitment to partner with others in working for the betterment of the whole. She never worked alone, but always invited others into the mission of Mercy. From the very beginning of her work, she sought and fostered the support of the wider public. When need arose, she went directly to benefactors, friends, coworkers, and church community, presented the need and helped them understand why their support was vital. Philanthropy and partnering went hand in hand with her works.

To foster support from the wider community, Mary Baptist founded benevolent societies such as the St. Mary's Society for Catholic Females. This society had both a spiritual and a monetary focus. Members committed themselves to prayer, exemplary life, and raising funds to be "expended for the spiritual and temporal benefit of the members." This unique partnership between the Sisters and lay partners provided an effective way to expand the mission. Persons linked to the works became identified with them and brought the Mercy charism to places where the Sisters were not directly involved.

These five characteristics of Mary Baptist's life and mission provide a solid framework for twenty-first century life. In an increasingly impersonal world, Mary Baptist's life witnesses to the primacy of authentic human relationships. In an age of disillusionment, she points to what is enduring, love of God and love for one's brothers and sisters. The example of Mary Baptist and her Sisters urges us to abandon a "flash and sound bite" world in order to embrace a manner of living based on core truths. People changed and adopted new ways of living, found a sense of self-worth because Mary Baptist and her Sisters honored their dignity as persons.

For the timid of heart, Mary Baptist presents a paradigm of trust. If the ministry is worth doing, if the undertaking is compelling, just do it. Nothing is guaranteed to succeed, but not to risk doing good never changed another's future. Her ministry also shows the importance of adapting to new circumstances, of being in touch with the culture of her times. She knew the realities that faced people on a day-to-day basis, and because of that knowledge, she was able to craft responses that were relevant and effective. One example of this acumen was her provision of new clothes for released prisoners. Without such clothing, finding a job was impossible.

Mary Baptist also provides us with a lesson in self-knowledge. She was an immigrant, like those she served. She fully acknowledged and took pride in her heritage while also becoming a woman of the American culture. Diversity for her meant learning the language of those she served, honoring their unique customs and opening the eyes of her understanding to welcome new insights. She was a woman with roots deep in Irish and in American soil.

Perhaps what is most striking in Mary Baptist is her ability to integrate the various streams of her life into one. She was both a woman of prayer and a woman of action, possessing a passion for learning and an openness to life. She lived a contemplative rhythm of life, carrying the poor to God and then, moved by that prayer, being impelled outward in service. The more she prayed, the more her heart expanded. It is true to say that she both cradled the poor in God and found God in the poor and broken. Through it all, Mary Baptist was exactly what she claimed to be: a woman in love with God, a lover of the poor, a Sister of Mercy.

Epilogue

Nestled in the foothills of Calaveras County is a grove of ancient sequoias. These natural giants were discovered during Mary Baptist's lifetime but many were skeptical that trees could be as round as a house or taller than any building of the time. How could anything so ancient and so big exist? To prove that the tales of these spectacular redwoods were true, lumbermen, in 1854, stripped the tallest sequoia in the grove of its protective bark. The bark was cut away in massive segments and preserved so that the shell of the sequoia could be reconstructed for a World Fair. The ravishing of this ancient tree gave birth to a movement to protect these wonders of creation. Today, the scarred and wounded tree, called the Sacrificial Tree, still stands, naked and unprotected. It has endured, and continues to speak its truth to the seekers who stand before it.

For me, this giant sequoia has become a symbol of Mary Baptist herself. To the contemporary mind, the full scope of her talents, devotion and accomplishments are almost as unbelievable as the sequoia groves were to people in the mid-nineteenth century. Her willingness to be stripped of all that she had for the sake of God's people, left her, like the Sacrificial Tree, vulnerable and open to whatever consequences came of her love. Like the sequoia, the witness of her love still endures. One hundred and fifty years later, Mary Baptist's story still inspires and challenges us. Her life is a deep well from which we can draw inspiration, guidance and hope.

Like Catherine McAuley before her, Mary Baptist made the spiritual and corporal works of mercy the business of her life. At the time of her death, the Rev. A. P. Doyle, a Paulist Father who knew her, wrote:

> I feel her loss as keenly as though she were of my own kith and kin, for she was associated with my earliest recollections of devoted religious work in San Francisco. There are few figures that stand out as prominently as hers in the history of the past forty years, and fewer still on whose bier are heaped the benedictions of the poor and unfortunate more abundantly than on hers. She goes down to her grace with the consciousness of having rounded out, in the fullest measure, years of usefulness for the Church and for poor humanity. She goes not unattended to her reward. A cloud of witnesses follow her to testify to her very great charity. It will be some consolation to her bereaved children to realize that though she is gone, her spirit still lives and will continue to make fruitful their lives.[1]

The words of Father Doyle still ring true today. The spirit of Mary Baptist is alive in each person who has a passion to serve those who are poor and in need. It continues in the work of everyone who labors to make the world a more loving place, in those who strive to create a society where the dignity and value of each person is honored. Our story of Mary Baptist has now come to its end, but it is not really finished. Her spirit and story continues wherever one comforts, consoles and responds to another in need. Mary Baptist Russell, California's Pioneer Sister of Mercy lives wherever Mercy is found.

*Sacrificial Tree which still stands in the Sequoia grove
at Calavaras Big Trees*

Part II

The Letters of
Mary BaptistRussell
1854–1898

In Her Own Words
1854–1860

A Note of Explanation

The following letters have been gathered from a variety of published and unpublished sources. The original letters of Mary Baptist were frequently devoid of any form of contemporary punctuation and used abundant capitalization. For ease of reading, I have chosen to insert punctuation where it seems feasible. Spelling has been adapted to the American usage. Each letter is prefaced with a brief annotation. Identification of sources has been abbreviated as follows:

Archives, Sisters of Mercy, Auburn Regional Community: Archives, SOMA

Annals, Sisters of Mercy, Auburn Regional Community: *Annals,* SOMA

Archives, Sisters of Mercy, Burlingame Regional Community: Archives, SOMB

Annals, Sisters of Mercy, Burlingame Regional Community: *Annals,* SOMB

Archives, Jesuit Province, Dublin: Archives, JPD

Russell, *Life of Mother Mary Baptist Russell:* LMMB

Russell, *The Three Sisters of Lord Russell of Killowen:* TTS

Other sources will be sited in full.

Mary Baptist and her sisters were entrusted with the management of the San Francisco County Hospital in October 1855. The contract required the County to reimburse the Sisters for expenses incurred. From the beginning of the contract, the government failed to meet its obligations. Economic depression had hit San Francisco and resulted in depleted county funds. The Sisters carried on as long as they could without reimbursement but finally were forced to send the following letter to the San Francisco Board of Supervisors.

Date: February 28, 1857
To: Board of Supervisors
From: Mary Baptist Russell
Source: *Annals*, SOMB, I: 88-89

To the Board of Supervisors:

Gentlemen,

Finding no notice taken by your honorable body of the communication sent you on our behalf by J. S. McGlynn, E. P. Seymour and others respecting the care and maintenance of the County Sick, we are obliged to address you directly.

It is now *nine* months since we have got any money from the treasury and [you] must be aware of the immense outlay necessary to carry on a Hospital such as this averaging one hundred & forty patients; it cannot, therefore, be a matter of surprise that we should be obliged to give up the contract. We would, indeed, be very anxious to continue the care of the Sick, and would also be anxious to accommodate the Authorities, especially in the present state of the city funds; but it is utterly impossible to hold out longer and we feel every just mind will exonerate us from all blame when they consider what a sum it requires *daily* to supply food, medicine, attendants, fuel, &c &c for such a number.

We are, therefore, obliged for the reasons given above to decline entering on another month except on the following terms: *1st* that the Board engages to *cash* on the first day of each month two of the audited bills now in our possession beginning with the one for July last. *2nd* that the terms of the monthly contract henceforth be $2800.00 in audited bills.

If these terms cannot be granted you will please consider the contract with us at an end on and after the *1st* day of April from which date no new patients will be admitted and the City and County will be charged for those remaining at the rate of $1.00 each per day.

Sister M. B Russell
Superioress of the Sisters of Mercy
February 28th, 1857.

Little of the early correspondence of Mary Baptist survived. This reality is noted by Matthew Russell in his life of Mary Baptist written in 1902. This is one of the few letters from the '50s. The letter reflects the strong family ties which existed among the Russell family. The scope and state of the California mission and the way in which Mercy communities supported other communities in need is also reflected in the letter.

Date: October 15, 1857
To: My dearest Mamma
From: Mary Baptist Russell
Source: Archives, Sisters of Mercy, Burlingame

St. Mary's Hospital
San Francisco
Oct. 15th

My dearest Mamma,

There is some fatality over your letters. I have not received one since the time you enclosed a certain document for me to sign tho' the Sisters have several times mentioned that you were writing to me. I can't understand what becomes of your letters. The London Post Master sent word by last Mail that a letter for us lay in his office in consequence of not being pre-paid and it may be from you. I hope you all enjoy the blessing of good health as I do, thank God. You have heard long ere this of dearest Mother de Sales' [Reddan] death. Should we ever depend on an arm of flesh? If we do, how sadly are we deceived. We say the power of the Saints in Heaven was never so clearly manifested as in her, for we attribute to her prayers the success that seems to follow many of our projects for God's glory which interested her most and for which she labored and prayed night and day with apparently little success. She used often laughingly remind me of your having placed me under her special care and she often prayed, too, you might have grace and strength to give Sarah also up to God's service if He called her during your life time.

I returned last Friday from our Branch House, St. Joseph's, in Sacramento, the capital of the State. Mother M. Gabriel and Sister Mary Francis [Benson] are the only members of the little Band that you know. They have with them three Novices and one Postulant who will P.G. be received on the Feast of the Presentation of the B.V.M. and one of the Novices will be professed in March. They will confine themselves for the present to the School and Visitation, but there is such pressing need of an Orphanage that I expect it will be built by May next, perhaps even sooner. They are in treaty for a nice Building in a good location, but for the winter they will occupy the Priests House which adjoins the Church, the Sacristy of which is their Choir, and the Basement makes a School capable of accommodating 500 children which is more than they could expect for years to come. Father Cassin, formerly of Arran Quay, Dublin, is assistant Pastor at Sac. and he, and indeed the whole community Protestant as well as Catholic, gave a hearty welcome to the dear Sisters and seem most anxious to make them comfortable. They have already met numbers of cases of *Spiritual* misery such as you would live and die in dear Ireland without meeting. There never was a country in which Religious are more required.

Do pray for us often and pray that we may get more Sisters. You may have heard how God has blessed us in this respect so much beyond our expectation, but yet we have not near enough for the duties that devolve on us, and besides, religious vocations are very rare among the educated portion of American Ladies so that out of the fifteen who have joined us in this country only nine were Choir Sisters, a small proportion in a Community like ours where so much of our time is occupied instructing. Besides the day school we have *fifty-three* in the Orphanage and are never without two or three adults, sometimes Grandees who come there to get instruction in Reading and Writing unknown sometimes to their Husbands, and it is quite common for people of this class thirty or forty years of age to be as ignorant of their Religion as a baby. This very week Sr. Mary [Howley] "laid hands" on a *hoary* headed man who came to visit his nephew who is in the Hospital and succeeded in inducing him to commence his confession. He comes now every morning at 7 o'clock to meet Father King and is making a regular *clearing out,* Thank God. His last confession was made in Tyrone *43 years ago!* Poor old man acknowledges now that since he began to grow old and lose his relish of the world, he has never been happy nor enjoyed any peace of mind and that often he would start out of his sleep frightened he knew not of what.

The Hospital is a great thing. It brings such number to a sense of their duty, not alone the sick but their family and visitors. If they had sufficient Sisters in Sacramento they might open one immediately there and it would be not alone *self supporting,* but many could be admitted free if necessary. You probably know well from our letters to Newry of how we are circumstanced here so I will say no more on that subject except that nothing has been done about Building nor can there be till Spring, however, we cannot complain as we are not by any means badly located where we are.

Last May Mother M. Catherine [O'Connor] sent a box of work, the produce of their Industrial School, with Capt. Burke of the "Scotland" hoping we might be able to sell it for them. It arrived about three weeks ago and after repeated journeys and explanations both written and verbal, Mr. Telly, our steward, succeeded in getting it from the Custom House. You may fancy, then, how provoked I was when I opened to find there was scarcely a saleable article in it. The children's aprons and some other articles of plain work I have converted to use in the orphanage and could have got sale for four times as much Chemises and aprons if they were of a size to fit girls of from four to ten years. I have disposed of the babys' shirts and a few collars and will enclose in a check for the amount, but you may tell the Sisters they must not look for any more as really and truly I may as well not show the remaining articles to any one. The collars would only fit children and the edgings are too coarse and badly done. I am sorry not to have a better account to give and I hope if another opportunity offers for sending a box that they will send a better assortment. I have a trunk full left from the Kinsale work which I can never sell, and I must only put Mother Catherine's with them and some fine night make a *bonfire*.

You will all say it is high time I should inquire after you all. I know so little about you now, thanks to your lazy fingers, that I scarcely know what to ask—from the last letters from Kinsale I learned that *you* are growing young, that Arthur and his family and affairs were in a happy and prosperous condition, that Matthew was with the Jesuits in England and that Sarah is still yearning for a Religious Life. To us all that was gratifying news and I hope if it is God's will that this state of things still continue but how are dear Charles, James, Margaret and all the younger branches? I would be so delighted to get a letter from these three. Has James any addition to his flock? And how [do] his affairs, Spiritual and temporal go on? Is there any change in Peter Gartlan's? And send what sort are Alice, Maggie, Anne. Have any of them a vocation for the order of Mercy? What a welcome I would give them. I only wish the California ladies would follow dear Margaret's example in patience and sweetness amidst their matrimonial trial, but alas, they do not, but almost on the first difficulty separate and too many violate the laws of God and man by marrying someone else with whom in all probability they will have just as short a time. God has indeed been good to dear Margaret. I hope and trust death will find her as true and faithful to her engagement as ever.

Our dear good friends in Belfast are, I hope, as usual happy and united. So give them all my most affectionate love. I trust dear J. W. Mulholland's affairs have prospered. Tell me of any change that may have occurred among them. I heard of a J. W. Brophey who lives in this country, could it be the doctor's brother-in-law? Have you heard lately of Miss Cunningham or from our poor afflicted friends in Columbus? It is a considerable time since they wrote to me. Tell Charles that poor Dr. Mahon who sent him the ring and breast pin is now in our hospital and very near death. Do you ever visit Killowen now? I think I mentioned that Richard Brennan was married and well married and doing well too. He works at Public Works and is well paid. A Mrs. W. O'Brien, formerly Miss Jordan, went last June to see her family in Newry but I was not at home or I might have had some communications. Her husband expects her home about the beginning of next year and it would be a good opportunity for sending out work if the Sisters had any for this market. You could hear of her at Frank Jennings on Mill St. as her sister is married to one of that family. What about our own Jennings? Is the old lady still living and poor? Kate and Margaret? Where are they? I would wish to be remembered most affectionately to them all. Do they ever hear from Joseph? Do you ever see dear Anita, Ann and Kate? When last I heard of them Aunt Margaret's health was very bad. You might, if you think well, send them this letter as I won't have time to write another.

Have I anything particular to say only to beg them never to cease praying for me. I wonder might I ask a mass from Uncle Charles. How grateful I would be for it. Has Roseanne Collins settled herself in any way yet? I have never lost my affect for her. Now I must send my letter to you as I have determined to write on business to dear Sarah and have not much time, but as a last request this time, I must ask you to pay St. Clare's a visit in my name and see do they still remember me particularly in choir. I do most earnestly beg their prayers, particularly dear Sr. Mary Bernard's. Is Mother Mary Michael still superioress? How is she? And also Sr. Mary Aloysius. How I could enjoy a stroll on a hill like theirs but that's what we shall never have in this country. Ground is too valuable near the towns.

When you write you will have all the news about your bazaar for me. Now, good-bye, dearest Momma. Fondest love a thousand times to yourself, James, Arthur, Margaret, Sarah, Charles and Matthew, also dear Mary and her little ones, Anne and her flock and to all the children at Matilda's. If Reverend J. W. O'Neil is still in Newry, I would wish to be remembered in a particular manner to him, implore him to pray for us. There is a Jesuit here who has been no small comfort to us, God bless him. Begging your blessing and unceasing prayer forever. I am ever, Your affectionate child, Sr. Mary Baptist Russell

Mary Baptist was very close to her sister Sarah. It had been Sarah's hope to join her in the San Francisco mission and even after entering the Newry foundation, still hoped that this would be possible. Mrs. Russell had already given three daughters to religious communities and one son to the Jesuits. While Mrs. Russell was at peace with Sarah's entry into Mercy, sending her as far away as San Francisco was more than she could bear.

Date: Winter, 1857
To: Sarah Russell (Sister Mary Emmanuel)
From: Sr. Mary B. Russell
Source: Archives, JPD

St. Mary's Hospital
San Francisco

My dearest Sarah,

You will be no little surprised at the contents of this letter my first, I believe, since I came to California. My time is *so precious* that I will come to the point at once for fear of interruptions. A very short time ago I was thinking about you all, how you were not circumstanced and what might be your destiny hereafter. Your own dear self is almost the only one unsettled and I began to wonder why you were so long so when I knew well your mind was decided long ago on which path you would chose. While I was thinking thus, letters from Kinsale arrived and as usual the dear Sisters sent along the news they were possessed of respecting my folks—"Sarah is most anxious to join the Sisters in Newry but Mamma tho' quite willing to part with her won't hear of her entering and wants her to go to Belfast which Sarah cannot bring herself to do."

What can all this mean, thought I. I know well neither Mamma nor Sarah would lightly throw obstacles in the way of God's designs. Perhaps this is one of the *little* things by which He works out His own all wise ends, like Saul's Asses straying away apparently by chance to bring him to the Prophet as the Lord appointed. So I half concluded in my own mind that the Almighty destined you to share in our Labor here and was making use of dear Mamma's opposition to your wishes to reserve you for us.

Now, dear Sarah, I don't wish to influence but merely give you the *Light* I got *in order* that you consider the matter. I need not tell you the field that lies open before you here now, how much Labors are required. We have been obliged to give up (for want of Sisters) altogether visiting the Jail and there are two Large hospitals to which we can never go for the same reason. Our own Hospital, Orphanage, Home of Mercy, Schools and Visitation of the County Hospital and of such as wish us to see them in their own Houses being as much as we can manage. Oh! What a welcome we would give you. As to the Journey it is *delightful* from New York here and from Liverpool to New York takes only one week. F. Dalton's Sister now at Cabian Convent has some idea of coming out to us so [you] might not be alone and M. M. Gabriel intends asking her Sister Fredrick Brown to think it over too.

I have told the Sisters my intention of writing to you about it and they are all praying for God's will to be accomplished whatever it may be. You must treat the matter with due respect and not too hastily dismiss the subject and be sure to write by return of Mail. I dare say Mother Catherine will think I am *somewhat selfish* but no selfish motive activates me I assure you and I shall sincerely rejoice should you get Mamma's permission to join her Community and Mamma too may say I should have more consideration than to take you from her. I would be sorry, indeed, to do it if *God* does not require the Sacrifice. If He does, I know she would die rather than refuse what He demands. Do you remember the contract we made for the *1st* Fridays? Now may God direct you.

Pray for your affectionate Sr. Mary B. Russell.

Early leaders of the Mercy community in the United States frequently wrote to each other concerning issues of mercy life. In this letter, Mary Baptist shares with Mother Francis Warde the progress of the mercy mission in California and addresses some broader questions facing the Order. In this letter there is mention of both a gathering of all leaders of Mercy and the need for some form of uniform customs. Also included in the letter is a brief discussion of the life of consecrated Magdalens, an important ministry of the sisters in San Francisco.

Date: December 28, 1859
To: Mother Frances Warde
From: Mary Baptist Russell
Source: *Annals*, SOMB, I:123

My dear Mother M. Francis,

Having heard that our mutual & good Friend Mrs.[name is unclear] is going by next Steamer to Manchester (New Hampshire)

I have determined she shall not go without a letter from me. I acknowledge it is a shame that we have been five years in America without writing altho' you have written to us more than once, but I will not spend time forming excuses & will merely say I am one of those who would wish a cordial, affectionate intercourse to be maintained as much as possible between the different Houses of our Holy Order, besides *you* are one of the *Old Heads* and I quite a young one so that it often occurred to me it might be very much for the glory of God for us to exchange views with regard to *ourselves* in this wonderful and trying country. Judging from the many Houses you have established, God's work must be flourishing with you.

We have opened a Branch in Sacramento, a city about one hundred miles from this, but there is daily communication by Steamer. Our community consists of thirty four, pretty nearly one half of whom are Lay Sisters, in fact we can have any number of *them* but desirable *Choir* Sisters are scarce; as yet we have only twelve professed and in this number I include those from Ireland, so you see we are but a small body yet.

Here our duties are onerous & most varied, in the *Hospital* we have an average of *thirty,* in the House of Mercy about the same number but instead of *young* Women able to assist in the Laundry &, they are for the most part old, infirm "Grandmothers," half recovered Patients, too poor to remain in the Hospital and too weak to work, or homeless children who for some reason or other cannot get admission into the Orphanages, in fact it is truly a *House of Mercy* to which every object of compassion is sent. The Servants of this country are still too highly paid to expect they will submit to the discipline of such an Institution if they can avoid it, neither do they like the hard work at which on principle we employ them, but they will soon be glad of such a home.

One wing of the Hospital we appropriate to the Penitents till a proper Asylum can be got for them. At present we have only six as it is a very short time since we transferred *three* of those longest with us to the Sisters of the Good Shepherd Louisville, Ky. and two more were very happily settled by their friends about the same time; in all there have been twenty four Penitents under our care, one died in most enviable sentiments, and alas a few also *left*. The Superioress of the Good Shepherds is a namesake of yours, perhaps you claim relationship, She is to receive two of those we sent into the Community of Consecrated Magdalens who make the vows of Poverty, Chastity, & Obedience, and are governed by one of the Good Shepherd Nuns; they have a regular Novitiate and Rules suitable to the life they embrace.

To continue with *our duties,* the Registry Office occupies a Sister entirely for about *four* hours each day. I often ask myself the question, does it *do good* in proportion? But, then, I think it does for truly there is no class needs instruction more than those it brings under our influence. For them we have established a Society which in time will I trust work a change; as it is, the greater number of them are half crazy for *dress jewelry* & high notions; the visitation is not much except the County Hospital & Jail which we visit generally four times a week. In Sac. City their labors are confined to a day School averaging One Hundred & twenty, and the Visitation; in time they expect to have a Half Orphanage but it is pretty hard to raise the necessary funds even in this so called Golden Country. We have got a lot for our intended Hospital and, please God, will make a beginning this Spring. In Sac. also they have a building lot secured but not the wherewithal to go further, however we console ourselves with the reflection that as a general thing great bodies move slowly.

We manage, if possible, to leave the Branch House under the superintendence of the Assistant. She would be much wanted at the Mother House but then it is necessary to have a Head at the Branch possessed of sufficient authority. I understand that in one or two Houses in Ireland they found so many difficulties in the government of Branch Houses (for which there is no provision in our Holy Rule) that with the approbation of their Bishops they have appointed a Second Mother Assistant (as it were) specially to preside over these Establishments. They say it works well, and now this brings me to a subject of great interest and *importance,* the necessity of a *general chapter.*

I do think that a similarity in customs &c as much as possible in *all* the Houses of our Order would be very much for the glory of God and unhappily it does not exist and never can as long as so many things are left to the judgment of individual Superiors; to be candid

I often feel a short of *shame* and know not what to say when Seculars remark the little uniformity of practice that exists among us. We were thinking by all the Professed sending a petition to Baggot St. to that effect, a General Chapter might be the result. I feel every effort should be made to bring this about before all the Old Heads drop off and I am sure you agree with me; now there is no one I know can do more for the good cause than you.

Every house in America with very few exceptions claims the honor of being founded by "Mother Warde" therefore a word from you would have great weight.

I am thinking of writing to good, affectionate, Mother M. Agnes O'Connor of New York to rouse her into exertion. I hope it is the Spirit urges me for tho' anything but an *enthusiast,* I feel quite anxious about this matter. I know dear Mother Mary Francis Bridgeman of Kinsale will go into it heart & soul, so will Mother M. Elizabeth Moore of Limerick and they, in my opinion, are real *Wise Heads*. We have been for the last eighteen months making mementoes in our Communions &c for the General Chapter as we understand it is in contemplation, I hope your dear Community will not fear but prayer will accomplish what appears so difficult....

This short letter from Mary Baptist to her mother gives insight into the types of correspondence which passed between Ireland and San Francisco. Mrs. Russell had sent Mary Baptist the latest work of her Uncle Charles dealing with the life of Cardinal Mezzofanti. Political addresses by Mary Baptist's younger brother Charles were also included. The building project refers to the New St. Mary's Hospital that was in its initial phase of construction.

Date of Letter: February 1860
From: Sister M. B. Russell
To: Margaret Russell (her mother)
Source: LMMB: 60-62

My Dearest Mamma:
    It is nearly two months since Mr. O'Connor delivered your fine collections of letters, also the "Life of Mezzofanti" and the pamphlet

by dear Charles. I must thank dear Arthur, Margaret, Matthew, etc., etc., *through you,* as I cannot write to themselves. I sent on your letters to Columbus by next mail. You must not be displeased, as it pleases the poor creatures there so much to hear all the particulars. I have not got a reading of Uncle Charles' book yet, as it has been borrowed by some of the priests. Poor Uncle Charles seems doomed not to enjoy the quiet of college life very long. I hear that he is surely to be Bishop this time. Mrs. Rose Kelly, whom I have often mentioned, was quite interested in dear Charles' articles on workhouses. She is matron of a large lunatic asylum about one hundred and fifty miles from this in a town called Stockton since the 1st of last June. She often tells us she will see our people yet, as she intends, please God, to visit the old sod once more. She has on an average one hundred and sixty female lunatics; and there are fully twice as many men. It is quite a remarkable fact that, though the population of California is for the greater part Catholic and Irish, there is quite a small proportion of either in the asylum, the effect of *religion,* of course.

We are going on here, thank God, as usual. We hope, too, that 1860 will surely see our building pretty far on. The contract for the brick required was duly signed on the 2d of this month. Our good Mother wants to signalize all her Feasts by something propitious. Sister M. Francis [Benson] sends you her love and desires me to tell you *I am very good.* I tell her you know that already. Dear Sarah is now in her second year; please God, she will be professed this time twelve months. I have hardly left myself room to send love to all. I would wish to begin with yourself, I send you my fondest love, dearest mamma, a thousand times, and I hope your love makes you pray and pray over and over for me and mine. To Arthur, James, Margaret, Anne, Mary and all the little ones, also to Aunt Anne, Kate, Elizabeth and all my dear uncles, my love.

I remain, dear Mamma, your affectionate child in Jesus Christ.
Sister M. B. Russell
Sister of Mercy

In Her Own Words
1861–1870

The period from 1857 through 1869 was a period of expansion and growth for the San Francisco community. During this period, Mary Baptist established foundations in Sacramento CA. and in Grass Valley, CA. The letters of this period reflect the struggles of selecting suitable leadership for the missions, remaining true to the charism of the community in the face of church needs and the challenge of interpreting the charism of Mercy in a new and different culture. This letter introduces a conversation about the interpretation of the Mercy educational charism. Strongly influenced by her own passion to serve those who are economically poor and the position of Mother Mary Francis Bridgeman on the issue, Mary Baptist explains her position on Academies.

Date: July 25, 1861
To: Mother Francis Warde
From: Mary Baptist Russell
Source: *Annals*, SOMB, I: 204-208

When I first addressed you on the important subject on which you write (the General Chapter) I was quite sanguine as to the result of our efforts but now it seems next to impossible to stir *all* up to the necessity of a general union; the greater number being withheld by a predilection for what they have been individually accustomed to and I am myself, perhaps, in this number. Since the date of my former letter some things have occurred which shew [sic] a sort of contradiction in those I was most disposed to yield to which inclines me to throw up the whole in despair. A general determination to be *frank* with each other should be our guide throughout the discussion that must take place if any general movement is to be made; by the time you finish this you will have *proof positive* that I for one am frank enough and I promise you I will take in good part all you will say to me.

Now dear M. M. Xavier, the difference between Sisters of Mercy in *Ireland* and Sisters of Mercy in *America* that strikes *me most* is that in the former we are devoted to the *poor suffering* Members of J. Christ, whereas in America with the exception of ourselves here, in California, and those in St. Louis, New York, Brooklyn & Cincinnatti, our Sisters are employed in conducting *Boarding Schools,* and now for the first proof of my frankness, *you* get the credit—deservedly or not I can't say—of introducing this change first. I know Londonderry and Down Patrick are exceptions to what I have said of Ireland. I have always been taught to consider Boarding Schools as entirely contrary to the Spirit of our Holy Rule every line of which breathes devotedness to the Poor and which even expressly forbids our receiving Boarders. Even day Academies for the children of the wealthier classes seems to me not in accordance with its Spirit, and the Right Revd. Dr. Leahy, when consulted on the Subject, gave it as his opinion that we could not conscientiously take charge of such establishments and in support of his opinion he quotes a portion of the Rules of the Presentation Order and he argues from the silence of our Rule on this point that we are entirely forbidden to undertake such schools, for as our Rules are in a great measure drawn from those of the Presentation Order, our Foundress would have embodied this *conditional* Sanction had she wished us ever to undertake such schools. This is Dr. Leahy's opinion. I know it is contradicted in part by the fact of our Sisters in Cork & Carlow having day Schools for the higher classes even in the life time of our dear Mother Foundress still in both these places they are so much employed about the Poor in Hospital, Visitation, House of Mercy &c they do not lose the character of *Sisters of Mercy* and they have besides the excuse of the Presentation

Nuns being settled in both places before them and having large poor schools under their charge.

I never could understand how the Sisters in Londonderry going direct from Baggot St. could be persuaded to open a Boarding School and now Down Patrick is said to have follow the example. I see it is only a Day Academy you have opened in Philadelphia, but will it not be your *principle* duty; won't the Free School be of *Secondary* importance; consequently, won't you be rather the Servants of the Rich rather than of the *Poor?* For my part I am altogether against both Boarding & Day especially the former, and in fact I would never have joined the Order had I thought they were a duty of the Institute. But, much as I am opposed to them, I could scarcely express myself more strongly on the Subject than Mother M. di Pazzi of St. Louis who, writing sometime since to one of our houses says, "I am even more opposed to pay schools or Academies than Mother M. Agnes [O'Connor]. I think it is much to be deplored that so many have departed from the true spirit of our Institute which it is evident from our Holy Rule is to devote our labors to the service of the Poor" from whom they cannot receive any temporal emolument" besides there are numerous convents in this Country who educate the Rich.

I know *necessity* has been made the plea, but my dear Revd. Mother used to say "Why give a foundation of our Order where such necessity exists?" She might have given many but never would if the Community should be obliged to have pay Schools to support them. Our Convent is small and we are much inconvenienced in it as well as in the House of Mercy, still I would not have recourse to such means but wait on Divine Providence; tho' our works may be more limited, still I believe more real good will be effected for the glory of God, our own sanctification, and the Salvation of Souls so long as the true spirit of the Institute is carried out; this is my *pride* and not extensive works at the expense of the *end* for which our Holy Rule was instituted. Our Schools are entirely free, no child has, up to this, paid us one cent. A great deal will be done for Religion by good free Schools taught by Religious. I hope you will never have any other but for the Poor. Still this same Mother de Pazzi [Bentley] (according to the Metropolitan Directory) has now an Academy with 180 and Mother M. Agnes [O'Connor]had a small one attached to their

House in Houston St. N. Y. in 1854 when we stopped there on our way to this Country, but the proceeds I know were expended on the Poor.

We have had a Magdalen Asylum (in embryo) ever since we came to this country and expect soon to erect a distinct House for themselves; still I have had doubts whether *it* is really an Object of our Institute, there is no work of charity to which I would more willingly devote myself and I think there is no doubt of its being in accordance with the *spirit* of our Rules, still it has often flashed across my mind that we are only preparing the way for the "Good Shepherds," however, since I heard of the Sisters in Dublin & Cork taking charge of such establishments I am beginning to think differently.

The *Spirit* of our Rule is to me sufficiently clear from the formula of our Vows—"The *Service* of the *Poor Sick, and Ignorant.*" In a letter received lately from Mother M. Paul Lemon of N. York she points our very clearly the difficulties presented by the words of our Rule on "Establishments" and the support of Communities but the remedy she hints at does not meet my ideas of "right." I would if it depended on me be strict in requiring the *spirit* of our Rule to be followed *everywhere,* but I would not be binding about customs and practices that do not interfere with that essential point. How glad we would be if it were God's Holy Will to have the Sweet Spirit and great experience of Mother Agnes to assist us now.

Once more Mary Baptist finds it necessary to ask the Board of Supervisors to honor its fiscal obligations to the sisters. Carefully, Mary Baptist points out the terms of the contract and seeks reimbursement.

Date: February 2, 1862
To: Honorable the Board of Supervisors
From: Sister Mary Baptist Russell
Source: *Annals*, SOMB, I: 227-229

To the Honorable the Board of Supervisors, Alameda Co.
Gentlemen,

In the month of Nov. 1859 a delegation from your Honable. Body waited on us to ascertain on what conditions the Indigent Sick of our Country would be received into St. Mary's Hospital; we then proposed to receive them at the rate of one dol. & twenty five cents (1-25) per day to be paid *in cash* every three months. Liquors if required in any large quantity and surgical appliances to be *extra,* yet we have never made any extra charges for these things tho' we have supplied them when called for by the exigencies of the case.

On the 7th of Feb.1860 your Board passed an Ordinance giving us the charge of the Sick of the County on the above conditions, a copy of said Ordinance being in our possession. On the presentation of our first bill, your Honble. Body finding it inconvenient to pay cash passed a second Ordinance to the effect that twenty per cent (20/100) additional should be allowed if you were obliged to issue Scrip; with this we were satisfied but after a time your Board began again to pay in *cash* giving of course only the net amount as per contract which was all right, but for the last year or more, your Honble. Body has not allowed either $1.25 *cash* nor the twenty per cent additional when issuing Scrip; neither have our Bills been paid quarterly as agreed to but at the end of seven or eight months as it suited the convenience of the Board. We consider it necessary in justice to ourselves to state these facts and hope your Honble. Body will give the matter due consideration and rectify the wrong that has been done us. On our part the contract has been faithfully carried out and we only regret your poor Patients are not with us *now* when our accommodations are so much superior to what they were in the old Establishment.

I have the honor to remain respectfully
Your Obt. Servant in J. Christ
Sr. Mary B. Russell
Super. *Sisters of Mercy*

San Francisco had large Chilean and Mexican communities. As a commercial center there was much traffic between San Francisco and South America. Mary Baptist seems to be aware that women were often left without recourse when employed outside the country. Sister Mary Stanislaus Rodriquez is the sister referred to in the letter.

To: Mr. Migan
From: Mary Baptist Russell
Date: March 31ˢᵗ, 1862
Source: Archives, SOMB

Dear Mr. Migan,

Would you do me the favor of writing in Spanish, an agreement between Caroline Cody and Fredrico Amana to the effect that she agrees to serve his wife as a Lady's maid and for $10.00 per month on condition that he will send her back to San Francisco and pay all her expenses any time she wishes to leave his family.

This Mr. F. Amana is the gentleman for whom you wrote a letter of introduction lately and as it is a far distant country to which she is going, I wish Caroline to have some guarantee for his fidelity to his promises. He and his Lady are staying in a private boarding house on Stockton St. west side, near Pacific and if it is not too much to ask I would be so deeply obliged if you would call and get the above mentioned paper signed.

I would not trouble you, thus, but the only Sister who speaks Spanish is confined to her bed at present and could not see Mr. A. when last here. I will send a messenger this evening at 8 o'clock for your answer as I will beg you to attend to this soon as they are to sail tomorrow at 9 a.m.

Most sincerely yours,
Sister Mary B. Russell

This lengthy letter continues the conversation with Mother Mary Frances Warde on the academy issue. Mother Frances correspondence is not found among the letters in the archives of the Sisters of Mercy of Burlingame but it is clear from the letter that she shared her knowledge and insights on Mother McAuley's educational views. Some of the information was quite new to Mary Baptist. While stating that she would not encourage boarding schools, it is interesting to note that Mary Baptist starts one in Sacramento later in the 1870's. Mary Baptist was always open to change in the face of new information or pressing need.

Date: September 24, 1862
To: Mother Francis Warde
From: Mary Baptist Russell
Source: Annals, SOMB, I: 241-245

St. Mary's Hospital
Corner 1ˢᵗ & Bryant

A week ago I received your letter and you see I am losing little time in answering it, not that I have anything of importance to say but because I do not wish our correspondence to be dropped. I hope it will lead to something in the end. Many things you say are rather startling to me. I was quite unprepared to find our holy Foundress quoted in support of Boarding Schools which I was always led to consider a sort of innovation; and does it not seem strange she should repeatedly express in our Rules our devotedness to the *Poor* without one word about educating the Rich or higher classes if she really intended her children to be employed in that duty. It seems to me that any Community with a Boarding School must give their whole attention to it, to the neglect of the direct duties of the Order.

As it occurs to me I will mention a little bit of information I learned lately from one of the Jesuits who came to this Mission within the last few months. I have seen him but once or twice, on the first occasion after shewing [sic] him thro' the House he inquired had we a Boarding School. I said no but we had a day School at our Branch House in *Sac* and hoped sooner or later to have one here also. He then asked did we contemplate ever having a Boarding School, to which I answered *no* and that we had already withstood a siege on that very account; he then said "You did *right.*" I have studied your Rules for I was obliged to do so and I tell you Boarding Schools are positively contrary to its spirit and to my own knowledge much mischief has been done by them. Ladies who are long accustomed to teach music and such accomplishments if sent to dress ulcers and other disagreeable duties won't always do them promptly, not being practically trained to regard the poor & afflicted as their proper charge, the maid will revolt against such duties as these.

Your Sisters in Chicago opened a Boarding School when they went there, I will not say they did *wrong* as there were no other

Religious near and it may have been a great charity to do so *for a time,* but some time ago the Superioress and the majority of the Sisters looked into the matter, concluded they had enough to do in their own proper sphere and with the approval of their Bishop wrote to the Ladies of the Sacred Heart telling them that Chicago was a good field for their labors and that if they would open a House there they (the Sisters of Mercy) would immediately close their Boarding School. In consequence of this invitation the Sacred Heart Sisters erected a House in that City but in the mean time a new Superior had been appointed who happened to be devoted to the Boarding Schools and after all, the Sisters of Mercy would not close their schools which continue to the present day and consequently neither institution flourishes.

These are not, of course, his precise words but are substantially correct, he also gave me to understand that great troubles had arisen in the Community from having received many Sisters who were devoted to the education of Ladies and who should have entered other Orders and who were therefore like bones out of joint in ours. I felt sorry the dear Sisters allowed such an opportunity of relinquishing this School (with honor) pass without embracing it. I take for granted you have frequent communication with the Sisters in Chicago as it is a filiation from Pittsburgh so you will know all these facts already. I merely mention them to let you see how many agree in pronouncing Boarding Schools *contrary* to our *Rules* whatever may have been the private views of Mother McAuley....

I intend telling Mother Francis [Bridgeman] what you heard Mother McAuley say and we will see what she thinks of it. It is easy for you to see the side to which I incline but I am prepared to agree to whatever may be decided on by the majority if a general conference is held, and I am sure Mother M. F. Bridgeman will do the same for I know she strictly adhered to the customs adopted in the General Chapter held in Baggot Street in 1845 or 46 though many things were not according to her "attrait" [Word is unclear] She was always scrupulous in following any regulations made by Authority and tried to impress all under her with the same strictness.

What you say about the Asylum had decided me on giving the one we have just built the name of the "House of the Good Shepherd." I suppose Mother E. Moore had our revered Foundress in her mind when she refused the charge of the Magdalen Asylum in Clare St. which was repeatedly offered her by its Foundress our late Sr. Mary de Sales Reddan

Archbishop Alemany had proposed that the House of Mercy serve a dual role as a shelter for domestic servants and as a home for aged ladies. Mary Baptist explains the reasons for not joining those two ministries into a single undertaking. She makes a practical appeal to experience and points out why such a venture would hinder the outpouring of charitable support.

Date: September, 1862
To: Archbishop Alemany
From: Mary Baptist Russell
Source: *Annals*, SOMB, I: 245-248.

If we understood aright what your Lordship said on last Sunday your idea is to establish a home in which all females of good character whether young or old, healthy or infirm can have a home for a shorter or longer term according to circumstances—the young & healthy to be employed at washing &c &c as a means of support for the establishment.

The "House of Mercy" properly so called is one of the chief objects of our Order and is intended as a temporary home for healthy able bodied women during the time that elapses between their leaving one situation and procuring another and to it is attached the Registry Office thro' which employment is provided for the Inmates of the House of Mercy as well as for all who attend the Office.

The Inmates of the House of Mercy are obliged on principle to rise very early, work hard &c &c in order to fit them for the hardships of service, but should there be among them persons not able to observe these regulations it creates jealousies, dissatisfaction and more or less disorder; and this is one of the difficulties we have had to contend with all along, for there being no home for the Aged & Infirm Females, no Alms House, we were obliged to throw all such on the House of Mercy. Some twenty or thirty I could name were not fit subjects for the proposed "Mater Miserecordiae" and were an encumbrance on the House of Mercy.

Another & a strong reason for not uniting the two objects together is that it would have the effect of depriving the Institute of the interest & charitable assistance of the Benevolent, for Servant Girls have been as a body hitherto so independent & even impudent in this country that the Public have no sympathy with them—think them no objects of charity and would say, as many do even now, that in providing a "Home" for them we are only encouraging them in idleness and that if they had not such a place to retire to, they would be satisfied to go to any place & at low wages. Now tho' this is the language of those who do not understand the system of the House of Mercy nor the real *facts* and must not deter us from doing what is right for our poor faithful & much abused girls, still I think it a reason against connecting their name with the proposed Establishment which in its other form will I am sure meet the warmest sympathy of the people. Neither is it intended to be entirely on the charity of the Public; in such Institutions at Home are found many who bring ample funds for their own support & often even more; even this moment we know several nice old Women in this country whose children are well off but live so far away from Church that they would be delighted to get into such an Institution just for the advantage of getting Mass & spiritual reading and their friends would pay for them. We would not wish the House of Mercy detached from the Hospital as the most useful thing of which there is an immensity to be done in this house.

I am strongly of opinion it would quite throw a damp on the people who advocate the "Home" if it is connected with the House of Mercy and experience proves they do not work well together. A school could well be undertaken in connection with the Home if in suitable location. This is a much longer production than I intended but it will be more satisfactory than if I tried to explain myself verbally.

Mary Baptist responded to an appeal for sisters by Bishop Eugene O'Connell. The mining industry had resulted in many orphans and children who were in need of care. Mary Baptist clearly outlines the objects of the Order and accepts the invitation. Part of her business sense is seen in the comments about clearing the debt of the Church first. She had already seen the results of a large church debt in Sacramento. In spite of unhealthy conditions there, the sisters were not permitted to raise funds to repair the convent until the church debt was cleared.

Date: Sometime in 1862
To: Bishop Eugene O'Connell
From: Sr. M. Baptist Russell
Source: O'Brien, Kathleen, *Journeys: A Pre-Amalgamation History of the Sisters of Mercy Omaha Province.* 1986, 23.

My Lord:

You are already aware of our late visit to Grass Valley to which place we were invited by Father Dalton for the purpose of judging whether a Branch of our Order was likely to succeed in that town. As far as I could see, our Institute is in every way suited to the wants of the place and F. Dalton and others whom I consulted seem to have no doubt of its being able to support a Religious Community. If, therefore, with your Lordship's cordial approval (of which I am not yet fully satisfied) our Sisters do go there, I trust they may be the means of helping many souls on the road to Heaven.

Since our return I have spoken to the Archbishop to know his wishes in the matter. He expresses himself under many obligations to your Lordship and would, therefore, wish to grant your request; otherwise, he would hardly consent to our leaving his own Diocese, particularly as our numbers are few compared with our duties. Before entering into any possible arrangements I would wish to ascertain if your Lordship is fully informed of the Spirit and duties of our Institute in order to avoid the possibility of a misunderstanding hereafter.... Our Sisters are especially devoted to the "Service of the Poor, Sick and Ignorant" in other words to a class whose very name precludes the idea of remuneration, therefore, in Ireland, the land of our birth as a Religious Order, no convent is established unless sufficient funds are provided for the support of the community. In this country we are satisfied to depend in a great measure on the charity of the Benevolent ... but we never undertake any duty however meritorious in itself for the purpose of supporting the Community. We do not charge the children who attend our schools but we take from their parents any voluntary offerings they make us. Our primary duties are the instruction of poor Girls, the protection of unemployed Women of good character, and the visitation of the sick. We do not exclude the Rich from our Schools. We endeavor to give all a thorough education, but we do not teach Music, Drawing, or any of those accomplishments that consume time, and are un-suited to the class to which we principally devote ourselves.... We are willing to conduct a school for Infant Boys. We also conduct Orphanages, Hospitals, Reformatories, visit public Hospitals, Prisons, Work-houses, etc. In short any work of Mercy in accordance with the Spirit of our Rule....

Father Dalton tells me there is still some six thousand dollars due on his Church which he would be satisfied to let lie by for a time in order to provide a common convent for the Sisters but I would consider it more advisable to clear the church first and then in the course of a year or so to collect funds for the erection of a dwelling for the Sisters. I would not think of accepting Father Dalton's generous proposal of giving them the use of his house while theirs is in progress. Better let them wait till a place is ready for them. It need not be so very expensive nor very grand; a plain, airy frame building is sufficient.

This letter seeks funds from the legislature for the care of women in the Magdalen Asylum. The women usually were placed at the Asylum by legal authorities because of prostitution, addictions or public behavior. Some women voluntarily came to the sisters in hopes of changing their situations.

Date: February 9, 1863
To: Honble. the Senate & Assembly
From: Mary Baptist Russell
Source: *Annals*, SOMB, I: 259-260

To the Hon<u>ble.</u> the Senate & Assembly
Gentlemen:

In presenting the foregoing Report of the State of the Magdalen Asylum, we beg to return our best thanks for the past liberality of the Legislature by which we have been mainly enabled to undertake this work of mercy; It must be gratifying to all who have taken any part in the good work to observe the great increase in the number of Penitents rescued during the short time that has elapsed since the opening of the present Establishment in March 1862, as also to know that their accommodation tho' necessarily limited and on a very humble scale, has been comfortable and healthy, very different indeed from the miserable quarters they formerly occupied.

The Sisters, in behalf of their charge, again throw themselves on the charity of the State in the persons of its Representatives and they feel they need not seek for forcible terms when making their appeal as every one is sensible of the necessity of an Institution where the unhappy Victims of crime & credulity can be sheltered & encouraged in their repentance, strengthened in their good resolutions, and protected during the Ordeal of conversion. In fact the *Magdalen Asylum* has very particular claims on the public and it is to be hoped will be in time one of the noblest Monuments of the charity of California as well as one of the most useful of its Benevolent Institutions.

Sr. Mary B. Russell
Super. Sisters of Mercy
San Francisco
Feb. 9th. 1863

The circumstances of this note are unknown. Mary Baptist seems skeptical that money meant for purchase of a grave site will be spent properly if given directly to the daughter of the deceased.

To: Mr. O'Regan
From: Sister Mary Baptist Russell
Date Feb. 26, 1863
Source: Archives, SOMB

Dear Mr. O'Regan

I have some money belonging to the late Mrs. Gunter and will pay for her grave (buy the ground) but I do not wish to give the money to the daughter. As soon as you let me know the cost of the grave, I will send you the money.

Yours truly,
Sister Mary B. Russell
Feb. 26th 1863

Every two years the sisters reported to the State Legislature on the status of the Magdalen Asylum. The reports provide a detailed listing of the progress of each resident. The cause for a woman's entry into the Asylum is listed as well as the outcome of her time there.

Date: Jan. 8th, 1864
To: California Assembly
From: Mary Baptist Russell
Source: *Annals*, SOMB, I: 280-284

MAGDALEN ASYLUM
Report of 1863

No.	Nativity	Age	Date	Remarks
1	New Orleans	40	Aug. 29, 1859	Still in the Asylum
2	New York	19	Jan. 23, 1860	Still in the Asylum
3	Virginia	21	Dec. 11, 1860	Still in the Asylum
4	Pennsylvania	18	Oct. 2, 1860	Went to a Situation Oct/63
5	Germany	19	Aug. 16, 1861	Still in the Asylum
6	Australia	18	Feb. 10, 1862	Still in the Asylum
7	California	19	Feb. 11, 1862	Still in the Asylum
8	Ireland	32	Mar. 19, 1862	Engaged in a Laundry Apr/62
9	New York	19	May 2, 1862	Still in the Asylum
10	New York	14	June 12, 1862	Still in the Asylum
11	Australia	18	July 16, 1862	Returned to parents Jan/63
12	Massachusetts	17	Aug. 3, 1862	Returned to parents Feb. 10, 1863

13	New York	16	Aug. 6, 1862	Still in the Asylum
14	New York	11	Aug. 6, 1862	Went to a Situation Nov/63
15	New York	23	Aug. 7, 1862	Sent to Hospital Jan. 3, 1864
16	Ireland	24	Sept. 3, 1862	Left March 10, 1863
17	Ireland	44	Sept. 12, 1862	Reconciled to her husband Aug/63
18	New Orleans	19	Oct. 21, 1862	Sent to a place Nov. 21, 1863
19	California	10	Oct. 25, 1862	Still in the Asylum
20	Ireland	40	Oct. 30, 1862	Still in the Asylum
21	California	20	Oct. 30, 1862	Still in the Asylum
22	Ireland	38	Nov. 17, 1862	Died Feb. 18, 1863
23	California	10	Nov. 17, 1862	In the Asylum
24	New York	15	Nov. 21, 1862	Ran away June 19, 1863
25	Ireland	23	Dec. 13, 1862	Sent to a place Jan/64
26	Ireland	40	Dec. 13, 1862	Left Jan. 29, 1863
27	Ireland	22	Jan. 2, 1863	Left July 26, 1863
28	Ireland	32	Jan. 9, 1863	In the Asylum
29	Ireland	38	Feb. 14, 1863	Left June 8, 1863
30	California	10	Feb. 14, 1863	In the Asylum
31	Maine	24	Feb. 27, 1863	Left May 9, 1863
32	Ireland	32	Mar. 14, 1863	Left July 9, 1863
33	Kentucky	15	Apr. 14, 1863	Ran away Apr. 24, 1863
34	Pennsylvania	18	Apr. 25, 1863	Sent to the States May 22, 1863
35	Ireland	32	May 9, 1863	Taken by husband May 30, 1863
36	California	12	May 9, 1863	Returned to parents
37	Pennsylvania	9	May 11, 1863	In the Asylum
38	Pennsylvania	18	May 14, 1863	In the Asylum
39	Massachusetts	15	July 4, 1863	In the Asylum
40	California	8	July 4, 1863	In the Asylum
41	Ireland	26	July 6, 1863	Sent to Hospital Aug. 29, 1863
42	England	30	July 29, 1863	Left Sept. 21, 1863
43	California	10	Aug. 2, 1863	In the Asylum
44	New York	15	Aug. 3, 1863	Ran away Aug. 7, 1863
45	Illinois	19	Sept. 16, 1863	Ran away Sept. 21, 1863
46	Ireland	38	Sept. 19, 1863	Left Oct. 4, 1863
47	New Orleans	14	Sept. 21, 1863	In the Asylum
48	Maine	14	Sept. 29, 1863	In the Asylum

49	Ireland	36	Sept. 29, 1863	Taken by husband Oct/63
50	New York	24	Jan. 30, 1863	Aug. 6th Dismissed Incorrigible
51	Australia	17	Oct. 29, 1863	In the Asylum
52	Ireland	24	Nov. 15, 1863	In the Asylum
53	California	7	Nov. 15, 1863	In the Asylum
54	Ireland	22	Nov. 26, 1863	In the Asylum
55	California	16	Nov. 26, 1863	Ran away
56	Maine	18	Nov. 18, 1863	In the Asylum
57	California	13	Dec. 16, 1863	In the Asylum
58	New York	12	Dec. 26, 1863	In the Asylum
59	Ireland	30	May 27, 1863	In the Asylum

Summary

In Asylum at date of last Report	26
Admitted since	<u>33</u>
Total	59
In the House at present	30
Variously provided for	13
Died	1
Sent away or left incorrigible	8
Returned to their friends	<u>7</u>
Total	59
Discharged prior to last Report	63
Total from beginning	122

In presenting the above Report of the state of the Magd. Asylum, the Sisters of Mercy beg to return thanks for the past Liberality of the Legislature by which they have been mainly enabled to undertake this work of Mercy. In behalf of their charge they again throw themselves on the charity of the State in the persons of its Representatives, and they feel it is unnecessary to seek for forcible terms, when making an appeal on behalf of the unhappy victims of crime or credulity, as every one feels the necessity of an Institute where they can be sheltered and encouraged in their repentance, strengthened in their good resolution, and protected during the ordeal of their conversion.

The Asylum is (on principle) conducted in the most economical manner; still the outlay is considerable, By reference to the Books of the Institute it is found that the average cost of each inmate for food, clothing, &c &c (everything) is about $19.00 per month making a yearly total of $8500.00. All of which is respectfully submitted.

Jan. 10th, 1864
Sr. Mary B. Russell
Supr. of Srs. of Mercy

Unlike the situation in Sacramento, it was twenty years after her arrival in California before Mary Baptist was able to open a lasting school for San Francisco. This letter refers to a request by Father Prendergast for the sisters to open a school at Mission Dolores. There was confusion about the terms of the request. Ultimately, Mary Baptist did not open a school there.

Date: March 4, 1864
From: Mary Baptist Russell
To: Archbishop Alemany
Source: *Annals*, SOMB, I: 290-91

Most Revd. Abp.:

The education of Poor Girls being the primary object of our Order, we always regretted not having a School in this City, therefore I unhesitatingly answered F. Prendergast in the *affirmative* with the *Solo proviso* that it would be a *Free* School and that the support of it did not fall on us. We have not, at present, too many Sisters for our duties but if Providence intends us to have the School I do not fear but we will have enough to manage it. Still, if there is any other Community willing to undertake it they will probably do it more Justice & we will be quite pleased.

I do not understand what Father Thomas says regarding a House of Mercy, we have had one ever since we came to the City. Over *eleven hundred* have been sheltered in it of which fact he surely cannot be ignorant. We have never less than a dozen and generally *twice* that number. Perhaps he wished to know did we intend transferring it to the Mission; *we did not,* as we think this is the most suitable place for it as they (the Inmates) are here employed doing the washing & ironing which is large and also the cleaning of the Hospital. The only thing we calculated on having at the Mission is the House for "Aged and Infirm Females of Good Character," a class for whom no provision has hitherto been made and who are pretty numerous. Your Lordship may remember that St. Mary's Society over a year ago donated $1000.00 from their funds for this object and they are willing to assist further as it goes on. I believe I have now replied to all your queries. This is all we had planned regarding the Establishment at the Mission but should your Grace desire any change it is not too late as nothing has been positively arranged.

The following six letters deal with a crisis of leadership at the Grass Valley foundation. Mary Baptist had established the house in 1863 as an affiliate foundation. At this time she still had the responsibility for its members. The letters outline a test of wills between a difficult bishop (O'Connell) and somewhat inflexible and fearful leaders of the Grass Valley community. The skill with which Mary Baptist moves through the ecclesiastical rapids shows her tact, practical wisdom and use of consultative processes.

Date: August 15, 1864
To: Bishop Eugene O'Connell
From: Mary Baptist Russell
Source: *Annals*, SOMB, I: 296-303

My Lord:

I was well aware that reports gave me credit for the rather ungracious act of removing Mother M. Teresa King from Grass Valley without even acquainting your Lordship much less getting your permission. Still, I would not think of clearing myself of the imputation had not your Lordship & Father Griffin directly charged me with it on occasion of your late visit to our Sisters in Sacramento. I have an instinctive horror of explanations and my little experience has convinced me they are generally worse than useless, but I feel it is due to your Lordship to satisfy you on this matter because I feel you would indeed have just reason for displeasure had it been as appearances would had you to believe, and even as it is, you have a fine opportunity of practicing forbearance.

I have merely to repeat what M. M. Gabriel told you on the occasion above referred to; that when Dr. Clayburn urged so strongly the necessity of Mother Teresa's removal to the City, I wrote saying if she herself really thought it advisable to do so, for her to write & inform your Lordship, and that if you approved of her coming I would myself go for her in order to avoid taking a second Sister from their small Community. M. M. Teresa did not seem willing to do even so little as that towards her own removal, and I believe your Lordship was away from home at the time. I then decided on taking that opportunity of paying them a visit not so much, as I said to Father King, on account of his Sister's delicacy, as in order to let M. M. Gabriel see how the Sisters there are placed as I wished to have her opinion on some points.

In the mean time, Dr. Clayburn came to the City and, in my opinion, went beyond a Physician's duty in urging me to bring Sister down forthwith. No doubt he laid me down as a most heartless being for taking her illness so coolly. He spoke in the same strain to her Reverend Brother who, at last, got so worried that he said he would get the Abp's permission to pay her a visit. It must have been on this occasion the Abp. desired him to bring her down *if he ever did so*, of which I am very doubtful as I think the Abp understands too clearly the relative position of Bishops & Religious to do so, but I am sure Father King in the excited State of his mind understood him to do so, or he never would have acted as he did.

When I arrived Mother M. Teresa was already gone, and, as I ascertained from the Sisters, much against her inclinations but under the impression she was acting in obedience. What was done, could not be undone so I said all that remained was, without delay, to acquaint you of the facts and make the best apology for the really unintentional want of proper deference for your Lordship's authority. This Mother Teresa somehow neglected to do up to the present moment; had I thought for a moment it would have gone on so long, I certainly would have written to your Lordship ere this, but I left it to her as the proper person. To this day she really thinks the Abp. sent for her and wonders at my doubting it. I have not yet told her I am writing, neither have I mentioned your interview with M. M. Teresa but I intend copying this letter in order to show it to her when she is stronger.

As to the difficulty regarding poor Miss Dalton, it does not seem to me such an insuperable affair. If the Sisters decide she has not the understanding for a Religious she must, of course, be dismissed and I don't think she will give any unnecessary trouble nor has her stay among them been in any way detrimental to their interests. Her brother, the Priest, will not be so very much surprised as is perhaps imagined at her dismissal. I told him nearly two years ago when she wanted to enter here that it seemed to me she was intended rather for a Saint in the World rather than for a Religious, for my part I would feel little difficulty in telling him, tho' I know the poor Man will be sadly disappointed but he has met so many heavy crosses he will not think much of so trifling a one. It might have been wiser not to have received her into the Community at all, but under all the circumstances, I do not see that it could have been avoided—her anxiety to try herself in Religion, the deference due to her Brother's wishes, the circumstances of the place, *all* seemed to concur in her being admitted, and even your Lordship said in one of your letters that she was ready to join the Sisters on their arrival so that altogether I feel it was impossible to get out of it particularly as the Presentation Nuns gave as their reason for not retaining her a mere physical infirmity which was long since removed.

I am satisfied it is the holy will of God for the Sisters to be in Grass Valley. How could I doubt it since every means was taken of ascertaining the Divine Will and the knowledge of this is to me a sufficient answer to all the difficulties proposed by Father Griffin but as your Lordship may be better satisfied by my entering into particulars I will endeavor to do so. In the first place I can name many houses of other Orders as well as of our own that began with even less than we sent to Grass Valley; secondly, wherever there are human beings there will be human miseries and, consequently, work for a Sister of Mercy not so much in Grass Valley as a matter of course as in a large City but still enough to employ usefully a small Community. As soon as it will be possible for the Sisters to open a half Orphanage even on a humble scale, it will add greatly to their usefulness and be a blessing to the poor children who are scattered over the Mountains without a chance of instruction. I shall indeed be glad when I hear of this good work being commenced. A.M.D.G.

As to the Spiritual wants of the Sisters, I really think they have no reason whatever to complain. It is certainly a privation to be without daily Mass but, when it is unavoidable, God will supply and we hope it will not be always so, at all counts let the Sisters made good use of all they have and in God's good time they will get greater.

As to F. Griffin's youth, it is a comfort that every day will lessen that defect and surely no one can blame him for not being older, so he need not be the first to state that objection, but I hope he will never again say there is any place shut out from God's grace. I agree with F. G. that anxiety about Community affairs &c preyed on Mother M. T's mind and had no small influence on her health, but I trust she will be wiser in future. Doctors Bowie, Celle, Clayburn all agree in saying she has no consumption, that extreme debility is her chief ailment, but that her heart is somewhat enlarged and that caused the difficulty in lying on the left side which was supposed to originate in the diseased state of her lungs. Dr. Celle says emphatically, that the climate of Grass Valley is much better for her than this, so under all these circumstances she will, with your permission, return towards the end of this month and continue her post so long as God leaves her strength to do so. I am sorry to hear of your Lordship also being delicate, but ill health is a very sanctifying cross particularly when one is obliged as you are to attend to so many fatiguing duties. From my heart I pray God to give you and all poor invalids' patience to bear uncomplainingly their sufferings and all their attendant ills. I understand you are soon to pass thro' this city on your way to Mendocino and that we may then expect a visit. I shall indeed be glad to see your Lordship and will take that opportunity of speaking to you further on the chief subject of this letter. You see I have interrupted my retreat to write this long epistle but I felt it my duty to do so and hope you will, in charity, give me an additional prayer.

I remain with deep respect, your Lordship's most obt serv in J. C.
Sr. Mary B Russell
Supr. Srs. of Mercy

Date of letter:1864
From:M. Baptist Russell
To:Sr. Gabriel Brown
Source: *Annals*, SOMB, I: 284-288

The Abp came last evening; he began his usual bantering about specimens of gold, &c. At last I introduced the topic by telling his Grace that Mother M. Teresa was not at all satisfied with Grass Valley & thought it would not be a *permanent* place and that it was not a fit place for any Sisters, at least not for Sisters of Mercy. I added it pleased me much she had come down as it would enable her to have a satisfactory conversation with him which I hoped would settle her mind and that then, if she was convinced on the points, she would mention she hoped to get a professed Sister back with her. He then asked the reasons which I need not repeat as you have heard them already. He replied that Grass Valley is a place of considerable importance & likely to remain so, that in his mind it would ulti-mately be the *See* of the Bishop, that it certainly would not grow much if the new mines in Nevada Territory continue what they promise to be; but that he does not anticipate their ruining Grass Valley entirely, that he hoped to see Sisters in places of far less importance before long, that San Juan, Monterey & Santa Barbara are nothing in comparison to it, and that the Sisters of Charity do much good in all these places, that she must not fear regarding the training of the Sisters, that all she has to do is to *plant* and that the Holy Ghost would water as there is no fear but the Holy Spirit will find His way to Grass Valley if they *pray*, that it was not absolutely necessary to be actually employed in *all* the duties, that the Presenta-tion Nuns used to say to him, "Oh, Abp. we may as well go home, we have only 40 children to teach" but I would tell them (said he) that soon they would have a Hundred or two Hundred and now they have from five to seven hundred. At length he ended by saying that everything regarding the foundation had been maturely & prudently considered and that he believed it to be the Will of God for them to be there and that if a wife is bound to her Husband as long as he lives so are they till Grass [Valley] dies away; that when that happens they will be free and then it will be time to see to what place they would remove. Sister said something about its undoubtedly failing and that Dr. O'Connell was of the same opinion. "Well then, said the Abp., if Bishop O'Connell sends you all down, I will receive you."

There was a long pause. At last his Grace got up to leave so, fearing he would go, I said that now P. G. Mother M. Teresa would feel better satisfied as she had explained herself and that she would now put her whole mind to the work but that she wanted a *third* professed choir Sister. He did not reply for some minutes, and then he said, "Well, I wrote to Dr. O'Connell. I thought we had done all we could for him in that way." After some further remarks he made a move to go, so I again asked would he allow us to give her a Sister, that we were willing if he was. He then asked how many sisters had they. I said *five* (for I was determined not to count Sr. M. Teresa nor Sr. Kate as neither will do). "Well," said he, "I think that is as many in proportion as ourselves." M.M. Teresa said her great dread was the responsibility of receiving & professing Sisters which fell entirely on her when the Chapter was not formed & added that Sr. M. Joseph her only councilor, thought just as she did, and that in fact they might not go back [illegible] without some arrangement being made. When the Abp. heard this he took up his hat and told her to tell Sr. M. Joseph from him to read three or four chapters of St. Liguori's "Man Sanctified" whenever Satan put such thoughts into her head. He begged Sr. M. Teresa to have more courage & confidence in God and that God would assuredly bless her, that Sr. Philip Neri began his foundation with a sum equal to $20 and when some persons saw the large building he was preparing to erect they remonstrated but he told them tho' he had only twenty dollars he had great confidence in *Divine Providence*. So his Grace went without another word.

I was quite unprepared for his refusal and M.M.T. felt it very much. She wrote him a very nice little note last evening telling him she was now determined to do her best to promote God's glory among the little flock of Christ in Grass Valley and begging his blessings & prayers and renewing her petition for a Professed Sister for even six or eight months. No reply has yet been received and no one can tell what his reply may be, therefore, I beg M.M.T. to keep her mind free.

In the course of the conversation the Abp. told us the Pope said to himself when coming to California that as so many came to get *gold*, he must come to carry the Cross of Jesus Christ and said he every Sister has her Crucifix from which she should learn the *Spirit of Sacrifice* which should make us willing to suffer for Him who had suffered so much for us. May God grant us all that Spirit. There were many other nice, holy, little things which I have forgotten but altogether I felt impressed with his prudence & sanctity

Date: March 12, 1865
To: Archbishop Alemany
From: Mary Baptist Russell
Source: *Annals*, SOMB, I: 319-322

Dear & Most Revd. Father:

The enclosed are copies of the letters from Grass Valley which I mentioned to your Lordship. It is evident matters there have come to a crisis and that some change must be made. I am still of opinion there are no very serious or insurmountable difficulties in the *place* itself but by these letters you will see the *Seniors there* think otherwise. Under these circumstances, the first idea would be to remove the Heads and send others with a different spirit but that cannot be easily done without running the risk of interfering with our Establishments here & in Sac. As far as any judgment goes, there could not be a better Head than Mother M. T. King if she followed her own views. Her health is, and always was poor, but I thought and *think* sufficient for all required of her if her *mind* was *settled*.

There was no formal arrangements made with Dr. O'Connell, but I was explicit in my letters as to the conditions on which our Sisters went there and said I addressed myself to *him* rather than to Father Dalton as Pastors in California are not very stationary. The Bishop made no demur to anything I said. Tho' it would be more agreeable to have a certain specific income I am sure they will never be allowed to want for *necessaries* and that should satisfy us in this country where every Institution has to struggle thru' difficulties in the beginning.

I send the Manuscript (The Guide) to which the Sisters allude and have marked the several passages to which they refer. I know well we are bound to receive back all professed here if it is found necessary to break up the Establishment and in that case we would gladly welcome them back. It appears by Dr. O'Connell's Pastoral the Orphanage is a settled thing now but then a new difficulty arises. If his Lordship contemplates removing all the Orphans belonging to his Diocese from San Rafael and opening a regular *Boys' Orphanage*, I would not approve of the Sisters undertaking the charge of it as it would not be suitable for them, but if his Lordship only expects them to take *very small* little creatures and will allow them to transfer to Father Lootens the grown ones on whatever terms may be agreed to (or otherwise provide for them) then I see no difficulty whatever and I feel satisfied this would be perfectly satisfactory to his Lordship.

The points on which I beg your Grace's opinion and *direction* are——

1st   Is the Establishment in Grass Valley to be given up or *not*.

2nd   If continued shall we change the Heads at all risks to our duties here or shall we endeavor to satisfy the Sisters *already there*.

3rd   Shall I require of Dr. OC. the written agreement spoken of in the enclosed.

4th   If your Grace decides on changing the Sisters shall *I* inform Dr. O'Connell and what shall I say, or will you write to him yourself.

Should I not have made matters sufficiently clear, I know you will have the goodness to give me an opportunity of explaining myself more fully, but I do not wish to intrude unnecessarily on your time. Recommending myself particularly to your prayers I remain Most respectfully in Jesus Christ.

March 12th. 1865   Sr. Mary B. Russell &c &c

P.S. Since writing the above I have received a letter from Grass Valley enclosing the accompanying from their Bishop. In no case would we agree to their being transferred to Yreka so that present appearances would lead one to expect them home again.

Date: Between March 13-24, 1865
To: Mother Mary Teresa King
From: Mary Baptist Russell
Source: *Annals*, SOMB, I: 324-330

My dear M. M. Teresa,

I must try to give you all the particulars of our interview with the Abp. as you will naturally wish to hear all.

Knowing his Grace is always pressed for time, I had Sisters M. Gab.[Brown] & Baptist [Mogan]in the Community room awaiting his arrival, after getting his blessing and some few ordinary words I began by saying I was sorry that I had been obliged to trouble him with all those letters. He looked at Sister M. G. & Ba. and asked "Are we all Freemasons," "Do they know this matter"? So when assured of that he said, "Well, it seems to me this great Mountain is all *Smoke*." The Bishop means well, the Sisters mean well, & Father Dalton means well but they got on a wrong line and are not now going right but it can be settled. Don't you at your profession make a promise to go wherever you are Sent? I answered *no*, not a direct engagement to that effect but that it is a sort of an understood thing and that I supposed no Religious would think of objecting unless for some weighty reasons.

Well now, said he, let us draw some line so as to bring matters to a point. Are you *forbidden* by your Rules to do anything for boys? No, I answered, but it is not one of the *real objects* of our *Order*. It is not, however, in my mind contrary to the *Spirit* of our Rules as it may very properly be ranked among our Services to the Poor, & Ignorant and is of course a work of Mercy. I added that we had never been in any place when it was undertaken & never heard the matter discussed. We would not think, at the same time, that it would be very Suitable for Nuns to have charge of *big* boys. "But," said the Abp., "Bishop O'Connell does not ask you to take *big* boys, he only says till they are at the age of discretion say from 7 to 8 years and if any larger have to be received, for a week or two while arrangements are being made to send them elsewhere it is no harm, it is only temporally."

I answered I was inclined to agree to all that, particularly as I know in this new country priests have many difficulties in providing for the wants of their people and that it was a mistake on your part to think I had disapproved so strongly of the charge. He then said that you were too pusillanimous, that you feared if you did *this* you could be required to do *that*, that you feared the place would not last &c so said I do not think she will ever get on, you had better recall her and send another. I said to him that he knows so little personally of the country I supposed there was no use asking to suggest which Sister to send. "Oh, yes," said he, "I know nothing, you must decide yourself, but you have to see that she be *pious, agreeable,* willing to do anything she can that her Bishop would wish, a Sister should not thwart a poor Bishop when he is trying to do the best he can for his flock. I am trying to arrange to send three or four Sisters to all the little towns so that they may teach children; this reminder now of what you said, that Grass Valley might do for a *Branch* but not for a place to train Novices, to this he made the same answer he did to yourself last summer.

He said (when asked) that Sr. M. Joseph [O'Rourke] should also be removed, for said he [censored by annalist] She is like Father Cassin "the Bishop is *very good, very holy, very wise;* a very good boy, *but*—does she think young priests can drive the Holy Ghost from a Bishop? If he asks their advice he is not obliged to follow it unless convinced by their reasons, besides those whose opinions are asked are supposed to be capable of giving a correct one. Sister M. Joseph [O'Rourke] has a great soul but she is not right in the way she speaks. You *must remove her also.*"

His Grace said he would himself write to Dr. O'Connell on Monday and for me also to write to him and to tell him my reasons for hoping the Sisters I send may suit but if I was mistaken in my judgement that I would be obliged by his writing me a line & I would try & send another. Hoping he would send us his letter to Dr. OC. I said to him "perhaps your Grace would let us know what you say to the Bishop." Well, said he, I will write in this form, it appears the two Sisters in Grass Valley now are a little timid, a little pusillanimous, rather scared at the ghosts of the place and that we are sorry for it as we expected they would have got on nicely, but that now we would send him two who were not so easily frightened and who would do all he would wish to have done—Here I interrupted saying, "not every thing he would want, but everything that was at all compatible with our Rules" that for instance if he wished us to open an Academy such as the Dominicans & Notre Dame Sisters conduct, I should remonstrate against it as contrary to the spirit of our Rule & Order which is entirely devoted to the Poor,

Sick, & Ignorant, but I added, I would not anticipate much difficulty in convincing his Lordship it was not unwillingness on our part to do all we could to please.

After hearing me out the Abp answered that as a matter of course he spoke of what was according to our Rules, that *no* Bishop could require anything else and that Dr. O'Connell would be the first to check you if you did undertake anything contrary to it; but that if he forgot himself you have your Abp to write to and if it was not settled for you by him, *Rome* would come forward to see that nothing was imposed on you contrary to your vocation; that the canons of the Church are very strict in defining the length to which each one's authority goes and that no Bishop could oblige a Religious to go contrary to her Rules but that the Rules do not name every little thing Sisters are to do but only the spirit by which they are to be guided and you know, said he, in an emphatic tone, a Bishop will give his blood for his Sisters.

This is the substance of all that passed. I had sent him as I told you copies of all your letters & Dr. O'Connell's and it was evident he had studied them for he came prepared to speak on *each* point and there was no need of questioning on our side at all. I will add nothing except to beg that you will now take it all in *good part* and with *grace*. Do not listen to all that nature & Satan may suggest to disturb your mind, and prevent you doing so—the past cannot be recalled, be it right or wrong it is over, and let all our endeavors now be to turn all these occasions to our Soul's benefit. Time may prove that your fears were well founded, but it will be then time enough to act. You will return to us at whatever time may be arranged and you will please God, be what I must say you always tried to be while here, a humble, good, child. We will all give you a hearty welcome and do all in our power for your happiness & perfection. What I say to you I say also to Sr. M. Joseph. So I need not write to herself.

I send you a copy of what I [have] written to Dr. O'Connell. I said after *Easter* because the roads are not now very safe and besides all this is so unexpected that I must get a little time to think—For the present at least you had better make no remarks to the Sisters. There is no necessity for them to hear anything except that your health obliged you to leave.

Now don't spend time pondering over the past or imaging what may be here after but meekly acquiesce in what has been arranged and keep your mind quiet, attend also to your health. You must pray fervently that God may now, in mercy, direct all to His own honor & glory.

Your ever affectionate &c &c

Date: Between March 12-24, 1865
To: Right Revd. O'Connell
From: Mary Baptist Russell
Source: *Annals*, SOMB, I: 331-332

Right Revd. O'Connell,
My Lord:

You cannot well imagine the surprise & horror your letters to Father Dalton & Mother M. Teresa received during the past week gave me. I know you must have been tried beyond measure to proceed to such lengths, but you must pardon the dear Sisters and attribute it all to ignorance, for willingly they would not do wrong in the least thing. We will hope God has allowed all for a good end. It has convinced us, however, that a change is necessary, so according to the Abp's advice we will (with your permission) recall Srs. M. T & J. at a fitting time, say Easter, and send in their stead two who will, I trust, do better.

In the mean time let the Orphanage be proceeded with, we must not stop the good work and one too so much needed. It is quite usual with our Sisters to have a Day School for young Boys but to have the entire charge of them as in an Orphanage is very rare with us, at the same time it is not contrary to the *spirit* of or Rules and may be undertaken when it is possible without interfering with our more immediate duties. It would be desirable, however, to have it distinctly understood that grown boys are not admissible, as it would be rather unseemly and, in fact, impossible for Sisters to manage them, but your Lordship's letter shews [sic] you do not require them to be received so it is unnecessary to say anything on the subject.

I must beg your Lordship to implore the Divine direction in the Selection of the Sisters to be sent to Grass Valley as that has yet to be arranged.

Be so good as to pray also for me in your charity and believe me to remain

Most respectfully your Lordship's obt. Sert. in J. C.

Sr. M. B. Russell &c &c

Date: Between March 12-24, 1865
To: T.J. Dalton, Grass Valley
From: Mary Baptist Russell
Source: *Annals*, SOMB, I: 332-333

Revd. T. J. Dalton,
Grass Valley

Dear Revd. Father,

When I wrote you last week I had little idea of the turn affairs were going to take. It is a happy provision of Providence that we know not what is coming. It is useless for me to enter into any details of our cogitations during the past few days. The decision is all that will interest you and I will save myself writing even that again by enclosing the copy I kept of my letter to Dr. O'Connell. I know the poor Sisters will feel and, perhaps deeply, lest they may have seriously erred and I need not ask you to make it as little painful to them as it may be in your power to do.

From this day till a Superior is appointed, you must look to me as at the head of affairs in Grass [Valley] so now I want to hear all about the proposed Orphanage, how much has been already collected, what are the prospects for more, what plans you are thinking of adopting. Is it to be frame or brick, in short all & everything about it. I hope with God's blessing, it will be quite a success and a blessing to many, therefore, I would like to see it started and I certainly will assist all I can to forward it. I will look for a line from you (if not on the Mission) this week without fail so please do not disappoint me.

Hope & praying this unpleasant affair is at an end and begging your prayers & blessing.

I remain &c&c

Sr. M. B. R. &c&c

This is another in the series of reports on the Magdalen Asylum made to the State Legislature.

Date: January 6, 1866
To: the Honorable the Assembly
From: Mary Baptist Russell
Source: Annals, SOMB, I: 346-348

To the Honorable the Assembly,

May it please your honble Body, it is now two years since we presented to your honorable body a report of the condition of the Magdalen Asylum. During that period material changes have taken place in that Institution which we beg leave to lay before you.

The number of Inmates increased so much that the frame Building in Hayes' Valley was found insufficient for their accommodation, and we were therefore obliged to provide a much larger house. About twenty thousand dollars were contributed for this purpose by a few charitable & kind friends who had formed a just appreciation of the necessity of extending the usefulness of this great work of mercy; but the outlay incurred in purchasing a suitable location, the erection of the present brick building, the enclosures, and other improvements, together with the increased expense of living—the number of Inmates being more than double, has left the Institute with a debt of more than eight thousand.

With the exception of a moderate annual appropriation by the State, and the offerings of a few private individuals, there is no income worth mentioning. Using the utmost economy, allowing but twenty dollars per month for the entire support, clothing, &c &c of each inmate, the expense cannot be reduced much, if at all, below fifteen thousand dollars a year.

All the circumstances herein stated we are prepared to prove, if an opportunity be afforded, to the satisfaction of any Committee that may be appointed to visit the institution.

In conclusion we entrust with the utmost confidence the cause of this most wronged & helpless class of God's creatures to the humane & generous consideration of your honble. Body.

Appended is a list similar to those hitherto furnished.

Sr. Mary B. Russell

Supr. Sisters of Mercy

Jan. 6th /66

The early Mercy superiors carried on a network of communication throughout the early years of the Order in the United States. Bonds existed across country and ideas were exchanged on basic questions of Mercy life. In this letter Mary Baptist shares the sad story of a former member of the Chicago community.

Date: July 1, 1866

To: Superior, Sisters of Mercy Chicago

From: Mary Baptist Russell

Source: *Annals*, SOMB, I: 362-364

I think it my duty to let you know of the death of your former Sister M. M. di Pazzi [Eagan] if it were only to secure your prayers for her eternal repose. I saw her but once since I last wrote to you until she came here to die. That once was nearly three years ago when she called to offer her Academy to us on condition of our charging ourselves with the support of her Mother. Of course, we would not accept it with or without conditions. The poor Soul was just as infatuated as ever. Soon after she went to Virginia City and the next we heard of her was that she was married by a judge to an infidel who spent all his time gambling.—About six months ago we found she was again in San Francisco, her Husband treating her cruelly, herself in bad health and an infant in her arms.

About the first week in May, a Lady called begging Sr. Mary Francis [Benson] to go see "Mrs. Barnes" but she being ill, another

Sister was sent who had never seen her but had heard her sad story and she very soon discovered who "Mrs. Barnes" was. She found her in a dying condition, a Protestant Society supporting herself, mother, & child. We then learned she had dismissed Barnes a few weeks before and had just been reconciled to the Church and received Holy Communion for the first time in two years. Next day we had her removed to our Hospital, a holy Jesuit attended, every three or four days she received the Sacraments and you may be assured we neglected nothing to procure her every assistance. Her Mother, a broken hearted Creature, has her child but hopes it will soon follow its Mother—She is depending on charity and, I fear, suffers many privations but feels her heart overflowing with gratitude to God for seeing her poor child die as she did, and says she saw plainly before she was one day in the country that she was half crazy and so she was I feel assured, for she repeated uncalled for, many absurd ridiculous stories of the Convent even since she came to the Hospital.

The day before she died she begged Sr. May Francis to ask you all to forgive her all she did to pain or grieve you and to say that she *forgave all who injured her*. This fretted dear Sr. M. F. a good deal for she would like her to have been all *self-accusing* but thanks be to God she died in the Sentiments and with the helps she did and not, as one might dread, hardened and impenitent. You would be astonished at the loving confidence she expressed all thro' her illness and the ardor with which she desired Holy Communion. At 10 OC. this forenoon (July 1st) her remains were deposited in Calvary Cemetery. The Abp. gave a free grave and we did the rest. I trust she will yet be an intercessor for us. I feel she was not really *right* in her mind and consequently not as accountable as we might imagine but oh! what trouble & sorrow one wrong headed person like her can create. May God preserve us from such another and may she rest in peace—

Most commentators believe that the Sacramento community became an independent congregation due to the creation of the Sacramento diocese in 1886. This earlier note indicates that plans for an independent foundation were discussed almost twenty years earlier. Mary Baptist gives no reasons for the Archbishop's decision in the matter.

Date: February 7, 1867
To: Mother Assistant residing in Sacramento
From: Mary Baptist Russell
Source: *Annals*, SOMB, I: 383

You will see by this that our good Abp does not approve of making St. Joseph's "Stand alone" yet awhile, so of course that point is settled——. F. Prendergast our recently appointed confessor is now engaged in the Choir at his new duty and I am just returned from a "Bath in the Precious Blood" as M.M. F. expresses it in the Guide. May God be praised for His infinite mercy in the institution of that sweet Sacrament. Tho' the Abp. still says *no* about the Fair I hope he may yet yield, but if *not,* it will be God's will and what else do we desire—I hope Sr. Francis will take the Infants as there are many objections (besides the trouble) to their being at the Asylum.

One of the qualities of Mary Baptist was her ability to enter into solid friendships with the church leaders of her time. Her relationship with Archbishop Alemany was one of respect, support and friendship. This letter reveals her freedom of spirit in requesting changes in church ritual as well as her spiritual insight into the liturgy.

Date: May 30, 1867
To: Rev. Joseph Sadoc Alemany
From: Sister Mary Baptist Russell
Source: *Annals*, SOMB,'I: 388-391

1867
Most Reverend and dear Father,

In a few days I expect to resign my post as Superior of this Community. I am sorry you are not here to give me a general *absolvo* for all my delinquencies, indeed had I known you were leaving I would have had many things to say to your Grace, but it is too late now. As you expect soon to be in Rome, I have decided on asking you to obtain some favors for us from the Holy Father. Many Indulgences have been from time to time granted to the "Sisters of Mercy" *residing* in *Ireland,* and it appears, it is necessary to apply *specially* for an extension of these privileges to those who reside in any other country. I was not aware of this until lately; hence, we never made the application till now, when we hope your Grace will petition them for us. I take for granted it is unnecessary to *specify* them.

We have long wished we had the privilege of solemnizing in some particular way the 5th of July, on which day in 1841 our Rules were confirmed by his Holiness, Gregory 16th , and the 12th of December, the day on which our Beloved Foundress and her first two companions made their vows. A. D. 1831. Being a Religious yourself, your Grace understands what is usually observed on such occasions in your own & other Orders, so we will leave it to you entirely what to ask, the usual Collects, etc., of thanksgiving occurred to me. If you are good enough to obtain any such privileges for us, please see that *all* Convents of our Order, no matter where located, share in them. Like Abraham in converse with the "Lord" as I proceed I feel encouraged to say more tho' what I am about to say may appear foolish & unreasonable, but no matter I will mention it and your Grace will let it go no further if it is, as I almost fear, foolish. Whenever the Feast of our Lady of Mercy occurs, I feel a regret we have not a *Mass* more appropriate to the Day, and the Order. I always feel a regret the Gospel is not that where our Lord is represented at the Day of Judgment granting the Kingdom of Heaven to the Elect in reward for exercising the *works of Mercy.* Then as *Collect,* I would suggest the prayer—

> O God, who under the protection of the Mother of Thy Son, was pleased, that the Order of Mercy, should be instituted, in Thy Church, for the relief of the suffering, and the instruction of the ignorant, vouchsafe that they to whom Thou has granted this holy vocation may faithfully and efficaciously dispense Thy mercies on earth and thereby come to the enjoyment of Thy Divine Presence in Heaven, thro' Jesus Christ, our Lord. Amen.

I fear this seems presumptuous of me, knowing the Ancient & much honored Order of Mercy for the Redemption of Captives still exists, but I do not mean to put our recent & humble Order in comparison with it, far less do I expect it to get the preference. All I mean is that if it were agreeable to the "Powers that be," we would be so grateful for the privileges of having the changes in the Mass on this day in our *Convent Chapels only.* Now tho' I have nerved myself to explain this, I am sensible it may be altogether preposterous and if so, I must only ask your Grace to *forget* it and to let it go no further. Sister Mary Francis begs to remind your Grace of the Petition presented with your permission some months ago begging the Apostolic Benediction for "St. Mary's Society" and that an Indulgence might be accorded to the Members (with the usual conditions) on the day of entrance, on the Feast of the Holy Name of Mary, and at the hour of death.

I will now bring this long epistle to a close by begging your blessing for myself and each member of the Community.

I remain your Grace's most obedient Servant in J.C.,

Sister Mary Baptist Russell,
Superior, Sisters of Mercy.

Response

Lucerne, Switzerland
September 10th, 1870

Dear in Christ Sister,

Having at last received the Spiritual favors which your good Society desired, I send them enclosed with a hearty Holy blessing from the Holy Father to them and to all the Sisters. The other favor about the Mass contains greater difficulty. I had expected that the Council would not take but a few months but it seems such important matters demand much time. In a few weeks the heavy work may commence again, and I may have to attend, unless troubles cause the postponement of the Council, in which case I would at once go home. Now I may have to visit Ireland on business, otherwise I would expect soon to return to the Holy City.

Ask all your Community and Sister M. Francis with all her Society to continue their holy prayers, which with those of others have no doubt done much to avert trouble in Rome. In particular I must ask a share in their prayers for myself.

Yours truly in Christ,
+Joseph Alemany, ASF

This letter is one which relates some of Mary Baptist's hospital stories. It is clear that the spiritual well-being on those served was foremost in her mind. Catholic belief during the period in which Mary Baptist lived, emphasized the importance of being baptized before death. In Mary's Baptist's mind, baptism was the doorway to heaven and all efforts to open that doorway for another were holy.

Date of Letter: March 27, 1869
From: Sister M. B. Russell
To: Rev. Patrick O'Neill, parish priest of Rostrevor
Source: LMMB, 77-79

Smallpox Hospital,
San Francisco, Cal., March 27, 1869.

Dear Rev. Father: As Sister Mary Aquin [Russell] is no longer in Rostrevor and as I am not sure of the name of any of the sisters, I will take the liberty of introducing to *you* my very dear friends, Mr. and Mrs. Kelly and their party, and beg you to introduce them to the inmates of your sweet little Convent.

They are traveling for the purpose of seeing the beauties of their native land, and, in my opinion, in no place could so many lovely views be found in so small a compass as in the vicinity of *Rostrevor.*

You will be glad to know that *this* Hospital has given us many opportunities for promoting the salvation of souls. I must tell you of one that was *undoubtedly* saved almost miraculously yesterday. The evening before, about seven o'clock, a carriage brought to this door a half distracted father and mother with their *only* son, aged six years, with the prevailing disorder in a virulent form. The rules of the Hospital require a *special* permit from the head officer of the Board to enable any friends to remain with the sick, so the poor mother had to leave the child with us and go back to the city for this document.

We soon saw the child was dying, and we thought he might not live through the night; and, knowing the negligence and want of faith of so many in this country, we began to fear it had never been baptized, and, not having in the hurry even ascertained the name or nationality of the parents, we had no means of judging. So at nine o'clock p.m., I gave it conditional baptism, and most providential it was I did so, as the mother returned soon after and turned out to be the most bigoted *Baptist,* but one that saw no use in baptizing a *child,* and, as she never left him one instant till he expired, we should have had no chance of pouring the regenerating waters on his head, had we deferred it one *half hour.*

This reminds me of a visit we paid once, ostensibly to comfort the *mother,* but in reality to baptize the *child* who was on the point of death. Sister Mary Francis, my companion, was provided a small bottle of water, and, by way of having better light to look at the little one, took him in her arms to the window, while I in the warmth of my sympathy pressed the mother's hands. Soon the little one was laid in its crib, the child of God, and very soon after it was, I trust, in the enjoyment of His presence.

It is terrible to reflect on the hundreds calling themselves *Christians* who have never been baptized, that are met with in this country. I do not know the exact number, but think it must now be over a hundred who have received that Sacrament during this epidemic in this one hospital. The Catholics afflicted have been very few indeed, and, as a general thing, very fine men. Often remarks have been made on their edifying deaths by persons of other denominations who were present.

Soon after Dr. Miller's appointment, I was assisting a fine young Irishman, "James Fennell," in his last moments; he was *choking,* and in as great agony as any mortal ever suffered, his face purple and his big frame convulsed. I thought him long speechless when the poor fellow, making a great effort, pronounced distinctly the holy names *Jesus, Mary* and *Joseph.* The doctor and nurse, both Protestants, were evidently much impressed but turned away and left me alone, much to my relief. I found afterwards that Sister M. Borgia [Ward], one of my companions, had explained to him the indulgence granted for repeating those holy names when dying. A German Lutheran said to me afterwards, "I see you Catholics do more for your dying than we do." And true for him, as the poor Protestants are left alone to breathe out their last and the instant they have ceased to breathe the sheet is drawn over their faces and off they are carried to the "dead house." We get too much gratitude, I fear, from the survivors. Still, as it is not *that* we seek, I trust it will not lessen our merit.

I will enclose an article in yesterday's *Pacific,* a religious journal of the Protestant stamp. You will please let James read it, as it may interest him, and I have no a second copy and neither have I now time to write to him. I have come to the end of my paper without expressing a hope that you are enjoying tolerable health, and that your flock in both the half parishes are your comfort *here,* and that they will be your glory *hereafter.* The Sister I mentioned above is a convert, and loses no opportunity of begging prayers for the conversion of her aged father, her brother, and two sisters. Please remember them sometimes at Mass, and I will feel very grateful; and pray for me sometimes also.

Begging your blessing, I remain, dear Rev. Father,
Ever most respectfully in Jesus Christ,
Your obedient, humble servant,
Sister Mary B. Russell,
Sister of Mercy.

Not every request for sisters could be granted. In this letter to Bishop Blanchet, Mary Baptist bases her decision to decline his invitation on the volume of work already undertaken by the small community.

Date: July 6, 1870
To: Revd. F. N. Blanchet, Abp of Oregon
From: Mary Baptist Russell
Source: *Annals,* SOMB, I: 504-505

Most Revd. Father,

I did not know that Father Delorme was acting *officially* when he called on his return from Europe and whatever promise I gave him was merely conditional. Since Father Delorme was here, our duties have increased so much that, far from having Sisters to spare, we have not sufficient for the work on hand. Besides the Hospital with an average of one Hundred, the Magdalen Asylum with from eighty to 90 Inmates and attached to it the Female Industrial School with over sixty young girls who are placed in it by the Authorities; besides these Home duties we visit the City & State Prisons, the Co. Hospital & Boy's Industrial School and the Sick in their own houses, so that I assure you we are not idle, and happy as we should be to labor in your Grace's portion of the Great Vineyard, it is impossible for us to accept your gracious invitation.

In Her Own Words
1871–1880

One of the great needs Mary Baptist identified in San Francisco was a home for a larger House of Mercy, a shelter for young working women. Sister Mary Francis Benson was a major proponent of the undertaking and was able to raise some funds through the St. Mary's Society to defray its cost. Sister Mary Francis was moderator of the Society which was dedicated to prayer and to raising funds to assist young women in need of housing. Since all Church property belonged to the Church, sisters were not allowed to purchase property, sell property or take on major indebtedness without the permission of church officials. Sister Mary Francis believed she had the permission of Archbishop Alemany to pursue the project. The Archbishop did not feel permission had been given. This letter, like those to Bishop O'Connell, shows the diplomacy with which Mary Baptist handled conflicts with Church authorities.

Date: June 2, 1873
To: Archbishop Alemany
From: Mary Baptist Russell
Source: *Annals*, SOMB, I: 561-562

Dear & Most Revd. Father:

I received your letter yesterday and would have answered it immediately, but that Sunday is always a busy day with us and in addition to our ordinary duties we yesterday held the Chapter for filling the Offices of Assistant, Bursar and Mistress of Novices. These posts were assigned respectively to Sisters Mary Gabriel [Brown], Rafael [McCormick], and Borgia [Ward]. I trust the Holy Ghost guided us and that we will have your Grace's blessing & prayers—

Now for the subject of your letter. Sr. Mary Francis thinks your Grace must forget the conversation she had with you on the subject when you held the Visitation. She considers you gave her a cordial approval and only warned her not to use up all she had for the support of the old women and she did not understand that you required her to apply to the *Council*. I do not know how to account for the misunderstanding, but I know Sister has ever since told us that your Grace gave her full power to carry out her design and if it were not that we have already enough work for half as many more Sisters, I would be more than delighted as the protection of young women is one of our primary duties.

The Building will cost about $6650.00. Sister has in Bank to the credit of the Home about $6000.00; to the credit of St. Mary's Society $3600.00 and she has collected $1500.00 for the House of Mercy & expects a considered amount in addition from girls who have been at various times in the house or look forward to being in it when unemployed. I beg an immediate reply as the work will of course be stopped until we hear from you.

Begging your Grace's blessing
I remain your obt. Sert in J. C.
Sr. Mary B. Russell
Sr. of Mercy

Sister Mary Baptist Mogan was sent to the Grass Valley foundation by Mary Baptist Russell. She became ill in 1872 and returned to San Francisco for cancer surgery. There was an attempt on the part of her sisters in San Francisco to recall her to that city since she was still a member of their foundation. Indications are that Sister Mary Baptist Mogan did not wish to leave Grass Valley. This most likely is the background for this inquiry by Archbishop Alemany.

Date: November 25, 1873
To: Archbishop Alemany
From: Mary Baptist Russell
Source: *Annals*, SOMB, I: 567-569
Most Revd. Father

According to your desire I will now endeavor to state briefly the circumstances under which Sister Mary Baptist Mogan was sent to Grass Valley and the bearings of the case with regard to her recall. She went there in January, 1863 at the request of the then Superioress Sr. Mary Bapt Synan, to assist her in any way she might find useful.

In the following May she was elected or appointed Superioress and a few months after, sent home Sr. Mary B. Synan whose health was very poor at the time, and Sr. Mary B. Mogan has continued in office ever since. No precise time was named for which she was lent, but there never was the slightest intention on our part of giving her up entirely and your Grace will see, by referring to the Chapter on "Establishment" in our Guide a copy of which I send, that this could not be done without her own formal application to the Chapter and the consent thereof ratified by your Grace's approval.

Our Rules do not prescribe all this form but our customs as expressed in the Guide are conformable to the usual practice of all Religious Orders; and the length of time that has been allowed to elapse, nor the fact of not naming any precise time for which she was lent does not alter the case in the least, as I know from facts that have come under my own observation.

The Convent in Kinsale sent a foundation to Derby, England from which every member of the original Community has been withdrawn with one solitary exception and the last was withdrawn after the lapse of full fifteen years. In this instance the House in Derby would fain have retained the Sister in question, and she herself would prefer to remain, but both yielded knowing the Community in Kinsale had the *right* and had reasons for what they did. If Sr. Mary Baptist Mogan wishes to withdraw from this Community, she should send in her petition to that effect which I will lay before the Sisters to ascertain if they are willing to accept her resignation. It will then be necessary to get your Grace's approval to make the act of Chapter valid.

Of our reasons for the change we proposed last Spring, I need say nothing as you already understand the matter sufficiently. I will not, therefore, enter on the disagreeable subject and will merely add that we will daily implore God to direct your decision for His own glory and the good of all concerned.

Respectfully begging your blessing
I remain your Grace's obt servant in J. C.
Sr. Mary B. Russell
Sister of Mercy

In order to obtain funding from the State for their charges, the sisters had to submit a report of their ministry every two years. Below is the report for the period 1873/74.

Date: Jan 2, 1874
To: Assembly
From: Mary Baptist Russell
Source: *Annals*, SOMB, I: 596-597

Gentlemen

We beg to present the Report of the Mgd. Asylum for the two years ending Jan 1ˢᵗ /74

Your Honorable Body are aware that for some years, the young girls committed to the Industrial School have been confided to our care. This year a large wing has been added to the Building for the special accommodations and they are now entirely separated from the other Inmates, so that henceforth they will form two distinct Institutions on the same premises. They took possession of the new apartments in Nov. of last year; but in order to avoid confusion & unnecessary trouble, the tabular statement appended is drawn up in the usual form; *hereafter* a distinct report of *each* department will be furnished. As the additional Building and other improvements have cost over $15, 090, the debt on the Institution is considerably increased. The Sisters will therefore feel doubly grateful for any assistance your Honorable Body may be good enough to award them.

Not wishing to intrude longer on your valuable time, we will conclude this brief appeal by respectfully recommending the Institution to the generous consideration of your Honble Body.

Sister Mary B. Russell

This long letter to Arthur and Mary Hamill contains not only family news but extensive information concerning the various works of the sisters at this time. Of particular interest is the description of the prison visitation at San Quentin and the various works done at the House of Mercy. Mary Baptist's love for nature is seen in the discussion of flowers.

Date of letter:February 8, 1874
From:M. Baptist Russell
To: Arthur and Mary
Source: Archives, JPD

St. Mary's Hospital, San Francisco, Cal.
Feb. 8th, 1874

My dear Arthur and Mary,

I am taking a big sheet, fit for a Lawyer's brief, to answer your last truly welcome and interesting package. It was the most satisfactory I have had for years, I may say since poor Mamma lost her power of letter writing. Her last would have been unintelligible had not SM Aquin accompanied it with an explanation. When I opened the package I remember putting it aside to read last, thinking it was from some of the *little* children just attempting to write. It was so unlike dear Mamma's legible hand.

Your photographs please me so much. I see very little change in either of you and what change I do remark is an improvement. You are both a little *fuller* in face and figure and have not such an anxious expression as I fancy you had. I hope you are both less so in reality as well as in appearance. Christian Philosophy is to be content with what God allows and this we must all aim at with God's help, but indeed, you have both reason to rejoice and be glad for you have many very great blessings and have been exempt from very severe trials. The death of your two fine girls was, of course, a trial but not a *bitter* one and their deaths must not be looked on as a loss for they are the only ones really safe and therefore the ones about whom you may most rejoice.

It seems to me Alice is like her Mother and Emily like her Father and so is Arthur John. I am sorry he is not as enthusiastic about his profession as you might desire, but he may come to like it with a little further experience or, like his father and uncle, may change it yet and still have no great reason to regret having devoted his early days to the study of law. I hope his eyes are perfectly strong now—You will, no doubt, miss Ellen Jennings but your Young Ladies have reason to be grateful for the advantages they enjoyed for so many years.

You don't know the pleasure it gave me to see you show the few remaining members of that admirable family all the little attention in your power. They are worthy of it and having been so severely tried, they will appreciate it all the more and it will have a hundred fold reward. You know the words of our Lord after He had denounced the Pharisees for entertaining only those who could invite them in return "But you, when you give a banquet, invite the *poor*, etc. etc. and recompense shall be made them by the Lord." I would like you always to say something kind to them for me even if hurry should cause me to forget it myself.

I heard of dear old Mrs. Hamilton's death soon after it occurred and did not fail to include her among our deceased friends. There is a Miss Cassin, sister of Mrs. J. Cassin, of somewhere *near* Dublin who knew her pretty well and from her I heard of the family for the last five years. She was very old even when I saw her *twenty-five* years ago, older I think than Mamma and see how long she survived her. May God have mercy on them all.

Is it in Glasnevin you have your two darlings laid? It is nicely kept, but the poor old graveyard in Newry, tho' a sanctified spot, was desolate looking in the extreme. Here the cemeteries are laid out with walks and trees and are cheerful looking but, in general, there is too much gingerbread show about the tombs etc. for my taste. In the work department of the "Mater Misericordiae," as we call our House of Mercy, we make Habits and Shrouds for Ladies and gentlemen young and old and I often contrast the grandeur of them with the plain calico shrouds I was accustomed to see at home. Quantities of white satin, cords, buttons and ribands [sic] and lace on those for Ladies and the coffins are just as great a contrast to our Home ones. I hear, however, I would hardly know Ireland. It is so changed since my time and may with regard to these things as well as others.

I wish you could see *our* sweet little cemetery. It is at the Magd. Asylum where we have about 7 acres of ground. We keep the cemetery green by constant irrigation. Without this it would be parched by the long dry season and fresh breezes that keep our summers so cool. We have eight Sisters already laid in their narrow homes and four or five of the Penitents. *They* have one half appropriated to themselves but only those who make their Consecration for life are buried there. The others are interred in the common Cemetery. We have in it a small mortuary chapel in which some of the Penitents say the office for the Dead on the first Sunday of each month and in which is a mock coffin with a skeleton (drawing) on top, appropriate pictures and mottoes as the dead Christ, death of St. Joseph and St. Patrick. All these little things help and interest the Inmates whose *world* is limited by the enclosure and for whom we have to provide every little comfort in our power. You would wonder how holy some of them are but, of course, it is the smallest number.

Besides the Magdalens we have in the same establishment, but entirely separated from them, from forty to fifty girls under 18 and some of them are not over 10 who are placed there by the City authorities for being found wandering thru' the Streets or in dangerous places. For these we have a regular school in the house to be taught the ordinary branches. The Penitents do very beautiful needlework of all description. They are just now embroidering four Banners for the 17 of March and a Canopy for St. Ignatius Church besides any quantity of the finest Baby linens and under clothes. They keep 14 machines in constant use tho' the greater part of their work is done by *hand*. The Asylum is over two miles from the Hospital but as Street Cars run in that direction it is quite convenient to go and come. The "Mater" and the "Home for Aged and Infirm Females" as also our Day Schools for Boys and Girls are on the same block as the Hospital but open on different Streets.

We have forty-five or fifty boys under 9 years of whom Sister M. Aquin (Mary Martin) has charge with a postulant to assist her. The girls are regularly graded and have a very convenient school with a half dozen classrooms besides the two principal assembly rooms, but it is only a frame one story building, so it does not present a very grand exterior.

In the Home are fifty one dear old women. Some knit, some sew, some do nothing, but all *pray* and indeed it often astonishes me to see some that are feeble enough, in the chapel before ourselves every morning and if we had a dozen Masses they would wait for all. I was showing a few ladies thru' the place lately when one old Soul, Mrs. Willet, astonished me by telling the Ladies that I used to sit watching her when she was in the cradle and when she had her own children she followed my example. This was the first sign of doting we had noticed but many times since we have heard her talking in a similar strain. Between Nurse Crisp and Kitty Murray you have a pretty good beginning for a similar Institution. It speaks well for all parties to hear you have them so long in your service. I remember Kitty and Nurse too. It was she had charge of Alice the day she visited me in Baggot St. when passing thro' Dublin coming here.

One of the branches of industry we carry on in the Mater is making *Bed Comforters* and the old women *open* the cotton batting for the more active hands. Here we have about as many machines as at the Asylum and lately we introduced *water power* to work some of the heavier machines. It is very simple and leaves the feet free and is, of course, less fatiguing. I believe California has the credit of first applying water to this purpose.

In one of the large work rooms we had the Crib for the last two years. Our Congregation has increased so of late that we could not spare the usual place in our Lady's chapel. Last year we got very fine figures almost five feet high, all except the Infant are *wood* elegantly carved and painted. We have one set of Kings *standing* who are used during the early part of the time to represent them on their journey and another set on their knees which we put in the Cave on Epiphany. We have also two B.V.M. one *kneeling* while the Divine Infant is in the Manger and one *sitting* in such a position as to hold the Infant in her arms in the most natural position. This one is used for the Epiphany and its Octave. These changes make the whole very much more interesting even to big people. These figures cost near a thousand dollars but the offerings of the people this year and the tickets of admission last year have already paid for them and how hereafter we will not have the trouble of dressing them each time as formerly. If I could send you a little poem written on our Representation of Bethlehem by a young lady you would be delighted with it. It was published in one of the weekly papers and I tried to get a dozen copies but could not. She very kindly wrote it in order to attract attention to the Industrial Department of the Mater which, being only lately established earns the patronage of the public.

We have had very *constant* but not very heavy rain this winter and Farmers expect plentiful Harvest in consequence. Indeed, all they need here to have two or three crops in the year is rain although great difficulty is the want of facilities for transporting their produce but this is lessening every year. We had a free pass on the boats to Sac. ever since we came to California until the great C.P.R.R. company bought out the C.S.R. Co. about two years ago. They then gave us half fare pass and this was a great matter but when we applied for a renewal of it at New Years it was refused. We still travel free all through the City; indeed, I doubt if there are many places where religious have been more favored hitherto but some prophecy that times will change soon with us as with the religious in Continental Europe. All the Public Institutions are open to us whenever we can visit them, and we do so all we can as so much good can be thereby accomplished.

The Sisters at the Asylum visit the Co. Hos. four days each week and go there without changing their dress as the Hospital adjoins their property and the authorities were kind enough to allow us to open a door between, the key of which we keep. This very day two Sisters are gone to San Quentin, the State Prison. The number in this Establishment is a thousand men on an average and about twenty women. We are the only Ladies admitted during the week when the men are in the yards or shops at their different occupations, but on Sundays the poor prisoners are kept in close confinement except for a short time in the foreroom and then Ladies are admitted.

The Sisters give them papers which we collect on purpose such as the Tablet, Pilot, Monitor, etc. etc. Also books, clothes and every thing they can pick up to add to the comforts of the poor creatures, very many of whom are really good hearted fellows and appreciate the most trifling kindness shown. We have gotten pardons of three or four who were condemned for life but were in consumption or some other incurable disease and then ended their days here. We have now one old man, entirely helpless, who we discharged a few months ago after spending sixteen years there. He could gladly have remained, as he has neither funds nor friends. They are provided with a certain *quantity* and *quality* of clothing while in prison, but as this would identify them as prisoners anywhere, nothing delights them more than the receipt of a valise on the eve of their departure with an outfit even if it is second hand. Indeed as we tell the Sisters who visit San Quentin they have a *pet* duty, at the same time it requires a little nerve to go there the first few times but we change the Sisters as little as possible in this and all such duties. San Quentin is on the opposite side of the Bay about an hour & half sail from the city and a delightful sail it is for the view is fine.

You know this bay is proverbial for beauty but it lacks one essential in my eyes, the proximity of high mountains, what made Carlingford Bay so lovely. I am sorry to hear of Ellen Russell's delicacy and hope it may not last. What a blessing good health is. May God be praised for the excellent health I enjoy all the time and the little sprain I gave my ankle has left no bad effect whatsoever. T.G. Neither of you ever pay a visit to Newry but it is surely recorded in the next letter. Such an event could not be overlooked. I heard already of the time you spent there. Indeed dear S.M. Aquin [Russell] is very good in writing but do you know that big brown package from S.M. Bernard [Hamill] did not contain one line from herself, all old letters. Still it was very interesting & she *promises* a letter soon. You will be amused to hear I am going to send your photographs *on a visit*. Our Cousins in Columbus will be glad to see them and I love to give them pleasure for they seem to cling to the *past* with great affection and love to hear of old friends—Mr. Fred Hamilton remained a long time a Widower. His daughter must be quite grown, older I think than your Alice, and I am sure is a nice girl if like her Mother.

Mary Martin was grateful for your kind inquiries and desires to be remembered to you both. She is somewhat frail but a sensible useful little body and very happy tho' her Brother in Law's unlooked for death made her anxious for a time regarding her dear old Mother. Tell Margaret my next letter will be to her surely. There is nothing but good news from her people too, thank God.

I suppose, dear Mary, you manage to have a garden at Howth at all counts as you were always so fond of flowers. We have a small hot house (but with no artificial means of heating it) and we place any nice plants on the steps of the Altar of our Lady when in bloom. There is now a lovely pink Camellia with twenty two flowers on it. The high wind impairs our flower garden very much in this City, otherwise the climate is extremely beautiful but, tho' unpleasant, I believe the winds are what we may thank for the moderate temperature we enjoy compared to places not far from us. Now my big letter is at an end and a very unladylike production it is, but as I write seldom and my letters have to travel so far, I feel they ought to be of some size. I wish you both an abundance of graces and blessings and the same to your loved family *each* and all. I hope you will all remember me in your prayers always. Ever your aft.

Sister M. B. Russell, S.M.

During the period of economic depression in the 1870s the sisters provided an employment office to find situations for those looking for work. While this was not a new ministry, the office was relocated at this time. In this letter Mary Baptist reports to Archbishop Alemany on the progress of the ministry.

Date: August 16, 1875
To Bishop Alemany
From: Mary Baptist Russell
Source: *Annals*, SOMB, I: 610-611

To His Grace, Most Revd. J. S. Alemany,

In the beginning of Feb., this Office was removed to it's present location. Since that date 1050 persons have applied for situations. Not more than 50 of these were under 18 years, quite a large proportion were new arrivals in the Country, among them natives of almost every Country in Europe but an overwhelming majority were Irish. During this period 764 families applied for help in various capacities, but owing to various circumstances, perhaps not more than half were supplied.

It may be well to explain that the names of servants are not entered a second time; while the names of families applying for help are entered every time they do so. The monthly expenditure of the Office is about $100.00 and to fit it up and supply the necessary furniture &c &c required an outlay of $129.00. The receipts during the past six months amount to $475.25 including $150.00 donated by Revd. J. Prendergast. The needle work sold for the Mater Misericordiae realized $228.30 which is, of course, a help, as the Inmates have to be instructed in that branch of Industry. In the expenditure we have not included what may be given to the Poor who apply in greater numbers than could be supposed.

The fact of the Office being patronized by so few of our Catholic families cannot be accounted for except by the supposition that they imagine all their little domestic difficulties will be revealed to the Sisters, not knowing the Rules of the Order forbid all inquiry on such subjects; and that what is unavoidably learned is never repeated nor commented upon. The girls are also in many instances, deterred from applying from the fear of their most trifling faults being reported to the Sisters. It is hoped time will remove all these prejudices and that all parties will ere long cordially cooperate with the Sisters in this good work which is certainly no small tax on their time & patience as well as on their funds. This latter difficulty will however be gradually removed and is, consequently, of minor importance.

Sr. Mary B. Russell, *Sister of Mercy*

Mary Baptist's response to an inquiry about the various works of the sisters provides a thumbnail sketch of the growth of the community during its first twenty years in California. In San Francisco, the first eight sisters had grown to a community of seventy. Mary Baptist also notes the other Mercy foundations found within the state and the numbers of persons served by them.

Date: Jan 3, 1876
To: Mr. J. OK. Murray
From: Sister Mary Baptist Russell
Source: *Annals*, SOMB, I: 616-618

Dear Sir,

Your Circular was only received a few days ago during our Annual Retreat and, consequently it was impossible for us to answer it sooner. I know so little of any of the Houses of our Order in the East, I could not answer any of your queries except the first three which have no doubt been answered already from other quarters.

In California there are six Houses 1st the one from which I write founded in 1854. 2nd St. Joseph's, Sacramento City a Branch from this House founded in 1857. 3rd The Magdalen Asylum in the suburbs of this City founded in 1860 and also a Branch of this House. 4th The Sacred Heart Convent in Grass Valley, Nevada Co. affiliation from this House and founded in 1863. 5th The Convent of Mercy, Yreka, Siskiyou Co. a filiation from New Hampshire and founded in 1870. 6th St. Joseph's Institute, Eureka, Humboldt Co. a filiation from New York and founded in 1871.

The first House mentioned & it's Branches have about 70 Members (including Novices) of whom 50 are Irish, 12 Irish descent, 2 Germans, 2 German descent, 2 Native American, 1 Spanish and 1 Canadian. In *this* City conduct a private Hospital with an average of 90 patients, a free school with 350 pupils; a Magdalen Asylum with about 80 Inmates, a Juvenile Reformatory with 60; a "Home for Aged & Infirm Females" with 90 poor old creatures; and a House of Mercy for Servants and other respectable young females without a home in which are usually about 45 Inmates.

In Sacramento we have a free school with an average of 250 pupils, and a half Orphanage with about 55 Inmates. In both these Cities, particularly San Francisco, we have extensive visitation of the poor & sick in their own Houses as also of the Prisons and other public Institutions in all of which we have ever since our arrival in the Country been most courteously received for which kindness we feel much indebted to the Authorities.

The Sisters in Grass Valley have large free schools for boys & girls and a large Orphanage for girls and another for Boys. The precise number of Inmates I cannot give but I know it is considerable. In Yreka I believe an Academy with the Visitation of the Sick is their only duty and in Eureka the same but you have probably communicated directly with these Houses.

I remain respectfully yours &c
Sr. M. B. Russell
Sisters of Mercy

This is another of the reports to the State Legislature required for funding. By 1876, 934 women had been served by the Asylum

Date: January 10, 1876
To: Honbl the Senate & Assembly
From: Sister Mary Baptist Russell
Source: *Annals*, SOMB, I: 632-4

Magdalen Asylum, San Bruno Road
San Francisco, Cal.
Jan. 10th, 1876
To the Honbl the Senate & Assembly of the State of California

Gentlemen:

We beg to present the Report of the Magd. Asylum for the two years ending Jan 1st, 1876

Your Honble Body is already aware that for the last two years the young girls of the Industrial School are entirely separated from the other Inmates and consequently they are not included in the tabular statement annexed——

It is not for us to speak of our labors in the charge of the Asylum. We will merely say that it calls for ceaseless exertion and much solicitude; but we feel more than repaid by the happy results of our labors evidenced by the numerable instances of thorough reform among the Inmates especially of late years. We need hardly remind you that for many reasons, the Inmates of the Asylum "Magdalens" as they are called are, as a class, the least adapted to contribute to their own support altho' those long in the Institute are now most industrious and have brought many branches of needle work to great perfection.

While gratefully acknowledging our past obligations, we must again respectfully recommend the Asylum to your charitable consideration, as, in addition to a small standing debt we are just now obliged to maintain a further burden of over $5,000.00 widening & grading the Streets, putting in Sewers and removing and building fences &c.

For whatever relief your Honble Body may kindly affort us in these circumstances, we, the Sisters in charge will feel most grateful.

Sr. Mary B. Russell, Mary G. Brown, & Mary C. Fleming.
Sisters of Mercy

Individuals frequently sought letters of recommendation from Mary Baptist. In these letters she is brief and candid. Below is a sample of one such reference she sent to Miss Armor, Foundress of the Holy Family Sisters.

Date of letter: March 9, 1876
From: M. Baptist Russell
To: Miss Armor
Source: Archives, Holy Family Sisters, Fremont, CA.

Dear Miss Armor

Mrs. Duffy the Bearer is quite a respectable young woman from Cincinnati. The Rev. D. F. Bender who was here for his health last Summer told us her family were excellent people and he felt very much grieved at the misfortunate marriage she had contracted. I think she is worthy of anything you can do for her.

Yours affect in J.C.
Sister Mary B. Russell
Sr. of Mercy

March 9th /76

It would seem from this letter that Archbishop Alemany sought Mary Baptist's opinion on the rules governing religious elections. No indication is given referring to any specific incident that prompted his request for information.

Date: May, 1876
To: Bishop Alemany
From: Sister Mary Baptist Russell
Source: *Annals*, SOMB, I: 660

Most Revd Father,

When the office of Superior becomes vacant by death, the election is held as soon as convenient no matter what part of the year it may be, but the *three years* during which a Superior governs is counted from the Feast of the Ascension nearest her Election; for instance *I* was appointed the first time in January and governed for three years from the *following* Feast of the Ascension. If the Bishop & Community accept the refusal of an Assistant during the short time that elapses between the death of one Superior and the election of another, I would imagine she would cease to be Assistant and that the Bishop should appoint one to take charge until the regular Election. Seven form our Chapter so until there are seven professed choir Sisters, there can be no Election and *all* the Offices must be filled by the Bishop who generally advises with the Senior.

Your Grace's most obt. Sert. in J. Christ
Sr. Mary B. Russell, *Sister of Mercy*

This letter was sent to Mother Dolores of the Holy Family Sisters upon the occasion of the dedication of their convent. Given her attention to detail and her love for fine craftsmanship, the tabernacle veil was not up to Mary Baptist's standards but, practical in nature, it had to do. Mary Baptist did not attend the open house but asked to come at a later time. Perhaps this was due to her dislike for crowds.

Date of letter:January 2, 1879
From: M. Baptist Russell
To: "My dear Sisters"
Source: Archives, Holy Family Sisters, Fremont, California

My dear Sisters,

I fear the veil for your Tabernacle is not exactly what you desired. I am not quite pleased with it myself. It is a little puckered and also there are other things I wish changed had I seen it in time, but such as it is, we send it as our offering to your little Choir and we hope it will remind you to recommend us occasionally to our Divine Lord & Master. I know you will have no objection to our visiting your new House and I intend some day, when I have leisure, to pay you a visit.

I hope you are all well and that this year may be one of blessings to you all.

Again begging your prayers I remain your affectionately in J. Christ

> Sister Mary Baptist Russell
> Sisters of Mercy

Magdalen Asylum
> Jan. 2nd 1879

Once in her lifetime Mary Baptist returned to her native Ireland. Mary Baptist returned as the companion of Sister Mary Columba Stokes who was called to Ireland on urgent family business. It was an opportunity for Mary Baptist to recruit new sisters for the California mission but it was also a time a great sadness. The following two letters tell of that trip. The first describes part of the journey while the second reveals the great pain Mary Baptist experienced in the death of her young companion. Mary Baptist's own sister Sarah, accompanied her for part of the journey.

Date: January 1879
To: Sisters in San Francisco
From: Sister Mary Baptist Russell
Source: *Annals*, SOMB, I: 675-679

We left the Convent Baggot St at 6 1/4. The Cars run out on the Pier at Kingstown so you have merely to step from them on the Steamer. Soon we were both sea sick so were not sorry when a good natured Sailor told us to look at the Breakwater & solid piece of granite masonry which runs out a mile & half into the Sea from Hollyhead with a light House at the point. The Express Train was in waiting, and in a few minutes, we were whirling along at a rapid pace with hot water at your feet which we appreciated doubly as Sea Sickness makes one so chilly.

The Isle of Anglesea is rocky & bare but the people must be comfortable for I did not see *one* poor hut. I was on the look out for the Memo Straits and had just pointed them out to my companion with a statue on the bank when all of a sudden we were in darkness, and I found the train runs thro' a tunnel *under* the Straits not *over* the well-known suspension bridge as I expected. The scenery of north Wales is picturesque in the extreme; a good part of the way the cars ran along the sea at the base of high & very precipitous mountains, most of them so rocky that even a blade of grass was not to be seen and at certain places the high mountains covered with snow could be seen at a distance.

The towns thro' which we passed seem to have sprung up recently, for I saw no *old* houses, all good stone structures with slate roofs, at Llanduck & Llandale as also at Bangor the majority are of an ornamental style with bay windows &c &c. The shore seems to be admirably adapted for bathing, the beach being sandy and protected by the Great & Little Armes' Head. I was only sorry we went so quickly but I was delighted with the view.

The first part of England we entered was flat & marshy in places but soon we got into rich farming land with neatly trimmed hedges and rows of trees and some towns with stacks of tall chimneys and big furnaces. One thing I remarked, from [when] we left Ireland we saw only three crosses tho' we passed many Churches, so I conclude Catholics are few in North Wales and the part of England thro' which we passed. At Litchfield we had to wait 1 hour for the Derby Train but the day was mild so we did not suffer by it. You will be amused to hear we had to pay P. 1 each for visiting the Ladies Toilet and 2 for washing our hands.

The poor Sisters here are obliged to go to the public church for Mass and indeed it is cold and very trying on the Sisters, the majority of whom are delicate but what can they do? Soon a detached school is to be opened at the other end of town. It will add greatly to their labors, and if they had the support of sympathizing Bishop & Priests it would be hard enough but, as it is, they are to be pitied and at the same time envied.

Date of Letter: April 20, 1879
From: Sister M. B. Russell
To: Arthur Hamill
Source: LMMB, 84-86

Convent of Our Lady of Mercy,
Kinsale, April 20, '79.

My Dearest Arthur:

You will be pained to hear that I have lost my dear Sister Mary Columba. She died at four o'clock yesterday morning and I am just now expecting her two brothers, brother-in-law and her sister; and I assure you I feel no little embarrassment meeting them, for they feel dear Sister's death very deeply. You know already she spent ten days in Tipperary where nothing would exceed the tender care she received. I left there and paid a hurried visit to Thurles and Limerick. While in the latter place, she got Sister M. Joseph Gartlan to write to hasten my return, saying she wanted to reach Kinsale before all her strength was gone. This was her only desire, for she looked on this as next to home, and whenever particularly ill, expressed the hope that, if she were going to die, it might be here. Still, neither of us really imagined she was in danger.

We rested two days in Cork to break the journey, and at last reached Kinsale, two weeks ago tomorrow, just about the time we shall be laying her in the grave. On Easter Eve she was so ill we gave her up, and on the following Monday she received the last Sacraments. I wrote to inform her brother of our fears, but being from home, he did not receive my letter till Tuesday evening. Next day he was here for several hours and found her so much better apparently than he expected that he went off quite relieved.

On Friday I saw her end was approaching, and so wrote him again, and he had my letter in time to prepare him for the telegram announcing her death. About half-past four on Friday she missed me, (I had gone to dinner) and sent for me, and, on my coming in, she embraced me so lovingly, and said: "Don't leave me any more, Mother. You won't have me long now; the great struggle with death is beginning; pray for me, pray for me, and get prayers for me. You won't fret, Mother; you know God's will is best; I am not sorry to die, God's will be done. Poor Michael and the girls. God help them and *He will.*" This was about all she said, except to ask for Reverend Mother, and when she came, she begged for *prayers* and *prayers;* and, when Mother was saying a few kind words, she said so earnestly, "O, don't mind me but pray." I tell you all this to secure your prayers and those of dear Mary, Arthur, Alice, Emily and dear old Kitty. I would be so glad and so grateful if you would all go to Holy Communion, and offer it for her soul on the third Sunday after Easter, the Patronage of St. Joseph.

During the eight or ten hours preceding her death, Sister could not speak, and, as far as we could see, was not even conscious, at least could make no sign of knowing what was said around, though she may have heard it all the time; we were saying to each other it ought to be a lesson to us all, to do all we can for our souls before death comes; for too often the struggle is such as to render it impossible to do much at that awful hour. Well, dear Arthur, all this may not be very interesting to you, but it occupies my mind at present, and I could speak of nothing else.

Now that I am no longer obliged to calculate *when* my sister would be strong enough for the journey, I believe I may say pretty determinedly that we shall sail, please God, on the 30th, and I am arranging to get a young Sister to bear me company, though I might go with one of my "recruits" by letting her enter here, even one week before our departure, but I think it is better to get one who has been some time in a convent. I will go now overland, as the chief reason for preferring the long sea-voyage was that it agreed better with Sister Columba.

I hope, therefore, to reach San Francisco about the 24th of May. I will write to some one and beg whoever it may be to inform the rest of my safe arrival, as I know you will all be anxious. I enclose an *Agnus Dei* and marker for each of you with my fondest love. You always have my prayers and deep affection, and if I never saw Mary, Alice, Emily and Arthur John, for *your* sake they would have the same, but I both know and love them, though I did not see very much of them; and I hope dear Arthur John will get really strong and have everything that the fondest heart could desire. Give each my love most affectionately.

Ever, dear Arthur, Your affectionate sister,

Mary. B. Russell,

Sister of Mercy.

Mary Baptist writes to let her family know that she has arrived safely back in San Francisco after her travels. The fragment also contains some of her humor.

Date of Letter: July 2, 1879 - finished on July 19
From: Sister M. B. Russell
To: Mother Mary Emmanuel, de Sales, Vincent and all in Newry, Rostrevor and Lurgan
Source: LMMB, 106-107

A joint letter is best, as I shall not have much time, and I ought to have written long before this. You know, from others, that I am safe at home since 23rd of May. Next Morning, at 10 o'clock, I got the keys of the house and the following Thursday was made *Boss*. So you see I was *just in time*. I found dear Sister Margaret Mary [Manning] wonderfully changed for the few months I was gone; but she has rallied since and may linger months yet. She came over here for the Election but did not venture to the Chapel. The Archbishop visited her afterwards in the Infirmary and gave her permission to receive Holy Communion twice a week without having kept her fast. I told him how good your Holy Bishop is to your sick, but he only smiled. Dr. Delany only allows it twice a week also.

****

We have a poor cripple here who asked to be enrolled in the scapular on the Feast of the Visitation. The Sister expressed some surprise that he had never been enrolled before. "Well, now, Sister," said the poor fellow, "how could I wear the Scapular of the Blessed Virgin and I telling the boys the cigars I was selling were the best that could be got, and I knowing they weren't? And I used to turn the spotted side to the oranges down, too." Had not the poor fellow a nice conscience? I think I told you of some of the out-of-the-way titles by which I am occasionally addressed. Since I returned I got a letter directed to the "Virgin Mother in Jesus Christ"; *that* was diametrically opposite to *"Baptist Russell, Esq."* I got on another occasion.

****

A thousand loves to each dear Sister in all the houses.

St. Mary's Hospital was often a stopping place for religious who were making their way to other mission. In this letter Mary Baptist describes her visit with the Ursuline sisters but she also befriended others such as the Holy Name Sisters and Franciscan refugees from Mexico.

Date of Letter: October 30, 1880
From: Sister M. B. Russell
To: Unknown
Source: LMMB, 109-111

Our Vicar General came to me last Tuesday to ask me to entertain for a few hours the Ursuline Nuns, who were expected to arrive the following day, en route for Santa Rosa, where they have purchased a house and three acres and are going to open a boarding school. We were, of course, happy to do so and prepared a good lunch in the Community Room for them, and General and Mrs. Rosecrans, young Mr. and Miss. Rosecrans, Father Prendergast the Vicar-General himself. One of the sisters was a daughter of the General, and that was the reason of the whole family's being here.

While the ladies were refreshing themselves after the long journey by the application of soap and water, I had the opportunity of getting into conversation with the gentlemen and having heard that the General owed his conversion to the politeness of a peddler, I had the curiosity to ask was it so. He said that, though that settled the point, he had often thought of it before while studying the military profession at West Point. He then told me that he and a brother officer were one day walking, the road was in a horrible condition and, at one point where it was particularly bad, a plank had been laid for foot passengers. Just as he and his companion got on it they perceived a poor man coming towards them and nearly half-way over, but as soon as he saw them back he walked to allow them to pass. The General turned to thank him for his politeness, and, seeing he carried a peddler's pack, asked what he had. The man answered: "I am selling Catholic books."

It seems that the General had often heard that Catholics had some dark secrets which they kept for themselves, so he said to his companion, "We have heard awful things of these Papists, let us see what they have to say for themselves." So saying he bought *The Catholic Christian Instructed* for himself and some other book for his friend, and you will say they studied their lesson well when I tell you the second officer is now a Paulist father, Rev. George Deshon, and General Rosecrans is ever since a practical Catholic and has brought up his children the same; his eldest son died a Paulist Father a couple of years ago, and two of his daughters joined the Ursulines. He was married at the time he became a Catholic, and his wife felt his change of religion deeply and seemed determined to supply or rather atone for his defection by increased zeal; but before many years she, too, opened her eyes to the true light and goes hand in hand with her husband in all good deeds.

Now about the Bishop. He was much younger than his brother and, at College, when he embraced the Catholic Faith. After leaving college he visited his brother, who wisely refrained from bringing the subject of religion much before him, but there were plenty of good Catholic books around, and the young man read them and they had the desired effect, but he was of a silent, thoughtful turn and said little or nothing. One day the General saw him apparently much amused at something he was reading and asked him what it was. The other answered, "Spalding's Critique on D'Aubigney's History of the Reformation, and I have just come to the story we used to be told of Luther's never once even hearing of the Bible until he accidentally met one and the reading of it opened his eyes to the errors of Popery. I confess it always struck me as a ridiculous story, but this writer tears it to pieces in style!"

Another day when they feared he had met some accident when boating and were rejoicing at seeing him safely on shore again, his brother said, "to be candid, Sylvester, I was worried about your soul more than your body, for I think you know too much for it to be safe for you to die as you are," and sure enough he did know too much to remain a Protestant any longer, and the very next day when the family were going to Mass he said to his brother, "You had better ask that priest if he would come and examine if I know enough to be baptized." This is all I had time to hear for the ladies returned and other things had to be discussed.

But though conversions to the Faith are delightful, conversions from sin are still better, so I will ask a fervent *Pater* and *Ave* for a young man who died on Thursday last, having within a couple of days, made a general confession, *been married,* anointed and received the Holy Viaticum.

Once more Archbishop Alemany turns to the sisters to provide necessary care for the homeless. While taxed to the utmost, Mary Baptist agrees to accept the task unless others can be found to do so. Her practical nature outlines the various business aspects that must be considered and she sets limits to the manner in which the sisters will carry out the request.

Date: December, 1880
To: Archbishop Alemany
From: Sister Mary Baptist Russell
Source: *Annals*, SOMB, I: 701-702

Most Revd. Father in God,

I scarce know what to say with regard to the Night Refuge, we are not by any means anxious to add to the number of our Houses but at the same time the object is one which excites our sympathy and, as I already informed your Grace, received the approval of the majority of the Sisters but only a *small* majority.

We would not *beg* in the style adopted by the Little Sisters of the Poor but we would do as is done by our Sisters in Ireland where similar charities are conducted by them, namely have a little cart with the name of the Institute on it in legible characters and supplied with proper vessels in which to put broken meat, bread &c donated by the markets, hotels & so forth. No doubt quite sufficient would be thus procured to supply food for such as you *now* contemplate and, as the necessity increases, so will the means too no doubt, particularly as we know from experience that charities such as that under consideration are always well supported, but there will be considerable outlay fitting up the place for the object proposed and supplying what would be necessary for the Sisters, and *we* could not undertake to supply *that.* We are already taxed to the utmost and would not be justified in undertaking more——We would like to know *who* occupies the second half of the Old Hospital Premises and, in fact, it would be desirable to see the place before concluding *finally.*

A lease of a Hundred years would be almost the same as a gift, provided possession and liberty to use the premises as we might wish be guaranteed for that time without being obliged to keep the Institute *there,* for it may, in time, prove an unsuitable location. We will, of course, engage to continue the Charity there or in some other part of the City. If your Grace has any other Community to undertake the work we will be only too happy, but if it should otherwise go to the City or to a Protestant Body, we would at almost any Sacrifice undertake it.

I remain most respectfully your obt. sert
Sr. Mary B. Russell,
Sister of Mercy

In Her Own Words
1881–1890

The large numbers of persons fleeing Ireland in search of a better life caused the population of the country to be greatly reduced. This reality caused Mary Baptist great pain. She was, like the rest of her family, rooted in Irish patriotism.

Date of Letter: May 3, 1881
From: Sister M. B. Russell
To: unknown
Source: LMMB, 108

I believe that the population of Ireland is less than it has ever been. I am sorry. I love my native land more and more each day.

This letter was written to a Catholic lady who had taken a position as governess for a Protestant family. At this time period Humboldt County, California, was a remote mining area. Mary Baptist seems to have corresponded with the lady frequently. Additional fragments of these letters were preserved in Matthew Russell's life of Mary Baptist.

In 1871 a residence for the elderly was attached to St. Mary's Hospital. Mary Baptist longed to have a Home constructed to replace this facility on Rincon Hill. It was the special project of Sister Francis Benson.

It is unclear whether the M. M. G. is Mary Gabriel Brown or Mother Mary Gertrude Ledwith of the Eureka foundation.

Date of Letter: June 26, 1881
From: Sister M. B. Russell
To: A lady who had previously appealed for hospitality while out of employment
Source: LMMB, 153-154

June 26, 1881.

My Dear Miss _____:

Your big letter was received on the morning of the 23d. I kept it until evening, when M. M. G. and I sat down and enjoyed it together. I say enjoyed, though we sympathize with you in your hard trials; and more than once tears were in Mother's eyes. I did not think such bigotry existed, but she tells me it is not much better in her part of Humboldt County. It arises from ignorance, and, when Catholics become more numerous, it will gradually disappear. But you have found a haven at last. The tender thoughtfulness displayed by placing all the Catholic books and pictures in your room was the only point that touched the soft spot in my heart. I pray God to bless your newly found friends. What inducement have people to settle in such a country as you describe, or how did they find out such a place? Truly this puzzles me.

Your description of your horseback ride adventures reminded me of myself. My dear old father (the Lord be merciful to him!) considered riding a part of our necessary training, and when mere children, we began on a donkey, but I never had courage to go farther; so when the other girls were sporting on horseback, the quiet donkey did for me, and the quieter he went, the better I was pleased, as I always had a book open before me. At last one day the poor brute got tired of my listlessness, and down it lay and I on its back. My poor father saw me in the distance, and when I got home said he supposed I had better give up riding, and so I did, and I am sure I would make a greater fuss than you did if obliged now to try it.

You say little of your eyes. I am so glad that you have so kind an amanuensis as Miss G. It will be one of the most improving exercises you can prescribe, so beg her to write as often as she can, and it will save your poor eyes. We did wonder we were not hearing from you. I hope you got the few letters we sent.

You will be glad to hear Sister M. Francis [Benson] is busy about the new home; not exactly the building, but preparing the ground and the plans. She has over thirty men grading for over six weeks, and probably six more will not see all finished.

We are rejoicing at one great blessing God has accorded her, a good well. Two weeks ago the men struck a good vein of water at 136 feet depth. All the money you send, I will lay up to secure you a home in the new building, so that you will feel independent. I often told you we did not hold you accountable for the time that you were here, except that you are bound to pray fervently for God's blessing on us all.

When there are so few Catholics in your part of the world, you have, of course, no priest and no sacrifice. How I pity you! But God is everywhere, and you are doing what seems to be your duty in the order of Providence. I will hereafter send you a *Monitor* as often as I can, or some Catholic paper. I see you get other papers with political news.

No mention is made in my family letters of my brother's being made successor to Forster, but unless it was a certainty, they would not mention such a thing. I am far indeed from wishing it for him; but, as God elevated Esther to the throne for the good of others and not for her own benefit, so it may be the Divine Will to make use of my poor brother for some wise end, and if so, provided he is true to God, all will go well. So far, mixing with the world has not lessened his fidelity to his religious duties, thank God! but pray for him. He is only 49 this October, and he has ten children.

Now I have dashed this off in double quick time, so your dear pupils must not take this as a pattern to imitate.

Ever yours in Jesus Christ,
Sr. M. B. Russell,
Sister of Mercy

While the recipient of this letter is unknown, it is typical of the types of letters that were sent by Mary Baptist to other religious leaders. This particular letter notes the fiftieth anniversary of the founding of the Order of Mercy.

Date of letter: November 30, 1881
From: M. Baptist Russell
To: Rev. Mother and Sisters
Source: Archives, Holy Family Sisters, Fremont, CA.

St. Mary's Hospital
San Francisco
November 30th 1881

Dear Reverend Mother and Sisters
    The approaching twelfth of December being the fiftieth anniversary of the Profession of our Beloved Foundress Mary Catherine McAuley, we very earnestly solicit your spiritual assistance on that day for all the members of our Order—Union of prayers being all-powerful in moving God to mercy, we hope to become the recipients of special graces from the merciful Heart of Jesus.
    Again recommending ourselves to your prayers
        I remain dear Reverend Mother & Sisters
            Very affectionately in J.C.
                Sister Mary B. Russell
                Sister of Mercy

St. Mary's Hospital
San Francisco, Cal.
Dec. 1st 1881

At the time of the profession of these sisters, Mary Baptist was ill and confined to the Magdalen Asylum. In her absence Mary Gabriel Brown, Mistress of Novices, took her place. This is one of the few extant reflections of Mary Baptist on the meaning of religious life.

Date: February 11, 1882
To: Sister M. Columba O'Kelly, Sr. M. Carmel Pidgeon and
Sr. Bernardine Ward
From: Mary Baptist Russell
Source: *Annals*, SOMB, II: 12-13

My dear Sisters,

As I cannot have the happiness of hearing you pronounce your vows, I will write a few lines to wish you all every happiness on the joyous occasion. I know you will all make your Consecration with fervor, from the very depths of your hearts, and I am sure dear M. M. Gabriel has made you fully sensible of the seriousness of the irrevocable engagements made by the Religious Profession.

I must acknowledge I had very vague ideas of it myself, when I was professed, but you are all more mature in your minds, and can enter into it more deeply. You must not now imagine all is done. On the contrary you are only now beginning. Hitherto you were apprentices, learning the principles & rules of religious life; now you must reduce them to practice in your daily life. Rev. Fr. Barchi S.J. said in one of his retreats, that "Religion is called by Spiritual Writers a 'Paradise on Earth' but he thought that 'Purgatory' would be a more appropriate name." The truth is both names are appropriate. It is a Purgatory, as it offers innumerable opportunities of performing acts contrary to nature, but it is also a Paradise on Earth, because of the peace enjoyed by humble, docile religious, who live by Faith and see God in their Superiors, and His Will in all the occurrences of life.

Our Lord assures us, a hair does not fall without His permission. If we really believe this, how then can we be over-anxious or worried? Let us then leave ourselves humbly & confidently in the Hand of Divine Providence, doing all we can to glorify Him, by living as true religious, real Sisters of Mercy—'gentle, patient, hard-working, humble, obedient, charitable and above all, simple and joyous.' You will recognize the words of Father Coleridge S.J., in his 'First Sister of Mercy.' They are beautiful and include everything necessary to make us Saints. The last is of more consequence than most persons imagine. "God loveth the cheerful giver" and it makes hard things easy & helps others on the hard road as well as ourselves. You know, besides, Sister M. Stanislaus [Rodriquez] grants an indulgence to everyone who causes a laugh at recreation, so gain all the indulgences you can, but it is more habitual, holy joy I advocate. May God bless you all.

Ever your affectionate Mother
Sister M.B, Russell.

This letter resumes the conversation with Mary Baptist's Humboldt correspondent. Here she indicates that financial troubles are delaying her hope of building the Home for the Aged. The fragment also hints at Mary Baptist's abiding trust in God's providence.

Date of Letter: April 13, 1882
From: Sister M. B. Russell
To: Same lady as in prior letter
Source: LMMB, 156

The work on the new Home is stopped for lack of funds. In God's own time it will get on.

Early religious women always lived in a state of tension around finance. Their ministry was usually supported by dowry but in the United States this proved nearly impossible. Bishops and pastors also wanted the limited amount of money available from the Catholic community. Mary Baptist makes her case in this letter that the financial demand to pay off the debt of St. Peter's was unjust and impossible.

Date: September 28, 1882
To: Rev. Father Grey, Chancellor
From: Sister Mary Baptist Russell
Source: *Annals*, SOMB, II: 20-24

St. Mary's Hospital
Sept. 28, 1882

Most Rev. Father:

On my return to the city, a few days ago, I received your letter of the previous week. I am indeed surprised at the 'unanimous decision' of your Council, but happily there is a higher Tribunal and we appeal from them to Your Grace with every confidence that you will considerably modify their decree, when you reconsider the matter. You say that Fr. Casey will refund the $1400 due us—*that* was *cash* we lent Fr. Gibney R.I.P. but it was not all that was due. I have already explained that the House and surroundings were in a most unfinished condition; no sewers, no closets, no cloakroom and the yard and garden a wilderness, so that when Dr. Kane made the public announcement, that the place was out of debt there was about $3500 due, besides what was due your Grace which must have been fully as much more for Fr. Casey handed you every cent realized by the Fair except $920.

If you intended St. Peter's schools to be *Pay schools*, we should have been informed by the fact; but far from it, Fr. Gibney announced publicly and privately that St. Peters was a *Free School,* that the parents had no excuse for sending their children to *Public* schools having one equally good and equally free at their door. No Parochial School can be supported without assistance. How could they, when the majority of the children are poor, and even those who are not poor expect the school to be free. Not to speak of the support of Teachers, there is considerable outlay in every school, keeping them in repair, cleaning, heating them &c &c. You cannot be ignorant that every Parochial School in the diocese is supported by the Parish. The Christian Brothers in Oakland and Brooklyn conduct the Boy's Schools & receive for their services $25.00 each per month and a horse & wagon goes twice a day, to convey them to the latter place because it is a few blocks from the cars.

Fr. Gallagher gave the Sisters who conduct the schools at 10th St. $50.00 a month and paid the salary for two secular teachers besides keeping the schools, dwelling-house & grounds in order and I many times heard the good Father regret he could do no more, but the Boys school was such a burden he found it impossible to be more liberal. Of the Presentation Schools I need not speak; naturally they had Fairs, Festivals and Lectures without end. The free schools of San Jose, Sacramento and our own one *here* are supported by various means. The Academy of the Notre Dame Sisters must bring in ample means: in Sacramento, the limited number of House children served to help us along, but since they have been so much reduced of late years, in consequence of the sickly location, their income does not equal their outlay, so they will need help in some form.

Our school here is supported by the Hospital and with the other drags on it, leaves it struggling year after year. We know the Schools conducted by Religious, male or female, give less trouble and cost less than those conducted by secular Priests: witness the great exertions required on the part of the late much to be lamented Fr. Gallagher, to support his school but no Parochial School can be carried on without more or less assistance from the Parish.

For four years and a half we have been left under the impression, St. Peter's was of this class, and now to be expecting us to pay off the accumulated debt is out of the question, in fact it is an utter impossibility. If that is paid off, we may manage by great exertions and a little assistance occasionally to make ends meet, but to undertake to pay off the debt we could not do. If the Sister there have to be supported by the Hospital, justice requires that the Hospital should get the benefit of their services and we can employ them all usefully if your Grace wishes St. Peter's closed, but I would be sorry to see that fine school disbanded & I hope you won't think it necessary to do so.

If you allow us a Fair about Xmas, I think we may make perhaps $4,000.00, provided the Priests are kind enough to lend their co-operation, and in eighteen or twenty months, another Fair will pay off the balance & enable the Sisters to continue. You will please let me know soon if we may act accordingly, as no time is to be lost. I am glad to hear the Parish is improving, for Fr. Casey told me more than once when the subject of a Fair or Festival was broached that the Priests could scarce get a living and Miss Mahoney says he spoke in even stronger terms to her, when she called regarding the Insurance. Hoping this matter may be now better understood, I remain

Your Lordship's obt. sert. in J. C.
Sister M. B. Russell, Sr. of Mercy

Lord Charles Russell, Mary Baptist's younger brother, was the only Russell sibling to make the trip to California. His skill in law had earned him the position of Lord Chief Justice under Gladstone. This meant much to the Irish community since he was the first Catholic to hold such a position since Reformation times. Throughout her life Mary Baptist was concerned about the demands made upon Charles and worried that he would not have sufficient leisure to tend his spiritual life. It was Charles that asked Matthew Russell to write the life of Mary Baptist which Matthew did in 1902. It was due to his book that much of her correspondence was preserved.

Date of Letter: September 21, 1883
From: Sister M. B. Russell
To: Matthew (her brother)
Source: LMMB, 98-100

St. Mary's Hospital, S. F.,
California, Sept. 21, '83.

My Dear Matthew: Before the day ends, I must write to you: first, as it is your feast, and we have all prayed for your every happiness as fervently as we could; and, secondly, to let you know that dear Charles is actually in California. He wrote me a couple of weeks ago from Winnipeg that I might expect to see him, if nothing unforeseen occurred, before the end of the month. On last Tuesday I happened to be in the parlor, when in walked a gentleman with gloves. "This is not a Californian," said I to myself. And lo! raising my eyes, I saw Charles, and, you will be glad to hear, looking remarkably well bronzed, no doubt, by his travels in this warm climate. He had arrived in this city the night before from Puget's Sound, by steamer, of course, and I think, like myself, the sea does not agree with him, for he was a little upset by the voyage and called on our doctor, who merely prescribed certain regimen.

Cousin Kate was delighted more than I can explain, to see Charles, and quite pleased to find the sweet, gentle expression of countenance so different from what his photograph would lead one to expect. He sat an hour or more, and then went to call on James Gartlan and Joseph Jennings. D. J. Oliver, one of our best and wealthiest Catholics, intended to have Charles as his guest, but he had already settled himself with his friend at the Palace Hotel and did not care to make a change. Mr. Oliver was watching the list of passengers expected overland, by which route we supposed Charles would come, and he intended to meet him; but he got here unknown to us all. He had calls from a half dozen gentlemen that night, and next morning, at 6:30, he drove in an open carriage to the Cliff House (via Golden Gate Park) where he and party had breakfast, and saw all that is to be seen there, in the way of seals, etc., etc., and got here at noon. He and I spent a quiet hour together, telling me of all at home, the *little ones* perhaps, getting an undue amount of time. I thought he had plenty of time at his disposal, and the sisters had lunch prepared for him in the Community Room, when we found he had arranged to start at three for Yosemite Valley and was to lunch with Mr. Martin before, so we had to let him go after a hurried visit to the Home or at least to a part of it.

In one room the tears came to his eyes, when he saw dear Mamma's obituary hanging in a central position—the room belongs to Mary Devlin who lived at Mr. Greer's and knew Mamma, and Sisters M. Aquin and Emmanuel well. He expects to return on Tuesday, and I must get one day to show him the asylum, schools, etc. The weather is pretty warm at present, and I fear where Charles is now it must be extremely hot. It is too bad he is so hurried. I hope he won't be half dead from fatigue, running as such a rate.

Now, my dear Matthew, may God bless you forever and ever. Pray for me.

Your affectionate sister,
M. B. Russell,
Sister of Mercy

Most likely this letter was written to a member of the Russell family. It refers to the ill health of Arthur Hamill, Mary Baptist's beloved step-brother. Arthur acted as a surrogate father to the younger Russell's after the death of their father.

Date of Letter: July 27, 1884
From: Sister M. B. Russell
To: Unknown
Source: LMMB, 169

Why should we desire to retard his happy entrance to the kingdom of God? He has had a long life, being seventy last April, and has, I trust, earned for himself a happy eternity. Often since I saw something of the world, I have reflected *with admiration* on what I recollect of Arthur, his wonderful respect and submission to mamma, his devotedness to *us* young ones, and the repeated journeys he took on Saturdays from Dundalk merely to spend Sunday with us in our quiet, old-fashioned home in Killowen, instead of enjoying himself with young people his own age.

Mary Hamill was closely linked to Mary Baptist. The preserved letters show a deep devotion to family and a kinship of heart. This letter is full of family news. The Gartlan family was related to Mary Baptist through marriage. Margaret Hamill, her step sister and Arthur's sister married James Gartlan. Two of their children became Sisters of Mercy.

Date: October 24, 1885
From: MB Russell
To: Mary Hamill (Arthur's wife)
Source: Archives: JPD

St. Mary's Hospital
San Francisco, Oct. 24th. 1885
California

My dearest Mary,

I had a letter sometime ago from good Father Matthew dated Down Patrick in which he mentioned his intention of going to see you at New Castle, Dundrum. He added that, in obedience to the Doctor's orders, dear Arthur was to refrain at least for sometime from attending Circuit. I was glad to hear it and I am sure you agree with me that even should he recover (comparatively), he has done enough work and may well *rest* the *rest* of his life. From what I hear he is affected, just like our dear Sr. Mary Francis, at times she is very much oppressed and the action of the heart weak and painful. She has been ailing a considerable time but gets intervals of ease and at present is wonderfully improved. I trust it is the same with dear Arthur, and that he will have a quiet winter with you in Dublin.

I believe your present residence is more cheerful than the old House in Eccles St. and I know Arthur has everything your loving heart can supply to lessen his sufferings and add to his bodily comforts and the spiritual, I am sure, is equally well attended to, so the thought of my dear Brother only excites in my mind deep feelings of gratitude to God. I am sure you all enjoyed your stay in New

Castle. It is a lovely spot. I suppose you don't recollect anything about the day a whole party of us spent at Bryan's ford and New Castle and returned next day to Newry via Green Castle and Rostrevor. I recollect it well and can fancy I see yourself and poor dear Sr. Mary Aquin arm in arm. If I am not much mistaken Arthur was the subject of your confidential chat. You and she were great Friends.

You see I have blotted my paper but will not rewrite this knowing you will overlook the unseemly paper—How are you yourself? I trust *well*. You were suffering for years, but I hope you are entirely recovered. You need strength now for the greatest part of the nursing will fall to your share had you fifty nurses. When you have a leisure I would dearly like to have a letter from you telling me what you really think about dear Arthur, and how he passes the day. Is he able to go to Church at all? He misses the Mass, for I think he used to go to daily Mass when in the City. "God hears the Man who often hears the Mass" is the motto on the ticket of admission to a Purgatorian Society in New York and one I fully endorse.

We in this House are singularly blessed in this point. We get *many* Masses, T. God. We have a Resident Chaplain who says daily Mass and we are seldom without *one, two* and sometimes *three* extra Masses, indeed we have every Spiritual advantage. We have a fine large Chapel and our Abp. is generous in allowing Benediction etc. etc. The only thing we seldom enjoy is a sermon; except at Receptions and Professions we get none with the exception of our two Annual Retreats but we make up for that loss by Spiritual Reading.

I am rambling on about my own surroundings and should rather ask about what I wish to hear regarding you one and all. Is Arthur able to enjoy reading? What pleasant evenings he gave so long, long ago reading aloud some of Dicken's works while we plied the needle. I suppose Arthur John is obliged to be a good deal from Home but you have Alice all the time and I imagine she is a happy, cheerful Companion and you have her all to yourselves since Emily's marriage. This reminds me. *Cousin Kate* was looking over her Album of Family Portraits lately and she remarked we have no likeness of Emily since she was in short dresses, so if you have a late photograph of herself, Husband & Baby please let us have it. I am sure the innocent smile of the little Baby brings joy to many. As for me there are few things so lovely as the eyes of children who know not guile.

Of course you know Jas. Gartlan is here & thro' him I hear occasionally of Emily etc. He has just commenced to practice as a Lawyer and tho' far from brilliant I have every hope will ultimately succeed in his Profession because he is persevering & earnest. In this Country we have not the distinction of Barrister and Attorney as at home. But my chief reason for commenting on his success is my confidence in the promises of our Lord that if we seek in the first place the Kingdom of God & His justice the rest will be added and I am happy to say James is an edifying, practical Catholic. He has just heard of his Cousin Maria Gartlan having entered in Sacre Coeur Convent. I hope she will happily persevere like her Sister Alice.

I don't know that I ever heard what your Niece did with herself. I mean Miss M. Hamilton. Is she married or has she entered a Convent? When you get time to write me about all your surviving Relatives. Are you near a Church, within easy walking distance? I hope so, for to have daily Mass is, I know, your comfort and support. You would be sorry to see how badly the week day Masses are attended in this Country altho' better a hundred times than when we came first. I believe I will add a few words to Arthur himself so I will close, dearest Mary, with my heart's best love and affection. I am yours in J.C.

Sr. Mary B. Russell
Sister of Mercy

Don't forget me *in your good prayers*. How is Alice Kenny? It is long since I heard of her.

This was part two of the letter above. The letter shows the great spiritual concern Mary Baptist had for her brother and provides insight into her spirituality. The second part of the letter gives us a window into the work the sisters did in the prisons.

Date: October 25, 1885
From: MB Russell
To: Arthur (her brother)
Source: Archives, JPD

St. Mary's Hospital
San Francisco, Oct. 25th 1885

My dearest Arthur,

At first I thought I would not bother you with a letter and so addressed dear Mary who will, I know, write me in return but now I am adding a few lines to you yourself. So death has sent you 'three warnings' that he will call for you some day. Please God you will not be found unprepared and so you do not dread his approach. I met sometime ago a few sweet lines on death which I would copy could I now lay my hands on them, but the substance was that we should welcome Death as an Angel for he alone shows us that *Man is immortal*, and *the Soul can never die*. Still, being the penalty of Sin, there is a certain solemnity about death that makes us naturally shrink from it and it is this very fact makes so pleasing to God our entire conformity to His holy will. Like every one, you feel, too, having to be separated from those you love but this separation is only *for a time*. We will all, please God, be reunited in Eternity. You willingly allowed Mary and the girls to go to Germany etc. etc. believing it was for their happiness and benefit and looking forward to the pleasure of meeting them again. In like manner you and they must rather anticipate the happiness of being reunited in a Blessed Eternity than dwell on the necessary separation in time.

You used to have rather too stringent ideas of the preparation required for Holy Communion, but you must lay that view aside and avail yourself of every opportunity of receiving Holy Communion and dwell not so much on the Infinite Justice and Sanctity of our Divine Lord as on His Infinite Mercy and Love. You have great advantages, dear Arthur, in such a City as Dublin with dear Mary and Matthew to urge you on in the path of sanctity and so many grateful loving hearts praying for you continually. You won't object to my alluding thus to your death, tho' you are better, Thank God, at present and may be spared to us a few years, yet at your age we know well it must be only *a few* and, as death is the only means by which we can be united to God never again to be separated, we should not shrink from it.

To make you still more grateful to God for the many blessings you enjoy, I must tell you about a death bed at which I assisted no later than yesterday. I was at the State Prison and found in the Hospital of that Institution a poor Spaniard dying of Cancer and his two Brothers at his Side, all three incarcerated for life and it is generally believed they are innocent. Indeed, I am satisfied they are. The eldest is only 35 and you can picture to yourself how depressed the poor souls look with such a prospect before them. Before the advent of the Americans into California their Family owned leagues and leagues of land and quite a flourishing town is named after them 'Alviso,' but like the greater number of the old Spanish Families, unscrupulous Americans have by degrees dispossessed them of almost everything. All I could say to cheer these poor Fellows was that a Day of Retribution is at hand and that their present degradation and suffering will only add to their glory and happiness for all Eternity, but it was not in my power to change the dejected expressions on their countenances, although it was as sad a sight as I have witnessed for many a day.

A good Jesuit goes there every second week. He spends Saturday afternoon hearing confessions and talking with the Inmates who may wish to speak to him and next day says two Masses, one for the Prisoners and another in the School House of the Village for the People and any of the Officers who may be Catholics.

Now is not the above sad picture calculated to make you feel very grateful for all the blessings you enjoy, but I should tell you something more cheering and could tell you many amusing things were I near enough to *speak*. I must, however, stop even *writing* as I have some thing to attend, but another time I will write more provided you are not mad with me for this production. I fear dear *Mary* will, but I am so familiar with death I half imagine you must be the same.

If you are not fatigued by writing, I would dearly like to have a few lines; 'Kate Russell' and I often speak of you. She has the most loving recollection of you, indeed she forgets none of the old family Circle and even the most minute circumstances and sayings are remembered by her. She unites with me in sending affectionate love. We both pray for you *every day* and I, at least, promise to pray more and more and I know she will do the same and you will say a little prayer for us both. I must now stop— Ever dearest Arthur. Your fondly attached and affectionate Sister.

> Sr. Mary B. Russell
> *Sister of Mercy*

Although she was far from Ireland, Mary Baptist kept up on all the family news, indeed, she took the responsibility for passing letters on to other Russell relatives within the United States. Matthew Russell was editor of the Irish Monthly and deeply involved in the Irish literary scene. Rosa Mulholland, also a Russell family member through marriage, was a writer of the period.

Date: October 28, 1885
From: Mother Mary Baptist Russell
To: Matthew Russell
Source: Archives, JPD

St. Mary's Hospital
San Francisco
California
Oct. 28th 1885

My dearest Matthew,

You are very good to write to me without waiting for an answer to your last. I know I was in your debt, but as dear Arthur is on the Invalid List, I gave him the preference. I wrote to him and to Mary but Cousin Kate says Mary will never give Arthur the one I wrote to him. She says it was a terrible letter to send a sick man so I added a P.S. telling her to use her own judgment about giving it or not. We are so habituated to the thought of death that it has lost its terror for us, but as Cousin says it is different with seculars.

You know dear Arthur was almost a *Father* to us, so don't let him die without sending me a special blessing—You regret not being able to send me Rosa Mulholland's Bust. There is nothing to prevent you sending me her photograph, so please send it and also Clare's. I have not either. We also ask for late ones of Charles, Arthur and Emily, as those we have are taken when they were children and we want to see them as they are now. We have a tolerably complete *Family Gallery.*

Revd. Mother says you may send us one doz. of the 'Book of Poems' and I will show it to some of the communities who conduct large Boarding Schools who may, perhaps, order some for premium. I hope it will be generally appreciated. You seem an admirer of everything she writes. Some who are reading 'Marcella Grace' consider it *her best.* I don't intend reading it till it is concluded so cannot judge.

Since I last wrote, we had a visit from Father Roman but it was a hurried one. He arrived in Cal. Thursday evening and left Monday Morning so of course we could not expect much of his time. He paid a long visit Saturday evening but I was on the Visitation. Next morning he gave us Mass and remained an hour or two after. He asked us to send James Gartlan and Henry Perry to him as they are his only acquaintance in San Francisco. I fear he did not see Mr. Perry for it being Saturday night his Office was closed and I am not certain that he was found—I notified Joseph Jennings of his being in the City knowing it would gratify his Friend at home to have Father see him but, as in the other case, I am not sure if any letter found him at home. Since his marriage, Joseph has never come to see me, but Mrs. John Jennings tells me he and his wife are regularly at 10 OC Mass at the Cathedral every Sunday. I am sure I would be far from blaming him for marrying, but I think his children felt it deeply. Mrs. J. Jennings was a Miss Jordan of Warrenpoint and her Husband was one of the Jennings of Mill St. She had a long and pleasant interview with F. Roman—

I may send the photographs of two side altars about to be erected in our Chapel to Newry but their destination is *Kinsale* as we always want our dear old Mother to see all we can of our surroundings—The Altars are to be erected at the expense of two Germans in gratitude for favors granted to prayers—They are carved wood, covered with some preparation that gives them the appearance of stone. We expect to have them completed for the Feast of the Im. Conception— Our present Revd. Mother has an Aunt and Cousin in Dublin. You may meet her Cousin sooner or later. His name is George Whitager M.D. and indeed he almost deserves the name of 'Confessor for the Faith'.

His father was so bigoted he never sanctioned his going to Mass or Sacraments and when dying, appointed a Renegade his Guardian with authority until the young man was 25, so he was kept at Trinity and every other means employed to crush out the Faith but no sooner could he throw off the Trammels than he declared himself a Catholic. You must pray for Rev. Mother Angela as she is very delicate. She kept up splendidly since her election until this week but was at last obliged to yield to weak nature and return to "Bedford Square" so please don't omit her in your mementoes—Ever dear Matthew your affectionate Sister.

Sr. Mary B. Russell, Sr. of Mercy

This letter reveals the attention to detail that Mary Baptist had when describing things of beauty or things of nature. She was alive to the arts, to literature and this appreciation shines through in her letters. Again, she comments on the success of Charles saying that what is really important is his integrity of life.

Date: February 3, 1886
To: Arthur Hamill
From: Sr. M. B. Russell
Source: Archives: JPD

St. Mary's Hospital
San Francisco, California
Feb. 3rd 1886

My dearest Arthur,

So you are *talking* of going circuit this coming summer. This is glorious news, as it shows you must feel an improvement tho' still suffering so much. But tho' it delights one to hear you speak in this way I must protest against you thinking of such a thing and I know dear Mary and *all* will cry out against it. Surely it is time for you to rest on your oars and, if I mistake not, you can retire on a pension unlike our judges here who must make hay while the sun shines as there is no such thing as a retiring pension and, worse still, they are almost sure to be turned out of office at each election. I only wish your position was *hereditary* and that dear Arthur John could step into your shoes and then you would *enjoy* your rest but in all things God's will be done.

So you had a long visit from Emily and her pet Agnes. How you must miss the little angel. Someone said she was like her Father but that gave me no idea of what she is as Alexander is the only one of the family I never met so I will be glad to get the photos Emily promised to send. My namesake here has a large collection of Family pictures and loves to go over them and she is as interested in those she never saw as if she knew them intimately. She speaks most affectionately of you and her love for dear Mamma is wonderful. You don't know how kind and attentive James Gartlan is to her; he spends every Sunday evening with her. While Mary lived they enjoyed a game of checkers or even of cards, but since she died, Kate cannot bear anything of that kind.

Are you able to amuse yourself by such games? Reading is no doubt your great recourse, not of course reading yourself, but others reading for you. It would seem a sweet return for the pleasure you gave so long ago reading aloud Dickens and Scott's works, etc.

I have just received a telegram from Father Malony of *Miniok*, Illinois informing that dear Charles is Attorney General for England. The news does not delight me as did what I heard of him in a recent letter that he and his four sons were side by side at Holy Communion at Christmas and that he goes frequently. Of course it is a wonderful thing to think of an *Irish Catholic* holding such a position and the way in which the news has reached me shows it is regarded as a *triumph*, but it will be an additional tap on the health and mind of dear Charles and unless he and *his* have uncommon Christian wisdom will not add to his happiness *here* and much less *hereafter* but we must hope for the best.

As you have time to spend at trifles during this forced leisure, I will tell you about a nice present we have just received for our Chapel. A few months ago a German who could barely make himself understood called with a letter he had received from a friend then in Russian America far from Church and Priest in which he told his friend that sometime previous he had promised to erect an Altar in honor of Our Mother of Sorrows in case a certain favor was granted him. God heard his prayer and he wished his friend to fulfill his promise as it was not possible for him to attend to it himself. He added that his *name* was to be kept private—the friend *JW Baggan-field* had been a patient of ours 13 years ago and at once thought of our Chapel so came to ascertain if we would have any objection. You may be sure we had none, but quite the contrary, we at once made arrangements and now we have *two* very pretty Altars for JW B. followed his friend's example and furnished funds for a correspond-ing one on the other side of the Sanctuary.

The *Altars* are alike with the exception of carved portions. *Under* one is the Dead Christ with the B. Virgin and Mary Magdalen bending over Him. Our Lord is *full* figure but the other two are in *high relief.* Under the second is Our Lord in His Agony at the moment the Angel presents the Chalice. This figure and surround-ings are painted in character but the Altars and Tabernacle are white and gold, but the table and slabs in front of each are marble—on the slab in front of our Lord in His agony are the words, "The Lord hath laid on Him the iniquities of us all" and before the Dead Christ, "He was wounded for our iniquities. He was bruised for our sins" both are from the 53rd chapter of Isaias. I think them most devotional, children especially seem much taken with them. We find groups of little ones kneeling before them continually. Almost the last thing I do at night before leaving the Choir ever since your first serious attack is to beg our Lady of Sorrows to take special care of you, dear Arthur, both spiritually and temporally.

Tell dear Mary when she has a little leisure to write. Give her my love, also to dear Alice and Arthur. I suppose you often see Alice Kenny. Her Son must be full grown now. Give all my love more particularly to dear Matthew. Ever your fondly attached Sister in J. C.

SM B. Russell
Sr. of Mercy

This letter is another of the "newsy" family letters sent by Mary Baptist to her brother Arthur. It hints at Mary Baptist's love for history and antiquities. This was a quality that was noted in her educational initiatives. The bond of affection that existed between Mary Baptist and Arthur is constant in all their correspondence.

Date of letter: June 18, 1886
From: M.B. Russell
To: Arthur
Source: Archives: JPD

St. Mary's Hospital
San Francisco, Cal.
June 18th 1886

My dear Arthur,

Would not this big Sheet remind you of the letter paper dear Mamma patronized? You remember she never liked the fancy note paper that was so fashionable. I trust this will find you tolerably well. M.M. Emmanual said in a recent letter that the latest accts. from you were most encouraging. [If] it's God's will, I shall be glad when I hear you are in Green Castle or rather New Castle or Rostrevor or some such sweet spot with dear Mary. Alice, Emity and of course, Miss Agnes, the pet of the House and Mouse of the cupboard. I think a House with young people must be lovely no matter how many in it. Dear Sr. M. Bernard H[amill] believes in praying and hoping you may go to Lourdes so our blessed Lady may cure you, but our Sweet Mother can do that wherever you are if she sees it is for your real good.

I must tell you what she did *this week* in response to a humble prayer. A young Lady who had been some years in a Convent School tho' fully convinced of the truth of the Catholic Church had not the courage to make profession of her faith until grace touched her heart while a patient in this Hospital a few weeks ago. She is only on a visit in Cal. and was nerving herself to meet a volley of abuse from her Relatives when she would return to them. So to have the worst over she wrote giving her reasons for the Step she had taken, but return of post she received a terrible letter from her Brother (the Head of the Family) telling her she had cut herself off for ever from them all; never again could she call their home *hers*. She would receive money to support her here, but they would neither receive her among them nor correspond with her. The present was *his last* letter to her and so forth. The poor Soul did not expect this and felt crushed, after giving vent to her feelings she went to St. Ignatius church and there begged the

B. Virgin to soften her Brother's heart and make him write again reminding our Sweet Mother that she had obtained for her many favors when she was not a Catholic and now that she was truly her *Mother* she must not refuse her request. Imagine her delight when a letter arrived just as quickly as it could reach her and began by saying he fully determined *never* to write to her again but that "Mother came to me in a dream and commanded me to write to J." He went over much he said before but no matter she feels [word illegible] convinced that all will be right *in time*. Would not this convince the most incredulous that every little petition is heard and granted *if for our real good*. So let us continue to ask and if the favor sought is not granted, a *better* will.

No doubt you recollect the charming bit of Biography which appeared some years ago in the *Irish Monthly* under the title 'Alive'. It is worth reading again and again. J. O'Dougherty whose family dear Matthew knows well, said he derived as much if not more strength and instruction from the perusal of it than from Books of Devotion.

I found Cousin Kate the other day so intent on the 'Inner Life of Père Lacordaire' that she did not hear the door open. She tells me it is intensely interesting and I can say the same of the Life of Père de Raoigini, S.J. He is truly a *grand* character. You recollect it was Lacordaire who delivered the panegyric on O'Connell in Paris and Père Venturin in Italy.

I hope Matthew continues to come as often as allowed to offer Mass for you in your room. Don't let him drop off this good practice, everyone finds a tedious illness *much trying* and one accustomed to such an active life as you must find it doubly so and therefore you need extra grace to bear it humbly. I was delighted to hear you had resigned your Judgeship. It only kept your mind on the strain and it is full time for you to retire to private life. I am still telling good St. Joseph not to forget you good *Arthur John* & James' poor *John Arthur* & we won't be disappointed, P. God.

You may have heard of some family relics preserved by the Columbus Russells which Kate gave Charles when he paid us a visit a couple of years ago. She has a few left which are to go to his young people also the first opportunity. For Lillian Russell she has a Box (carved ivory) which my Father brought when returning from one of his voyages when Aunt Elizabeth and Uncle Peter were one week old. That must be 72 years at least but I intend to ascertain the precise date. He brought two, one for Aunt Anne and the other for Eliza Russell & had their initials carved on them. The lining and cushion on top are faded but these we are getting renewed and otherwise, it is wonderfully preserved. When it was so long religiously preserved would it not be a pity having it left when it would not be appreciated.

Then for Mary Gertrude she has an Album belonging to Jane. The first piece in which is written by Father Murray and dated Maynooth March 2nd 1833—There is an original piece by dear Mamma, a farewell before they sailed for America. It is written by Margaret in a hand very different indeed from her style as long as I recall it and there are some pieces written by Mamma. Uncle Charles etc. etc. besides some little painting by Margaret and Ellen Russell of Dublin whom you may recollect but I do not. I intend to copy into it Lord O'Hagan's Obituary on Brother Thomas. I dare say not one of the family preserved it and Cousin has it treasured in a prayer Book. Now don't you think these two young ladies are honored in getting these keepsakes. We must hunt up something for dear Mamma's little Namesake as she is the only *Girl* not supplied.

I *pity* poor Charles dragged into such Public life. So seldom is it that the peace of Home and Soul are not thusly interfered with but St. Thomas More will I hope be his Model and St. Charles who kept his heart on God in the midst of Grandeur will help him I trust, as Providence seems to have brought things around to the present position. Robert Russell resides in Dublin now and has nothing to do. No doubt he would gladly sit and read for you if you only let him know you would like it and this would give dear Mary and Alice a chance of getting a walk occasionally. Thank God they are both enjoying such excellent health, but poor Mary had her years of delicacy. See how good God is to have her well now when you so much need her care. I am sure she is a devoted nurse and you have 'Nurse' with you still have you not?

I fear you see but little of dear Margaret. Her visit was so hurried and she had to go to Tipperary, of course, to her dear Louisa and Agnes. But I believe she is to settle permanently in Dublin this year.

Then you will see her often. Does your old Friend D.C. Jennings call to see you? You know Joseph is here in the Insurance Business. His first wife died many years ago leaving two sons and two daughters very nice and nicely educated. They reside in Chicago where they visited me when enroute for Ireland 8 years ago. He married a second time nearly 2 years ago and both he and Mrs. Jennings are most edifying attendants at every exercise in St. Mary's Cathedral. He is tall and slight, much respected for his Gentlemanly manner and strictly honorable principles in business. He calls once in a while to see me and talks of *long ago*. He has the deepest reverence for dear Mamma, as indeed have all who knew her. May she rest in peace.

Now dear Arthur have I not penned a regular newspaper? I hope it may help to divert you a little from your sufferings. I place you every night the last thing before leaving the Chapel, in the arms of our Sorrowful Mother. Could you be in better keeping? I must now bid you good bye for the present, give my fondest love to dearest Mary and Alice, Matthew and if writing to Mother M. Emmanual and Bernard. See in how many Convents prayers are being offered for you. Well time flies and eternity approaches when we hope all to be united in blessing and praising God forever—

Your affect. and grateful Sister in J.C.
Sr. M. B. Russell
Sister of Mercy

Arthur's ill health continues and Mary Baptist continues to encourage him and assure him of her prayer. In this letter is found a reference to the ongoing tension between the Irish Catholic community in San Francisco and members of anti-Catholic/anti-Irish groups. Some of Mary Baptist's Irish nationalism shows in her comments. San Francisco Irish had keen interest in the politics of the day in Ireland. Home Rule was a hot topic of the period. Charles Russell was linked to these politics as was James Gartlan, their brother-in-law. It also should be noted that one of the original founding sisters, Mary deSales Reddan was the cousin of Daniel O'Connor, known as the Irish Liberator.

Date: July 7, 1886
From: MB Russell
To: Arthur, her brother
Source: Archives: JPD

St. Mary's Hospital
San Francisco
California
July 7th/86

My dear Arthur,

In a few hours our Annual Retreat begins, but before entering the Desert as we call it, I must write you a letter. I trust it will find you doing well; and whether *better* or *worse,* dear Arthur, it is *well* for whatever happens is by the will of our loving Father without whose permission not a hair fall from our heads. What a Source of Sweet tranquility is this faith in the tender Providence of God. Of course we have many occasions of exercising resignation, but in the *end* we will see that what He allows is best. What a trial on our Blessed Lady and St. Joseph to be obliged to go among Strangers at such a time and yet their public registration in the Records of Bethlehem as belonging to the Tribe of Juda and family of David has naturally been one of the most powerful means of convincing the Jews that J. Christ was truly the promised Messiah. Now, when God tried thus and in others far more severe ways His Chosen Servants, *we* certainly ought not to expect to escape trials. *They will come* but we can lessen their bitterness by accepting them humbly and as cheerfully as we can and this I hope you will do.

I went last evening to say farewell to Cousin Kate and found J. Gartlan with her. He went to announce that Charles has been reelected but with only 100 majority whereas the last time he had a much larger majority. Folks here do not seem quite so confident of Home Rule as they were a few weeks ago but all seem to say it must come *in time.* Our Catholic Paper the *Monitor* gave last week a letter from 'Margaret Sullivan' correspondent of the N.Y. Sun in which she gives a pleasing account of the scene in the Commons when Charles delivered his Speech on the Topic of the Day. I will send you the paper and you will show it to Matthew. You may have seen it already but as I am not certain I will send it.

Sr. Mary Aquin [Martin] is with us at present and she too came to see Miss Russell so we had a *Family Reunion* as it were. You who have never left home can scarcely understand the *warm* feeling you have to any one from the same quarter who can speak of persons and places you love. Sr. M. Aquin has been of late years principally in Sacramento and only comes here for Retreats and such like. She is an affectionate little soul and has a special love for all our people. She is most anxious about your health and does not neglect praying for its restoration if God s will and for all you intentions and I need not tell you I do the same—I hope dear Mary keeps up both mentally and physically. Her strength of mind and body is well taxed but God will fit the Back to the Burden. I trust as He promises to do so we must never be discouraged however hard things may seem—I have just referred to my copy of the Baptismal Register and find dear Sr. M. Bernard [Hamill] will be 57 years in the Convent in August while I thought she would only then complete her Jubilee. I referred to it to ascertain *your* age and lest you should not know must tell you that you were 72 last April. I heard lately of the Father of Lady Kenmark who had been a Minister in the Church of England and is now a Catholic being ordained Priest in his 70th year. He must be an energetic old man surely. I see also that Charles was born in Oct. 1832 whereas a newspaper acct. sent me lately said he was born in 1833. It made another mistake in saying he was not a pledged Teetotaler. I think he took the pledge with a crowd in Warrenpoint from F. Matthew himself.

July 4th is a great day in this Country. Processions and Addresses, Fireworks, etc. etc. This year a certain Mr. Pixley, Editor of a violent anti-Catholic Paper, was somehow elected President of the Day much to the dissatisfaction of the Catholic Party and all liberal minded peoples. What did they do, think you? They left him in his glory. The different Regiments went off camping one here and one there. The Emmet Guards leading and so there was no Procession for the first time in the annals of the City. I think this will teach him 'The Pope's Irish' are not to be insulted with impunity.

Does your old Friend, or rather the Friend of your youth, Daniel Jenning go to see you frequently? I think he resides in Dublin. If you see him you can tell him Joseph is well and happy in his second marriage, business not very flourishing but moderation is best in all things. Truly I dread too much success for myself or those I love. Probably you never heard of D.J. Oliver of this city but he was one of the most uniform in his friendship to us and one of the few I could introduce a friend in need to when occasion offered. I made him acquainted with J. Jennings and he never failed to show him attention and assist him in business. When he heard of dear Charles' visit he called on him and insisted on his meeting some Friends at Dinner. Charles called him my 'Good natured Friend'. Well he was Grand Marshall on last St. Patrick's Day and seemed in good health yet he died on the 18th of Ap. and if you look over the *Monitor* I send you you will see his only surviving daughter followed him to the grave on the 24th of June. He leaves one son and three grandsons but their name is *Tobin*. He was an excellent Man. He got a very handsome oil painting in Rome representing the Pope's private chapel and His Holiness Pius IX giving 1st Holy Communion to his second daughter. The whole family are present, himself and Mrs. Oliver, four daughters and son also. This Mass for Cecelia who is just dead was then about four years old. Of course there are also a few Priests, *all* the faces are portraits and altogether it is a very interesting painting— Now dear Arthur I hope this will divert your mind for a little time at least and remind you to say a little prayer for me. I have barely room to send my fondest love to dear Mary, Alice, Arthur John and Emily. Ever your aff. Sister in J.C.

Sr. M. B. Russell
— Sister of Mercy —

This letter was written after the death of Arthur Hamill. It contains descriptive information about the Magdalen Asylum and the life of the penitents. The Sister Mary Aquin mentioned in the letter is Sister M. Aquin Martin, a relative of Mary Baptist's who was a member of the San Francisco community. She spent much of her ministry life in Sacramento.

Date: Jan. 23rd, 1887
To: Mary Hamill (Arthur's wife)
From: MB Russell
Source: Archives, SOMB

Magdalen Asylum
Potrero Avenue
San Francisco
California
Jan. 23rd. 1887

My dearest Mary,

I have not written since you settled *pro tem* in Newry but I sent a few papers to let you see it was not forgetfulness kept me from doing so; the six months for which you leased your Dublin House is well nigh up but, as it must be too large for your present small number, I hope you will be fortunate enough to get it rented for a longer time; of course you rent it *furnished*.

What became of good faithful Nurse when you were obliged to break up, fortunate for poor old Kitty Murray that she was called to her Happy Home. Are you still with Emily? Little Agnes and Irene come in for a fine share of petting if you are, for like all Grand Mammas you are, of course, devoted to the little Ones; is it one of the row of houses in which the poor Duffs lived that Emily occupies. I recollect them well and I think they were the nicest residences in that part of the town. I suppose there is not one of that family living. What a blight that one unhappy child brought on the whole household but, truth to say, they were all spoiled by weak over indulgence of their too loving parents.

You are a considerable distance from Church and to miss daily Mass is something you would scarcely agree to. Now more than ever, it must be your comfort and support. You are, however, so light on your feet that a good walk won't frighten you and in any case it is not farther than from Ballybot and you remember we used all trudge to the Cathedral every day. I am sure this is an anxious time with you and Arthur John. I always think of you when I hear people exulting that JW this and JW that had to reduce their rents 30/00 and 40/00, but no matter you will come out all right in the end, P. God, tho' not just as independent as poor Arthur hoped. Even when his father lived, I believe A.J. was obliged to reside on some of the property away from home, so you don't miss him as much as if he had been able to stay at home always. I never forget asking St. Joseph to bless and prosper him and *you* I leave in the care of our Mother of Sorrows. Dear Alice must not think I forget her, indeed I do not.

We heard of the death of Thomas Gartlan of Monalty. What a ripe old age he attained. I understand he was 86. Now only Mrs. McMahon and George remain. I was thinking the other day that there are few families where so few deaths occurred as the Jennings of the Quay. There are ten of them living still and Letitia the youngest, so the elder ones must be a venerable age now. You never saw Joseph. I think, he and Sr. M. Aquin were about the same age. He resides in this city with his second wife but his family two sons and two daughters reside in Chicago. He resembles his Mother and is very much respected and deservedly too. Charles the youngest of all is in New York and has a nice family

I was looking lately over dear Arthur's last letter (penned by dear Alice). He says he will ask Matthew for the Sketch of 'Alive' in an old *Irish Monthly* which I recommended him to read. Poor fellow, he seems to have had no idea his summons was so near. In it is related an interview which the heroine had with the Saintly Cure of Ars. Her heart was crushed by the sudden death of her Husband, who to all appearances, was ill prepared to undergo the Searching Scrutiny of the Divine Judge but the holy Man cheered her with an assurance, well founded too, of his salvation but at the same time impressed on her to pray much for him and especially to offer the Stations of the Cross as the most efficacious prayer she could offer.

This is brought to mind frequently in *this House* when that devotion goes on almost from morning till night. The Penitents have the greatest devotion to the Stations and seldom or rare is the chapel without some one or other *going the rounds* and certainly no more suitable devotion could be found for them. We have a sweet little Chapel both here and at St. Mary's. When I say *little* I speak in comparison to a *Church,* for they are far from small ones being 100 x 50 and the one here 90 x 40. The Altar stands in a deep recess with a small Stain glass window at each side, in one, the *Good Shepherd* in the other Mary Magd. with the Cross, skull and book. We have many saintly souls among the Inmates and are often consoled by visits from those who have left and are now doing well outside, but once in a while are grieved, as happened last week, by the news that one had died miserably, perhaps by her own hand. I recommend our dear charges to your prayers.

I suppose you see S. M. Bernard [Hamill] occasionally. She seemed to feel Arthur's death even more than Margaret's. I have both their obituary cards in our Chapel so as to secure them many prayers from the Sisters etc. etc. We have about 7 acres at this Establishment and our Cemetery is here, a sweet little spot with fine Trees and green grass but to keep it so we are obliged to irrigate except for a couple of months in the rainy season. We have had summer weather until the last couple of weeks when it became pretty cold, but as yet we have had very little rain. The washing for the Hospital, Home, St. Peter's and Lourdes is all done here so our laundry is a big affair. The washing, wringing and mangling are done by steam but the girls do the starching and ironing. We also keep here cows sufficient to supply all our city houses with milk but men do all milking in this country and, of course, we have to buy all the feed. It is like coming to the country to come here tho' we are not out of the city limits.

I saw an article recently on this city in which it was mentioned that 300 was the population in 1848. Now it is a big city with some 50,000 children attending school so you may judge what the entire population must be— We have two schools *here* in the City and two others elsewhere. Our present Abp. is urging all the Pastors to provide schools, not alone for the girls, but also for the Boys who have hitherto been rather neglected.

I have not written very frequently of late to Sr. M. Emmanual [Russell]. I trust her eyes will not trouble her long, but I suppose she will be obliged to have the cataracts removed. I use glasses at night and if reading fine print but not as a general thing. Thank God for the exceptionally good health I enjoy. I am sure you are *thin;* it is your nature but I trust you feel well. Tho' I may not be prompt in replying, I am always glad to hear from you so don't wait for me but write when you can. Is your old Landlady Mrs. Purdor still alive? I have an idea she is not but forget and St. M. Aquin [Martin] is not at hand to assist my memory. She is in Sacramento at present. Now is not this a long letter and little in it but having a free afternoon you have got the benefit of it. From my heart I wish you all a happy year—To all I send afft. love and am as ever yours in J.C.

Sr. M. B. Russell. *Sister of Mercy*
P.S. Miss Curoe cousin of Mrs. G. Hamilton of High St. has a Brother in Mo. whom she is writing by this mail to call on Mr. Gartlan to arrange his affairs and draw up his will. She begs Mr. G. will keep the will, for her Brother is soft and foolish, easily led and might be made a fool of by designing persons. He wrote to her he was about to make his will in her favor.

The following letter is another example of the direct, familial and chatty style Mary Baptist used in writing to her family. It exhibits both her humor and concern as well as her spiritual insight.

Date: July 27, 1887
To: Mary Hamill (Arthur's wife)
From: MB Russell
Source: Archives, SOMB

St. Mary's Hospital
San Francisco, Cal.
July 27th. 1887

My dearest Mary,
    I heard of Emily's delicacy and of your having taken her to England etc. so I knew what kept you from writing. Thank God her health is improved. Her little ones would suffer if she continued delicate, so for their sake she must be prudent. She sent me Agnes' photograph and indeed she does look a darling child. Well indeed you must feel half lost in the big House now that the family is reduced to yourself and dear Alice. Could you not let it for the whole term of your lease? But just because you would feign do so it will be the more difficult to get a Tenant. One of our wealthiest families here wished to sell their House and right away a purchaser offered and truly I could not help thinking if they were poor and the sale seemed a

necessity there would not be one to buy, and it seems so almost always but God knows what is best and his Providence regulates these things so we must try to bow humbly to His Holy Will.

You have one great comfort in all your trials; loving good children and lacking that would anything satisfy you? Oh! If you only knew the unfeeling, selfish children we meet here frequently, you would bless God a thousand times for the devoted love your children have always shown you and their Father. His anniversary could not pass unnoticed and when I told Sr. M. Aquin [Martin] of you reminding her to pray for him she told me to say she could *never* forget him. She esteemed him too much for that. She is ashamed that she never wrote you a line but the truth is she is the laziest person at her pen I ever saw. It takes her *an age* to make up her mind to write even to her family and once her poor Mother is gone, I doubt if they will ever hear from her. She is with us at present for a couple of weeks but Sacramento is her Home for the time being.

You heard dear Arthur speak of an Old Friend Miss Kate Russell of Columbus. She is failing a good deal and as she loves dear S. Mary Aquin much and they can talk of mutual Friends in *Heaven* or in the *Green Isle*—we brought Sr. M. Aquin down.

With so much anxiety on your mind, I fear you did not enjoy your visit to London very much otherwise it would surely have been a great treat. I believe your Brother Frederick resides in that great City. Is his daughter still unmarried? What a lovely woman her Mother was and I believe she was as sweet in disposition. I see you are still as great a Beggar at Heaven's gate as ever. You are quite right never give up. Are not these words of our Lord unconditional, "Ask and you shall receive" and we know when He delays, it is for some wise end, to try us, to increase our merit, or because He who is infinitely wise sees the thing we seek is not for our good and then He is sure to give something more beneficial. Well I remember your *urgent* appeals in the dear old Cathedral in Newry. You and poor Lilly were kindred spirits as far as that went, but she was always more buoyant than you. Oh! Indeed she was a loving soul and she was very fond of you. I suppose you took a peep at Ballybot when you were in Newry but it is much changed since the time we use to go in a group to Mass etc. Of course you went to see Anne. I suppose she is getting old altho' her health has always been so good and her life so uniform and quiet she may hold out many a year yet. I must write to her for the Feast of St. Bernard as she has not now dear Margaret to do so.

Our visiting Surgeon is a son of Sir Robert Kane of Dublin. He and Mrs. Kane went home on a visit in the beginning of May and returned this week. He is delighted to get back to California and gives a sad description of our dear Native Land. Irish men *out here are not so despondent.* The majority of them think good times are at hand and that this coercion Bill will only hasten the advent of better days, but all changes, even for the best, entail many present troubles and difficulties. Some of Mrs. Kane's family is connected with Mrs. P. Russell but I never inquire into the matter. I think her name was Kavanagh. She is a fine woman. You may know her.

Does Lady O'Hagan continue to spend a portion of the year in Dublin and is she as friendly as ever. I would also like to know what became of Dr. Macdonald's daughter. Her cousin J. Gartlan is here as you, of course, from Alexander. He is doing his best to get up the ladder and finds it is hard work but he is *truly good* and had good health so may hope to succeed p.G., sooner or later. Your good old Mother was acquainted with Miss Cassin and you may have known her too, so you will be glad to know she has a quiet home with our Sisters in Sacramento where she is employed as Music teacher and to accompany the Intern pupils to Church etc.

You may be sure *I will do all I can to obtain* from *Heaven all you desire* for yourself and dear Alice and Arthur, to both of whom I send my afft. love. Did you ever think of asking dear Arthur now that He has more influence with God than we mortals can have to help you? I am a firm believer in the departed interesting themselves for those they leave still struggling in the world. So now ask him to get you what is needful, and Agnes and Charlotte who are surely in the presence of God, don't cease to love and sympathize with their dear Mamma, and so ask them too to pray for all your wants. If you worry much it will tell on your health, so try to resign yourself to the care of Divine Providence with loving confidence. Pay Matthew a visit and give him my love—Now, dear Mary, good bye. Pray for your ever affectionate Sister in J.C.

Sr. Mary Baptist Russell
Sister of Mercy

Sister Mary Bernard was the elder sister of Mary Baptist and the first of the siblings to enter a convent.

Date of Letter: prior to June 5, 1888
From: Sister M. B. Russell
To: Sister Mary Bernard Hamill
Source: LMMB, 166

The year 1901, if I ever see it, will be my golden Jubilee. But I don't expect to live so long, nor do I wish it either; in fact I wish for nothing, knowing that the very thing I might be naturally inclined to desire may be the least desirable for me, so I have no wishes whatever, except to be a good religious, and for that I beg your prayers always. May God graciously hear all the prayers offered for your Golden Jubilee, and may eternity be for you one long jubilee of love and praise.

This chatty letter to Matthew Russell includes descriptions of the Grass Valley foundation and its environs. It also expresses Mary Baptist's appreciation for support of the Jesuit Fathers in California. The Jesuits provided retreats, direction and support for the sisters throughout the early years of the community. Although Matthew places the letter inscription as 1868, internal evidence indicates that the letter was written in 1888, thirty four years after Mary Baptist's arrival in California.

Date of Letter: September 20, 1888
From: Sister M. B. Russell
To: Matthew Russell S.J.
Source: LMMB, 148-151

Convent of our Lady of Mercy,
Grass Valley, Nevada County, California,
September 20th, 1868.

To-morrow being the feast of your holy patron and not claimed by any one nearer or dearer than yourself, you shall get all my days' doings' good and bad, and I trust the former may predominate. It seems to me it is unusually long since you wrote, but I believe the

Retreat season is a busy one with you. It would astonish you the number of Retreats your Fathers here are called on to conduct. The late Provincial, Father Congiato, told us more than once that whatever community might be disappointed, we never would, and you must know we require three, two for the Sisters and one for the penitents. You recollect Father Raffo; he gave our first retreat this year, Father Calzia the second, and Father Neri the one for the penitents. We say truly the Jesuits are the greatest blessing we enjoy in California. God bless them everywhere.

I have given you above my present address in full, not that I expect you to send your reply to this place. I came here this day three weeks and hope to leave this day week. My throat was somehow a little troublesome, and the doctor said a short time in this pine district would be beneficial, and so it has, thank God, both to me and my two companions, Mother Mary Gabriel [Brown] and a young professed Sister [M. Ignatius Stafford] who claims your holy founder for her patron. This is a real primitive country place and we can do here what would be unusual elsewhere. For instance, we three, and three of the Grass Valley Sisters, went on Monday morning after breakfast out at the rear gate of the Boys' Asylum and in five minutes found ourselves in a primeval pine forest through which we wandered *ad libitum* a few hours, resting occasionally and not meeting a living creature save a few cows with bells on their necks and some birds, lizards, and such like. The morning was cloudy, for which reason it was selected, as usually at this season the sun is very hot. We were not home over an hour when loud rolling thunder was heard and plenty of lightning also, soon followed by heavy rain, which was welcomed by every one and has made the country sweet and fresh since.

Through thirty-four years in California, it is only this week I saw a mine. You may be sure we did not descend the shafts, but we saw the cages ascending and descending with men and rocks, and saw the whole process required for getting the gold from first to last; and surely it is no wonder it is valuable, for it costs great labor. The process would be too tedious for me to explain in writing, but truly, it is interesting. Some sad accidents occur. The employed are obliged to change their clothes before leaving the building, and are examined, fearing they might secrete valuable specimens; and to the honor of our holy Faith, it is a fact that never yet did a Catholic attempt such a thing, though that cannot be said of Cornishmen. Yet the latter get the preference, the present proprietors being nearly all Protestants. The two mines we visited are the Idaho and North Star; the former goes a perpendicular depth of 1600 feet, the latter goes only a depth of 600 feet, but runs over 1800 feet, following the ledge of gold-bearing quartz. There is in each a machine for forcing fresh air into the mine. I am bringing several specimens to our cabinet.

Now I must tell you about this establishment, which is our first filiation. It is twenty-five years since it was started, a mere mustard seed; now it is a large institution, including an asylum for orphan and half-orphan boys (about eighty-five in number), one for young orphan and half-orphan girls, and a third for the more grown girls, amongst whom are the children of families living in remote districts where no good schools are to be found; the girls in both mount up to pretty nearly two hundred. Ground is not so valuable here as in the city, so they are not stinted. It would delight you to see the boys chasing each other through the pines, or playing ball, etc. The whole enclosure of six of seven acres is left free to them. The Sisters find it costs less to buy fruit and vegetables than to cultivate them.

**Matthew edited his sister's letter at this point and no copy of the missing content exists today. The sentence below was at the conclusion of the longer letter.

I was told lately I look as young as I did twenty years ago. The truth is I never looked young.

Mary Baptist was blessed by robust health until the last two years of her life. At an earlier period, however, she did have a short interruption to that physical well-being. She writes to assure her sister Sarah that all is well.

Date of Letter: 1888
From: Sister M. B. Russell
To: Mother Mary Emmanuel (Sarah Russell)
Source: LMMB, 172-173

I fear Sister Mary Francis' [Benson] letter may make you more or less anxious about my health; so I will tell you I have since had an examination, and it is found that the first opinion given by the doctor was not correct. My case is not so serious as he feared, and in the course of a month or so, I will, please God, be all right. But he keeps me lying either on a lounge or in bed, and has ordered me lots of good things to take, even meat on Fridays! *So my day has come.*

Few of the letters that Mary Baptist sent to Charles still exist. She followed her brother's political career with great concern but, as the following letter indicates, her deeper concern was his spiritual well-being. The trial referred to is the Parnell trial in which Charles was involved. Parnell was a leader in the fight for Irish Home Rule.

Date: April 29, 1889
To: Charles Russell
From: Sister Mary Baptist
Source: TTS, 103

My Dearest Charles:

I need not tell you we are watching with intense interest your struggle with the powers of the land, and glory in the success that seems to attend your efforts. Three things especially rejoice my heart: First, that you are true to your Faith, then to your country, and last to the principles of temperance. May God bless you, my dear brother, and preserve you ever true to these three points, and then your glory *here* will not lessen your glory *hereafter*. This is my prayer; for would I care for all the good you procure for the cause in which you are engaged if it deprived you of one degree of happiness hereafter? "What doth it profit a man to gain the whole world if he suffer the loss of his own soul?"

To give you an idea of how the poor Irish out here watch the progress of the trial, I will tell you how one of our patients, after weeks of delirium in fever, only just got a gleam of consciousness when he asked the doctor how the Parnell case was progressing; and, when told how gloriously everything was going on, the poor fellow uttered a heartfelt "Thanks be to God!" and declared that the news did him more good than a dozen bottles of medicine.

Now, dear Charles, I want you to send a little remittance to _____ in Brooklyn. I believe it is *needed*, though it may not be *deserved*; but we must overlook that fact once more.

I had a little share of sickness myself this last year, but now, thank God, I am all right. We may thank our good Mother's wise rearing for very many of the blessings that we enjoy. May God bless you, my dear Charles. When you make your Easter Communion, give me a memento.

Your ever affectionate
Sister M. B. Russell
Sister of Mercy

Sister Mary Agnes Stokes was a vital member of the San Francisco community for many years. Her impending death evokes a reflection on death from Mary Baptist.

Date of Letter: @August 27, 1889
From: Sister M. B. Russell
To: community members
Source: LBBR, 166

Our dear, kind-hearted, devoted sister Mary Agnes is to all appearances near death.

****

Certainly we will do everything in our power to honor the day when it comes; but who can tell how many of us will then be in the land of the living?? Let us learn a lesson from our poor dear sister now lying in the infirmary. Not a prayer can she say, not a look can she cast on her crucifix. Even when Father Prelato called and tried to rouse her to consciousness, she could give no sign that she had even heard him, though it is possible she may know what is going on. She has not opened her eyes since she was anointed. It is indeed little we can do when dying. I will send you a few lines each day as long as she is in this precarious state.

The letter following is another in the series of letters which were exchanged between Mary Hamill and Mary Baptist. In addition to chatting about family concerns, Mary Baptist describes some of the poor families she assisted through her lifetime.

Date: Nov. 24, 1889
From: Mary Baptist Russell
To: Mary
Source: Archives, Sisters of Mercy, Kinsale

St. Mary's Hospital
S. F. California
Nov. 24th, 1889

My dearest Mary,

This day 41 years, I entered Kinsale Convent, do you recollect that time? You were only married a few months. Well I remember the delight with which you made a run up to Dublin leaving me in Dundalk where I went to say farewell to all our friends there, how few of them survive but 41 years is a long time. I was very glad to receive your prompt reply to my last letter. I was not quite certain of the address and now I am in the same predicament but if you give me the full address in your next, I will make a memorandum & won't be in a difficulty again. I don't know how I heard of Cootehill being in County Caven and I only hope I am correct.

You have just enough of ground to occupy you. It must be a nice place from your description. I hope Alice inherits your love of gardening. Would you like California seeds, not indeed that I see many, if any, flower I did not see in some place in Ireland. I hope you will soon be able to treat yourself to a phaeton and pony so you can not only drive to Mass but take an airing occasionally. Here Ladies drive themselves continually, but in any case, I am sure Alice can master a Horse, not to speak of a pony. You are quite venerable with your *four* grandchildren. May God bless them all. I suppose their Grandfather Gartlan is quite proud of them too as they are his *only* grandchildren. I am glad there is a Convent of our Order in your little town. Sarah will have no excuse for not going should you be sick. I suppose it is a Branch House from some larger establishment. From which?

Too bad you are so far from Church but you can have an oratory and when you get the pony you will be able to pay a visit every day and that will be the next best thing with Spiritual Communion. You will be lonely while Alice is in London but you will share her recreation in spirit. I hope she will enjoy her visit & have as the people say here *a good time.*

Has Lord Dartry any family? It is a pity there are not any Catholics with whom you could associate—We had a sick priest here lately who was a native of Cootehill (Smith) he described the scenery as really beautiful—Don't forget we got photos of none of Emily's little ones except Agnes—I sent a *Monitor* last week. Let me know if you get them. I will send you one occasionally so as to show I am not forgetting you tho' I may not write.

If you had paper like this you could write a longer letter but that thick paper is too heavy. Your last was over weight, [an] ounce is all that can be sent for 2 1/2. How proud dear Arthur John must be to keep a nice home for you and dear Alice. Thank God for this & that you all enjoy good health.

Is there much distress around you in Cootehill? You must know we meet cases equal to any we met in Ireland. In the land of gold even yesterday I was [with] two families in misery. In one the father is laying with cancer in the stomach and the mother blind for 5 years, and five children. In the other the father is paralyzed and the poor Mother has terrible ulcerated legs. Their eldest child, who is their support, is now in consumption & they have two girls half grown, but both these families are a credit to their country and creed and worthy of assistance whereas unfortunately we meet too many who might be comfortable but for their low dissipated habits. Our Lord's words, "The Poor you have always with you" are verified even in this golden country.

Christmas will have come and gone before I write again so I must wish you all the blessing of our Infant Savior. I want you all there to pray for me. We have quite a nice Crib in our Chapel every year, very large fine figures carved of wood & all in proper proportions but we have no *scenery* merely the cave. Good bye, dear Mary.

Ever believe me your affly in J. C.
S.M. B. Russell
Sister of Mercy

Death was a frequent visitor to the San Francisco community. Mary Baptist loving spoke of her deceased sisters in letter sent to other Mercy foundations.

Date: November 17, 1889
To: unknown
From: Mary Baptist Russell
Source: *Annals*, SOMB, II: 95.

"Now all is over for our good, little Sister Mary Ambrose [Flemming] & indeed I trust confidently there is a great reward laid up for her. She was a wise, prudent, sensible religious and anything more edifying than they way she bore her illness could not be imagined. She was young in years & in religion but I verily believe old in virtue." R.I.P.

This letter was written to the sisters in Sacramento. The climate of the city often led to illness and Mary Baptist shows her practical concern in recommending a hot water bottle. Likewise, her belief that daily experience provided sufficient mortification is reflected in the letter.

Date of Letter: December 1889
From: Sister M. B. Russell
To: The Sacramento community
Source: LMMB, 139-140

I know you will each do all in your power to contribute to the general happiness during this joyous season, and that you will make good use of the quiet three days to lay in spiritual strength for the coming year, and repair the rents caused by your struggles during the time that is past. You can renew your vows in concert as we will do here, that is, you [Sr. M. Nolasco Coghlin] say the words aloud, and the others join you.

I hope you are keeping a good fire, and that those who have cold feet, which I dare say all have, get a jar of hot water in their bed at night. We are not so mortified as to wish to be kept awake all night with cold feet. Our mortification must be bearing with all that is disagreeable in each other, laboring hard with stupid, willful children, accepting humbly the thanklessness of their dissatisfied parents and the many other disagreeable things we meet with in our daily life. All this is true mortification, and very pleasing to God, besides showing more of a really mortified spirit than any corporal penance we could undertake.

Now, my dear Sisters, one and all, may God bless you, and may you be every one more pleasing to our sweet Infant Savior than you ever were, and you know that means may you be meek, loving, humble, laborious, forbearing, etc. Let us pray fervently for each other. I hope that you have a little Crib, and that you will be happy in God.

In this letter to her sisters, Mary Baptist gives a mini-sermon on Charity. It was foremost among the virtues treasured by her.

Date of Letter: February 16, 1890
From: Sister M. B. Russell
To: To the Sacramento community
Source: LMMB, 138-139

You must all pray that God will bless us, and all try to be extra good, exact and pious this Lent. Of course fasting from food is not included in the good things, but cheerfulness at duties, exactness, charity, silence, attention and fervor at prayer, etc. At our last meeting I said a good deal on the evil of repeating remarks we may have heard to the person of whom they were made. It is no palliation of the fault, or at least very little, to say, "We did not divulge the name." If the one of whom the remarks were made, and to whom they are repeated second hand, has the heavenly wisdom to take no notice further than to humble herself and resolve on amendment, if culpable, it would do her good instead of harm, and the chatterer would be the only one injured; but unfortunately some persons do not alone feel hurt, but express their displeasure, never cease till they find out who made the remark, or perhaps settle on one that is innocent, and will then rake up the faults of this person, as if that would lessen their own guilt, and their poor minds become embittered and disturbed all from the unguarded tongue and their own pride. Now I do not know that this applies to any of you but it is no harm to be forewarned; so think it over, and you will be less likely to fall into this serious fault. I also spoke of the evil of curiosity and inquisitiveness. Let us think of St. Paul's words, "I know nothing among you but Jesus Christ and Him crucified." Well, my dear sisters, God bless you all.

Mary Baptist mentored Mary Michael Cummings and was partially responsible for Mary Michael's establishment of the Mercy foundation in San Diego. In 1922 the San Diego foundation merged with the San Francisco foundation and became part of the Burlingame Regional Community.

Date: July 20, 1890
To: Mother Mary Michael Cummings
From: Sister Mary Baptist
Source: *Annals of St. Joseph's Hospital, San Diego*, 169

My dear Mother Michael:

The first retreat was in progress when your photograph album and gloves arrived and though not dead myself, I was not able to write as I was very busy. Then a few days later my own retreat began and ever since one thing of other has kept me busy. So only now I can say

'Many thanks' ... I think your plan of renting a house, a wise one. I have do doubt but you will succeed, please God, especially as your climate is so pleasant and healthy.

When you see the Sisters at the Academy and at the Indian School, please remember me very affectionately to them. They were very kind to us, and please tell Father Ubach that I say as it was impossible for me to go to his mission, I did the next best thing and sent you. I know he has a kind heart, but not much management, I fear.

Now goodbye, dear Mother Michael, with love to Sister M. Alphonsus [Fitzpatrick].

Ever yours in J. C.
Sister M. B. Russell,
Sister of Mercy.

Mary Baptist shares with Mary Michael news of another death. The letter contains indications of the exchange that went on between the various California foundations even though they were independent of each other at this period of history.

Date: October 8, 1890
To: Mother M. Michael Cummings
From: Sister Mary Baptist
Source: *Annals of St. Joseph Convent, San Diego*, pg. 174

St. Mary's Hospital
San Francisco, Cal.
October 8th, 1890

My dear Mother M. Michael:
I little thought when I wrote a few days ago, that soon I would have to enclose dear Sister M. Joseph's [O'Rourke] Obituary. You know she looked poorly and felt poorly this long time and within the last month or so she had two severe attacks of heart trouble, but they did not last long. Yesterday she went with the rest to dinner and as we were about half through dinner, she was observed to drop her hands and, when a moment after, my attention was drawn I actually

thought she was dead. Her eyes wide open and fixed as I have seen with so many dead persons, and her face exactly that of a corpse, but in a few minutes it passed away. With help and leaning on the baluster she made her way upstairs. No sooner, however, had she reached the landing than she sank and for several moments all thought she was dead. We had a priest in the house and he was instantly summoned. The doctor and the nurses carried her to the infirmary and from that until she expired her sufferings were terrible. The doctors said it was Angina Pectorus, and from the first, they said it would be fatal. At the same time, they did all in their power, but nothing seemed to even relieve her. She never open her eyes and scarcely spoke, though she was perfectly conscious to the last and her lips never ceased to move in prayer and about one half hour before she died, she told where her own crucifix was to be found. We have already secured about fifty Masses for her. The Requiem will be at nine o'clock tomorrow, the funeral after. Sister M. Francis [Benson] and indeed all got a shock at her sudden summons. You will pray for her and so will good Father Walsh who recollects her well. Please mention her death to him. Yesterday forenoon, Sister went all through the Home, attic and all, it would look like a farewell visit. What a warning to us all to be 'Always ready' as our Lord enjoins. Mother M. Teresa [King] is going to Sacramento. I trust the change may benefit her. Mother Vincent [Phelan] paid an unexpected visit and took her up. Pray it may do her good. Give my love to all your little flock.

Ever yours affectionately in J. C.
Sister M. B. Russell
Sister of Mercy

The following fragment provides insight into Mary Baptist's encouragement of vocations not only to the San Francisco community but to her other affiliations.

To: Miss Mary Murray
From: Sister Mary Baptist Russell
Date: 1890
Source: Archives, SOMB

My dear Mary

If you still have the desire of devoting the rest of your life to God in the service of His little Orphans in Grass Valley, come here to see two sisters who are down here at present and will be for a few weeks. As they have to attend to some business and are occasionally out, you had better send a postal saying when you will call if you wish to see then.

Yours' as ever in J.C.,
S. Mary B. Russell
Sister of Mercy

In Her Own Words
1891–1898

In this letter Mary Baptist describes to her aunt the latest addition to St. Mary's Hospital. True to the intention of the sisters to provide excellence in care, St. Mary's was designed to have the most advanced equipment and accommodations possible.

Date of Letter: September 8, 1891
From: Sister M. B. Russell
To: her aunt, Sister Mary of Mercy Russell
Source: LMMB, 144

Every one says the Hospital is very perfect. There is every convenience that could be imagined: electric bells and lights, speaking tubes, a passenger elevator, chutes for soiled clothes, letters, dust, etc., etc. The three principal corridors are 200 feet long with large triple windows at each end; there are thirty-five private rooms, about a dozen of which are double, and there are eighteen wards, but none large, the largest only accommodating twelve. The bathrooms, water-closets, and lavatories are all nicely tiled, both floors and walls, to the height of six feet; and the basins, slabs, etc., are all marble. The house is heated throughout by steam. But the grandest part of all is the mansard story, in which the operating rooms are situated. There are two antiseptic rooms, the ceiling, walls and floors are tiled, the basins and slabs marble, and they are so constructed that the whole can be

315

hosed out, and the water flows to one corner and runs off down a marble gutter. The operating tables are heavy plate glass in nickel-plated frames. The ophthalmic and electric rooms are furnished in hard wood with oilcloth on the floor. There is a large waiting room off which these rooms all open. We have got the attic hard finished, and one end is for the female employees, the other for the male. The operating rooms are placed between them and only reached by the elevator. There are three flights of stairs, one in our end of the building. We have better and more ample accommodation than formerly, the chief things being fine offices for the Superior and Bursar, which we needed much. All this, of course, has increased our debt, but I have no doubt with the blessing of God we shall pay it off in due time. We have an elegant suite of offices: a dining room, drug-store, and a private parlor for the doctors on the first floor; also parlors and a very neat mortuary chapel from which funerals take place without being obliged as formerly to go from the hall door. Altogether, our place is now very complete.

The stature of Lord Charles Russell caused great interest in him within the Irish Catholic Community. Sister M. Mildred, a Presentation Sister from Chicago, writes requesting information about his early life. The letter provides Mary Baptist's own sense of growing up in Ireland.

To: Sister M. Mildred Flannery, P.V.B.M.
From: Mary Baptist Russell
Date: July 1890 or 1891
Source: *Academy Scrapbook*, (Academy of California Church History: Fresno, CA.), 318-19
A copy is also found in: Archives, SOMB

My dear Sr. M. Mildred,

I would willingly do what you ask but truly I have little to say. My brother's youth was very uneventful & quiet. We had a *truly grand* good Mother to whom we all owe any good that is in us. She gave us practical lessons in obedience, temperance, and all virtues. We were so accustomed to prompt obedience that no one ever thought of questioning any direction we received. One lesson she impressed on us was to take whatever was given to us to eat without remark and I recollect one amusing little incident illustrating this, over which we often laughed. When Charles was about 4 years, he made a lengthened visit to our Grandfather's place and, being the first boy after four girls and being moreover named for my Grandfather, he was a great pet with the old gentleman and still more with our four young Aunts who no doubt indulged him a good deal. A day or two after his return there happened to be fowl for dinner and the gizzard was put on his plate. He put it aside saying he did not like that. When Mamma checked him reminding him that every one [should] eat whatever was given them & and that poor children would be delighted to get what he was rejecting. Of course he had no redress and so the gizzard was demolished, but when saying grace he made a change in the formula by thanking God for his good dinner "Except the gizzard."

From his 5th to his 13th year, we lived in the country and had, I may say, no companions outside our own family. There were no picnics, matinees, theatres, nor anything of the kind to disturb the even tenor of our lives, very little was spent in providing amusements & and we never got candy & such like, yet we had innocent unalloyed happiness. All this time his only Teacher was the Governess provided for us three girls, all his seniors, and I don't think he showed any particular talent, nor was he urged on by anyone and I think he was most generally below Matthew (who was younger) in any lessons they recited together. One [Our] House, a very old fashioned one was at the base [of] a low range of Mountains & ... [*a page of the letter seems to be missing*].

... of them by my Father who was frightened at their not making an appearance when Supper was announced.—After my Father's death when Charles was about 13 he was sent to Catteknock and was, at an early age, apprenticed to my step-brother Arthur Hamill, then practicing as an Attorney. I left him an Apprentice when I went to the Convent & all I know of him since is public. I suppose you know what your Chicago papers said of his having eleven daughters & two sons is untrue. He had five sons and five daughters, but one daughter died in infancy.

Father McElhatton paid us a visit on his arrival. Even tho' warned by your letter of his coming, I did not recognize him. He is now in the Hospital. He got an attack of gastric fever; he will be up today or tomorrow. We are still surrounded by Mechanics & don't expect to be freed from them for a month or more. Won't we rejoice when they are gone.

You must excuse this scribble, I really have not time to rewrite it. I hope it won't make some folks mad at my being foolish enough to write as I have, but I never refuse anything I can grant without serious difficulty & your little journal goes only among your own circle.

We are always glad to hear from you. Our Retreats are all over & the Schools reopened on Monday.

The Penitenta(e) are now in Retreat previous to the Feast of St. Mary Magdalen.

I never see Father Prendergast. The Sisters will be glad to hear that the Ab [Archbishop] is getting strong. He spends a week occasionally in the country with Mrs. Wensinger & she tells me he no longer requires the little soups & so forth that he did.

Affect love to your Rev. Mother.
Ever yours in J.C.
S. Mary B. Russell, Sist of M.

Benefactors were an essential part of the Mercy mission. Without the support of dedicated friends and collaborators, the sisters would not have been able to finance many of their works. Here, Mary Baptist expresses her thanks and appreciation for the support of Mr. Flynn.

To: Mr. Flynn
From: Sister Mary Baptist Russell
Date: May 17, 1892
Source: Archives, SOMB

May 17th, 1892
Dear Mr. Flynn,

I fear you laid out much more on the concert than you acknowledge, and it is scarcely fair to allow you to do so particularly as so much of the labor of getting it up fell to your share. Mr. Hassett told me it was you secured the service of the majority of the talent. We are certainly under many obligations to you and we are most grateful. I shall still be more grateful if you do me another favor, namely to express our grateful acknowledgements to each of the Ladies and Gentlemen when you have an opportunity. They received nothing but plaudits from every one who had the pleasure of being present, which is a great satisfaction to all parties.

Wishing you and yours every blessing,

I remain, dear Sir, yours sincerely in Jesus Christ.

S. Mary B. Russell

Sr. of Mercy

Mary Baptist shares with her sister Sarah, her hopes for the Home for Aged. The project was postponed due to the economic conditions which caused great suffering.

Date of Letter: August 2, 1893
From: Sister M. B. Russell
To: Mother Emmanuel (Sarah Russell)
Source: LMMB, 156

I told you some time ago about a lovely spot we had set our hearts on for the Home, Peralta Park. Well, the Archbishop did not approve of it, so we gave it up. The location was grand, such a fine view of the bay, Golden Gate, Yerba Buena and Alcatraz islands, etc., etc. This very thing, however, was objectionable, as it thus gets the full benefit of the winds and fogs; but it so happened that we went on an exceptionally lovely day. We have since bought five acres in Fruitvale, a suburb of East Oakland, and intend, please God, to build there in time. Our reasons for selecting this place are, first, the climate, which is mild, and, secondly and principally, we are within a few hundred feet of a church belonging to the Franciscan Fathers, where our old people can have the advantage of numberless Novenas and devotions of all kinds. Besides, religious priests are usually more numerous than secular priests, so we are not likely to have any difficulty about securing daily Mass, paying a certain amount annually, of course.

Until we dispose of the property we purchased so long ago for the Home in this city, we cannot think of building, and at present everything here is not dull, but dead. Crowds of people are out of employment, and several of the banks are closed.

This brief note is one of the letters that went between Mary Baptist and other religious women of the City. Mother M. Dolores is the foundress of the Holy Family Sisters.

To: Mother M. Dolores
From: Mary Baptist Russell
Date: November 2, 1893
Source: Original Letter, Archives of the Holy Family Sisters
Fremont, CA

Nov. 2nd 1893
My dear Mother M. Dolores

We received your invitation to the Dedication of your new Convent but we prefer going to see you and it some other day when you will not have such a number of the grand folks as you will no doubt have on that occasion. We congratulate you on accomplishing so much in so short a time. I pray God may continue to bless you & your works for His own glory & the comfort & salvation of souls.

　　With kindest wishes to yourself & Community
　　I remain ever yours afft in J.C.
　　Sr. Mary B. Russell
　　Sister of Mercy

The tenderness and thoughtfulness of Mary Baptist is seen in this letter to a young girl confined to bed. Most likely they met through the hospital or during the various home visitations carried on by the sisters.

Date of Letter: December 14, 1893
From: Sister M. B. Russell
To: Gussie (a young girl confined to bed by a disease of the spine)
Source: LMMB, 122-123

San Francisco, Dec. 14, 1893.

My Dear Gussie:

Knowing you have to act 'Santa Clause' for the little people, I send you this box of different things to help sustain the Saint's good name.

I trust, dear Gussie, you are a little easier, a little improved; still, whatever God allows is for your good, so continue to say often, 'God's holy will be done.' One such act of conformity in time of trial is, according to St. Augustine, more meritorious than thousands of love when all goes smoothly.

I hope your dear mamma is well. Give her my love and best wishes, and your papa, too, the same. Ask them to pray for me sometimes. I need not say a few lines, when you feel able to write, will give me pleasure. Wish all a happy, holy Christmas for me. Have you still a sister with the sisters of the Holy Names? I hope Louis and Lander continue a comfort to their parents, and Joseph also.

Ever, dear Gussie, yours affectionately in J. C.,
Sr. M. B. Russell,
Sister of Mercy.

Economic conditions continued to deteriorate during the mid '90. Distress was great in the cities. The sisters did what they could and St. Mary's Hospital became a social center reaching out to the public. Unfortunately, not all could deal with the hardship.

Date of Letter: February 6, 1894
From: Sister M. B. Russell
To: her sister in Newry
Source: LMMB, 152-153

There is great distress among the working classes here and everywhere. About five hundred men are coming daily for something to eat. We give them coffee and bread. We have twelve dozen tin cups; when these are served out they are dipped into a pail of water and used again. The poor men stand in the open air in a long line, two abreast, and we hand the coffee and a portion of bread out the window. It is considerable work serving so many, but we are thankful that we are able to do it. Of course, we get help. A poor young man hired a room last week in Third Street, and after cutting marks from his clothes and destroying all papers and anything that could identify him, shot himself, leaving in writing that he did it rather than beg, and he could get no employment. I trust we may be the means of preventing such an act. But workmen and tradesmen are not provident; they spend every cent they earn on dress and amusements beyond their rank in life.

The system of choir and lay sisters was outlined in the Mercy rules and customs. Lay sisters, responsible for domestic work and care of the orphans, wore a distinctive dress. American bishops objected to this practice, considering a sign of class separation. Archbishop Riordan asked Mary Baptist to abolish the practice. Always concerned with fidelity to the Rule, she consulted with other Mercy leaders to see what was common practice.

Date: May 9, 1894
To: Archbishop Riordan
From: Mother Baptist Russell
Source: *Annals*, SOMB, II: 148-149
May 9, 1894

Most Rev. Archbishop,

I have consulted the seniors of the community with regard to the change your Grace considers desirable in the dress of the lay-sisters & our opinion is that we are bound to follow the words of our Holy Rule, "The lay-sisters shall be distinguished by a white apron which shall receive the benediction of the Bishop together with the Habit & Veil and be always deemed an essential part of the religious dress." But if the majority of the Houses of the Order in America agree in your Grace's views we shall readily unite with them in requesting the Holy See to add a codicil to our Rules expunging the foregoing paragraph. If you so desire, I shall write on the subject to the Houses in Pittsburgh, Chicago, New Hampshire, New York, Cincinnati & c, but I would request your Grace at your leisure to write me a letter I could copy when addressing them.

Mary Baptist and her sisters were women of their time. In an age prior to ecumenism, great emphasis was placed upon leading persons to a particular religious tradition and to "saving souls." This was not only true within the Catholic community but within Protestant denominations as well. In this letter, Mary Baptist describes the length to which the sisters went to make sure that a dying Catholic was able to receive the sacraments of the Church. The rest of the letter focuses on internal news between Kinsale and San Francisco.

Date: May 15, 1894
To: Mother Mary Evangelist (Fallon)
From: Mary Baptist Russell
Source: Archives: Sisters of Mercy, Kinsale, Ireland

St. Mary's Hospital
Bryant and First
San Francisco, Cal.
May 15th, 1894

My dear Revd Mother,

The above will do for *any one* but as you, dear M.M. Evangelist, have been only three years in office, it is probable it is yourself I am addressing. How astonished you will be to hear *I* am my own Successor. I remember writing to my Aunt M. M. of Mercy in Dundalk when she told me their Bishop got a dispensation & that M. M. de Sales [Vigen] was in the 4th time without interruption. I wrote saying they were *cruel*, they ought to give the poor Mother the respite our Rules allowed, and ever so much more in that style, and now the same has been done to myself; won't you redouble your prayers; the reason for this is that his Grace intends amalgamating Rio Vista to this Community pretty soon. Were you near at hand I would enjoin secrecy, but you may talk of it if you choose, as your words will not reach Cal. S. Mary de Sales [Bouse] is Assistant, my late Asst. M. M. Columba [O'Kelly] is now Bursar, and SM Nolasco [Coghlin] is again Mistress of Novices.

You have received, I hope, a '*Monitor*' I posted Saturday last in which I placed [the notice] announcing the death of our dear Sister [Sister Martha McCarthy]. I will ask Sr. M. deSales to describe her lovely death, only one week sick, died on the 9th & buried Friday 11th but, dear Mother, a holy death is not a *real cross* as you know. I never grieve over the sisters who die holy deaths, in fact, I feel more real happiness than at a Profession. For years we offer Holy Communion on the 1st Monday for our deceased Sisters & Benefactors & on the 8th of May for those interned in our cemetery which we name Mount St. Michael's as that angel is to blow the trumpet at the Last Judgment.

We read with interest all the particulars of your Jubilee celebrations, not one of us understand what is meant by *Ceclian Altar Rails.* I hope 'America's Wonderland' reached safely. We did not *time* the departure of our gifts very exactly. I am glad to see Fr. O'Callaghan is walking in Dr. Delany's footsteps.

You will be sorry to hear _____ are both Protestants, altho' their Mother promised her husband on his death bed that she would bring them up Catholic & for some time did send to the Presentation nuns for instruction. So much for mixed marriages, too common here. I must tell you of an instance of the Divine goodness that occurred here yesterday. A man named Edward Worton in the last stage of consumption was brought yesterday about noon; Between the journey & excitement when Sister got in she found him evidently *dying.* She raised the eyelid *no sight,* no feeling of breath from his nostril or mouth & the faintest pulse. She instantly called the Resident Physician, but he shook his head, *too far gone, dying.* Sister begged him to inject Brandy, something to rouse, as she did not know if he was a Catholic or not. Accordingly the Doctor worked over him injected strychnine, ether & fully a wineglass of Brandy in the arms, around the heart & limbs. Sister at the same [time] giving all the whiskey & water she could get him to swallow and hot applications at his feet. At last to their great delight he opened his eyes and Sister saw he was conscious, so she asked at once if he was a Catholic. "Yes, Sister & for God's sake bring me a Priest." You may be sure no time was lost. It was then 2 o'clock and F. Gannon was with him until 3:50 being obliged, of course, to rest frequently. When the poor young priest came out he looked exhausted & Sister gave him a glass of lemonade. He was hesitating whether he would anoint the man then or in the evening, but Sister said, "In the name, finish the work now." So he administered Extreme Unction and gave the Last Indulgence and sat down to rest in the room with a sick Priest while Sister remained with the man, who expired without a struggle in about 5 minutes—Some time after she met F. Gannon who asked, "How is he now, Sister?" You may imagine his surprise and also his gratitude at being the means of saving that soul.

A poor fellow was hanged last month in San Quentin. As my namesake [Sister M. Baptist Mogan] who has charge of that Institution was ill at the time, I went in her place. It is when death is at hand you see the beauty of faith and the peace it brings to the soul—

S. M. Michael [Kennedy] and Stanislaus [Rodriquez]returned from G. Valley in time for the resignation, but much improved in health. S. M. M. is to return for the summer taking one other invalid S. M. Salette [Lynch] with her. I think it may restore her health. I have just found out that the Abps. has made no secret of the Rio Vista affair, several Priests know it already so, of course, we are no longer bound to secrecy.

How do you manage with the vocals at the Branch Houses? Any lights you can give will be gratefully received— I am so glad you are getting a sketch of M. M. Francis [Bridgeman], our venerated Mother. I think S. M. F.[Benson] has a few letters stored away which I must hunt up for you. No chance of my getting home alas, alas miles when en route for the Eternal Shore.

M.M. Magd's handwriting does not indicate delicacy of age. I think in a little time she may be as strong as ever. I hope M.M. Philomene is over her long delicacy and the young Sisters mentioned as unwell. You did not say what the Cin. frame contained but I will hear that from M. M. Bapt.—the Chonakilty 'Gathered Home' was indeed a lovely idea and I am sure nicely got up. Have you a picture of Mother McAuley. I know Mother Francis was not pleased with any portrait she saw so she said none of them had our Holy Foundress' expression. I pray we inherit the spirit of our *two* Mothers that is more important than having their features—Now dear Mother, won't you continue to pray for us and ever more than ever. Our four senior Novices are in distant retreat for Profession and two pos. for reception, a poss [posulant] left and one entered last week and a novice at Easter. 48 is the number of vocals included S.M F.

[Benson] who did not vote, she has lost all her old interest in what is going on around her, so we think her end must be near—Good bye and God bless you.

Always and ever your affection. J. C.
S. Mary B. Russell
—Sister of Mercy—

This letter contains an abundance of detail about the works of the sisters in the late 1890s. It also provides some anecdotes of humor and insight into the day to day life of the community.

Date: Nov. 6th, 1894
To: M.M. Evangelist (Fallon)
From: Mary Baptist Russell
Source: Archives: Sisters of Mercy, Kinsale, Ireland

St. Mary's Hospital
Bryant and First,
San Francisco, Cal
Nov. 6th 1894

My dear M.M. Evangelist,
    Your good little Postulant arrived yesterday. She made many delays on the way but reached her journey's end in good trim tho' pretty tired. She will not don the cap until Sunday, meanwhile, she will see all that is to be seen in the city. She is out now in the Park & chaperoned by one of our pupils, a school teacher, but who, unfortunately, has no position this term. She will write herself soon. Her Revd. Brother bid her good-bye in N.Y. & proceeded to the Cath. University where he is to spend a year, a great advantage for any young man before going on the mission.
    The Abp. administered confirmation at the Asylum yesterday to twenty one of the Inmates &, as he always does, gave a nice Sermon & Benediction. Dear S.M. Francis [Benson] was delighted to see him, kissed his hand more than once and asked for a Play Day in honor of the 49th anniversary of her entrance, but I suspect some of the young one suggested this. She was in her propelling chair when he

arrived; altogether she is wonderfully well for some time but looks *very ancient*.

You ask is the Asylum attached to St. Mary's. *No*, it is nearly two miles from here on the outskirts of the City but an electric car goes direct from the corner of our street out past the Asylum door & we are *free* in all the cars. St. Peter's Convent is a few blocks from the Asylum but in a more thickly populated part of the City & is fully two miles from us, the cars go direct there also. It was open in the spring of 1878. These schools are considered very fine, but you would not think them large as the Irish schools are so much larger. St. Peters number on the roll is only about 400 and about 345 in attendance. East Oakland is, I dare say, 12 or 13 miles, half of which is the Bay, but it takes just *one hour* to go that distance on the steam cars run every half hour from 5 a.m. to 11 p.m. That House is under the Patronage of Our Lady of Lourdes and sometimes we speak of [it] as 'East Oakland' at other times as 'Lourdes' which made you imagine they are different places—

The works attached to St. Mary's are Hospital, Home, St. Brendan's School and House of Mercy & from it also the visitation of the jail, State Prison & House of Corrections and considerable visitation of the Sick—In St. Brendan's the number is not quite as many as St. Peter's, not over 350 including primary boys. At Lourdes the day school numbers about 225, and they have from 12 to 16 children in the House and extra classes for the Mill children three nights in the week & visitation.

In Grass Valley our Sisters have two orphan Asylums, Male & Female, with 125 in one & 150 in the other and day school for the poor children besides & of course, visitation. In Sacramento they have extensive Visitation & day school and about 25 or 30 boarders. The Sisters in Grass Valley had a poor shabby chapel, but the Superior did not dare to add to the debt but one of the Sisters asked leave to *beg* for means to improve the chapel. Her appeal was so kindly met that she was encouraged to *build* and on the 21st of this month a fine large Chapel will be blessed to their great delight. Their own Bishop gave her 500.00. Our Abp 50.00 and she raffled various articles, some donated & some made by the Sisters. We have sent her a handsome carpet for the Sanctuary and four branches of lovely lilies

(St. Joseph's) made of feathers. S Mary Augustine [Crofts] makes them very perfect. Our two invalid Sisters are there all summer & don't seem in any hurry home but are much improved by the dry mountain air & the exhalations from the Pine forests.

We sent you the obituaries for dear SM Paul [Looby] one month dead yesterday. She was not well for years but, with an occasioned interruption, was able to act as Portress one half the day until Retreat. Since that she failed rapidly. In September it was thought a change might benefit her so we sent her to the sanitarium conducted by the Sisters of Charity in San Jose but she could not bear the heat & returned in ten days. Mother M. Columba [O'Kelly] accompanied her. Good F. Calozio S.J. made her last days very holy & happy, may God bless him. The same time she was sick, SM Carmel [Pigeon] was very ill but thank God she is up & around once more.

I had a little attack myself only a few week ago. I believe it was bilious fever & it has left me not quite as strong as I was—during the summer we had two Sisters of the Im. Heart from Los Angeles & a Sister of St. Joseph from Oakland but for serious operations which were, thank God, successful.

M.M. de Sales [Bouse] has at last come to St. Mary's for good. SM Joseph [O'Rouke], Peter, Augustine [Crofts], Agatha [Ladrigan], Cecilia [Downing] & Vincent [White] are Mother Gabriel's [Brown] staff with the usual number of lay Sisters. S. Mary [Howley], Alphonsus [Riely], Evangelist [Kiernon], Elizabeth [Riely], Dominic [Kelly], Paula [Hughes], Antonia [Gillespie], Zita [Holland] and Fachman [Phelan] nd in addition dear old SM Francis and her nurse S. Agnes [Quinlan] only take care of *each other*.

We are making up our minds to try & commence the Home in Fruitvale next Spring, You must help us by your prayers. Many say SM Francis [Benson] will live to see it up but even if living I don't see how we could get her to it as she cannot put a foot to the ground. We *wheel* her from the Infirmary to the Comty room, Chapel, Balcony etc. She has a *sweet tooth* & sometime ago she [managed] to edge her chair over to the table on which stood a sugar bowl & *helped herself.* SAgnes made fun of her for there was a trail of sugar from the bowl to her mouth. Next time F. Demensini came she must have told him for she announced triumphantly that he said she might take sugar as often as she wished. Well I am near the end of my paper without a word of inquiry about any one but you know we like to hear everything about our Alma Mater. Dear Mother Magdalen is your greatest invalid. I hope she and all are improved. How we rejoice at the happiness of the poor in the workhouse. Thanks be to God, what a change!

Aff. & love to yourself and all & everyone from us all
Ever your aff.
SM. B. Russell
Sister of Mercy

This is a circular letter sent to various Mercy houses to inquire about the dress of lay sisters. Archbishop Riordan was strongly in favor of adapting the dress.

Date: Jan. 31, 1895
To: Dear Rev. Mother....
From: Mother Mary Baptist Russell
Source: *Annals*, SOMB, 149-150

Jan. 31, 1895

Dear Rev. Mother,

For the past two or more years our honored Archbishop, Most Rev. R.W. Riordan, has many times spoken to me about doing away with the white aprons worn by our lay-sisters, telling me that it is the subject of much comment among seculars and consequently of mortification to the Sisters. Whenever his Grace mentioned the subject I merely answered, it was not in my power to make any change—previous to our last Election in May, he urged the point so strongly that I promised that I would consider the matter. After due consideration I wrote to his Grace that as long as our Holy Rule says "They shall be distinguished by a white apron" I could make no change but that if he would give me in writing his views on the matter I would have the subject brought before the Superiors of the Principal Houses of our Order in America and if the majority agreed to the change we would petition the Holy See to expunge that paragraph or add a Codicil annulling it. His Grace has recently given me directions to write myself & therefore, it is I now address you. Please let me hear from you as soon as convenient & when replies have been received from all to whom I am writing, we will let you know the result.

Yours &c
Sr. M. B. Russell

Mary Baptist writes to the Kinsale community to share with them the death of Sister Mary Francis Benson. Sister was one of the founding sisters from Kinsale.

Date: March 6, 1895
To: Mother Mary Evangelist (Fallon)
From: Mary Baptist Russell
Source: Archives, Sisters of Mercy, Kinsale, Ireland

St. Mary's Hospital
S. F. Cal.
March 6, 1895

My dear M. M. Evangelist,

At last our dear SM Francis (Benson) is at the end of her earthly suffering. She died on the 25th. I told you she was failing and tho' very busy, I spent the last few Sundays with her altho' she could not utter a sentence but I felt it pleased her to see me. On the 24th I was as such with her and marked the change more than ever. Next morning I sent M.M. deSales [Igo] and Assissian [Blackiston]. No difference was observed until she was dressed and wheeled into the Comty room, then they saw how altered her appearance and about 11 a.m. M.M. Gab.[Brown] wrote to the Priest to come soon instead of waiting for next morning as had been arranged, so holy lying in her chair, she was anointed in the comty room. The Priest imagined she was unconscious and that he could not give Plenary Indulgence but M.M. G. said "Cannot you *sweet Jesus.*" At the sound of the Holy Name the dear old soul bowed her head most reverently & satisfied the Father she was conscious but by the time I got over she was in her agony & expired with us all around her at 5 p.m. Knowing the crowds of poor old people that would wish to visit her remains, we had [her] brought next day to St. Mary's where she was laid out all Tuesday afternoon, Wednesday & at 9:00 Thursday the Requiem Mass took place. The Abp. presided & preached a little sermon that won him many hearts. Fathers Nugent, Coyle & Gannon were Priest, Deacon and Subdeacon and there were about 13 or 14 Priests in the sanctuary, a wonderful number of this country.

She did not look much spent in the coffin. When the lid was closed and the pallbearers were approaching, one of the old women (Mde Jonventin) almost bent in two made her way over and reverently kissed the coffin. I think you know it is our custom to meet the funeral at the Asylum entrance in choir cloaks and follow the hearse up the avenue to the cemetery, the Priests & Acolytes with Cross, lanterns preceding but omit candles as the wind so often extinguish them. She is laid between S. Madeleine [Murray] and S. Mary Dominic [Quinn], two of the early sisters and the 3rd & 4th to die. When we laid out the cemetery we planted a tree between every two graves but afterward we had to remove them and so those who died recently are buried between the early departed where the trees formerly stood. MMdeSales wrote to Derby and I wrote to M. Gertrude and as soon as we get a few obituary cards I will write to Kingstown for I know the Dominicans will pray for her.

We had two Sisters of the Holy Family & two of the Holy Names of Jesus and Mary at the funeral; so now our dear old Sister is gone & we don't expect to see her like again. She had a heart for everyone. She is the last of her family and may she rest in peace. She seems to understand when told of dear SM Raphael's [McCormick] accident. Tell MM Meg_____[unidentified] her message to the abp and also one from MM Joseph who wished his Lordship to know her two sisters and Brother Tim had all died within the last few months. Bishop Manogue of Sacramento died about 12 hours after SM Francis and was interred yesterday. He was kind to our Sisters. May God send a good one to fill his place.

Among the patients, we generally have one or two Priests but only once before had we a Jesuit. Now we have a holy old man here, F. Berchi with cancer in his tongue. He is to be operated on tomorrow. He gave us many retreats and was our Confessor for some years. Is edifying to see all the time he spends before the Blessed Sacrament. We are making the *Novena of Grace* which is a great favorite with the Jesuits. If you do not know of it, I will send the form up if you tell me. With best love to all the Sisters and hope the Workhouse Chapel has our Divine Lord entroned in the Tabernacle.

I am ever dear M.M. Evangelist yours affectionately J.C.
SMary B. Russell
Sister of Mercy

The Sisters were excellent educators and Mary Baptist did everything in her power to encourage education. In 1895 she prepared a box of materials for a natural history exhibit for St. Joseph Academy in Sacramento. Her knowledge and love of science is evident.

Date: September 30, 1895
To: Sister Mary Aloysius [Nolan]
From: SM B. Russell
Source: Sisters of Mercy, Auburn Regional Community

Sept 30, 1895

My dear SM Aloysius,

I sent today a box of sundries for museum and at the bottom 4th vol of annals and some hymns for Choir Sisters. You will laugh at the *big* box half full and some will be amused at its contents but anything valueless can be thrown aside—The *corals* can be made white by boiling or even by washing and drying in the sun and I am sure some of your chemists know some preparations that will do the work well—I will give a list as well as I can so you can, at your leisure, mark and a big piece of brown marble as one of our tables was broken just as I was collecting these things—you will find a *box* with a good many *varieties of postage stamps* to start your albums. You will find a pair of walrus' teeth and I don't recollect anything else but only wish they were more worthy of being sent so far—I hope your hand improves with time and that SM Berchmanns [Kast] is much better—SM Lorenzo[O'Malley] getting on splendidly, SM Aloy [Reichart]again laid up and SM Angela [Synott] the same but no one in danger of death.

Love to all ever your affect...
SM B. Russell
Sister of Mercy

[List attached to letter]

Plate of whale bone: from 300 to 400 of these plates are found in the mouth of a full grown whale of the species found in the Arctic and Antartic oceans. They [are] 12 to 16 ft. long, the fringe on end and sides acts as a strainer to catch the jelly and other fish on which the whale subsists. When taken from the whale these plates are hard and inflexible but become pliable by being boiled; its elasticity renders it valuable for many purposes—The whale can remain under water a whole hour at a time—The blubber which is many feet thick lies immediately under the skin. Whales are 30 to 100 feet in length according to the species. A large whale yeilds about 40 tons of oil which is very valuable—

Division	Vertebrates
Class	Mammalia
Order	Cetacea
Family	Baloenida
Genus	Balaena
Species	————

The shells I should have marked separately for it will be hard to distinguish many of these but you have portions of pearly nautilus, a pair of pearl oysters, a pair of spiney oysters (broken), several varieties of cowies and I don't know the names of the greater number. There is some Alga (sea weed) across them which adds much to the value and interest.

1st: Sword Fish

Division	Vertebrates
Class	Pisces (fish)
Order	Osseous (bony)
Family	Scombridae

Genus   Xiphias
Species   Xiphias Gladius

The swordfish inhabits the Mediterranean Sea and Atlantic Ocean and occasionally makes its way into smaller seas—A full grown one measures from 15 to 20 ft. the sword being nearly one third the length. It is formed by the elongation of the upper jaw in a horizontal line and is so strong in some species that with one thrust they have pierced the hardest timber several feet. The flesh is palatable either fresh or salted—

2nd: Piece of Pear Tree over a hundred years old, planted at San Raphael mission of the Franciscan Fathers, cut down to make room for the T.O Fellow's Lodge in 1891 before which a photograph was taken.

3rd: Brush (handmade) from Mission of San Juan Captistrano

4th: Model of canoe (Alaska)

5th: Irish Peat (turf)

6th: Indian dish (Arizona) and straw dish, etc.

In an effort to raise funds, Mary Baptist sends out an appeal letter to her benefactors. Some donors were known to her; others were recommended to her attention. She lets the need make the case.

To: Mrs. Robert Baker
From: Mother Mary Baptist Russell
Date: October 10, 1895
Source: Archives, SOMB

October 10, 1895

Dear Madam:

We are making an effort to erect a Home of the Aged & Infirm of both sexes, not a new establishment, for it has been in existence for years but the present house which was erected in 1872 is much too small and very inconvenient. We have secured a very desirable location, paid for it and have the concrete foundation ready, and this had made a big hole in our purse so we are obliged to appeal to the charitable and your name was mentioned as one who would undoubtedly contribute more or less. For a number of years the State allowed all such Institutions as ours a small amount for each really poor Inmate over 65 years but alas, just as we started work it was withdrawn. While it paid, we refused no applicant we could possibly manage to accommodate, the consequence we have now a very large proportion entirely dependent on us and we could not think of dismissing them now, it would be cruel.

It is scarcely necessary to remark that our old people can do nothing to contribute to their own support. They are too feeble from age & infirmities, in fact, this greater number have to be washed & dressed like infants & some even *fed*. About eight are blind so that altogether they are a serious charge. Those [who] had a little saved for old age give it, of course, and when we have better accommodation there are many who intend to buy their Homes in the new Establishment.

May we, dear Madam, hope for a favorable reply to our appeal at your leisure? Please [do] not disappoint us and our poor old people will pray for you and our good God will not reject their prayers.

Believe me, dear Madam
Very sincerely yours in J. C.
S. Mary B. Russell
Sister of Mercy

The depression continues to block plans for the new Home. Mary Baptist comments on the gap between the rich and those in need in this letter.

Date of Letter: December 7, 1895
From: Sister M. B. Russell
To: Matthew Russell
Source: LMMB, 156-157

Business of every kind is depressed and taxes are extra heavy; so, contrary to our expectations, we are getting no contributions to the

Building Fund of the new Home. We are consequently resting on our oars for the present. When I hear of the amount expended for useless decorations, as at young Mackay's funeral and at Miss Vanderbuilt's wedding, I am half provoked. At the last 120,000 dollars worth of cut flowers. It is almost incredible, but even here 500 dollars for a pall of violets has been paid more than once. We are in Calafornia 41 years to-morrow, Feast of the Immaculate Conception, and the day Pius IX proclaimed it a dogma of our Faith. Dear old Mother de Sales [Reddan] threw a miraculous medal into the mud as we drove from the steamer to St. Patrick's Church and begged our Blessed Lady to take us under her protection; and no doubt she preserved us from many dangers, notwithstanding our shortcomings. Ask her to help us now to finish the Home; it is too long on the Hospital premises for the good of either institution, and I could wish (if God's will) to see the new and permanent building erected before I retire from work, and you know my years cannot be many. So, pray, and God bless you.

This is another "letter of recommendation" letter frequently given to persons looking for work.

To: Rev. P. Mulligan
From: Mary Baptist Russell
Date: December 27, 1895
Source: Archives, SOMB

Dec. 27, 1895
Revd. P. Mulligan
Cathedral

Dear Revd. Father

I am much obliged for your letter of this morning and pleased to find that terrible accusation is not down against us in the records of the City. I had not heard anything further on the matter until the receipt of your letter.

I am sending this by Nicholas Powers who is like too many without steady employment and [word is unclear] being and having six children only one of whom is able to work, he is badly off. He has been told you are about to engage two men to work in Calvary Cemetery near where he lives and he hopes, if possible, you will give him the position. You will find him a good sober man, his brother is in the Hospital, an invalid for life.

Hoping you may be able to give the poor man this work. I remain, dear Revd. Father, with many thanks.

Yours respectfully in J. C.
S Mary B. Russell
Sister of Mercy

Mary Baptist continued the conversation with Gussie, encouraging her in her illness. In the next letter, she writes to Gussie's sister, Katherine.

Date of Letter: March 18, _____
From: Sister M. B. Russell
To: Gussie (a young girl confined to bed by a disease of the spine)
Source: LMMB, 120-121

My Dearest Gussie,

I think you must have made the prayer of St. Augustine your own! "Here burn, here cut, here do not spare, but spare me for eternity." Your mother tells me your sufferings are greater than ever. God's will be done. He promises to fit the back to the burden, and I am sure He will not fail to increase His grace and strength in your soul as He increases your pains, and then, dear Gussie, a moment of pain will be followed by an eternity of joy.

Your dear mother, father and sister suffer at the sight of your sufferings, but do not let that grieve you. God will sustain them, and even reward them for all they suffer, and by being conformed to His will, you will draw down many blessings on them. I do not fail to place you daily in the tender care of the Mother of Sorrows, but you know it was not God's will that she should have the consolation of assuaging the pains of her divine son, and it may be that she sees it is more for God's glory, and your real good that you suffer more, and knowing you desire only God's will, she does not relieve you. But never fear, she will support and strengthen you; so, dear Gussie, do not lose courage. What you have gone through is past forever, but the merit of it is before you.

I missed your letters, and I am glad Mother has broken the ice. I know she will write again, hurried though she be. To-morrow will be the feast of St. Joseph. I give you special prayers on that day and during his octave. I don't ask you to pray for me, just one aspiration. May God continue to bless you, my dearest Gussie.

Every yours affectionately in J. C.,

Sr. M. B. Russell.

Date of Letter: April 24, 1896
From: Sister M. B. Russell
To: The younger sister of Gussie (see above)
Source: LMMB, 121-122

San Francisco, April 24, 1896.

My Dear Little Namesake:

I was very much pleased to get your little note, but it had one great defect. You never mentioned Gussie. How came such an omission? Now you have to write soon again, and tell me all about her, for I am always anxious to hear of her. Had you signed your letter Jean Redman, I would know very well who you are, but don't you think as you are a little girl, you would better make it feminine and write Jeanne Baptiste? That is the way little Jeanne Fottrell writes her name. Both her grandmas are Jane, and to distinguish her, she is called Jeanne.

It will be very useful to learn German, so I hope you will avail yourself of the opportunity you now enjoy with the German Sisters, and learn to speak it. I suppose Eva knows last Sunday was the feast of St. Expedit, to whom she introduced us. We had never heard of him until she sent his litany. Tell her we all said a Novena in his honor, and think he did hurry up some matters for us, but much is needed, so let her continue to remind him of our needs. He did something good for a poor little orphan who invoked his aid, and the child sent me word that she will be "Sister Expedit" when she is grown.

Your good Bishop Montgomery called to see Father McManus when he was sick in our hospital, and then came to see me. I was delighted to see him looking so well. I said the climate of Los Angeles must agree with him, and he replied, "Yes, indeed it does."

Now, dear Jeanne, I must bring this to a close, and wish you good-bye. Remember me in your prayers, and give my love to mother and all the family, but in a special manner to dear Gussie. I send a prayer to St. Joseph to keep in your prayerbook to remind you to pray for me at Mass.

Ever, dear Jeanne, your affectionate

Sr. M. B. Russell,
Sister of Mercy.

Mary Baptist was always moved by stories of suffering. She relates one sad story in this letter to an unknown correspondent. The reference to the "Drummond Castle" refers to a ship wreck which occurred this year.

Date of Letter: 1896
From: Sister M. B. Russell
To: Unknown
Source: LMMB, 119-120

The Hospital keeps pretty well filled, notwithstanding the open opposition from many quarters. A young woman died here some time ago of consumption; death was at hand when she came, but the good priest who sent her said it was a charity to take her, though nothing could be done, if it were only to give her a few hours' quiet before death. The poor soul had close quarters and her two children were pulling and pulling at her all day long, and their noisy plays were distressing to her. She lived only a couple of days. When the poor, desolate husband brought the little ones to the funeral, she looked so nice in her coffin, the children did not seem to know she was dead; the eldest, about five years old, said to her father: "Mamma's not coughing now. She's not sick now;" and she kept going from the coffin to her father, evidently puzzled; but when the last prayers were said, and the undertakers put the lid on, she burst into tears and threw herself into her father's arms, "Why did you let my mamma die. O papa, why did you do it?" The poor man could do nothing but cry; and, indeed, many present were also moved to tears. It was as touching a scene as I would care to witness, and we see many such. What a sad thing was the wreck of the 'Drummond Castle!' No wonder the bed of the ocean is called the largest cemetery in the world.

What follows is a very "chatty" family letter from Mary Baptist to Mary Hamill. Like most of her family letters, it is focused on persons. Reflections on the events of the day are woven in and around stories of the many people she loved.

Date: November 24, 1896
To: Mary Hamill (wife of Arthur)
From: MB Russell
Source: Archives: JPD

Convent of Our Lady of Mercy
East Oakland, Cal.
Nov. 24th. 1896

My dearest Mary,

On this dark day 48 years dear Mamma left me in Kinsale. One way it looks very long and in another light *very short*. I am weatherbound and will avail myself of the enforced leisure to write to you. I trust my letter will find you well and all things doing well. I saw dear Alice's name among the attendants at Mrs. Mulholland's Requiem Mass. I hope she is well; and (much as you might like to see her with a house of her own) I congratulate her on being in the enjoyment of single blessedness and liberty. Has Arthur obtained any position since he took up his abode in London? I fear not as I heard nothing of such good fortune being his, and I know such a thing is not easily got. But you have enough to keep you comfortably and cannot be too grateful for that same.

This week we have a national Feast 'Thanksgiving Day' which, if observed as originally intended, is worthy of imitation by all Nations. I recollect many years ago reading in the 'Catholic World' a very interesting sketch of a French Lady, then recently dead, who had thoughts of forming an Association whose object was to make reparation for the neglect of the generality of people to return thanks to God for His many unmerited favors. She mentioned her design to a venerable Jesuit and he gave every encouragement, among other things he told her he had been in many different countries, among so many different classes of people and had been requested to offer Mass for almost every blessing for soul and body that could be named and to rout every imaginable evil but only *once* had he been asked to offer a Mass of Thanksgiving. These are the words of a priest of vast experience, but I think the custom of having Masses offered in thanksgiving is more general now, for I have heard many speak of doing so.

I met a warm friend of yours a short time since. I think her name was Miss Gercim. She brought a letter to M. M. Gabriel (Miss Brown of Limerick) from a cousin of her's who now resides in London. I enjoyed her visit very much. Being quite a traveled personage she had many interesting things to tell. None of you will be in love with San Francisco from her description. She considered it the most ill kept City she had met and she is not exaggerating, for our streets are not in good condition, we much acknowledge—She spoke highly of dear Arthur, may he rest in peace. Just at the time she was here, Charles had arrived in New York and there were frequent items about him in the daily journals. Sr. M. G. asked if she knew him. She did of course. "But," she said, "he is nothing in appearance and manner to his elder Brother Mr. Hamill."

A great fuss was made over Charles. Of course you will hear all about the trip from themselves, but I will tell you what he may not mention and what pleased me more than all the fine things said in the papers; he spent a full hour with John Hamill in his poor place, took the poor foolish fellow gently and kindly, and did not reproach him with his past misdeeds. He gave him L5 and promised to give him L100 to enable him to get a little cigar stand as something of that nature the unfortunate young fellow is fitted for. This I heard from John himself, and it did please me indeed.

We were no little amused when the report reached us that Lilly, only in her 19th year, was to wed Boneke Corkran! As both he and his late wife are relations of one of our Sisters, we knew all about his being a second time a widower, and one of his loving effusions after the death of his last wife happens to be in my hands. I believe he is an excellent man and a practical Catholic. It is not so long since the papers had it he was about joining the Jesuits, so there is little dependence to paid to any public report. How much Ellen would have felt, had her good Mother died during her absence! Indeed at the age of the old Lady, she ran quite a risk; but thank God they were all at home in time.

I see the worst has come with poor dear Mrs. B. Hagan. No wonder she was in a hurry to get rid of Townly Hall and grounds. The unfortunate woman, she must feel wretched. Tell me about her when you write. Has she induced his son and daughter to go with her? Oh! how sad and she is so charitable.

Matthew told me of the handsome Altar erected by Mrs. J. O'Hagan in the Chapel of the Poor Clares Newry. Of course you know he spent four days in Newry on the occasion of its consecration and on his way back saw Aunt Elizabeth who is nearing death. She is very old but not as old as Mrs. Mulholland. I felt a little uneasy at M.M. Emmanuel's [Russell] hiccoughs. Generally they are a bad sign but Matthew tells me some Dublin Physician pronounced her all sound, of course whatever God allows is all I wish done—

Well, dear Mary, I should have inquired about your health the first thing. I trust you are well. Are you like your Mother as you grow older. You recollect Father James Cassin? His oldest Brother and one of his youngest Sisters, now quite aged, are in our Home for Aged and Infirm for years and another Sister died in same years ago. Pray if it be God's will we may be enabled to erect the new Home soon. I never neglect to place you and yours in the loving compassionate Heart of Mary every day. I hope you and Alice pray for me. I will look for a letter about New Years. It is not wonderful how quickly and safety letters travel from side to side of the globe and how little the expense? I *recollect* when it was 2 2 from Newry to Dundalk, precisely what is now charged from Europe to California.

I hope you continue to like London. Dear Margaret enjoyed every spiritual consolation from the Fathers of the Oratory—are you near them? But of course you have Electric cars running in every direction and can easily go wherever you desire without fatigue.

When you write, tell me everything about Charles' family. None of them write so I will be glad to hear of them. Mary seems to be more retiring than Lilly tho' several years her senior. I wish they would give Margaret her name and not call her that foolish *Daisy*. To me Margaret seems a noble name and the other sounds silly. Remember me to dear Emily when you write. James Gartlan is getting *white* but he is a young man no longer. I don't think he is overrun with work but indeed it has been dull with every one. I must not run on longer. I wish you and your little household and all you love the blessing of our Infant Lord. Pray for me at the Crib. I won't forget any of you. Ever dear Mary your afft. Sister in J.C.

　　Sr. Mary B. Russell
　　Sister of Mercy

Mary Baptist relates the news of Mary Gabriel Brown's death to one of her relatives. The letter has a special affect to it in which is seen the sense of loss Mary Baptist experienced.

Date: June 21, 1897
To: Mary Ellen
From: Sister M.B. Russell
Source: Archives, SOMB

St. Mary's Hospital
June 21, 1897

My dear Mary Ellen,

　　You know why I did not sooner reply to your letter—All is over now. About eleven a.m. yesterday we laid your loved Mother Mary Gabriel [Brown] in her grave between her companions crossing the Atlantic, Mother Mary de Sales Reddan and Sister M. Paul Beechi-' nor. Your brother was one of the Pall Bearers. We kept her as long as we could and she looked lovely when we closed her coffin after a second Mass at 7 A.M. She had two funerals, for to gratify the dear Penitents who loved her so much, we allowed them to follow the Hearse Saturday afternoon when her remains were brought over here. They walked in procession, the Consecrated immediately after the

Hearse which went up the circular Avenue and down the one leading to the street. The Sisters stationed themselves at certain distances and gave out the Rosary for the Dead as they walked along. I won't enter into further particulars and indeed I should apologize for saying so much on such a subject but 'From the abundance of the heart the mouth speaketh' and besides I know you loved our dear Mother.

Wednesday, the day on which she received the Holy Viaticum and Extreme Unction, she told me not to forget that you were to be married on the 23rd., so you see she did not forget you in her extremity, indeed she forgot nothing, the mind was as clear as crystal to the last moment. What puzzled me is that she did not really think she was dying; to me she said she would be around again, please God, and Mother M. de Sales [Boase] asked her where she kept certain Papers of importance. "Oh, they are all right. I'll get them for you when I get up" was her answer. Here I am still on the same subject.

Well my dear child, we intend offering Holy Communion for you in the morning and humbly pray and trust your marriage will be blessed by God as I am sure it will. Give my best wishes to your husband whose name I have not heard. Wedded life is placed under the protection of the great St. Joseph, the Head of the Holy Family and he will guide and protect you always. May God and His Blessed Mother bless you and grant you health and happiness and above all Eternal happiness hereafter.

Ever yours affectionately in J. C.
Sister M. B. Russell,
Sister of Mercy

Dr. Luke Robinson was a long-time friend of the sisters. It gave Mary Baptist great joy to have him convert to Catholicism prior to his death.

Date of Letter: October, 1897
From: Sister M. B. Russell
To: Unknown
Source: LMMB, 146-147

He was a good man, and God rewarded him with the true Faith. Many times we feared he might be carried off suddenly without having taken the final step, and Mrs. R. suffered great anxiety on this account, for she understood the precarious state of his health; but, as I dare say you have heard, he had the grace to call for the priest when he found himself sinking on the train, although surrounded by Protestants. And, indeed, no Catholics could have behaved better than they did. They got the car, in which the doctor was, detached from the train, and they brought the priest from the town at which they stopped. After the priest had paid him a long visit in private, the gentlemen were summoned and knelt (not a usual thing for non-Catholics) while the last Sacraments were being administered, one of them removing the doctor's socks. When the priest had taken his departure, the poor doctor said to those present, "Now, thank God, I have received the Sacraments of the Catholic Church, and if you can only bring me home to die, it is all I ask." The poor man expired when only half-way on his journey. It was a terrible shock to his wife, but all the bitterness was gone when she thought of the wonderful grace accorded to him.

This might be termed an "insider" letter. It is filled with the internal news of the community and written to one of its members. Of particular interest is the description of the visitation to Mrs. Phelan. The Corbett referred to is "gentleman Jim Corbett, a champion prize fighter of the period.

To: Sister Mary Helena O'Brien
From: Mary Baptist Russell
Date: @ November 29, 1897
Source: Archives: SOMB

My dear S Mary Helena,

What in the world has happened [to] your poor Brother? I don't think we even heard him being ill and sincerely trust it is a false alarm and that he is already over the worst. Your poor dear Mother must be spared that sorrow after all she had gone thro' and his wife and children still more. We were really stunned when we heard of his illness and are praying & will get prayers that it may be God's will to restore him to his family, tho' as you know, death is not the greatest affliction and may be a blessing in disguise. We shall look anxiously for the next letter. Sister said you were not feeling very well yourself. I hope you are well by this time.

We were both amused & astonished at the Abps. estimate of Cardl. Manning, but he atoned for objectionable remarks by saying His life was *spiritual* and *intellectual*. For surely that was a high compliment and true. I would have been rendered *speechless* had he answered me in the way he answered SM Lorenzo [O'Malley]

I am sure F. Casey must have been pleased that the "Great Day" passed off so well but St. Patrick's Church celebration was *grand* in my mind and Patrick's Day was the same, barring the unhappy, inhuman, brutal fight at Carson. I never could understand how a man with the education & training of Corbett could demean himself by adopting such a profession and I sincerely hope his humiliation has taught him a useful lesson & that he will withdraw at once.

We are being coaxed by Sisters & seculars to remain for the fiesta but I say it would hurry me away, so much do I shrink from *crowds* all my life. We called yesterday on 1st Miss Phelan, 30th and Grand Avenue, a long & easy drive. When within a block of her house a carriage passed us and MMC [M.M. Columba O'Kelly] said she thought it was Miss Phelan, but we walked up the steps & the maid who opened said Miss Phelan had just gone out. We were prepared for this emergency, so Mother gave her our card and we were just descending the steps when Miss P returned. As she is lame, I got into her carriage for a moment or two and then, not wishing, to delay her, we bad her good bye. Imagine her wrapped in furs and a muff and we found the day warm. This morning she sent a large bunch of white and blue Iris with enclosed card.

We next drove to Mrs. Mockles, but the House [was] open on all sides with a dog guarding but no human being to be seen. We left our card & two little prayer books in return for the flowers the Boys gave us last day on the sewing machines. We drove then to M. Getlish (Agnes Dawson) who is suffering with a carbuncle on her upper lip and no one could be more delighted to see another than she was to see us from her house. We went to hunt up S Antonia's [Gillespie] sister and with considerable difficulty found her, and fortunately she was at home, which she seldom is, as she goes from one patron's house to another. She and her brother are both well. She is to call on Sunday next. We want to make her acquaintance with the Sisters here. It was just 6 when we got home and, as usual, I went straight to bed & was only just settled when sister brought in my supper, broiled fish and a honey comb, our Lord's dishes which I kept but sent away milk toast and apple sauce. This will give you an idea how I feel. This morning we had Mass at 6 instead of 61/2 so M. M. C and I were not in choir in time to receive Holy Communion with the rest *before* Mass. I am allowed to go to refectory in honor of the day. We did act for SM Claver today and I believe Mary Meehan enters the Novitiate today also.

We are going with several Sisters to the Ostrich Farm this afternoon & M.C. is prepared to take views with his Kodak. We did intend to go to San Diego the end of this week but may not go before Monday. I intend sending the letters from the children at Lourdes for St. Brendan's children's use and benefit, for I think it the second best way to learn the art of letter writing is to read nice letters, the *first* being to *practice.*

Angelus bell has rung and dinner follows the Angelus, so good bye dear Sister & hoping for good news of your brother & with *love* most affectionately to *all.*

& everyone in all the Houses I am as ever
Yours afft in J. Christ
S Mary B Russell
Sister of Mercy

This letter reveals Mary Baptist sense of coming to the end of her life and her regret that so many of her Sisters have died in such a short period of time.

Date of Letter: @1898
From: Sister M. B. Russell
To: Mother Gertrude [possibly Mother Gertrude Ledwith]
Source: LMMB, 166-168

You know I will be fifty years in religion next November, if I live so long. Dear Mother Gabriel [Brown] and others wanted me to celebrate my Golden Jubilee then, but I objected. I think they feared I might not live for my jubilee of profession; but if I do not, I will, please God, be sooner in heaven. Though life is precarious, and I am perfectly indifferent on that point, I am inclined to think I will see August 2, 1901, which will by my golden Jubilee.

****

I intend sending you a sketch of our cemetery with the names of all our dear departed. Our dead form a goodly company.

It seems to me we lose more in proportion to our number than any community I know—forty-five in not quite forty-four years— and the climate is good, proverbially pleasant, and we give them good food and plenty of it; but the doctors have many times said that the air breathed in the schools, home and hospital was not the best, as we know well; but we rejoice at having now a quiet little spot by the seaside, where we can spend a week or two in turn during vacation, and have salt-water baths. I enjoyed it so myself in the early part of last summer; but, as I got some serious or rather alarming attacks in the fall, no one will hear of my venturing near the water again.

****

One of the Sisters, seeing the dead the chief subject of my letter, remarked that it was scarcely a suitable subject for a jubilee letter, but I know you are like myself, thinking more of the dead than of the living, and among our dead are some very dear to you, so I think you will not object to all I have said.

I must tell you about myself. I do not know whether you heard of the rather alarming attacks I had many times last fall and winter. They have almost disappeared, and, as I sleep well, eat well and am not allowed to do much, I am getting fat; but that does not make long life any more certain, as we see day after day; so I must try to be prepared, should God call me out of life suddenly. I therefore recommend myself earnestly to your prayers, and, as you are naturally expecting your summons before long, I will not fail to recommend you often to St. Joseph, the patron of a holy death. In our infirmary at the asylum we have a picture of that saint, with Our Lord on one side, and the Blessed Virgin on the other. No wonder he is invoked for that great and supreme blessing of a happy death

The last sister we lost, Sister Mary Cecilia [Downing], was not long ill, about ten days, but very sick from the first. It was that fatal pneumonia that carried her off. When scarcely able to articulate, I could hear her repeating, though half raving:

"O Mary, when I come to die,

Be thou, thy spouse and Jesus nigh."

Indeed, all our dear departed had enviable deaths, thank God! I love to reflect on some of them, they were so especially holy and edifying.

****

And now, once more, farewell, my ever dear Sister, until we meet in the everlasting jubilee of heaven.

The last two years of her life found Mary Baptist in ill health. Here, she speaks of the suddenness of her "attacks." The next letter continues that theme.

Date of Letter: January 17, 1898
From: Sister M. B. Russell
To: Unknown
Source: LMMB, 173

At present I am very well; but, as those attacks have come back unexpectedly, I cannot say I am all right. If it be God's will, I should like much to build the Home next summer. Pray for this intention.

Date of Letter: January 27, 1898
From: Sister M. B. Russell
To: Unknown
Source: LMMB, 173

I shall be sixty-nine in April. My health has been shaky all last year, and I may say I did nothing during that time but rest and nurse myself. *Now,* thank God, I feel well, and hope to continue so for a few years with the blessing of God.

This is one of the last extant letters of Mary Baptist. She often lamented that she did not get enough information about Charles' family and that their letters were few. All contact with him was counted as blessing by her.

Date: March 18, 1898
To: Charles Russell
From: Mary Baptist Russell
Source: Archives: JPD

St. Mary's Hospital,
Bryant and First
San Francisco, Cal.

March 18, 1898

My dearest Charles,

Your welcome letter and your enclosure came safely yesterday and I immediately forwarded it to John Hamill. He cannot blame any one but himself if he does not do better than he has heretofore. Please God he will, poor fellow, and you will have your reward a hundred fold. In fact you are singularly blessed, dear Charles, and I am sure your heart is full of gratitude and that you are glad to contribute to the happiness of others. Tho' I appreciate a line from yourself more than a budget from any other, I still look for a letter from Lilly or Margaret with a full account of the all the Little People and all about Mary's Reception and her Order of which I know nothing.

I wrote you a line re. Dr. Mc Nutt's son, of late we have increased our Medical Staff which formerly consisted of only one Visiting Surgeon and Physician and a Resident. Now we have a number and among them is a young Practitioner George Childs Macdonald who told me recently he had been at College with Cyril or Frank. He is Scotch. Another of their School Mates, a Mr. O'Brien (John I think,) called on me a couple years ago. He had no profession and had considerable uphill work but at last got a nice position and is doing well. He seemed an exceedingly good pleasing, young man and a practical Catholic. He is married for some years.

There is another Gentleman Mr. Stanley who has not, I fear, been so fortunate but I never see him of late. He had letters from influential men at home to some of our prominent Catholic Gents here so I fancied he would at once get a position but *no,* he is still without employment. I am sorry to say James Gartlan is *plodding* along but he is so reliable and good that he has the respect of all with whom he comes in contact. I fear our little business is nearly all he has on hands. We are glad to have a person on whom we can depend.

Well, good bye dear Charles, I wish you and all your Household the plenitude of Easter Joys and Eternal Happiness hereafter.

Ever your affectionate Sister in J. Christ.

Sr.Mary B. Russell

Sister of Mercy

Increasingly there are signs of the danger of ill health in Mary Baptist's letters. In this fragment, she speaks of stroke like symptoms.

Date of Letter: June 7, 1898
From: Sister M. B. Russell
To: Mother Emmanuel (Sarah Russell)
Source: LMMB, 173-174

Mother Austin Carroll says she has not one delicate Sister in her community of sixty! I envy her. We have many, and I head the list; but I am not suffering in any way. Yet, without any premonitory symptoms, I lose for an instant the power of my right side; and, as long as I am subject to such attacks I can't say I am *well.* Still I am stouter than ever, and no wonder for I sleep well, eat well, and cannot go around as much as formerly. These symptoms ceased for several months, but have returned of late, though I still follow the doctor's regimen.

****

I am glad Mr. Fegan has acted so nobly.

****

(In a postscript)

How grand the workhouses are getting! Nothing will do them but trained and certificated nurses. The world is changing; it must be coming to an end.

The message of this final fragment was not to prove true. Mary Baptist died five weeks later on August 6, 1898.

Date of Letter: June 28, 1898
From: Sister M. B. Russell
To: unknown
Source: LMMB, 173

You will be glad to know, to hear that my health is as good as it was years ago.

Fragments
and Undated Letters

A variety of small excerpts of letters from Mary Baptist were related in
The Life of Mother Mary Baptist Russell , Sister of Mercy *by Matthew*
Russell. (New York: The Apostleship of Prayer, 1901.) Here are a few of
those which do not have exact dates.

Our own dear Charles seems to prosper in every way. I only hope
God is not allowing more success than is good for his eternal interests.
His 'Woes to the Rich' are frightful. As charity is one of the chief
means of turning riches to good account for hereafter, I must [then
she suggests certain charitable works.] I must also find out if he has
sent a piano I asked him to send to our poor Sisters in a very poor
place in England. (Page 9)

Is Sally Bradley gone to her heavenly home? Will you ever forget
the holly and ivy about the altar in Killowen from Christmas to
March? Poor old soul, she was good and simple.
(Dated l892, page 22)

I need not say pray for her, and ask Father Gleeson to please
remember her at the altar. She was a noble woman and a holy
religious.
(Page 32, on the death of Mother Mary Francis Bridgeman)

"Our doctors don't like our taking these dying cases in, as it necessarily makes our death rate high; but what do we care for that? Many souls are saved, and they will pray for us."

(Page 147)

Fragments or short letters previously unpublished are included below:

Date: Unknown
From: M. Baptist Russell
To: unidentified 'Sister'
Source: Archives, Sister of the Holy Family, Fremont, CA.

Dear Sister,

I have only known the Bearer Mrs. Craig for a couple of week[s] but I am satisfied she is a hard working, good woman and it is a real charity to keep her poor little infants so as to have her free to do a day's work.

Very affectionately in J.C.
Sr. Mary B. Russell
Sister of Mercy

This particular fragment is difficult to translate for the contemporary reader. Phrasing in the third paragraph is unclear and some of the language unintelligible for modern times.

To: unknown
From: Mary Baptist Russell
Date: unknown
Source: Archives, SOMB

Xmas, p. God. She is probably 10 years younger then S Anna. There is a nice little lay sister on the topic also—You must all be earnest in begging God to direct about our three Senior Novices whose fate must be settled pretty soon—Is it true that your trees have all been trimmed already? I am glad you got the gravel before the wet weather. Our Hill looks lovely at present and some beautiful flowers.

Sr. Raphael, as usual, brought a superabundance of the handsome bouquets, the three altars were well supplied.

SM Francis [Benson] our Chronicler reminds that on the 24th Oct.,1855 we took possession of the County Hospital on Stockton St. & same day in 1854 dear Mother M. M. Fr. Bridgeman, at the head of thirty Sisters, sailed from Ireland for the Crimea. SM F is *really* very well, for *years* was not so well.

Father Fassoernott still in G. He's got a number of presents from Ladies. Those who have a taste for fancy work admired very much a couple of Kerchiefs. SM Gertrude went thro the presser [word unclear] three times and thro' yards & yards of the tape worm [??] it head still in possessing

S M Eva. Is waiting in Sac for Sis—

Affc & love to each and all every your aft.
SM B Russell
Sister of Mercy

The following fragments were transcribed in typescript form in the archives of the Sisters of Mercy in Burlingame. There is no notation was made on which communities received the letters.

Archives: SOMB

"It is an ill wind blows no good," & tho' we cannot but regret the circumstances that caused it we at the same time rejoice you are all together once more,—I sent you off this morning our Christmas Box & hope it will be with you by this day week. Its contents are fixings for an Oratory. I hope our blessed Lady and the sweet Infant Jesus will bring you many blessings. Be as cheerful as you can, little as you have of bodily comforts, you have more than they had at this season and when you can receive Our Lord into your hearts in Holy Communion you have more than all the world.

I send some pictures that you may give them to your little children at Xmas. The little Donkey whom you think is rusticating at Fruitvale is now in the hands of the Taxidermist & I expect will have the honor of adorning the Crib at Christmas.—I am told that Sr. M.

Francis [Benson] is failing visibly. I am going to the Asylum this evening to remain over Sunday with my dear old Sister. Don't on any account send money for [the] cloak, it is a gift.

******

How lonely you & your companion must be during this forced idleness. Sister looked for a letter yesterday but looked in vain. She fears you have not received the one she posted this day week—By this time you are wondering why I write & not dear Sr. M.M. I must explain. We found out what you probably knew. That she has been long suffering from a certain distemper & we thought while she was here it would be the part of wisdom to see the Doctor & so by his orders she is in bed yesterday and today. Don't you think we did right? What would be the use of sending her half cured when she could be made all right.

She is looking much better than you left her & is making noble efforts not to worry but to leave everything to Divine Providence,—Sister hopes you have enough to eat. Surely F … will see to that, he is not the good hearted man I consider him if he lets you suffer. We sent our Sr. M. Paul to the "Sanitarium" San Jose yesterday as she was not rallying here & the Drs. said a uniform heat was what she needed. M.M.C. [Mother Mary Columba O'Kelly] is her companion.—

Internal evidence shows this letter to be written sometime in 1888, the year Bishop Manogue had the fence built around St. Joseph's in Sacramento.

Your letter reached us Monday. You had not a pleasant trip after all but, thank God, you reached your journeys end safely.—Poor Sr. must have been overjoyed to see you once more. I hope Sr. M.M. remained quietly in "Bedford Square" for a couple of days. M.M. deS. is getting your cloak made & I hope will have it finished Friday evening. Your clothes are packed ready to start. Mrs.—sent the enclosed. I thanked her for it, tho' in my heart I grumbled that it was not more. You had better send a few lines, they say "Ingratitude dries up the source of benefits" & I suppose gratitude has a contrary effect so it is well to express our thanks to these rich people. I enclose her address. I hope the other two Millionaires to whom I wrote may be heard from later on. I told the "Oil Company" to send you the receipted bill in order that you may be able to judge if it is really a saving to send for it.

I wish it were in my power to send you good Helpers. Let us pray & hope God will send the Laborers in due time. The new Chapel in Grass Valley is to be dedicated on the 12th. I hear Bishop Manogue is now erecting a nice fence all around the Convent Block & putting in artificial stone sidewalks. This is in his Episcopal city, Sacramento. God bless him. The poor Sisters there would never do it. They find it no easy matter to make ends meet.

Friday night I got a Postal from Rev. Fr. Guerin saying "I send two donkeys by freight" & sure enough two white donkeys, mother and child arrived last night. The young one will be killed and stuffed for the Crib & the old one goes to Fruitvale. At first I was disappointed at the color but I find all the donkeys in Palestine & the East generally are white.—I do pray for you all every day & will continue. I will be anxious to hear from you when long enough in _____ to understand matters.

**

Internal evidence indicates that this letter was written around 1897, the year when Mary Gabriel Brown died.

I am thinking you are now poking your own way through the "Desert." Well, God will enlighten you if a visible Guide be wanting. You will get this by the 15th so I welcome you after your stay in the wilderness & hope you are all in good health. Father——called twice, once I was in bed, not a usual thing for me, but I was miserable a few days, next time I was out. The good Fr. has most likely gone home I suppose, as there would be nothing to keep him in this city I imagine.

Under this impression I mailed him a letter yesterday. It contained one from a Millionaire enclosing 10 dollars. Poor Fr. was mightily disappointed no doubt, at his appeal meeting such a poor response from the rich folks down here.—

I sent this week's *Monitor.* It contains our Archbishops address at Archbishop Croke's Jubilee. From friends I heard his speech at

Maynooth Banquet was the best on the occasion—his appearance &
his address are in his favor.—

Pelagia, one of the consecrated penitents, died on Wednesday &
was buried at 3 p.m. Friday. We give them exactly the same honors we
do our Srs. And truly they deserve all we can do for them. Pelagia was
21 yrs. In the Asylum & a holy soul, tho' not the saint of the
Establishment. Magdalen has that happiness. Only the consecrated
rest in our Cemetery, the others go to the Public one.

Dear M.M. G. [Brown] is, I fear, failing fast, suffering almost
without intermission and no appetite, she will be missed should God
call her as she has been a tender wise head to the dear penitents.___

**

It is hard to advise, certainly you must leave no matter how
friendly a few may be. You cannot remain without the Abp. Permission.—My poor souls, you are in a sad predicament, only God can
bring things to a happy end. You can remain, of course, as long as you
like but you can not do anything about settling yourself in that
diocese as long as the Bishop keeps to his present resolve.—Our Sr.
M.M. is failing fast, this climate does not agree with her. We feel sorry
to lose one so very useful. Well, let us try to do what we see is right &
to the best of our knowledge & leave the result to God. "Whatever is
not eternal is unworthy of a thought"——

Nov. 22, 1897

I am losing my name as a prompt correspondent but I believe you
know why? I am here [Oakland] three weeks this morning, I must say
I am a different being &, please God, I will go back to St. Mary's this
day week. It was too bad we let Sr. M.M. undertake that trip South.
It shows what short sighted beings we are. On her account I watch the
accounts of the Yellow fever & I am sorry to see it is still unchecked.
From the first M.M. Austin [Carroll] said they could hardly hope for
its disappearance before the February frosts.

Remembrances and Tributes

Father Matthew Russell, S.J. asked Archbishop Riordan to send him recollections and observations about Mary Baptist. The following is the personal recollection of Archbishop Riordan sent to Fr. Russell in response to that request. The complete text is located in the San Francisco Archdiocesan Archives.

July 16, 1912

Rev. Matthew Russell, S.J.
St. Francis Xavier's Church,
Upper Gardiner Street,
Dublin, Ireland

My dear Father Russell:

You must excuse me for my delay in answering your letter. I was in Chicago when it reached here, and when I came home I found so much to be done that I put it off from day to day, until at last it was time for the retreat of the Clergy, which I was obliged to attend. I returned Saturday evening, the 13th, and immediately set to work to answer your request. The enclosed I deducted quite hurriedly; look it over, change what is not correct and polish it up the best way you can. You have my full permission to make any changes, amendments or corrections as you think fit.

Dear Mother Russell was a wonderful woman in many ways, and she has left the impress of her life and work upon her Community in this city of San Francisco. She was eminently fitted for the pioneer work which she came to do, and her name will be held in veneration by all who knew her.

I do not wish this letter of mine to go to the press as you receive it, without first having been corrected by your own hand. I cannot tell you how busy we are here. Six years ago the great work of fifty years was in ruins, and we have been trying to rebuild our institutions from that day to this. Thank God we have accomplished wonders, and almost everything has been rebuilt. The city will be better and more beautiful than before, and all the Catholic institutions destroyed have been replaced by larger and more substantial buildings, but it has taken all my time from morning till night, and I am just about tired out.

With kind remembrances to all my friends of Upper Gardiner Street, I remain,

Yours faithfully,

The recollection follows:

July 16, 1912

Dear Father Russell,

It gives me great pleasure to write the following lines about your saintly sister, Mother Baptist Russell:

Mother Baptist Russell arrived in San Francisco December 7th, 1854. The city was small, as it had been organized only in 1849, and had the appearance rather of an overgrown village than of a settled, well organized city. The Catholic population was small, and very few of them people of means. They had come here attracted by the discovery of gold, and most of them were on their way to the mines. In those early days few people came to remain long. Their object was to get some portion of the wealth that was to be found here, and then return to their homes in the east. Such a population, being unstable, is not apt to take much interest in religious institutions, and having drifted away from their old, well ordered homes, they are apt to become very careless in the practice of the duties of their religion.

Mother Baptist was not here long before she realized that there was a great work to be done to save this floating population to the

Church, and lost no time in beginning it. She was a gentle, calm, silent but strong woman, who took in at a glance the necessities of the situation, and laid her plans accordingly. A hospital had to be built for the infirm; a house of protection and reformation for the erring ones of her own sex; a house of Providence for the unemployed; a home for the aged, both men and women; and above all, and most necessary, Catholic schools in which the children of our Catholic people while learning the things that would be useful for this life would, at the same time, be solidly instructed in the principles of their religion which would sanctify their lives here on earth, and bring them to their eternal home after this life is over.

At the present time, when churches and schools are numerous, it is not easy to understand the tremendous difficulties that confronted her on all sides, difficulties that would have deterred one less hopeful and less courageous than Mother Baptist Russell. She had a great work to do, and with the courage of the saints she put her hands to do it without delay. She had God with her, and with His assistance all obstacles could be surmounted. She remembered the saying of St. Teresa, towards whom she had a great devotion: "Teresa is nothing. Teresa and two ducats are nothing. But Teresa, two ducats and Almighty God are very powerful," and so, although Mother Baptist and her small Community were poor, their Divine Master would see that the means needed for the work they had at heart would not be wanting. When she passed to her eternal reward she left as monuments of her great zeal a well equipped Hospital; a Home of Providence for aged men and women; a Magdalen Asylum; a large school for boys and girls in St. Peter's Parish; a school in St. Brendan's Parish; a school in St. Anthony's Parish, Oakland, and a Retreat for the members of the Community who needed rest now and then from their exhausting labors.

These material works would, of themselves, be sufficient evidence of the very great business qualifications which she possessed, and also of her tact and influence in bringing people to place at her disposal the means necessary for their construction and maintenance. The principle source of her ability to interest her lay friends in her works of charity was her deeply spiritual character. All who came in contact with her soon recognized that she was a woman of deep faith, great piety and most affectionate love for the poor. She accomplished much because she was entirely disinterested, asking nothing for herself, nothing for personal needs or comfort, but always for others; always thinking for others, planning for others; she was in every fibre of her being a perfect Religious. If I were to single out from her many virtues those most characteristics and prominent, I should name her obedience and her charity. The rule of her Community was the law of her entire life.

She inculcated by counsel, and above all by example, that victory over one's self comes only to the obedient. As our Divine Master was obedient, even to the death of the cross, and hence was given a name above all other names, so Mother Russell instructed her spiritual daughters that progress in the religious life could only be attained by a strict observance of the letter and spirit of the Rule under which they had made their vows. It might seem to others who did not know her well that her government was severe, but her spiritual children forgot that she was the Superior, because her authority was applied so gently, so affectionately, that the name of Superior was lost in the more endearing name of Mother of the Community. She never issued commands, she politely and gently made requests, and her requests were always granted. The union between her and her spiritual children was perfect. She had obtained from Almighty God the gift of government, and obedience on the part of her subjects was an easy thing because it was prompted by a very deep affection.

Her charity towards all, and especially towards the poor, was boundless; no poor person was ever turned from her door. The care of the sick was always without compensation for those who were unable to make it. It was enough to be destitute to receive her most careful consideration. The words of the Book of Proverbs find an application in her life: "She hath opened her hand to the needy, and stretched out her hand to the poor." (Prov. 31. 20.) In her dealings with all classes of people she was the personification of courtesy and kindness, and we may apply to her the words of Proverbs (31. 26.), "She openeth her mouth with wisdom; and in her tongue is the law of kindness."

Her voice was low, sweet and deliberate. One always felt when speaking with her that she realized that words were the expression of thought and were to be used with deliberation. As age came on, her activities seemed to increase, and she was every day planning something new for the good of her Community, and ultimately for the good of our Catholic people, so when the end came it found her vigilant and working for her Lord. Death came sweetly and gently; she was conscious even to the last. It was a consolation to myself to have her recognize me and speak to me shortly before she passed into eternity. When it became known that Mother Baptist Russell had died the whole city seemed to feel that a great woman had gone from it. Thousands visited her bier, and the large chapel was filled with a multitude that overflowed into the street as the last solemn rites of the Church were held over her remains.

She left her impress on her Community. It is today what she made it, and her words and example are quoted as authority on all questions by the members of it. We all felt that a special blessing was left by her to her spiritual children.

Her great devotion was to our Lord in the Blessed Sacrament. She was always the first to offer Him her homage in the morning, and the last to leave Him at night. She seemed to realize always that she was speaking and acting in His presence. He was indeed a companion to her during life; may we not feel certain that she is His companion now in His eternal home.

I remain, my dear Father Russell,
Faithfully yours,

The following collection of memories from Sisters who knew Mary Baptist are preserved in the archives of the Burlingame Regional Community. They were gathered as living memories long after Mary Baptist's death.

Remembrance of Sister Mary Lawrence Comyns

During early days when Nuns first began to ride free on the street cars, Sister M. Lawrence, a postulant, was assigned to accompany Mother Russell on her round of visitation. Both Mother and Sister had wrapped extra sheets or blankets under the cloak, and were carrying hampers containing soup, jelly, etc. They were permitted to ride on the first street car. On the second car the conductor demanded their fare. Mother Russell courteously acknowledged she had none. The conductor put them off. They went to 6ᵗʰ and ___, where Sister M. Helena's father had a livery stable. Mother Baptist asked for fare. Mr. O'Brien was very much annoyed at the conductor and demanded his number. Mother Baptist asked him to overlook the incident for she feared for the man's job. Mr. O'Brien gave them a carriage and driver. They rode in state that day. The visitations were all the way from South of Market to Silver Avenue.

Remembrance of Sister Martina Nolan

Sister Martina—young—was hurrying to get patients ready before 9:00 a.m. when lecture took place. Sister delayed. Realizing that she was late and that no one was in the convent corridor Sister began to run. She ran *into* Mother Russell. Mother said sweetly, "My dear, there is no need of such rush. You are late for lecture. Do not go in this morning." Sister Martina with greater love for God in her heart, returned to the patients.

To write the life of Mother Russell you would have to have known her. She was so motherly, so kind. Once I went to complain that while I was getting a tray for a priest, some other nun had taken him to the nurses' dining room. This meant that I had to let my own work go and all in vain. My resentment instantly disappeared when Mother so sympathetically said, "Oh, my dear, did they do such a thing to you."

One day I paused to let Mother Baptist pass me on the stairs. She looked at me and to my surprise said, "My dear, you look so very tired. Go now and lie down for a while."

Once we came with Mother Baptist to Fruitvale. Mother was working in the garden when a well-dressed man passed by. He and Mother began a conversation which became quite serious. Later Mother said to me, "That gentleman is in great trouble and needs help." "But Mother, he is so well dressed!" She sorrowfully explained that that was all the more reason for sympathy. It is so difficult for those who have seen better days to acknowledge their dependence.

Remembrance of Sister Christine O'Connor

Mother's manners, for a great lady, were so very simple.

Remembrance of Sister Mary Agnes Quinlan

Absolutely without vanity. As simple as a child.

When we read *The Three Sisters of Lord Russell*, we catch her simple, friendly, unaffected spirit. On her return from Ireland with the postulants one of them called her, "Reverend Mother." "I am not the Reverend Mother, but I have a good chance of being so when I return home.

Remembrance of Sister Mary Regis Wallace – Sept. 19, 1944

When Mother would go for Chapter of Faults she would often take the young Sisters with her. They loved to go. Before going to Chapel she would tell them to be good Sisters, to show what nice novices they were, to walk around the gardens and the grounds. At St. Catherine's good Miss McDonald at the door was always so happy to see Mother. One day she was taking a poor girl, so young looking to the two Sisters, to the hospital to have a baby. They innocently asked Mother if she were married. Mother answered, "No, that is the sad part." Here conferences were like those of a mother to a daughter. She would say, "I noticed last week that some Sisters came noisily into Chapel; I know this will not happen again. When on time we come in any door to the Chapel. When late, we come in the front door; we do not give a quick bow as though someone were chasing us, but we give a religious inclination. I know that this will not happen again; the Sisters will come reverently and quietly into our dear Lord's Eucharistic presence."

Shortly after Sister M. Regis and Sister M. Philippa were professed Mother N.[Nolasco] or C. [Columba] called them and told Sister M. Regis she was sending them over to St. Hilary's with dear Mother M. Russell. She instructed Sister M. Regis to be kind, thoughtful and watchful of the courtesies, to do all she could for Mother Baptist who was not well, to make the bed to her use, to take up hot water, do up the cell, and spare her a step here and there. Sister was delighted but found that it was impossible to have Mother rest. However she graciously accepted Sister's little services; she could receive as graciously as she could give—a real Mother's trait. However, she delighted to get down early to the old oil stove and make coffee. She would fry the meat and really cook the meals. Mother would also help with the dishes and prepare the dishes that the young Sisters would take to Sister M. Lorenzo and to Sister M. Raphael, although they would urge the young Sisters not to let dear Mother do so much work. Mother would go bathing daily with the Sisters and after throwing a dipper of water on them would tell them to plunge in. Even though they did not swim, they promptly obeyed her, for with their love was a deep reverence and respect for her mere wish. Sister M. Regis lost the profession ring in the bay while bathing and she cried out, "I would just as soon lose my finger." Mother answered, "Sister, such a thing to say. You might not be of much use to the community without a finger." As it was getting dark Mother advised Sister to come down early in the morning and if she were not too attached to the ring Our Lord might let her find it. If not, Mother promised that at the next profession she would have one blessed for her. This she did.

Dr. Lyford asked Mother to come over and select a site that he wished to donate to the community. She took the two young Sisters with her and told them that Doctor had gone through fifty six law suits to hold the property, and how grateful she was. She explained to them that the piece of property on the hill appealed more to her than the property on the low land which was damp and marshy while the hill site invigorated one. Besides this health standpoint Mother looked to the future as she explained that when the public came and the property had to be sold or turned into a sanitarium she felt that the community would realize more from the hillside. She planned a bulkhead so that bathing would always be good and water available for swimming. As a girl in Ireland she loved to swim and she kept up the practice at St. Hilary's. Mother died before the plans for St. Hilary's were completed. She saw only the site and lived in the old cottage, never in the present house. Mother had asked the opinion of the Sisters regarding the proposed site; they agreed with Mother's selection. Afterwards, the other site was given or sold to the Sisters of the Holy Family. Although her last illness was creeping upon her and she had to take her medicine, Mother enjoyed the talk and pranks of the young Sisters and she had as enjoyable a two weeks as they had. The young Sisters and the sick Sisters never forgot the last vacation that Mother had made so pleasant for them. After Dr. L. death, Mother had wanted to buy the land from gulch to gulch but the heirs would not sell.

The Sisters loved to go on visitations with Mother. When ill health was upon her and the Sisters wished to spare her carrying heavy baskets to the poor she thought of a way to spare them anxiety. Under the cloak and habit she fastened sheets, towels, linen and dressings she would need; in the large pocket other articles would fit. Mother looked so dignified in the long cloak and with the light looking bag that the Sisters did not worry. The young Sister carried the bread, tea, meat and potatoes, etc. While on the visitation Mother's partner was often surprised; out of nowhere would appear all that was needed in the sick room of the poor. The dear Sister, who on arrival from school, was Mother's partner, would have been only too happy to have carried all these for mother. Sister Philomene knew just how to pack for Mother. Many a time this dear nun was held up as a model to the young Sisters for her common sense, generosity, spotlessness and saintly life. One day, after the bag was packed Mother said, "I think Sister M. Regis can carry the basket today." Happy Sister M. Regis set off and soon arrived at the home of a drunkard. The poor refined young mother and wife was dying. As Mother excused herself she took from under the cloak the necessary bed linen with which to make the bed; at the same time she sent Sister to wash the face and hands of the five dear little children. When the patient was about ready to receive the last Sacraments, her husband came in. As Mother shook her finger at him and asked him why he did not show more appreciation for his lovely wife and five beautiful children, he was ashamed; at the same time he was most respectful and grateful for what the Sisters had dome for his family. Mother had brought medicine for the sick woman, a bit of nourishing food, and good wholesome food for the children which we prepared as we cleaned the rooms.

After another visitation before leaving she said to the poor woman, "Have you paid the rent?" The poor woman answered, "O

Mother, where would I get the money?" Mother handing her the wherewith said, "Take this, say nothing, and pay a month's rent." On another occasion when a girl in reduced circumstances was to be married Mother fitted her out in some of the embroidered gowns and linens that the postulants had brought. Many postulants were sent home if Mother and the Council did not feel that they would make good Sisters of Mercy. Eight had been dismissed before Sister M. Regis' profession. When clothes would be airing the Sisters were relieved to hear that they were for the poor and not for themselves to wear home. Mother helped six little children on Perry Street and another group on Baldwin Alley; the latter was a dirty, smelly place, no outlet, just a short alley; their father drank heavily.

Sister M. Rose made many of the clothes for the poor. Sister M. Emmanuel, a true daughter, walked in Mother's footsteps. One day after Mother Euphrasia gave her $20 for a poor family she returned and asked for $20 for another family; Mother felt that she could not possibly give it to her. Just then a loud knock on the door was heard and Archbishop Riordan entered. He was always happy to see Sister M. Emmanuel and he asked, "Are you in trouble, Sister?" Mother Baptist told him, "Begging, Archbishop, and I was telling Sister I did not have it this time." He asked, "How much do you need, Sister?" When Sister answered, $25, your Lordship the Archbishop wrote the check and handed it to Sister. When Sister exclaimed, $1,000, $1,000, O Archbishop, $1,000, he told her, "Never mind, Sister, only this morning a wealthy man was so grateful to God that during this awful flu epidemic not one of his several sons and their families had been afflicted; in gratitude to God he asked me to see that this $1,000 would be distributed among the deserving poor without any red tape as some who had been reduced would be embarrassed going through the Red Cross. He said, "Jot down the names on a slip of paper, Sister Emmanuel, so that if I die before the $1,000 has been accounted for I can leave a record that I had placed it in good hands. When work was scarce and food less plentiful, Mother Baptist started the Soup Lot. This brought vocations among the girls who saw as many as 400 poor people a day receiving the help of the Sisters. One day as the Sisters were standing on a corner, a big teamster jumped off his truck, handed Mother $10.00 and said, "to do good among the poor." He shook her hand and jumped back to his truck.

Remembrance of Sister M. Leo Mahoney

In the year 1871, dear Rev, Mother built a school house on a lot adjoining the Hospital. There was no Catholic school in that part of the city. When the school opened I was one of the first pupils. When the school was in its infancy, we had the pleasure of having Rev. Mother come for a half hour each day to teach us Christian Doctrine. All loved her dearly, there seemed to be a charm about her, every word she uttered formed an impression. She had such nice stories to tell us, she won the hearts of all the children. When the school became well established we only had occasional visits from her and we looked forward with pleasure to the time of her coming. She would always be present at our Exhibitions and encourage us in all our endeavors. I think it was on the occasion of our first Public Exercises, she entered the room in which were assembled the children that had taken part; I was one of the number. I cannot remember her exact words but they were to this effect: My dear children, I am well pleased with you all, and what is better still, I am sure you are all pleasing to Almighty God; and those who have not done so well have the same merit in God's sight. He looks to the intention and I am certain all tried to do their best. These were cheering words for the unfortunate ones like myself, who did not do so well.

A Sodality of the "Children of Mary" was established in the school. Rev. Mother took the deepest interest in it. Even after we left school, she kept track of us all. She would send her Sisters to visit us in our times of sorrow and if possible would go herself to offer consolation. The old pupils of St. Mary's could not forget her. She gave them every encouragement to lead good, holy lives. She entered into the spirit of all their little amusements and before she left would always impress them by relating some little incident that had happened. On one occasion when Rev. Mother was present at one of our Sodality meetings, we were drawing the virtues for the month; when I drew mine, Rev. Mother asked, "What did you draw, Kate?" I said, "Perseverence." Mother asked, "Remember, Kate, it is only she who perseveres to the end shall be saved." She said it in such a way I could not easily forget it.

When I was fourteen my dear father was on his death-bed. Dear Rev. Mother heard he was ill; accompanied by another Sister she visited him and gave him such consolation in his dying hours. When she left the house, turning to my mother, he said, "I think those Sisters are ministering angels sent from God." The saying could be well applied to dear Rev. Mother, she was an angel on earth, ready and willing to sooth all that were in affliction.

When my school days were finished, I only had the pleasure of meeting Rev. Mother occasionally. The old pupils of the school would generally meet at the Reception or Profession of one of our old schoolmates. On one of these occasions, after the Profession of one of our companions, now Mother Nolasco, dear Rev. Mother invited the old pupils into one of the parlors, sat down in our midst and related to us all about her vocation. Rev. Mother said, in speaking of her own vocation, "I picked up a Catholic Paper and glancing over it the first thing that attracted my attention was an article explaining about the "Order of Mercy" in Kinsale. It gave an account of the good done by the Order and stated that they were greatly in need of Sisters. There were plenty of Convents in my own part of the country, but the caring for the Sick, visiting the Poor and Distressed was the field of labor I desired; so I made up my mind to go to these Sisters if possible. I stated my desire to my Confessor who put no obstacle in the way, but said he would speak for me to my parents and obtain my desired request. This he did, no objection was made and shortly after my dear mother accompanied me to Kinsale." She explained why it was she became attracted to the "Order of Mercy;" how she broke the news to her father, that she wished to devote her life to God. She also related to us her trip to Ireland, 1879; told us she had stopped at Omaha, visited the Convent of Mercy there and was entertained by two of the old pupils of St. Mary's who were then Professed Sisters. She was in hopes some present on that day had a vocation, she thought we were very slow. A remark she made that day struck me. "What grieves me most," she said, "is that I have not more to give to the poor." Her heart was centered in them. At that time she was doing great good for the poor of the city.

A few years later my sister chanced to meet Rev. Mother, she enquired for me. My sister informed her that I had still the desire to become a Religious, but could not leave home at present. Rev. Mother said, "We will take Kate at any time." She always had the good kind word. Those few words, coming from the kind heart of dear Mother, gave me courage and consolation in many a weary hour. When I would think all hope is gone and I must content myself to remain in the world, those kind words would build up my hopes and give me courage. When I felt I was free, at the age of 38, I took the courage to beg admittance into the Order. Dear Rev. Mother received me kindly. I was the last Postulant she took to the Altar for Reception and the day I was one year received, on the sixth of August, our dear Mother was called to receive the reward promised to the good and faithful servant.

Notes

Introduction

1 A woman religious is a woman who has made vows within the Catholic Church. She is commonly called a Sister.

Chapter One

1 Matthew Russell preserved the family recollections in two books: *Mother Mary Baptist Russell,* (Dublin, Apostleship of Prayer, 1902), which will be noted as *LMMB* and *Three Sisters of Lord Russell of Killowen and Their Convent Life,* (London, Longmans, Green and Co., 1912).

2 O'Brien, Barry, *The Life of Lord Russell of Killowen.* (London, Thomas Nelson &Sons, 1901), 21-23.

3 During the 1600's supporters of Oliver Cromwell sought to suppress the Catholic faith in Ireland in an effort to control the Irish people. During this period there was fierce opposition against what the Irish deemed an English invasion. Catholic lands were confiscated and given to Protestant nobility loyal to the British crown.

4 O'Brien, *The Life of Lord Russell of Killowen*, 24.

5 The penal laws, lasting from the 1600's until 1829, placed limits on the participation of Catholics in public life, restricted the ownership and inheritance of land, forbade Catholic education, and interfered with freedom of worship. The intent of the laws was to force Irish Catholics to forsake their religion of birth and enter the English Church.

6 O'Brien, *The Life of Lord Russell of Killowen,* 33.

7 O'Brien, *The Life of Lord Russell of Killowen,* 26.

8 The Orange Party refers to a Protestant fraternity named for William of Orange. It was closely aligned with Protestant governmental control over the Catholic majority of Ireland.

9 John Mitchel's *Jail Journal* is an important chronicle of the movement for Irish self-determination and Home Rule. He was jailed by the British for his activism and became a symbol of the Irish resistance.

10 Russell, *LMMB*, 9-10.

11 Russell, *LMMB*, 9.

12 Russell, *Three Sisters*, 175.

13 Russell, *Three Sisters*, 178.

14 Russell, *Three Sisters*, 181.

15 Russell, *Three Sisters*, 179.

16 Russell, *Three Sisters*, 178.

17 Russell, *Three Sisters*, 180-181.

18 Russell, *Three Sisters*, 172.

19 Russell, *Three Sisters*, 181.

20 Russell, *Three Sisters*, 185.

21 In the early 1800's the British government dissolved the Irish Parliament and gave the Irish people representation in the British Parliament. The percentage of Irish representatives was not sufficient to have significant influence on policies that effected the Irish population. The "Repeal" movement was aimed at canceling the Union Act that created this structure and, thereby, reestablishing an Irish Parliament.

22 Russell, *Three Sisters*, 188.

23 Russell. *Three Sisters*, 184.

24 Daniel O'Connell was the Irish politician and legislator who led the fight against the oppressive governance of Ireland by British authorities. His activities eventually led to the establishment of home rule for the Irish people.

25 Russell, *Three Sisters*, 185.

26 Russell, *Three Sisters*, 184.

27 Russell, *Three Sisters*, 177.

28 Russell, *Three Sisters*, 174.

29 Private notes of Mrs. Una McClafferty of Newry who extensively researched the life of Lord Charles Russell.

30 Russell, *Three Sisters,* 177.

31 Russell, *Three Sisters,* 186.

32 Russell, *Three Sisters,* 187.

33 O'Brien, *Life of Lord Charles Russell of Killowen,* 25.

34 Russell, *Three Sisters,* 192.

35 Russell, *Three Sisters,* 189.

Chapter Two

1 Russell, *Three Sisters,* 192.

2 Russell, *Three Sisters,* 192-3.

3 Author unknown, "A History of Newry Workhouse, A Collector's Item Magazine," 1996, 2, 12.

4 The Irish were unaccustomed to using Indian meal, a coarsely ground substance that needed cooking to be digestible. Ignorance of how to prepare this food and lack of cooking facilities made the rations ineffective.

5 Author unknown, "A History of Newry Workhouse," 11.

6 Robert Kee, *The Most Distressful Country, Volume 1 Of the Green Flag.* (London, Quartet Books Limited, 1976). 247.

7 Kee, *The Most Distressful Country,* 247.

8 Russell, *Three Sisters of Lord Russell,* 193.

9 Russell, *Three Sisters,* 193.

10 Bishop Blake was both friend and advisor to Catherine McAuley. It was with his encouragement and support that Mother McAuley founded her order. Like the Sisters of Charity, the Sisters of Mercy were devoted to the service of those who were poor, ignorant, or infirm, especially women and children. The style of their work was to be in the midst of the people. Visitation of the sick poor in their homes, the protection of young women, and the instruction of youth were foremost in their commitments.

11 Since pension schools charged tuition for their students, they were not focused upon service to the economically poor. The free schools were open to every child and supported through outside funds.

12 Russell, *Three Sisters,* 195.

13 Johanna O'Mahony Walters, *Merci Beaucoup A Story of Courage and Compassion, Convent of Mercy, Kinsale 1844-2002.* (Johanna O'Mahony Walters, Church House, 2001), 14.

14 Handwritten notes from Kinsale annals found in Kinsale archives, annals entry 1847.

15 Handwritten notes from Kinsale annals found in Kinsale archives, annals entry 1847.

16 Russell, *Three Sisters,* 195.

17 Russell, *Three Sisters,* 195-196.

18 The House of Mercy was a ministry established by most early Mercy foundations. It housed young women who were employed as domestic servants or in employments. These women often needed safe shelter to avoid being exploited by their employers.

19 "Memoir of Mother Mary Francis Bridgeman," typescript copy found in Kinsale archives, pg. 11. Parts of document are identical to an article published in the *Irish Monthly* by Mother Mary Austin Carroll, but she is probably not the author of this memoir. It is most likely the work of Mother Mary Evangelist Fallon.

20 Walters, *Merci Beaucoup,* 18.

21 In Katherine's time, new members began their religious life as postulants. This was an initial period of testing whether they were called to be Sisters. The next step in the process was becoming a novice. During the period of her novitiate, the woman would intensely study the charism of the order, the ways of religious life and its commitment. The last stage was first vows which, when completed, led to a profession of vows for life.

22 Russell, *LMMB,* 39.

23 Guardians were an oversight group that set policy and direction for the workhouses. They determined workhouse capacity, quantity of food distributed and monitored health conditions. Some did their jobs better than others.

24 Walters, *Merci Beaucoup,* 16.

25 The "fever" was mostly likely typhoid fever.

26 Walters, *Merci Beaucoup,* 16.

27 Walters, *Merci Beaucoup,* 17.

28 "Memoir of Mother Mary Francis Bridgeman," 16.

29 Board Schools were under the jurisdiction of the Board of Education. They determined curriculum, approved teachers and paid the cost for instruction. Because of the climate of prejudice at the time, certification of teachers was, at times, subject to unjust evaluation practices.

30 "Memoir of Mother Mary Francis Bridgeman," 17.

31 "Memoir of Mother Mary Francis Bridgeman," 2.

32 "Memoir of Mother Mary Francis Bridgeman," 3.

33 "Memoir of Mother Mary Francis Bridgeman," 6.

34 "Memoir of Mother Mary Francis Bridgeman," 6.

Chapter Three

1 Thomas Gallagher, *Paddy's Lament Ireland 1846-1847 Prelude to Hatred* (New York: Harcourt Brace Jovanovich, 1982), 16.

2 Gallagher, *Paddy's Lament,* 117.

3 Gallagher, *Paddy's Lament,* 119.

4 Gallagher, *Paddy's Lament,* 204-206.

5 Gallagher, *Paddy's Lament,* 210-211.

6 John B.McGloin, *San Francisco, The Story of a City* (San Rafael, Ca.: Presidio Press, 1978), 33.

7 John B. McGloin, *California's First Archbishop the Life of Joseph Sadoc Alemany, O.P. 1814-1888* (New York: Herder and Herder, 1966), 74.

8 JoAnn Levy, *They Saw the Elephant: Women in the California Gold Rush* (London: University of Oklahoma Press, 1992), 217. The mission referred to is Mission Dolores.

9 Sister Andrea Vaughn, "Bonnets by the Bay" in *The Academy Scrapbook,* Vol. III, No. 2 (October 1952), 66.

10 Vaughn, "Bonnets by the Bay," 67.

11 Vaughn, "Bonnets by the Bay," 68.

12 A charism is the special gift or spirit given by God to a religious community for the sake of others.

13 *Annals of the Sisters of Mercy,* Archives, Sisters of Mercy, Burlingame Regional Community (SOMB) 10, 11.

14 *Annals,* (SOMB), 15.

15 *Annals,* (SOMB), 22-23.

16 Russell, *LMMB,* 55.

17 Russell, *LMMB,* 38.

18 Russell, *LMMB,* 39.

19 Russell, *LMMB,* 42.

20 Mother Mary Austin Carroll, *Leaves from the Annals of the Sisters of Mercy, Vol. 3* (New York: Catholic Publication Society, 1889), 471.

21 Carroll, *Leaves from the Annals, Vol. 3*, 472.

Chapter Four

1 *Annals*, SOMB, 25.

2 Carroll, *Leaves from the Annals, Vol. 3*, 473.

3 Carroll, *Leaves from the Annals, Vol. 3*. 474.

4 Carroll, *Leaves from the Annals, Vol. 3*, 474.

5 This term refers to a very small vessel which could usually navigate in shallow waters. Here the waters were so shallow that even such a boat or raft could not be used.

6 Carroll, *Leaves from the Annals, Vol. 3*, 474-475.

7 *Daily Alta California*, December 10, 1854: 1.

8 *Annals*, SOMB, 27.

9 The correct name of the "Know-Nothing" party was the National Council of the United States of North America. It was a secret society growing out of a fear and dislike of foreign-born residents in the U.S. It was particularly hostile to those of the Catholic faith tradition. The name "Know-Nothing" referred to their usual response when asked about their group or activities: "I know nothing."

10 *Christian Advocate*, December 9, 1854.

11 *Annals*, SOMB, 28-29.

12 The gold rush brought peoples from all nations to California. Among these new Californians were criminals and adventurers who took advantage of the absence of a strong legal structure. Groups like the "hounds" and "ducks" were ethnic gangs who victimized other immigrants.

13 John B. McGloin, *San Francisco, the Story of a City*,(San Rafael, Presidio Press, 1978.), 60.

14 McGloin, *San Francisco, the Story of a City*, 60.

15 Thomas Denis McSweeney, *Cathedral on California Street*,(Fresno, Ca: Academy of California Church History, 1952), 19-20.

16 This title was given to the Sisters during the small pox epidemic of 1868 by a grateful patient. *Annals*, SOMB, 473.

17 By custom, the title "Mother" was given to sisters who served in leadership roles within the Mercy community. It applied to superiors, assistant superiors and mistresses of novice. In Mother Reddan's case, she was the assistant to Mary Baptist.

18 Russell, *LMMB, 53-54*.

19 Russell, *LMMB,* 55.

20 Russell, *LMMB,* 56.

21 Russell, *LMMB,* 57.

22 The allusion to Mary and Martha refers to the Gospel sisters, one engaged in serving while the other listens at the feet of Jesus.

23 Russell, *LMMB,* 83.

24 Mother Mary Austin Carroll, "Joanna Reddan" in *The Irish Monthly,* (Vol. XX, No. 227, May, 1892.) 228.

25 Carroll, "Joanna Reddan," 229.

26 Carroll, "Joanna Reddan," 232-233.

27 Carroll, *Leaves from the Annals,* Vol. IV, 16.

28 *Annals,* SOMB 435.

29 The conflict in Grass Valley arose from two different interpretations of the Mercy Rule. The Sisters believed they should not teach boys. Bishop O'Connell, determined to provide education for boys, expected the Sisters to comply with his wishes.

30 Sister Mary Francis' sister was Mother Evangelist, superior of Derby, England; Sister Mary Bernard's sister was Sister Gertrude, a member of the Cincinnati foundation. Perhaps all these family ties contributed to the large volume of correspondence that passed among the Mercy missions.

31 McArdle, Sister Mary Aurelia, Private notes on Sister Mary Bernard O'Dwyer. 1

32 *Annals,* SOMB, 480.

33 *Annals,* SOMB, 477.

34 Small pox caused great fear in the public because of its highly contagious nature. Anyone who was in contact with a person who had the disease was considered a danger. The sisters were aware of the measures that needed to be taken to avoid contamination but the mere presence of someone from the "pest house" could have caused alarm.

35 *Annals,* SOMB, 479.

36Sister Mary Aurelia McArdle, Private notes on Sister Mary Francis Benson, Archives, SOMB.

37 *Annals,* SOMB,Vol. II, 158, 159.

38 *Annals,* SOMB, 250.

39 The Office refers to the Liturgy of the Hours, a liturgical prayer of the Catholic Church. At the time Mary Baptist lived, it was prayed in Latin.

40 Sister Mary Aurelia McArdle, Private Notes on Sister Martha McCarthy, Archives, SOMB.

Chapter Five

1 Carroll, *Leaves from the Annals, Vol. III*, 478.

2 Mary C. Sullivan, R.S.M., "Catherine McAuley and the Care of the Sick," *The MAST Journal*, Vol. 6, No. 2 (Spring, 1996), 11.

3 Sullivan, "Catherine McAuley and the Care of the Sick," 18.

4 Carroll, *Leaves from the Annals, Vol. III*, 478.

5 Sullivan, "Catherine McAuley and the Care of the Sick," 11.

6 As quoted in Sister Mary Aurelia McArdle, *California's Pioneer Sister of Mercy*, 39-40.

7 As quoted in Sister Mary Aurelia McArdle, *California's Pioneer Sister of Mercy*, 39-40.

8 As quoted in Sister Mary Aurelia McArdle, *California's Pioneer Sister of Mercy*, 39-40.

9 As quoted in Roy J. Jones, MD, *Memories, Men and Medicine: A History of Medicine in Sacramento, California* (Sacramento: The Sacramento Society for Medical Improvement, 1950), 38-39. Used with permission of the Sierra Sacramento Valley Medical Society.

10 *Alta California,* April 3, 1855.

11 *Alta California,* April 6, 1855.

12 *Alta California,* April 9, 1855.

13 *Annals*, SOMB, 33-34.

14 *Annals*,SOMB, 35.

15 Charles Caldwell Dobie, *San Francisco A Pageant* (New York: D. Appleton-Century Company, 1939), 126.

16 Kevin Starr, *Americans and the California Dream 1850-1915* (New York: Oxford University Press, 1973), 94.

17 *Annals*, SOMB, 45-46.

18 *Annals*, SOMB,43.

19 *San Francisco Daily Evening Bulletin,* April 9, 1856.

20 *Annals*, SOMB, 57.

21 As the Irish Catholic population grew in San Francisco, so did their political influence. This was seen as a challenge to the nativist segment of the city. The work of the sisters at the hospital was caught up in that powerful struggle.

22 *San Francisco Daily Evening Bulletin,* April 8, 1856.

23 *San Francisco Daily Evening Bulletin,* April 17, 1856.

24 *San Francisco Daily Evening Bulletin,* April 25, 1856.

25 *Annals,* SOMB, 54-56.

26 *Annals,* SOMB, 58.

27 *Annals,* SOMB, 59-60.

28 Carroll, *Leaves from the Annals, Vol. III,* 485.

29 *Annals,* SOMB, 73.

30 *Annals,* SOMB, 88.

31 McArdle, *California's Pioneer Sister of Mercy,* 56.

32 McArdle, *California's Pioneer Sister of Mercy,* 60.

Chapter Six

1 *San Francisco Evening Bulletin,* August 4, 1856. This text differs from the text found in the Annals of the Sisters. It was most likely edited by the gentlemen who placed the advertisement.

2 Carroll, *Leaves From, the Annals, Vol. IV,* 6.

3 *Annals,*SOMB, 104.

4 *Annals,*SOMB, 91-92.

5 Carroll, *Leaves From the Annals, Vol. IV,* 24.

6 *San Francisco Herald,* quoted in McArdle, *California's Pioneer Sister of Mercy,* 69.

7 Russell, *Three Sisters,* 199.

8 McArdle, *California's Pioneer Sister of Mercy,* 106.

9 McArdle, *California's Pioneer Sister of Mercy,* 106.

10 McArdle, *California's Pioneer Sister of Mercy,* 108.

11 Church law limited the time of office for religious superiors. After two terms superiors were not eligible for reelected.

12 *Annals,* SOMB, 434-435.

13 Carroll, *Leaves from the Annals, Vol. IV,* 51-52.

14 McArdle, *California's Pioneer Sister of Mercy,* 114.

15 Russell, *LMMB*, 144-45.

16 Letter to Sister Mary Evangelist Fallon, May 15, 1894. Original: Archives of St. Joseph Convent, Kinsale, Ireland.

17 Russell, *LMMB*, 147.

Chapter Seven

1 B. Vicuna Mackenna, "Selection from the Diary of B.Vincuna Mackenna: Winter of 1853 in San Francisco", trans. Brother Veronius Henry, FSC., in *Academy Scrapbook,* (Fresno, California: Academy of California Church History, 1959), 150.

2 Mackenna, "Winter of 1853 in San Francisco," 161.

3 Anne Seagraves, *Soiled Doves Prostitution in the Early West* (Hayden, Idaho: Wesanne Publications, 1994), 137-138.

4 Seagraves, *Soiled Doves,* 137-138.

5 Carroll, *Leaves from the Annals, Vol. 3,* 493.

6 Carroll, *Leaves from the Annals, Vol. 3*, 492.

7 *Annals*, SOMB, 85-86.

8 Seagraves, *Soiled Doves*, XVII.

9 McArdle, *California's Pioneer Sister of Mercy*, 90-92.

10 *Annals*, SOMB, 280-284.

11 *Post* news article, "The Magdalen's Home Compared with the Branch Jail", copy, Burlingame Regional Community Archives, undated.

12 The Children of Preservation were young children found wandering the streets of San Francisco. They often were caught stealing just to survive. Such children were placed in the charge of the Sisters.

13 Typescript notes from Good Shepherd Sisters, Archives, SOMB.

14 *Annals*, SOMB, 283.

15 *Annals*, SOMB, 310-311.

16 *Annals*,SOMB, 312.

17 *Annals*,SOMB, 313.

18 *Annals*,SOMB, 476.

19 McArdle, *California's Pioneer Sister of Mercy, 97-98.*

20 Carroll, *Leaves from the Annals, Vol. IV*, 45.

21 This Intelligence Office acted as an employment agency. It connected those looking for prospective employees with those who were looking for jobs.

22 *Annals*, SOMB, 656-657.

23 Typescript notes, Archives, SOMB.

24 *Annals*, SOMB,591-592.

25 McGloin, *San Francisco The Story of a City*, 58.

26 Carroll, *Leaves from the Annals, Vol. III*, 497.

27 Mary Gabriel's brother was a lawyer.

28 McArdle, *California's Pioneer Sister of Mercy*, 100-101.

29 McArdle, *California's Pioneer Sister of Mercy*, 102.

30 McArdle, *California's Pioneer Sister of Mercy*, 99-100.

31 McArdle, *California's Pioneer Sister of Mercy*, 102-103.

32 As quoted in McArdle, *California's Pioneer Sister of Mercy*, 104.

Chapter Eight

1 Catherine McAuley, *Original Rule of the Sisters of Mercy*, Chapter II, #5.

2 McArdle, *California's Pioneer Sister of Mercy*, 134.

3 Hinston Helper, *Dreadful California, 136,* quoted in: McArdle, *California's Pioneer Sister of Mercy*, 79.

4 Sister Mary Evangelist Morgan, *Mercy Generation to Generation*, (San Francisco: Fearon Publishers, 1957), 90.

5 Sister Gertrude King, *Annals of the Sacramento Foundation, 1857-1905*.

6 King, *Annals of the Sacramento Foundation, 1857-1905*.

7 *Annals*, SOMB, 77-79.

8 *Annals,* SOMB, 204-208.

9 *Annals*, SOMB, 204-208.

10 *Annals*, SOMB, 204-208.

11 *Annals*, SOMB, 241-245.

12 *Annals*, SOMB, 244.

13 Kathleen O'Brien, RSM, *Journeys, A Pre-amalgamation History of the Sisters of Mercy, Omaha Province* (Omaha, Nebraska, 1987), 23.

14 Jones, *Memories, Men and Medicine*, 457.

15 *Sacramento Daily Union*, July 24, 1860.

16 King, *Annals of the Sacramento Foundation, 1857-1905*.

17 Carroll, *Leaves from the Annals, Vol. 4*, 32-33.

18 Carroll, *Leaves from the Annals, Vol. 4*, 33.

19 King, *Annals of the Sacramento Foundation, 1857-1905*.

20 *Annals*, SOMB 284-286.

21 At the time seven choir Sisters were required for an independent Chapter, the governing group of a foundation. Since Grass Valley had only two, all responsibility rested on the Superior for local decisions. Mother Teresa found this responsibility too great.

22 *Annals* SOMB, 323.

23 *Annals*, SOMB, 324.

24 *Annals*, SOMB, 326.

25 *Annals*, SOMB, 326-327.

26 *Annals*, SOMB, 330.

27 *Annals*, SOMB, 423.

28 *Annals*, SOMB, 424.

Chapter Nine

1 *Annals*, SOMB, 396.

2 *The Sacramento Directory for 1854-55*, 13.

3 Quoted in "Knowledge is Power: Sacramento Blacks and the Public Schools, 1854-1860" in *California History*, Vol. 75:3, Fall, 1996, 216.

4 Richard C. Rogers, "The First One-Hundred Years of the Sacramento City Schools, 1854-1954," 9.

5 *Annals*, SOMB, 82.

6. Rogers, "The First One-Hundred Years of the Sacramento City Schools, 1854-1954," 9.

7 Typescript of Notes of Sister Mary Berchmans Kennelly, Archives, Sisters of Mercy, Auburn Regional Community, 3.

8 Typescript of Mother Mary Clare Lunney, *History of the Sacramento Community*, Archives, Sisters of Mercy, Auburn Regional Community, 3.

9 Lunney, 5.

10 Quoted in, McArdle, *California's Pioneer Sister of Mercy,* 137.

11 Steven M Avella, "Phelan's Cemetery: Religion in the Urbanizing West, 1850-1869, in Los Angeles, San Francisco and Sacramento,", in *Rooted in Barbarous Soil, People, Culture, and Community in Gold Rush California,* (Published for the California Historical Society by the University of California Press), 272.

12 Sister M. Regis Wallace, typescript memoir, Archives, SOMB, 10/8/44.

13 Sister M. Regis Wallace, typescript memoir.

14 Russell, *LMMB,* 129.

15 Russell, *LMMB,* 179-180.

16 Sister M. Monica Carroll, typescript of interview with Mrs. Fitzgerald, 1977. Archives, SOMB.

17 Avella, 'Phelan's Cemetery," 272.

18 Typescript memoir of Sister M. Leo Mahoney, archives, SOMB.

19 Mother Mary Francis Bridgeman. *God in His Works.* (Dublin: John Mullany, 1878, Vol.I & II; London: Burns & Oats, 1880, Vol. III; London: Society of St. Anne, 1887, Vol. IV), 4 Volumes.

20 Original Letter, Archives, Sisters of Mercy, Auburn Regional Community.

Chapter Ten

1 Sister Mary Regis Wallace, Interview, 9/19/44, Archives, SOMB.

2 Letter to Mother Mary Evangelist Fallon, Archives of Sisters of Mercy, Kinsale, Ireland.

3 Letter to Sister Mary Helena O'Brien, Archives, SOMB.

4 Russell, *LMMB*, 175.

5 Russell, *LMMB,* 174.

6 Russell, *LMMB,* 177.

7 Carroll, *Leaves from the Annals, Vol. IV,* 23-24.

8 Letter of Mother Russell to Rev. Joseph Sadoc Alemany, May 30, 1857 in *Annals,* SOMB, 388-391.

9 Russell, *LMMB,* 114-119.

10 Russell, *LMMB,* 125.

11 Letter of Mary Baptist to Margaret Russell, October 15, 1857. Jesuit Archives, Dublin, Ireland.

12 Letter of Mary Baptist to Sisters M. Columba, Carmel and Bernardine, February 11, 1882, Archives, SOMB.

13 In the Catholic tradition there is an understanding that God is revealed through matter. Things like water, bread, events carry the believer beyond what they behold to God. In this context, sacramental vision means seeing God in all things.

14 Carroll, *Leaves from the Annals, Vol. IV,* 58-59.

15 McArdle, *California's Pioneer Sister of Mercy,* 181-182.

16 Letter of Mary Baptist to Gussie, date uncertain, but probably during the 1890's quoted in Russell, *The Life of Mary Baptist Russell,* 120-121.

17 Memoir of Sister Martina, Archives, SOMA.

18 The word "cell" was used when referring to one's bedroom. They were normally very small and devoid of any excess.

19 Russell, *LMMB,* 57.

Epilogue

1 Russell, *LMMB,* 184.

Bibliography

The Letters of Mary Baptist Russell and information about the early history of the Sisters of Mercy in California have been gathered from the following archival repositories:

Archives of the Sisters of Mercy, Auburn Regional Community
Archives of the Sister of Mercy, Burlingame Regional Community
Archives of the Sisters of Mercy, Kinsale, Ireland
Archives of the Sisters of Mercy, Newry, Ireland
Archives of the Sisters of Mercy, Omaha Regional Community
Archives of the Sisters of the Holy Family, Fremont, California
Archives of the Society of Jesus, Dublin, Ireland
Archives of the Archdiocese of San Francisco, California

Major Sources

Annals of the Sisters of Mercy, Burlingame Regional Community, Vol. I and II. 1854-1898.

Archival collection, letters and memoirs of Mary Baptist Russell. Sisters of Mercy, Burlingame Regional Community.

Barker, Malcolm E. *More San Francisco Memoirs 1852-1899.* (San Francisco: Londonborn Publications, 1996).

Carroll, Mother Mary Austin. *Leaves from the Annals of the Sisters of Mercy. Volumes III and IV.* (New York: The Catholic Publication Society Co., 1889).

Clear, Caitriona. *Nuns in Nineteenth-Century Ireland.* (Washington, D.C.: The Catholic University Press, 1988).

387

Hurley, Frank. *St. Joseph's Convent of Mercy, Kinsale, A Celebration of 150 Years! 1844-1994.* (Kinsale, 1994).

Jones, J. Roy. *Memories, Men and Medicine, A History of Medicine in Sacramento, California.* (Sacramento, California: The Sacramento Society for Medical Improvement, 1950). Permission granted by Sierra Sacramento Valley Medical Society.

Kennelly, Sister Mary Berchmans. Typescript of Notes. Archives of the Sisters of Mercy, Auburn Regional Community.

King, Sister Mary Gertrude. *Early History of the Sisters of Mercy in Sacramento from 1957.* Archives of the Sisters of Mercy, Auburn Regional Community.

Lunney, Mother Mary Clare. *History of the Sacramento Community.* Archives of the Sisters of Mercy, Auburn Regional Community.

McArdle, Sister Mary Aurelia, S.M. *California's Pioneer Sister of Mercy, 1829-1898.* (Fresno, California, Academy Library Guild, 1954).

McClafferty, Una. Collection of private notes on Russell family.

McGloin, John B., S.J. *California's First Archbishop, The Life of Joseph Sadoc Alemany, O.P. 1814-1888.* (New York: Herder and Herder, 1966).

Morgan, Sister Mary Evangelist, S.M. *Mercy Generation to Generation: History of the First Century of the Sisters of Mercy, Diocese of Sacramento, California.* (San Francisco: Fearon Publishers, 1957).

O'Brian, R. Barry. *The Life of Lord Russell of Killowen.* (London: Thomas Nelson & Sons, 1901).

O'Brien, Kathleen, R.S.M. *Journeys, A Pre-amalgamation History of the Sisters of Mercy, Omaha Province.* (Omaha, Nebraska, 1987).

O'Fallen, Mother Mary Evangelist. *Memoir of Mother Mary Francis Bridgeman.* Typescript manuscript, Archives, Sisters of Mercy, Kinsale, Ireland.

Póirtéir, Cathal, ed. *The Great Irish Famine.* (Dublin: Mercer Press, 1995).

Russell, Matthew, S.J. *The Life of Mother Mary Baptist Russell, Sister of Mercy.* (New York: The Apostleship of Prayer, 1901).

Russell, Matthew, S.J. *The Three Sisters of Lord Russell of Killowen and Their Convent Life.* (London: Longmans, Green and Co., 1912).

Sheridan, Sister Mary Athanasius. *And Some Fell on Good Ground, A History of the Sisters of Mercy of California and Arizona.* (New York: Carlton Press, Inc., 1982).

Walters, Johanna O'Mahony. *Merci Beaucoup, A Story of Courage and Compassion, Convent of Mercy, Kinsale 1844-2002.* (Johanna O'Mahony Walters, 2001).

Woodham-Smith, Cecil. *The Great Hunger.* (New York: Harper & Row, Publishers, 1962).

Background Sources

_____ *Memoir of Rev. Mother Mary Teresa Comerford, Foundress of the Convents of the Presentation Order on the Pacific Coast.* (San Francisco: P.J. Thomas, Publisher, 1882).

A History of Newry Workshouse, Collector's Item Magazine.

Altrocchi, Julia Coley. *The Spectacular San Franciscans.* (New York: E. P. Dutton and Company, Inc.,1949).

Avella, Steven M. "Phelan's Cemetery: Religion in the Urbanizing West, 1850-1869, in Los Angeles, San Francisco and Sacramento." *Rooted in Barbarous Soil, People, Culture, and Community in Gold Rush California.* Eds. Kevin Starr and Richard J. Orsi. (Published for the California Historical Society by the University of California Press.) 250-273.

Bragg, Susan. "Knowledge is Power: Sacramento Blacks and the Public Schools, 1854-1860." *California History,* Vol. 75:3, Fall, 1996. 215-221.

Brechin, Gray. *Imperial San Francisco: Urban Power, Earthly Run.* (Berkeley: University of California Press, 1999).

Bridgeman, Mother Mary Francis. *God in His Works, Vol. I & II.* (Dublin: John Mullany, 1878).

Bridgeman, Mother Mary Francis. *God in His Works, Vol. III* (London: Burns & Oats, 1880).

Bridgeman, Mother Mary Francis. *God in His Works, Vol. IV.* (London: Society of St. Anne, 1887).

Callaghan, Mary Rose. *'Kitty O'Shea'. The Story of Katherine Parnell.* (London: Pandora, 1989).

Dobie, Charles Caldwell. *San Francisco A Pageant.* (New York: D. Appleton-Century Company, Inc., New York, 1939).

Donnelly, James S., Jr. "The Administration of Relief, 1847-51." *A New History of Ireland, Vol. V: Ireland Under the Union, 1801-1870.* (Oxford: Clarendon Press, 1989). 316-331.

Dwyer, John T. *Condemned to the Mines, The Life of Eugene O'Connell 1815-1891, Pioneer Bishop of Northern California and Nevada.* (New York: Vantage Press, 1976).

Egli, Ida Rae, ed. *No Rooms of Their Own: Women Writers of Early California, 1849-1869.* (Berkeley: Heyday Books, 1977).

Eifler, Mark A. *Gold Rush Capitalists, Greed and Growth in Sacramento.* (Albuquerque, New Mexico: University of New Mexico Press, 2002).

Gallagher, Thomas. *Paddy's Lament, Ireland 1846-1847 Prelude to Hatred.* (New York: Harcourt Brace Jovanovich, 1982).

Hendrick, Irving G. "From Indifference to Imperative Duty: Educating Children in Early California." *Rooted in Barbarous Soil, People, Culture, and Community in Gold Rush California.* Eds. Kevin Starr and Richard J. Orsi. (Published for the California Historical Society by the University of California Press). 226-237.

Holden, William M. *Sacramento, Excursions into Its History and Natural World.* (Fair Oaks, California: Two Rivers Publishing Company, 1988).

Holmes, Kenneth L., ed. *Covered Wagon Women, Diaries & Letters from the Western Trails, 1854-1860.* (Lincoln, Nebraska: University of Nebraska Press, 1987).

Kee, Robert. *The Most Distressful Country, Vol. 1, Of the Green Flag.* (London: Quartet Books Limited, 1976).

Levy, Jo Ann. *They Saw the Elephant, Women in the California Gold Rush.* (Norman, Oklahoma: University of Oklahoma Press, 1992).

MacKenna, B. Vincuna. "Winter of 1853 in San Francisco." *Academy Scrapbook, Vol. V.* Translator, Brother Veronius Henry, FSC. (Fresno, California: Academy of California Church History, 1959). 139-171.

McAteer, Seamus. "The Life and Times of John Mitchel of Newry." *Seanchas Dhroim Mor, Journal of the Dromore Historical Society.* 1990. 14-23.

McGloin, John B., S.J. *San Francisco, The Story of a City.* (San Rafael, California: Presidio Press, 1978).

McKanna, Clare V. Jr., "The Origins of San Quentin, 1851-1880." *California History,* Vol. 66:1, March, 1987. 49-55.

McSweeney, Thomas Denis. *Cathedral on California Street, The Story of St. Mary's Cathedral, San Francisco, 1854-1891 and of Old St. Mary's, a Paulist Church, 1894-1951.* (Fresno, California: Academy of California Church History, 1951).

O'Sullivan, Florence. *The History of Kinsale.* (Dublin: James Duffy & Co. Limited, 1916).

Rathmell, George. *Realms of Gold: The Colorful Writers of San Francisco 1850-1950.* (Berkeley: Creative Arts Book Company, 1998).

Rogers, Richard C. "The First One-Hundred Years of the Sacramento City Schools, 1854-1954."

Schlissel, Lillian. *Women's Diaries of the Westward Journey.* (New York: Schocken Books, New York, 1992).

Seagraves, Anne. *Soiled Doves, Prostitution in the Early West.* (Hayden, Idaho: Wesanne Publications, 1994).

Stellman, Louis J. *Sam Brannan Builder of San Francisco.* (Fairfield: James Stevenson Publisher, 1996).

Stone, Irving. *Men to Match My Mountains: The Opening of the Far West, 1840-1900.* (New York: Berkley Books, 1956).

The Sacramento Directory for 1854-55.

Vaughn, Sister Andrea. "Bonnets by the Bay." *Academy Scrapbook, Vol. III.* (Fresno, California: Academy of California Church History, 1959). 65-69, 112-115, 150-160.

Walsh, Henry L. *Hallowed Were the Gold Dust Trails, The Story of the Pioneer Priests of Northern California.* (Santa Clara, California: University of Santa Clara Press, 1946).

Wells, Evelyn. *Champagne Days of San Francisco.* (New York: D. Appleton-Century Company, New York, 1941).

Acknowledgments

I gratefully acknowledge the following organizations for permission to use copyrighted materials from their holdings:

The Apostleship of Prayer for use of materials from *Life of Mother Mary Baptist Russell* by Father Matthew Russell, S.J.

Diocese of Fresno for permission to use materials from *California's Pioneer Sister of Mercy* by Sister Mary Aurelia McArdle.

Irish Jesuit Province for permission to use writings of Father Matthew Russell, S.J.

Sierra Sacramento Valley Medical Society for permission to use excerpts from *Memories, Men, and Medicine* by Dr. J. Roy Jones.

Sisters of Mercy, Auburn and Burlingame Regional Community for use of archival materials.

Index

About
the Author

Katherine Doyle, RSM, is a member of the Sisters of Mercy, Auburn Regional Community. Trained in history and spirituality, she has spent twenty years studying the life and works of Mary Baptist Russell. She has ministered in education, faith formation and retreat ministries, formerly serving as the Director of Catholic Faith Formation in the Diocese of Sacramento and as Director of Mercy Center Auburn. Currently she continues to work in communications, retreat ministry and spiritual direction.